Hypertext 2.0

PARALLAX:
RE-VISIONS
OF CULTURE
AND SOCIETY

Stephen G. Nichols,

Gerald Prince,

and Wendy Steiner,

Series Editors

Hypertext 2.0

Being a revised, amplified edition of

Hypertext: *The Convergence of Contemporary Critical Theory and Technology*

George P. Landow

The Johns Hopkins

University Press

Baltimore + London

© 1992, 1997 The Johns Hopkins University Press

All rights reserved. Published 1997

Printed in the United States of America on acid-free paper

04 03 02 01 00 99 98 97   5 4 3 2 1

The Johns Hopkins University Press

2715 North Charles Street

Baltimore, Maryland 21218-4319

The Johns Hopkins Press Ltd., London

ISBN 0-8018-5585-3

ISBN 0-8018-5586-1 (pbk.)

Library of Congress Cataloging-in-Publication Data

will be found at the end of this book.

A catalog record for this book is available from

the British Library.

For Ruth, Shoshana, Serena, and Noah

Contents

Acknowledgments

I would like to thank the former members of Brown University's Institute for Research in Information and Scholarship (IRIS), which shut its doors in 1992. I owe special thanks to its founding director, William G. Shipp, to its later co-directors, Norman K. Meyrowitz and Marty J. Michel, and to my friend and colleague Paul Kahn, who was project coordinator during the creation of *The Dickens Web* and later Intermedia projects and who served as the Institute's final director. Nicole Yankelovich, IRIS project coordinator during the initial development and application stages of Intermedia, always proved enormously resourceful, helpful, and good humored even in periods of crisis, as did Julie Launhardt, assistant project coordinator. The IRIS facilities engineers, Todd VanderDoes and Larry Larrivee, maintained the hardware and software amidst conditions of continual change.

In 1988, Brown University's Computing and Information Services, in the Center for Information Technology, took over responsibility for the Intermedia lab from the IRIS team; and until 1992 Steve Andrade, Chris Chung, and Vic Nair made teaching and research with Intermedia possible. In the final years of the project, the late James H. Coombs, who created many of the key parts of the second stage of Intermedia, provided invaluable assistance.

Jay Bolter enticed me into using Storyspace, and I am most grateful to him, Michael Joyce, and Mark Bernstein of Eastgate Systems for their continuing assistance.

I owe an especial debt to my enthusiastic and talented graduate and undergraduate research assistants between 1987 and 1992, particularly Randall Bass, David C. Cody, Shoshana M. Landow, Jan Lanestedt, Ho Lin, David Stevenson, Kathryn Stockton, Gary Weissman, Gene Yu, and Marc Zbyszynski. My students at Brown University, both those in my more orthodox literature courses and those studying hypertext and literary theory, have provided a continual source of inspiration and delight.

The development of Intermedia was funded in part by grants and contracts from International Business Machines, Apple Computer, and the Annenberg/Corporation for Public Broadcasting Project, and I am grateful to them for their support. A Mellon Foundation grant and one from Dr. Frank Rothman, the provost of Brown University, enabled me to transfer the Intermedia materials created for English and creative writing courses into Storyspace. The generosity of Daniel Russell of Apple Computers has enabled

ACKNOWLEDGMENTS   me to carry out my research since the closing of IRIS, when my university found itself able to offer little assistance or encouragement.

I also owe a debt of gratitude to many colleagues and students who shared their work with me: Mark Amerika, J. David Bolter, Alberto Cecchi, Robert Coover, Daniela Danielle, Jay Dillemuth, Carolyn Guyer, Terence Harpold, Paul Kahn, Robert Kendall, David Kolb, Deena Larson, Gary Marchionini, Stuart Moulthrop, and Marc Nanard kindly provided me with draft, prepublication, or prerelease versions of their work; and Cambridge University Press, Dynamic Diagrams, Eastgate Systems, MetaDesign West, PWS Publishing, Oxford University Press, Routledge, and Voyager have provided published versions of their electronic publications.

I would also like to thank for their advice, assistance, and encouragement David Balcom, Bruno Bassi, Gui Bonsiepe, George Bornstein, Katell Briatte, Hugh Davis, Marilyn Deegan, Emanuela del Monaco, Jacques Derrida, Umberto Eco, Susan Farrell, Patrizia Ghislandi, Antoni J. Gomez-Bosquet, Diane Greco, Robert Grudin, Wendy Hall, E. W. B. Hess-Littich, Jean-Louis Lebrave, José Lebrero, Michael Ledgerwood, Gunnar Liestøl, Peter Lunenfeld, Cathy Marshall, Tom Meyer, J. Hillis Miller, Elli Mylonas, Geoffrey Nunberg, Allesandro Pamini, Paolo Petta, Allen Renear, Massimo Riva, Peter Robinson, Lothar Roisteck, Luisella Romeo, Daniel Russell, Ture Schwebs, Christine Tamblyn, Jeff Taylor, Robert Trappl, Paul Tucker, Frank Turner, Gregory Ulmer, Karin Wenz, Rob Wittig, and the members of CHUG.

When I presented the first edition of this work to the Johns Hopkins University Press, Eric Halpern, then editor in chief, was open-minded enough to have enthusiasm for a project that editors at other presses thought too strange or too unintelligible to consider. I greatly appreciate the encouragement I received from him and the support for the second edition by Douglas Armato and Willis Regier, director of the Press. Jim Johnston, design and production manager when the first edition was produced, and Glen Burris, the book's designer, deserve thanks for tackling something new in a new way. Anne Whitmore, my copyeditor, knows how much I owe to her rare combination of knowledge, rigor, and skepticism. She has contributed greatly to whatever grace, clarity, and accuracy this book may possess.

Finally, I must acknowledge the support and encouragement of my wife, Ruth, and my children, to whom this volume is dedicated. They have all listened for years to my effusions about links, webs, lexias, web views, and local tracking maps, and they have responded with enthusiasm and understanding. Of all the debts I have incurred while writing this book, I enjoy most acknowledging the one to them.

Hypertext 2.0

Hypertext:

An Introduction

The problem of causality. It is not always easy to determine what has caused a specific change in a science. What made such a discovery possible? Why did this new concept appear? Where did this or that theory come from? Questions like these are often highly embarrassing because there are no definite methodological principles on which to base such an analysis. The embarrassment is much greater in the case of those general changes that alter a science as a whole. It is greater still in the case of several corresponding changes. But it probably reaches its highest point in the case of the empirical sciences: for the role of instruments, techniques, institutions, events, ideologies, and interests is very much in evidence; but one does not know how an articulation so complex and so diverse in composition actually operates.

MICHEL FOUCAULT, *The Order of Things*

Hypertextual Derrida, Poststructuralist Nelson?

When designers of computer software examine the pages of *Glas* or *Of Grammatology,* they encounter a digitalized, hypertextual Derrida; and when literary theorists examine *Literary Machines,* they encounter a deconstructionist or poststructuralist Nelson. These shocks of recognition can occur because over the past several decades literary theory and computer hypertext, apparently unconnected areas of inquiry, have increasingly converged. Statements by theorists concerned with literature, like those by theorists concerned with computing, show a remarkable convergence. Working often, but not always, in ignorance of each other, writers in these areas offer evidence that provides us with a way into the contemporary *episteme* in the midst of major changes. A paradigm shift, I suggest, has begun to take place in the writings of Jacques Derrida and Theodor Nelson, Roland Barthes and Andries van Dam. I expect that one name in each pair will be unknown to most of my readers. Those working in computing will know well the ideas of Nelson and van Dam; those working in literary and cultural theory will know equally well the ideas of Derrida and Barthes.[1]

All four, like many others who write on hypertext and literary theory, argue that we must abandon conceptual systems founded upon ideas of center, margin, hierarchy, and linearity and replace them with ones of multilinearity, nodes, links, and networks. Almost all parties to this paradigm shift, which marks a revolution in human thought, see electronic writing as a direct response to the strengths and weaknesses of the printed book. This response has profound implications for literature, education, and politics.

The parallels between computer hypertext and critical theory are of interest at many points, the most important of which, perhaps, is that critical theory promises to theorize hypertext and hypertext promises to embody and thereby test aspects of theory, particularly those concerning textuality, narrative, and the roles or functions of reader and writer. Using hypertext, critical theorists will have, or now already have, a laboratory in which to test their ideas. An experience of reading hypertext or reading with hypertext greatly clarifies many of the most significant ideas of critical theory. As J. David Bolter points out in the course of explaining that hypertextuality embodies poststructuralist conceptions of the open text, "what is unnatural in print becomes natural in the electronic medium and will soon no longer need saying at all, because it can be shown" (*Writing Space,* 143).

The Definition of Hypertext and

Its History as a Concept

In *S/Z*, Roland Barthes describes an ideal textuality that precisely matches that which in computing has come to be called hypertext—text composed of blocks of words (or images) linked electronically by multiple paths, chains, or trails in an open-ended, perpetually unfinished textuality described by the terms *link, node, network, web,* and *path:* "In this ideal text," says Barthes, "the networks [*réseaux*] are many and interact, without any one of them being able to surpass the rest; this text is a galaxy of signifiers, not a structure of signifieds; it has no beginning; it is reversible; we gain access to it by several entrances, none of which can be authoritatively declared to be the main one; the codes it mobilizes extend *as far as the eye can reach,* they are indeterminable . . . ; the systems of meaning can take over this absolutely plural text, but their number is never closed, based as it is on the infinity of language" (emphasis in original; 5–6 [English translation]; 11–12 [French]).

Like Barthes, Michel Foucault conceives of text in terms of network and links. In *The Archeology of Knowledge,* he points out that the "frontiers of a book are never clear-cut," because "it is caught up in a system of references to other books, other texts, other sentences: it is a node within a network . . . [a] network of references" (23).

Like almost all structuralists and poststructuralists, Barthes and Foucault describe text, the world of letters, and the power and status relations they involve in terms shared by the field of computer hypertext. *Hypertext,* a term coined by Theodor H. Nelson in the 1960s, refers also to a form of electronic text, a radically new information technology, and a mode of publication.[2] "By 'hypertext,'" Nelson explains, "I mean non-sequential writing—text that branches and allows choices to the reader, best read at an interactive screen. As popularly conceived, this is a series of text chunks connected by links which offer the reader different pathways" (*Literary Machines,* 0/2). *Hypertext,* as the term is used in this work, denotes text composed of blocks of text— what Barthes terms a lexia—and the electronic links that join them.[3] The concept of hypermedia simply extends the notion of the text in hypertext by including visual information, sound, animation, and other forms of data. Since hypertext, which links one passage of verbal discourse to images, maps, diagrams, and sound as easily as to another verbal passage, expands the notion of text beyond the solely verbal, I do not distinguish between hypertext and hypermedia. *Hypertext* denotes an information medium that links verbal and nonverbal information. I shall use the terms *hypermedia* and *hypertext* interchangeably. Electronic links connect lexias "external" to a work—say, commentary on it by another author or parallel or contrasting texts—as well as within it and thereby create text that is experienced as nonlinear, or, more properly, as multilinear or multisequential. Although conventional reading habits apply within each lexia, once one leaves the shadowy bounds of any text unit, new rules and new experience apply.[4]

The standard scholarly article in the humanities or physical sciences perfectly embodies the underlying notions of hypertext as multisequentially read text. For example, in reading an article on, say, James Joyce's *Ulysses,* one reads through what is conventionally known as the main text, encounters a number or symbol that indicates the presence of a foot- or endnote, and leaves the main text to read that note, which can contain a citation of passages in *Ulysses* that supposedly support the argument in question, or information about the scholarly author's indebtedness to other authors, disagreement with them, and so on. The note can also summon up information about sources, influences, and parallels in other literary texts. In each case, the reader can follow the link to another text indicated by the note and thus move entirely outside the scholarly article itself. Having completed reading the note or having decided that it does not warrant a careful reading at the moment, one returns to the main text and continues reading until one encounters another note, at which point one again leaves the main text.

This kind of reading constitutes the basic experience and starting point of hypertext. Suppose now that one could simply touch the page where the symbol of a note, reference, or annotation appeared, and thus instantly bring into view the material contained in a note or even the entire other text—here all of *Ulysses*—to which that note refers. Scholarly articles situate themselves within a field of relations, most of which the print medium keeps out of sight and relatively difficult to follow, because in print technology the referenced (or linked) materials lie spatially distant from the references to them. Electronic hypertext, in contrast, makes individual references easy to follow and the entire field of interconnections obvious and easy to navigate. Changing the ease with which one can orient oneself and pursue individual references within such a context radically changes both the experience of reading and ultimately the nature of that which is read. For example, if one possessed a hypertext system in which our putative Joyce article was linked to all the other materials it cited, the article would exist as part of a much larger totality, which might count more than the individual document; the article would now be woven more tightly into its context than would a printed counterpart.

As this scenario suggests, hypertext blurs the boundaries between reader and writer and therefore instantiates another quality of Barthes's ideal text. From the vantage point of the current changes in information technology,

Barthes's distinction between readerly and writerly texts appears to be essentially a distinction between text based on print technology and electronic hypertext, for hypertext fulfills

the goal of literary work (of literature as work) [which] is to make the reader no longer a consumer, but a producer of the text. Our literature is characterized by the pitiless divorce which the literary institution maintains between the producer of the text and its user, between its owner and its consumer, between its author and its reader. This reader is thereby plunged into a kind of idleness—he is intransitive; he is, in short, serious: instead of functioning himself, instead of gaining access to the magic of the signifier, to the pleasure of writing, he is left with no more than the poor freedom either to accept or reject the text: reading is nothing more than a referendum. Opposite the writerly text, then, is its countervalue, its negative, reactive value: what can be read, but not written: the readerly. We call any readerly text a classic text. (S/Z, 4)

Compare the way the designers of Intermedia, one of the most advanced hypertext systems thus far developed, describe the active reader that hypertext requires and creates:

Both an author's tool and a reader's medium, a hypertext document system allows authors or groups of authors to link information together, create paths through a corpus of related material, annotate existing texts, and create notes that point readers to either bibliographic data or the body of the referenced text. . . . Readers can browse through linked, cross-referenced, annotated texts in an orderly but nonsequential manner. (Yankelovich, Meyrowitz, and van Dam, 17)[5]

To get an idea of how hypertext produces Barthes's writerly text, let us examine how the print version and the hypertext version of this book would differ. In the first place, instead of encountering it in a paper copy, you would read it on a computer screen. Contemporary screens, which have neither the portability nor the tactility of printed books, make the act of reading somewhat more difficult. For those people like myself who do a large portion of their reading reclining on a bed or couch, screens also can be less convenient. At the same time, reading on Intermedia, the hypertext system with which I first worked, offered certain important compensations.[6]

Reading an Intermedia or Storyspace version of this book, for example, you could change the size and even style of font to make reading easier. Although you could not make such changes permanently in the text as seen by others, you could make them whenever you wished. More important, since on Intermedia you would read this hypertext book on a large two-page graphics monitor, you would have the opportunity to place several texts next to one another. Thus, upon reaching a note number, you would activate the hypertext equivalent of a reference mark (glyph, button, link marker), and this action would bring the endnote into view. A hypertext version of a note differs from that in a printed book in several ways. First, it links directly to the reference symbol and does not reside in some sequentially numbered list at the rear of the main text. Second, once opened and either superimposed upon the main text or placed alongside it, it appears as an independent, if connected, document in its own right and not as some sort of subsidiary, supporting, possibly parasitic text.

Although I have since converted endnotes containing bibliographic information to in-text citations, the first edition of *Hypertext* had a note containing the following information: "Roland Barthes, *S/Z*, trans. Richard Miller (New York: Hill and Wang, 1974), 5–6." A hypertext lexia equivalent of this note could include this same information, or, more likely, take the form of the quoted passage, a longer section or chapter, or the entire text of Barthes's work. Furthermore, in the various hypertext versions of this book, that passage in turn links to other statements by Barthes of similar import, comments by students of Barthes, and passages by Derrida and Foucault that also concern this notion of the networked text. As a reader, you must decide whether to return to my argument, pursue some of the connections I suggest by links, or, using other capacities of the system, search for connections I have not suggested. The multiplicity of hypertext, which appears in multiple links to individual blocks of text, calls for an active reader.

A full hypertext system, unlike a book and unlike some of the first approximations of hypertext currently available (HyperCard™, Guide™), offers the same environment to both reader and writer. Therefore, by opening the text-processing program, or editor, as it is known, you can take notes, or you can write against my interpretations, against my text. Although you cannot change my text, you can write a response and then link it to my document. You thus have read the readerly text in several ways not possible with a book: you have chosen your reading path, and since you, like all other readers, will choose an individualized path, your hypertext version of this book would take a different form from mine, perhaps suggesting the values of alternate routes and probably devoting less room in the main text to quoted passages. You might also have begun to take notes or produce responses to the text as you read, some of which might take the form of texts that either support or contradict interpretations proposed in my texts.

Vannevar Bush and the Memex

Writers on hypertext trace the concept to a pioneering article by Vannevar Bush in a 1945 issue of *Atlantic Monthly* that called for mechanically linked information-retrieval machines to help scholars and decision makers faced with what was already becoming an explosion of information. Struck by the "growing mountain of research" that confronted workers in every field, Bush realized that the number of publications had already "extended far beyond our present ability to make real use of the record. The summation of human experience is being expanded at a prodigious rate, and the means we use for threading through the consequent maze to the momentarily important item is the same as was used in the days of square-rigged ships" (17–18). As he emphasized, "there may be millions of fine thoughts, and the account of the experience on which they are based, all encased within stone walls of acceptable architectural form; but if the scholar can get at only one a week by diligent search, his syntheses are not likely to keep up with the current scene" (29).

According to Bush, the main problem lay with what he termed "the matter of selection"—information retrieval—and the primary reason that those who needed information could not find it lay in turn with inadequate means of storing, arranging, and tagging information:

Our ineptitude in getting at the record is largely caused by the artificiality of systems of indexing. When data of any sort are placed in storage, they are filed alphabetically or numerically, and information is found (when it is) by tracing it down from subclass to subclass. It can be in only one place, unless duplicates are used; one has to have rules as to which path will locate it, and the rules are cumbersome. Having found one item, moreover, one has to emerge from the system and re-enter on a new path. (31)

As Ted Nelson, one of Bush's most prominent disciples, points out, "there is nothing wrong with categorization. It is, however, by its nature transient: category systems have a half-life, and categorizations begin to look fairly stupid after a few years. . . . The army designation of 'Pong Balls, Ping' has a certain universal character to it" (*Literary Machines,* 2/49).

In contrast to the rigidity and difficulty of access produced by present means of managing information based on print and other physical records, an information medium is needed that better accommodates the way the mind works. After describing present methods of storing and classifying knowledge, Bush complains, "The human mind does not work that way" but by association ("As We May Think," 31). With one fact or idea "in its grasp," the mind "snaps instantly to the next that is suggested by the association of thoughts, in accordance with some intricate web of trails carried by the cells of the brain" (32)

To liberate us from the confinements of inadequate systems of classification and to permit us to follow natural proclivities for "selection by association, rather than by indexing," Bush therefore proposed a device, the "memex," that would mechanize a more efficient, more human, mode of manipulating fact and imagination. "A memex," he explains, "is a device in which an individual stores his books, records, and communications, and which is mechanized so that it may be consulted with exceeding speed and flexibility. It is an enlarged intimate supplement to his memory" (32). Writing in the days before digital computing (the first idea for the memex came to him in the mid-1930s), Bush conceived of his device as a desk with translucent screens, levers, and motors for rapid searching of microform records.

In addition to thus searching and retrieving information, the memex also would permit the reader to "add marginal notes and comments, taking advantage of one possible type of dry photography, and it could even be arranged so that he can do this by a stylus scheme, such as is now employed in the telautograph seen in railroad waiting rooms, just as though he had the physical page before him" (33). Two things demand attention about this crucial aspect of Bush's conception of the memex: First, he believed that while reading, one needs to append one's own individual, transitory thoughts and reactions to texts. With this emphasis Bush in other words reconceived reading as an active process that involves writing. Second, his remark that this active, intrusive reader can annotate a text "just as though he had the physical page before him" recognizes the need for a conception of a virtual, rather than a physical, text. One of the things that is so intriguing about Bush's proposal is the way he thus allowed the shortcomings of one form of text to suggest a new technology, and that leads, in turn, to an entirely new conception of text.

The "essential feature of the memex," however, lies not only in its capacities for retrieval and annotation but also in those involving "associative indexing"—what present hypertext systems term a link—"the basic idea of which is a provision whereby any item may be caused at will to select immediately and automatically another" (34). Bush then provides a scenario of how readers would create "endless trails" of such links:

When the user is building a trail, he names it, inserts the name in his code book, and taps it out on his keyboard. Before him are the two items to be joined, projected onto adjacent viewing positions. At the bottom of each there are a number of blank code spaces, and a pointer is set to indicate one of these on each item. The user taps a single key, and the items are permanently joined. In each code space appears the code word. Out of view, but also in the code space, is inserted a set of dots for photocell viewing; and on each item these dots by their positions designate the index number of the other item. Thereafter, at any time, when one of these items is in view, the other can be instantly recalled merely by tapping a button below the corresponding code space. (34)

Bush's remarkably prescient description of how the memex user creates and then follows links joins his major recognition that trails of such links themselves constitute a new form of textuality and new form of writing. As he explains, "when numerous items have been thus joined together to form a trail . . . It is exactly as though the physical items had been gathered together from widely separated sources and bound together to form a new book." In fact, "it is more than this," Bush adds, "for any item can be joined into numerous trails" (34), and thereby any block of text, image, or other information can participate in numerous books.

These new memex books themselves, it becomes clear, are the new book, or one additional version of the new book, and, like books, these trail sets or webs can be shared. Bush proposed, again quite accurately, that "wholly new forms of encyclopedias will appear, ready-made with a mesh of associative trails running through them, ready to be dropped into the memex and there amplified" (35). Equally important, individual reader-writers can share document sets and apply them to new problems.

Bush, an engineer interested in technical innovation, provided the example of a memex user

studying why the short Turkish bow was apparently superior to the English long bow in the skirmishes of the Crusades. He has dozens of possibly pertinent books and articles in his memex. First he runs through an encyclopedia, finds an interesting but sketchy article, leaves it projected. Next, in a history, he finds another pertinent item, and ties the two together. Thus he goes, building a trail of many items. Occasionally he inserts a comment of his own, either linking it into the main trail or joining it by a side trail to a particular item. When it becomes evident that the elastic properties of available materials had a great deal to do with the bow, he branches off on a side trail which takes him through textbooks on elasticity and tables of physical constants. He inserts a page of longhand analysis of his own. Thus he builds a trail of his interest through the maze of materials available to him. (34–35)

And, Bush adds, his researcher's memex trails, unlike those in his mind, "do not fade," so when he and a friend several years later discuss "the queer ways in which a people resist innovations, even of vital interest" (35), he can reproduce his trails created to investigate one subject or problem and apply them to another.

Bush's idea of the memex, to which he occasionally turned his thoughts for three decades, directly influenced Nelson, Douglas Englebart, Andries van Dam, and other pioneers in computer hypertext, including the group at the Brown University's Institute for Research in Information and Scholarship (IRIS) who created Intermedia. In "As We May Think" and "Memex Revisited" Bush proposed the notion of blocks of text joined by links, and he also introduced the terms *links, linkages, trails,* and *web* to describe his new conception of textuality. Bush's description of the memex contains several other seminal, even radical, conceptions of textuality. It demands, first of all, a radical reconfiguration of the practice of reading and writing, in which both activities draw closer together than is possible with book technology. Second, despite the fact that he conceived of the memex before the advent of digital computing, Bush perceived that something like virtual textuality is essential for the changes he advocated. Third, his reconfiguration of text introduces three entirely new elements—associative indexing (or links), trails of such links, and sets or webs of such trails. These new elements in turn produce the conception of a flexible, customizable text, one that is open—and perhaps vulnerable—to the demands of each reader. They also produce a concept of multiple textuality, since within the memex world *texts* refers to (1) individual reading units that constitute a traditional "work," (2) those entire works, (3) sets of documents created by trails, and possibly (4) those trails themselves without accompanying documents. '

Perhaps most interesting to one considering the relation of Bush's ideas to contemporary critical and cultural theory is that this engineer began by rejecting some of the fundamental assumptions of the information technology that had increasingly dominated—and some would say largely created—Western thought since Gutenberg. Moreover, Bush wished to replace the essentially linear fixed methods that had produced the triumphs of capitalism and industrialism with what are essentially poetic machines—machines that work according to analogy and association, machines that capture and create the anarchic brilliance of human imagination. Bush, we perceive, assumed that science and poetry work in essentially the same way.

Forms of Linking,

Their Uses and Limitations

Before showing some of the ways this new information technology shares crucial ideas and emphases with contemporary critical theory, I shall examine in more detail the link, the element that hypertext adds to writing and reading. The very simplest, most basic form of linking is unidirectional lexia to lexia (see Figure 1). Although this type of link has the advantage of requiring little planning, when used with long documents it disorients readers, who do not know where a link will lead them in the entered document. It is best used, therefore, in brief lexias or in systems that use card metaphors. Next in complexity comes bidirectional linking of two entire lexias—identical to the first form except that it includes the ability to retrace one's steps (or jump). Its advantage lies in the fact that, by permitting readers to retrace their steps, it creates a simple but effective means of orientation. This mode seems particularly helpful when a reader arrives at a lexia that has only one or two links out, or when readers encounter something—say, a glossary definition or image—that they do not want to consult at that point in their reading.

Linking a string—that is, a word or phrase—to an entire lexia, another form of linking, has three advantages: First, it permits simple means of orienting readers by permitting a basic rhetoric of departure. When readers see a link attached to a phrase, such as "Arminiansm" or "Derrida," they have a pretty good idea that such a link will take them to information related in some obvious way to those names. Because string-to-lexia linking thus provides a simple means of helping readers navigate through information space, it permits longer lexias. Furthermore, since one can choose to leave the lexia at different points, one can comfortably read through longer texts. Third, this linking mode also encourages different kinds of annotation and linking, since the ability to attach links to different phrases, portions of images, and the like allows the author to indicate different kinds of link destinations. One can, for example, use icons or phrases to indicate that the reader can go to, say, another text lexia, one containing an illustration, bibliographical information, definitions, opposing arguments, or whatever.

The difficulties with string-to-lexia links, the form most characteristic of links in World Wide Web documents, arise at the destination lexia. Readers can find themselves disoriented when entering long documents, and therefore string-to-lexia linking works best with brief arrival lexias. Another variety of linking occurs when the link joining a string to an entire lexia is bidirectional. (Most linking in HTML [HyperText Markup Language] documents takes this form in effect—"in effect" because the return function provided by most viewers creates the effect of a bidirectional link.)

Lexia to Lexia Unidirectional

Advantage: simple, requires little planning.

Disadvantage: disorients when used with long documents, since readers do not know where link leads; best used for brief lexias or in systems that use card metaphor.

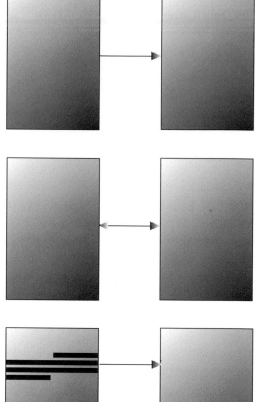

Lexia to Lexia Bidirectional

Advantage: by permitting readers to retrace their steps creates simple but effective means of orientation. Particularly helpful when arriving at lexias that have only one or two departure links.

String (word or phrase) to Lexia

Advantages: (1) allows simple means of orienting readers; (2) permits longer lexias; (3) encourages different kinds of annotation and linking.

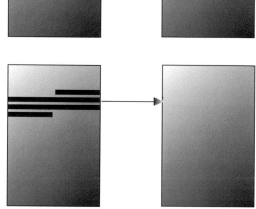

Disadvantage: disorients when used with long documents, since readers do not know where link leads; best used for brief lexias or in systems that use card metaphor.

Figure 1. Three Forms of Linking: unidirectional lexia-to-lexia, bidirectional lexia-to-lexia, and string-to-lexia

Unidirectional string-to-string linking (see Figure 2) has the obvious advantage of permitting the clearest and easiest way to end links and thereby create a rhetoric of arrival. By bringing readers to a clearly defined point in a text, one enables them to perceive immediately the reason for a link and hence to grasp the relation between two lexias or portions of them. Readers know, in other words, why they have arrived at a particular point. The possible disadvantage of such a mode to authors—which is a major advantage from the reader's point of view—is that it requires more planning or, at least,

String to String

Advantage: permits clearest way to end links.

Disadvantage: requires more planning than do links to full lexias.

One-to-Many

Advantages: (1) encourages branching and consequent reader choice; (2) permits efficient author-generated overview and directory documents; (3) when combined with systems that provide link menus and other preview functions, helps greatly in orienting readers.

Disadvantage: can produce sense of an atomized text.

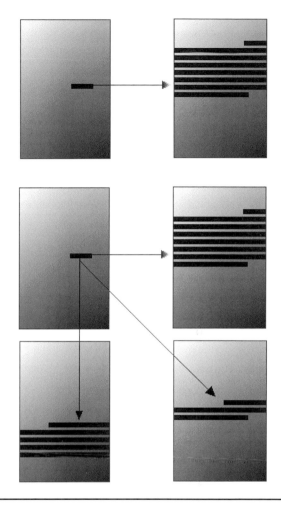

Figure 2. Two Forms of Linking: unidirectional string-to-string and one-to-many

more definite reasons for each link. Making such links bidirectional, which creates yet another category, makes navigating hyperspace even easier.

Full hypertextuality in a reading environment depends, I argue, on the multisequentiality and the reader choices created not only by attaching multiple links to a single lexia but by attaching them to a single anchor or site within a single lexia. A fully hypertextual system (or document) therefore employs a particularly important form, one-to-many linking, which permits readers to obtain different information from the same textual site. One-to-many linking supports hypertextuality in several ways. First, it encourages branching and consequently multiplies the reader's choices. Second, at-

Many-to-One Linking

Advantages: (1) handy for glossary functions or for texts that make multiple references to a single text, table, image, or other data; (2) encourages efficient reuse of important information; (3) allows simple means of producing documents for readers with differing levels of expertise.

Disadvantage: systems that create many-to-one linking automatically can produce a distracting number of identical links.

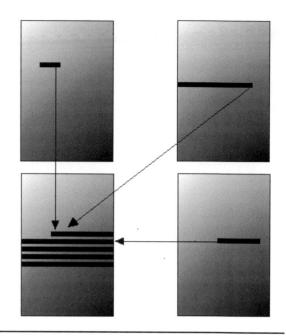

Figure 3. Many-to-One Linking

taching multiple links to a single text allows hypertext authors to create overviews and directories that serve as efficient crossroad documents, or orientation points, that help the reader navigate hyperspace. Multiple overviews or sets of overviews have the additional advantage of easily permitting different authors to provide multiple ways through the same information space. Third, when combined with software, such as Microcosm, Storyspace, or Intermedia, that provides link menus and other so-called preview functions, one-to-many linking greatly helps in orienting readers. The major disadvantage of this kind of link, which plays a large role in most hypertext fiction, lies in its tendency to produce a sense of atomized text.

A method called many-to-one linking (Figure 3) proves particularly handy for creating glossary functions or for creating documents that make multiple references to a single text, table, image, or other data. DynaText, Microcosm, and the World Wide Web exemplify hypertext environments in which one can have many links that lead to a single document, an arrangement that has advantages in educational and informational applications. In particular, many-to-one linking encourages efficient reuse of important information. For example, having once created an introductory essay on, say, Charles II, Lamarkianism, or Corn Law agitation, the original author (and later authors) simply uses linking to provide access to it as the occasion arises. Furthermore, by providing an easy, efficient means of offering readers glossaries and other basic information, many-to-one linking also permits webs easily to be used by readers with differing levels of expertise.

The major disadvantage of such linking involves not the links themselves but the means a system uses to indicate the links' presence. Systems that allow many-to-one linking, particularly those that create it automatically, can produce a distracting number of link markers. The World Wide Web uses colored underlining to indicate hot text; in the DynaText version of the first edition of this book, Paul Kahn chose red text to signify the presence of links. In both WWW and DynaText documents the reader encounters distracting markup intruding into the text. Experience with these systems quickly convinces one of the need for a means of easily turning on and off such link indicators, as one can do in Eastgate Systems' Storyspace. The disadvantages with many-to-one links derive not from this form of linking itself but from other aspects of individual hypertext environments.

As we shall observe shortly, some systems, such as Microcosm, include an especially interesting and valuable extension of many-to-one linking that permits readers to obtain a menu containing two or more glossary or similar documents. While creating a hypertext version of my book on Holman Hunt and Pre-Raphaelite painting for the World Wide Web, an environment that does not permit either link menus or one-to-many links, I had to choose whether to link all the mentions of a painting, say, the artist's *Finding of the Saviour in the Temple,* to an introductory discussion of the picture or to an illustration of it. In contrast, while creating a hypertext version of the same book in Microcosm, I easily arranged links so that when readers follow them from any mention of the painting, they receive a menu containing titles of the introductory text and two or more illustrations, thereby providing readers with convenient access to the kind of information they need when they might need it (see Figure 6, below).

Typed links, our last category of author-created links (Figure 4), limit an electronic link to a specific kind of relationship, such as "exemplifies," "influences," "contrary argument," "derives from" (or "child of"), and so on. Software that includes such link categorization ranges from proposed research systems that, in attempting to help organize argument, permit only certain kinds of connections, to those like Marc and Jocelyne Nanard's Mac-Web that permit authors to create their own categories. In fact, any system, such as Intermedia, Storyspace, or Microcosm, that permits one to attach labels to individual links allows one to create typed links, since labels permit

Typed Links

Advantages: (1) if clearly labeled, acts as a form of link preview and aids reader comfort; (2) can produce different kinds of link behavior, including pop-up windows.

Disadvantage: can clutter reading area or confuse by producing too many different actions when one follows links.

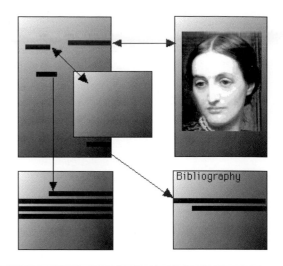

Figure 4. Typed Links

authors to indicate everything from document type (essay, illustration, statistics, timeline) to a particular path or trail of links that overlies a number of lexias.

The advantages of typed links include that, when clearly labeled, they offer a generalized kind of previewing that aids reader comfort and helps navigating information space. Such labeling can take the form of icons in the current lexia (the method used by DynaText, Voyager Expanded Book, WWW), similar indications in a second window (as in Intermedia's Web View and similar dynamic hypergraphs, like that created experimentally for Microcosm), and dynamic link menus (Intermedia, Storyspace). In systems that include pop-up windows overlying the current lexia (DynaText and the proprietary one created by Cognitive Applications for the *Microsoft Art Gallery*), typed links can also produce different kinds of link behavior. A potential disadvantage of the typed link for readers might be confusion produced when they encounter too many different actions or kinds of information; in fact, I have never encountered hypertexts with these problems, but they might exist. A greater danger for authors exists in systems that prescribe the kind of links to be made. My initial skepticism about typed links arose from doubts about the effectiveness of creating rules of thought in advance and from an experience I had with Intermedia. The very first version of Intermedia used by faculty developers and students differentiated between annotation and commentary links, but since one person's annotation turned out to be another's commentary, no one lobbied for retaining this feature, and IRIS omitted it from later versions.

An equally basic form of linking involves the degree to which readers either activate or even create them. In contemporary hypertext jargon, the opposition is usually phrased as a question of whether links are author or (w)reader determined, or—putting the matter differently—whether they are hard or soft. Most writing about hypertext from Bush and Nelson to the present assumes that someone, author or reader functioning as author, creates an electronic link, a so-called hard link. Recently, workers in the field, particularly the University of Southampton's Microcosm development group, have posed the question, "Can one have hypertext 'without links'?"—that is, without the by-now traditional assumption that links have to take the form of always-existing electronic connections between anchors. This approach takes the position that the reader's actions can create on-demand links. In the late 1980s, when the first conferences on hypertext convened, on-demand linking might have been a difficult, if not impossible, conception to advocate, because in those days researchers argued that information retrieval did not constitute hypertext, that the two represented very different, perhaps opposed, approaches to information. Part of the reason for these views lay in the understandable attempts of people working in a new field in computer science to distinguish their work—and thereby justify its very existence—from an established one. Although some authors, such as the philosopher Michael Heim, perceived the obvious connection between the active reader who uses search tools to probe an electronic text and the active reader of hypertext, the need of the field to constitute itself as a discrete specialty prompted many to juxtapose hypertext and information retrieval in the sharpest terms. When the late James H. Coombs created both InterLex and full-text retrieval in Intermedia, many of these oppositions immediately appeared foolish, since anyone who clicked upon a word and used Intermedia's electronic version of the American Heritage Dictionary—whether they were aware of it or not—inevitably used a second kind of linking. After all, activating a word and following a simple sequence of keys or using a menu brought one to another text (Figure 5).

Microcosm, a system on which work began in the early days of Intermedia, has built this idea of reader-activated links into its environment in two ways. First, using the Compute Links function, readers activate what are essentially information-retrieval software tools to produce menus of links that take exactly the same form as menus of links created by authors. Soft links, links created on demand by readers, look the same as the hard ones created

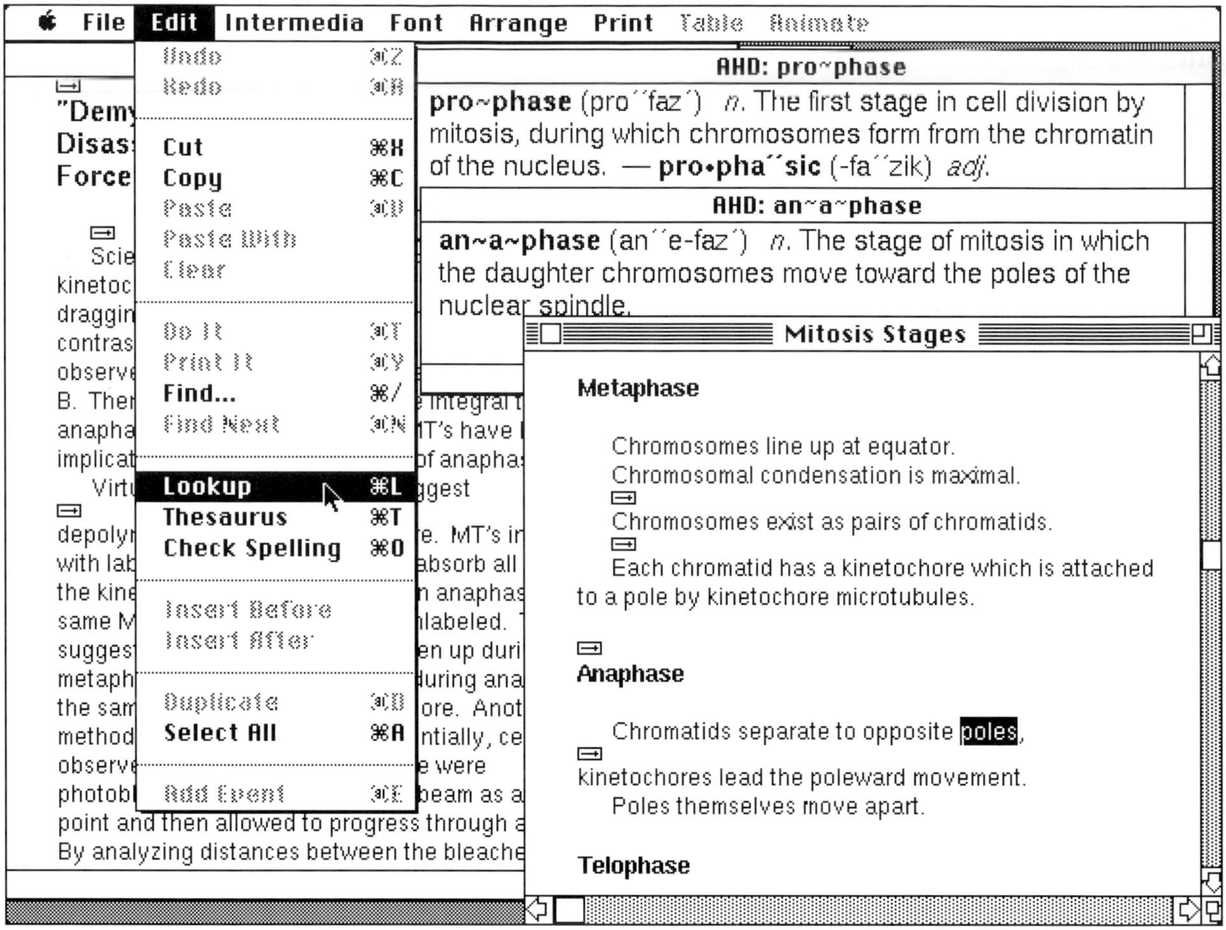

File Edit Intermedia Font Arrange Print Table Animate

Undo　⌘Z
Redo　⌘R

Cut　⌘H
Copy　⌘C
Paste　⌘B
Paste With
Clear

Do It　⌘T
Print It　⌘Y
Find...　⌘/
Find Next　⌘N

Lookup　⌘L
Thesaurus　⌘T
Check Spelling　⌘0

Insert Before
Insert After

Duplicate　⌘D
Select All　⌘A

Add Event　⌘E

AHD: pro~phase

pro~phase (pro´´faz´)　*n*. The first stage in cell division by mitosis, during which chromosomes form from the chromatin of the nucleus. — **pro•pha´´sic** (-fa´´zik) *adj*.

AHD: an~a~phase

an~a~phase (an´´e-faz´)　*n*. The stage of mitosis in which the daughter chromosomes move toward the poles of the nuclear spindle.

Mitosis Stages

Metaphase

Chromosomes line up at equator.
Chromosomal condensation is maximal.

Chromosomes exist as pairs of chromatids.

Each chromatid has a kinetochore which is attached to a pole by kinetochore microtubules.

Anaphase

Chromatids separate to opposite poles,
kinetochores lead the poleward movement.
　Poles themselves move apart.

Telophase

"Demy
Disas
Force

Scie
kinetoc
draggin
contras
observe
B. Ther
anapha
implicat
Virt
depoly
with lab
the kine
same M
sugges
metaph
the sam
method
observe
photob
point and then allowed to progress through a
By analyzing distances between the bleache

integral t
MT's have
of anapha
ggest

e. MT's i
absorb all
n anaphas
labeled. T
en up duri
during ana
ore. Anot
ntially, ce
e were
beam as a

Figure 5. Hypertext Links and Information Retrieval: The InterLex feature in Intermedia.

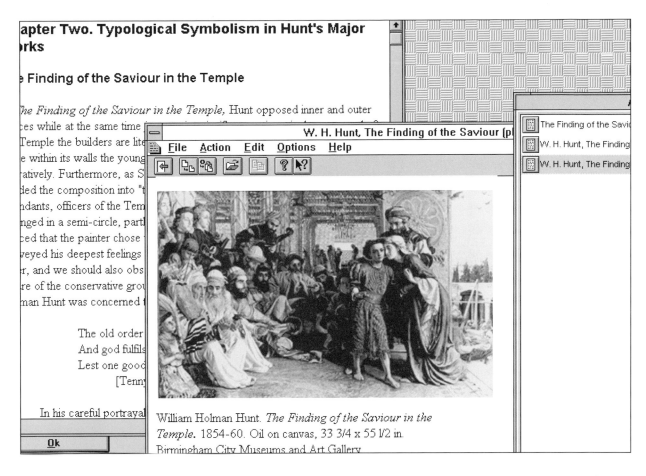

Figure 6. Generic Linking in Microcosm. This screen shot shows the results of following a generic link either from the word "Finding" or from the phrase "Finding of the Saviour in the Temple" in the Microcosm version of my book *William Holman Hunt and Typological Symbolism*. This action produces a menu (*at right*) with three choices, a section of my original book containing the principal discussion of this painting and illustrations of two versions of it. Since choosing "Follow Link" (or double clicking) on any word or phrase that serves as an anchor produces these three choices, this screen shot represents many-to-many linking. Furthermore, although readers experience the results of generic linking (here the menu with three destination lexias) just as if the author had manually linked each anchor to the discussion and two illustrations, in fact the links only come into existence when readers call for them. One can therefore consider this screen to exemplify soft many-to-many linking. Although Microcosm permits authors to create the usual manual forms of one-to-one and one-to-many links, the generic link function takes a great deal of the work out of creating informational hypertext webs.

by authors. Second, readers can activate implicit or generic links. When readers click upon hard links, they activate a connection established by a hypertext author, who, in some systems, could be a previous hypertext reader. When readers activate Compute Links, they create a dynamic relation between one text and another. In contrast to both these approaches, Microcosm's generic link function produces a different form of electronic connection that we call term "soft linking," linking activated only upon demand. Essentially, Microcosm's generic links appear only when a reader asks for them. No link marker, no code, indicates their existence, and nothing deforms the text in a lexia to announce their presence. In fact, only a reader's energy, active interest, or aggressive relation to the text brings such a link fully into being. Readers will recognize that this approach, this kind of linking, permits the many-to-more-than-one linking that permitted me to have readers obtain an introductory discussion and two plates of a painting by a Victorian artist by clicking upon the title of one of his paintings (Figure 6). Microcosm's generic linking facility, in fact, permitted me to recreate in a matter of hours links that had taken weeks to create manually in another system.

The final forms of linking—action links, warm (reader-activated data-exchange) links, and hot (automatic data-exchange) links—represent, in contrast, hard, author-created linking in other directions. These author-created links do more than allow readers to traverse information space or bring the document to them. They either initiate an action or they permit one to do so.

In later chapters, when we examine hypermedia containing animation and video, we shall observe yet other permutations of the link. Nonetheless, these preliminary remarks permit us to grasp some of the complex issues involved with adding the link to writing, with reconfiguring textuality by using an element that simultaneously blurs borders and bridges gaps, yet draws attention to them.

Virtual Texts, Virtual Authors, and Literary Computing

The characteristic effects that computing has had upon the humanities all derive from the fact that computing stores information in electronic codes rather than in physical marks on a physical surface. Since the invention of writing and printing, information technology has concentrated on the problem of creating and then disseminating static, unchanging records of language. As countless authors since the inception of writing have proclaimed, such fixed records conquer time and space, however temporarily, for they permit one person to share data with other people in other times and places. As Elizabeth

Eisenstein argues, printing adds the absolutely crucial element of multiple copies of the same text; this multiplicity, which preserves a text by dispersing individual copies of it, permits readers separated in time and space to refer to the same information (116). As Eisenstein, Marshall McLuhan, William M. Ivins, J. David Bolter, and other students of the history of the cultural effects of print technology have shown, Gutenberg's invention produced what we today understand as scholarship and criticism in the humanities. No longer primarily occupied by the task of preserving information in the form of fragile manuscripts that degraded with frequent use, scholars, working with books, developed new conceptions of scholarship, originality, and authorial property.

Although the fixed multiple text produced by print technology has had enormous effects on modern conceptions of literature, education, and research, it still, as Bush and Nelson emphasize, confronts the knowledge worker with the fundamental problem of an information retrieval system based on physical instantiations of text—namely, that preserving information in a fixed, unchangeable linear format makes information retrieval difficult.

We may state this problem in two ways. First, no one arrangement of information proves convenient for all who need that information. Second, although both linear and hierarchical arrangements provide information in some sort of order, that order does not always match the needs of individual users of that information. Over the centuries scribes, scholars, publishers, and other makers of books have invented a range of devices to increase the speed of processes that today are called information processing and information retrieval. Manuscript culture gradually saw the invention of individual pages, chapters, paragraphing, and spaces between words. The technology of the book found enhancement by pagination, indices, and bibliographies. Such devices have made scholarship possible, if not always easy or convenient to carry out.

Electronic text-processing marks the next major shift in information technology after the development of the printed book. It promises (or threatens) to produce effects on our culture, particularly on our literature, education, criticism, and scholarship, just as radical as those produced by Gutenberg's movable type.

Text-based computing provides us with electronic rather than physical texts, and this shift from ink to electronic code—what Jean Baudrillard calls the shift from the tactile to the digital (*Simulations,* 115)—produces an information technology that combines fixity and flexibility, order and accessibility—but at a cost.[7] Since electronic text-processing is a matter of manipulating computer-manipulated codes, all texts that the reader-writer en-counters on the screen are virtual texts. Using an analogy to optics, computer scientists speak of "virtual machines" created by an operating system that provides individual users with the experience of working on their own indi-vidual machines when they in fact share a system with as many as several hundred others.[8]

Similarly, all texts the reader and the writer encounter on a computer screen exist as a version created specifically for them while an electronic primary version resides in the computer's memory. One therefore works on an electronic copy until such time as both versions converge when the writer commands the computer to "save" one's version of the text by placing it in memory. At this point the text on screen and in the computer's memory briefly coincide, but the reader always encounters a virtual image of the stored text and not the original version itself; in fact, in descriptions of elec-tronic word processing, terms such as *text* and distinctions such as originality do not make much sense.

As Bolter explains, the most "unusual feature" of electronic writing is that it is "not directly accessible to either the writer or the reader. The bits of the text are simply not on a human scale. Electronic technology removes or abstracts the writer and reader from the text. If you hold a magnetic tape or optical disk up to the light, you will not see text at all. . . . In the electronic medium several layers of sophisticated technology must intervene between the writer or reader and the coded text. There are so many levels of deferral that the reader or writer is hard put to identify the text at all: is it on the screen, in the transistor memory, or on the disk?" (*Writing Space,* 42–43).

Jean Baudrillard, who presents himself as a follower of Walter Benjamin and Marshall McLuhan, is someone who seems both fascinated and appalled by what he sees as the all-pervading effects of such digital encoding, though his examples suggest that he is often confused about which media actually employ it. The strengths and weaknesses of Baudrillard appear in his remarks on the digitization of knowledge and information. Baudrillard correctly per-ceives that movement from the tactile to the digital is the primary fact about the contemporary world, but then he misconceives—or rather only partially perceives—the implications of his point. According to him, digitality involves binary opposition: "Digitality is with us. It is that which haunts all the mes-sages, all the signs of our societies. The most concrete form you see it in is that of the test, of the question/answer, of the stimulus/response" (*Simula-tions,* 115). Baudrillard most clearly posits this equivalence, which he mistakenly takes to be axiomatic, in his statement that "the true generating formula, that which englobes all the others, and which is somehow the stabilized form of the code, is that of binarity, of digitality" (145). From this he concludes that the primary fact about digitality is its connection to "cybernetic control . . . the new operational configuration," since "digitalization is its metaphysical principle (the God of Leibnitz), and DNA its prophet" (103).

True, at the most basic level of machine code and at the far higher one of program languages, the digitization, which constitutes a fundamental of electronic computing, does involve binarity. But from this fact one cannot so naively extrapolate, as Baudrillard does, a complete thought-world or *episteme*. Baudrillard, of course, may well have it partially right: he might have perceived one key connection between the stimulus/response model and digitality. The fact of hypertext, however, demonstrates quite clearly that digitality does not necessarily lock one into either a linear world or one of binary oppositions.

Unlike Derrida, who emphasizes the role of the book, writing, and writing technology, Baudrillard never considers verbal text, whose absence glaringly runs through his argument and reconstitutes it in ways that he obviously did not expect. Part of Baudrillard's theoretical difficulty, I suggest, derives from the fact that he bypasses digitized verbal text and moves with too easy grace directly from the fact of digital encoding of information in two directions: (1) to his stimulus/response, either/or model, and (2) to other nonalphanumeric (or nonwriting) media, such as photography, radio, and television. Interestingly enough, when Baudrillard correctly emphasizes the role of digitality in the postmodern world, he generally derives his examples of digitalization from media that, particularly at the time he wrote, for the most part depended upon analogue rather than digital technology—and the qualities and implications of the two technologies differ fundamentally. Whereas analogue recording of sound and visual information requires serial, linear processing, digital technology removes the need for sequence, by permitting one to go directly to a particular bit of information. Thus, if one wishes to find a particular passage in a Bach sonata on a tape cassette, one must scan through the cassette sequentially, though modern tape decks permit one to speed the process by skipping from space to space between sections of music. In contrast, if one wishes to locate a passage in digitally recorded music, one can instantly travel to that passage, note it for future reference, and manipulate it in ways impossible with analogue technologies—for example, one can instantly replay passages without having to scroll back through them.

In concentrating on nonalphanumeric media, and in apparently confusing analogue and digital technology, Baudrillard misses the opportunity to encounter the fact that digitalization also has the potential to prevent, block, and bypass linearity and binarity, which it replaces with multiplicity, true reader activity and activation, and branching through networks. Baudrillard has described one major thread or constituent of contemporary reality that is potentially at war with the multilinear, hypertextual one.

In addition to hypertext, several aspects of humanities computing derive from the virtuality of its text. First of all, the ease of manipulating individual alphanumeric symbols facilitates word processing. Simple word processing in turn has, ironically, made vastly easier the old-fashioned job of traditional scholarly editing—the creation of reliable, supposedly authoritative texts from manuscripts or published books—at a time when the very notion of such single, unitary, univocal texts may be changing or disappearing.

Second, this same ease of cutting, copying, and otherwise manipulating texts permits different forms of scholarly composition, ones in which the researcher's notes and original data exist in experientially closer proximity to the scholarly text than ever before. According to Michael Heim, as electronic textuality frees writing from the constraints of paper-print technology, "vast amounts of information, including further texts, will be accessible immediately below the electronic surface of a piece of writing. . . . By connecting a small computer to a phone, a professional will be able to read 'books' whose footnotes can be expanded into further 'books' which in turn open out onto a vast sea of data bases systemizing all of human cognition" (*Electric Language,* 10–11). The manipulability of the scholarly text, which derives from the ability of computers to search data bases with enormous speed, also permits full-text searches, printed and dynamic concordances, and other kinds of processing that allow scholars in the humanities to ask new kinds of questions. Moreover, while one writes, "the text in progress becomes interconnected and linked with the entire world of information" (161).

Third, the electronic virtual text, whose appearance and form readers can customize as they see fit, also has the potential to add an entire new element—the electronic or virtual link that reconfigures text as we who have grown up with books have experienced it. Electronic linking creates hypertext, a form of textuality composed of blocks and links that permits multilinear reading paths. As Heim has argued, electronic word processing inevitably produces linkages, and these linkages move text, readers, and writers into a new writing space.

The distinctive features of formulating thought in the psychic framework of word processing combine with the automation of information handling and produce an unprecedented linkage of text. By *linkage* I mean not some loose physical connection like discrete books sharing a common physical space in the library. *Text* derives originally from the Latin word for weaving and for interwoven material, and it has come to have extraordinary accuracy of meaning in the case of word processing. Linkage in the electronic element is interactive, that is, texts can be brought instantly into the same psychic framework. (160–61)

The presence of multiple reading paths, which shift the balance between reader and writer, thereby creating Barthes's writerly text, also creates a text that exists far less independently of commentary, analogues, and traditions than does printed text. This kind of democratization not only reduces the hierarchical separation between the so-called main text and the annotation, which now exist as independent texts, reading units, or lexias, but it also blurs the boundaries of individual texts. In so doing, electronic linking reconfigures our experience of both author and authorial property, and this reconception of these ideas promises to affect our conceptions of both the authors (and authority) of texts we study and of ourselves as authors.

Equally important, all these changes take place in an electronic environment, the Nelsonian docuverse, in which publication changes meaning. Hypertext, far more than any other aspect of computing, promises to make publication a matter of gaining access to electronic networks. For the time being, scholars will continue to rely on books, and one can guess that continuing improvements in desktop publishing and laser printing will produce a late efflorescence of the text as a physical object. Nonetheless, these physical texts will be produced (or rather reproduced) from electronic texts, and as readers increasingly become accustomed to the convenience of electronically linked texts, books, which now define the scholar's tools and end-products, will gradually lose their primary role in humanistic scholarship.

Books Are Technology, Too

We find ourselves, for the first time in centuries, able to see the book as unnatural, as a near-miraculous technological innovation and not as something intrinsically and inevitably human. We have, to use Derridean terms, decentered the book. We find ourselves in the position, in other words, of perceiving the book *as technology*. I think it no mere coincidence that it is at precisely this period in human history we have acquired crucial intellectual distance from the book as object and as cultural product. First came the distant hearing—the telephone—then the cinema and then the distant seeing of television. It is only with the added possibilities created by these new information media and computing that Harold Innis, Marshall McLuhan, Jack Goody, Elizabeth Eisenstein, Alvin Kernan, Roger Chartier, and the European scholars of *Lesengeshichte* could arise.

Influential as these scholars have been, not all scholars willingly recognize the power of information technologies upon culture. This resistance appears in two characteristic reactions to the proposition that information technology constitutes a crucial cultural force. First, many humanists assume that before now, before computing, our intellectual culture existed in some pastoral nontechnological realm. *Technology,* in the lexicon of many humanists, generally means "only that technology of which I am frightened." In fact, I have frequently heard humanists use the word technology to mean "some intrusive, alien force like computing," as if pencils, paper, typewriters, and printing presses were in some way *natural.* Digital technology may be new, but technology, particularly information technology, has permeated all known culture since the beginnings of human history. If we hope to discern the fate of reading and writing in digital environments, we must not treat all previous information technologies of language, rhetoric, writing, and printing as nontechnological.

As John Henry Cardinal Newman's *Idea of a University* reminds us, writers on education and culture have long tended to perceive only the negative effects of technology. To us who live in an age in which educators and pundits continually elevate reading books as an educational ideal and continually attack television as a medium that victimizes a passive audience, it comes as a shock to encounter Newman claiming that cheap, easily available reading materials similarly victimized the public:

What the steam engine does with matter, the printing press is to do with mind; it is to act mechanically, and the population is to be passively, almost unconsciously enlightened, by the mere multiplication and dissemination of volumes. Whether it be the school boy, or the school girl, or the youth at college, or the mechanic in the town, or the politician in the senate, all have been the victims in one way or other of this most preposterous and pernicious of delusions. (103)

Part of Newman's rationale for thus denouncing cheap, abundant reading materials lies in the belief that they supposedly advance the dangerous fallacy that "learning is to be without exertion, without attention, without toil; without grounding, without advance, without finishing"; but like any conservative elitist in our own day, he fears the people unsupervised, and he cannot believe that reading without proper guidance—guidance, that is, from those who know, from those in institutions like Oxford—can produce any sort of valid education; and, one expects, had Newman encountered the self-taught mill workers and artisans of Victorian England who made discoveries in chemistry, astronomy, and geology after reading newly available books, he would not have been led to change his mind.

Like Socrates, who feared the effects of writing, which he took to be an anonymous, impersonal denaturing of living speech, Newman also fears an "impersonal" information technology that people can use without supervision. And also like Socrates, he desires institutions of higher learning—which for the ancient takes the form of face-to-face conversation, dialectic—to be sensitive to the needs of specific individuals. Newman therefore argues that "a University is, according to the usual designation, an Alma Mater, knowing her children one by one, not a foundry, or a mint, or a treadmill."

Newman's criticism of the flood of printed matter produced by the new mass-publication technology superficially echoes Thomas Carlyle, whose "Signs of the Times" (1829) had lambasted his age for being a mechanical one whose "true Deity is Mechanism." In fact, claims this first of Victorian sages,

not the external and physical alone is managed by machinery, but the internal and spiritual also. Here too nothing follows its spontaneous course, nothing is left to be accomplished by old, natural methods. . . . Instruction, that mysterious communing of Wisdom with Ignorance, is no longer an indefinable tentative process, requiring a study of individual aptitudes, and a perpetual variation of means and methods, to attain the same end; but a secure, universal, straightforward business, to be conducted in the gross, by proper mechanism, with such intellect as comes to hand. (101)

Several things demand remark in this passage, the first and most obvious of which is that it parallels and might have provided one of the major inspirations for Newman's conceptions of education. The second recognition, which certainly shocks us more than does the first, is that Carlyle attacked those like Newman who proposed educational systems and design institutions.

In sentences that I have omitted from the quoted passage, Carlyle explained that, for his contemporaries, everything had "its cunningly devised implements, its preëstablished apparatus; it is not done by hand but by machinery. Thus we have machines for education: Lancasterian machines; Hamiltonian machines; monitors, maps, and emblems." Or, as Carlyle might say today, we have peer tutoring, core curricula, distribution requirements, work-study programs, and junior years abroad.

What is not at issue here is the practicality of Carlyle's criticisms of the mechanization of education and other human activities—after all, it would seem that he would attack any organizational change on the same grounds.

No, what is crucial here is that Carlyle, who apparently denied all possibilities for reforming existing institutions, made a crucial recognition about them that Newman, the often admirable theorist of education, did not. Carlyle recognized that all institutions and forms of social organization are properly to be considered technologies. Carlyle, who pointed out elsewhere that gunpowder and the printing press destroyed feudalism, recognized that writing, printing, pedagogical systems, universities are all technologies of cultural memory. Newman, like most academics of the last few hundred years, considered them, more naively, as natural and inevitable, and consequently noticed the effects of only those institutions new to him or that he did not like.

The great value of Carlyle's recognition to our project here lies in its reminding us that electronifying universities does not technologize them or add to them technology that is in some way alien to their essential spirit. Digital information technology, in other words, is only the latest technology to shape an institution that, as Carlyle reminds us, is both itself a form of technology, a mechanism, and has also long been influenced by those technologies on which it relies.

A second form of resistance to recognizing the role of information technology in culture appears in implicit claims that technology, particularly information technology, can *never* have cultural effects. Almost always presented by speakers and writers as evidence of their own sophistication and sensitivity, this strategy of denial has an unintended effect: denying that Gutenberg's invention or television can exist in a causal connection to any other aspect of culture immediately transforms technology—whatever the author means by that term—into a kind of intellectual monster, something so taboo that civilized people cannot discuss it in public. In other words, it takes technology, which is both an agent and an effect of our continually changing culture(s), and denies its existence as an element of human culture. One result appears in the strategies of the authors of historical or predictive studies, who relate cultural phenomena to all sorts of economic, cultural, and ideological factors but avert their eyes from any technological causation, as if it, and only it, were in some way reductive. The effect, of course, finally is to deny that this particular form of cultural product can have any effect.

We have to remind ourselves that if, how, and whenever we move beyond the book, that movement will not embody a movement from something natural or human to something artificial—from nature to technology—since writing, and printing, and books are about as technological as one can get. Books, after all, are teaching and communicating *machines*. Therefore, if we find ourselves in a period of fundamental technological and cultural change analogous to the Gutenberg revolution, one of the first things we should do is remind ourselves that printed books are technology, too.

Analogues

to the Gutenberg Revolution

According to Alvin Kernan, "the 'logic' of a technology, an idea, or an institution is its tendency consistently to shape whatever it affects in a limited number of definite forms or directions" (49). What can we predict about the future by understanding the "logic" of a particular technology or set of technologies? The work of Kernan and others, like Roger Chartier and Elizabeth Eisenstein, who have studied the complex transitions from manuscript to print culture suggest three clear lessons or rules for anyone anticipating similar transitions into electronic culture.

First of all, such transitions take a long time, certainly much longer than early studies of the shift from manuscript to print culture led one to expect. Students of technology and the practice of reading point to several hundred years of gradual change and accommodation, during which different reading practices, modes of publication, and conceptions of literature obtained. According to Kernan, not until about 1700 did print technology "transform the more advanced countries of Europe from oral into print societies, reordering the entire social world, and restructuring rather than merely modifying letters" (9). How long, then, will it take computing, specifically computer hypertext, to effect similar changes? How long, one wonders, will the change to electronic language take until it becomes culturally pervasive? And what byways, transient cultural accommodations, and the like will intervene and thereby create a more confusing, if culturally more interesting, picture?

The second rule of technological transition is that studying the relations of technology to literature and other aspects of humanistic culture does not produce any mechanical reading of culture, such as that feared by Jameson and others. As Kernan makes clear, understanding the logic of a particular technology cannot permit simple prediction, because under varying conditions the same technology can produce varying, even contradictory, effects. J. David Bolter and other historians of writing have pointed out, for example, that initially writing, which served priestly and monarchical interests in recording laws and records, appeared purely elitist, even hieratic; later, as the practice diffused down the social and economic scale, it appeared democratizing, even anarchic. To a large extent, printed books had similarly diverse effects, though it took far less time for the democratizing factors to triumph over the hieratic—a matter of centuries, perhaps decades, instead of millennia!

Similarly, as Chartier and Marie-Elizabeth Ducreux have shown, both printed matter and manuscript books functioned as instruments of "religious acculturation controlled by authority, but under certain circumstances also supported resistance to a faith rejected, and proved an ultimate and secret recourse against forced conversion." Books of hours, marriage charters, and so-called evangelical books all embodied a "basic tension between public, ceremonial, and ecclesiastical use of the book or other print object, and personal, private, and internalized reading" (Chartier, *Culture of Print,* 139).[9]

Kernan himself points out that

> knowledge of the leading principles of print logic, such as fixity, multiplicity, and systematization, makes it possible to predict the tendencies but not the *exact* ways in which they were to manifest themselves in the history of writing and in the world of letters. The idealization of the literary text and the attribution to it of a stylistic essence are both developments of latent print possibilities, but there was, I believe, no precise necessity beforehand that letters would be valorized in these particular ways. (181)

Kernan also points to the "tension, if not downright contradiction, between two of the primary energies of print logic, multiplicity and fixity—what we might call 'the remainder house' and the 'library' effects" (55), each of which comes into play, or becomes dominant, only under certain economic, political, and technological conditions.

The third lesson or rule one can derive from the work of Kernan and other historians of the relations among reading practice, information technology, and culture is that transformations have political contexts and political implications. Considerations of hypertext, critical theory, and literature have to take into account what Jameson calls the basic "recognition that there is nothing that is not social and historical—indeed, that everything is 'in the last analysis' political" (*Political Unconscious,* 20).

If the technology of printing radically changed the world in the manner that Kernan convincingly explains, what then will be the effects of the parallel shift from print to computer hypertext? Although the changes associated with the transition from print to electronic technology may not parallel those associated with that from manuscript to print, paying attention to descriptions of the most recent shift in the technology of alphanumeric text provides areas for investigation.

One of the most important changes involved fulfilling the democratizing potential of the new information technology. During the shift from manuscript to print culture "an older system of polite or courtly letters—primarily oral, aristocratic, authoritarian, court-centered—was swept away . . . and gradually replaced by a new print-based, market-centered, democratic literary system" whose fundamental values "were, while not strictly determined by print ways, still indirectly in accordance with the actualities of print" (*Print Technologies,* 4). If hypertextuality and associated electronic information technologies have similarly pervasive effects, what will they be? Nelson, J. Hillis Miller, and almost all authors on hypertext who touch upon the political implications of hypertext assume that the technology is essentially democratizing and that it therefore supports some sort of decentralized, liberated existence.

Kernan offers numerous specific instances of ways that technology "actually affects individual and social life." For example, "by changing their work and their writing, [print] forced the writer, the scholar, and the teacher—the standard literary roles—to redefine themselves, and if it did not entirely create, it noticeably increased the importance and number of critics, editors, bibliographers, and literary historians." Print technology similarly redefined the audience for literature by transforming it from

a small group of manuscript readers or listeners . . . to a group of readers . . . who bought books to read in the privacy of their homes. Print also made literature objectively real for the first time, and therefore subjectively conceivable as a universal fact, in great libraries of printed books containing large collections of the world's writing. . . . Print also rearranged the relationship of letters to other parts of the social world by, for example, freeing the writer from the need for patronage and the consequent subservience to wealth, by challenging and reducing established authority's control of writing by means of state censorship, and by pushing through a copyright law that made the author the owner of his own writing. (4–5)

Electronic linking shifts the boundaries between one text and another as well as between the author and the reader and between and the teacher and the student. It also has radical effects upon our experience of author, text, and work, redefining each. Its effects are so basic, so radical, that it reveals that many of our most cherished, most commonplace, ideas and attitudes toward literature and literary production turn out to be the result of that particular form of information technology and technology of cultural memory that has provided the setting for them. This technology—that of the printed book and its close relations, which include the typed or printed page—engenders certain notions of authorial property, authorial uniqueness, and a physically isolated text that hypertext makes untenable. The evidence of hypertext, in other words, historicizes many of our most commonplace assumptions, thereby forcing them to descend from the ethereality of abstraction and appear as corollary to a particular technology rooted in specific times and places. In making available these points, hypertext has much in common with some major points of contemporary literary and semiological theory, particularly with Derrida's emphasis on decentering and with Barthes's conception of the readerly versus the writerly text. In fact, hypertext creates an almost embarrassingly literal embodiment of both concepts, one that in turn raises questions about them and their interesting combination of prescience and historical relations (or embeddedness).

Hypertext
and Critical Theory

Textual Openness

Like Barthes, Foucault, and Mikhail Bakhtin, Jacques Derrida continually uses the terms *link (liaisons), web (toile), network (réseau),* and *interwoven (s'y tissent),* which cry out for hypertextuality (*La dissémination,* 71, 108, 172, 111; *Dissemination,* 96, 63, 98, 149). However, in contrast to Barthes, who emphasizes the writerly text and its nonlinearity, Derrida emphasizes textual openness, intertextuality, and the irrelevance of distinctions between inside and outside a particular text. These emphases appear with particular clarity when he claims that "like any text, the text of 'Plato' couldn't not be involved, at least in a virtual, dynamic, lateral manner, with all the worlds that composed the system of the Greek language." Derrida in fact here describes extant hypertext systems in which the active reader in the process of exploring a text, probing it, can call into play dictionaries with morphological analyzers that connect individual words to cognates, derivations, and opposites. Here again something that Derrida and other critical theorists describe as part of a seemingly extravagant claim about language turns out precisely to describe the new economy of reading and writing with electronic virtual, rather than physical, forms.

Derrida properly recognizes (in advance, one might say) that a new, freer, richer form of text, one truer to our potential experience, perhaps to our actual if unrecognized experience, depends upon discrete reading units. As he explains, in what Gregory Ulmer terms "the fundamental generalization of his writing" (*Applied Grammatology,* 58), there also exists "the possibility of disengagement and citational graft which belongs to the structure of every mark, spoken and written, and which constitutes every mark in writing before and outside of every horizon of semiolinguistic communication. . . . Every sign, linguistic or non-linguistic, spoken or written . . . can be cited, put between quotation marks." The implication of such citability, separability, appears in the fact, crucial to hypertext, that, as Derrida adds, "in so doing it can break with every given context, engendering an infinity of new contexts in a manner which is absolutely illimitable" ("Signature," 185, quoted in Ulmer, *Applied Grammatology,* 58–59).

Like Barthes, Derrida conceives of text as constituted by discrete reading units. Derrida's conception of text relates to his "methodology of decomposition" that might transgress the limits of philosophy. "The organ of this new philospheme," as Ulmer points out, "is the mouth, the mouth that bites, chews, tastes. . . . The first step of decomposition is the bite" (57). Derrida, who describes text in terms of something close to Barthes's lexias, explains in *Glas* that "the object of the present work, its style too, is the 'mourceau,'" which Ulmer translates as "bit, piece, morsel, fragment; musical composition; snack, mouthful." This mourceau, adds Derrida, "is always detached, as its name indicates and so you do not forget it, with the teeth," and these teeth, Ulmer explains, refer to "quotation marks, brackets, parentheses: when language is cited (put between quotation marks), the effect is that of releasing the grasp or hold of a controlling context" (58).

Derrida's groping for a way to foreground his recognition of the way text operates in a print medium—he is, after all, the fierce advocate of writing as against orality—shows the position, possibly the dilemma, of the thinker working with print who sees its shortcomings but for all his brilliance cannot think his way outside this *mentalité.* Derrida, the experience of hypertext shows, gropes toward a new kind of text: he describes it, he praises it, but he can only present it in terms of the devices—here those of punctuation—associated with a particular kind of writing. As the Marxists remind us, thought derives from the forces and modes of production, though, as we shall see, few Marxists or Marxians ever directly confront the most important mode of literary production—that dependent upon the *techne* of writing and print.

From this Derridean emphasis upon discontinuity comes the conception of hypertext as a vast assemblage, what I have elsewhere termed the metatext and what Nelson calls the "docuverse." Derrida in fact employs the word *assemblage* for cinema, which he perceives as a rival, an alternative, to print. Ulmer points out that "the gram or trace provides the 'linguistics' for collage/montage" (267), and he quotes Derrida's use of *assemblage* in *Speech and Phenomena:* "The word 'assemblage' seems more apt for suggesting that the kind of bringing-together proposed here has the structure of an interlacing, a weaving, or a web, which would allow the different threads and different lines of sense or force to separate again, as well as being ready to bind others together" (131). To carry Derrida's instinctive theorizing of hypertext further, one may also point to his recognition that such a montagelike textuality marks or foregrounds the writing process and therefore rejects a deceptive transparency.

Hypertext and Intertextuality

Hypertext, which is a fundamentally intertextual system, has the capacity to emphasize intertextuality in a way that page-bound text in books cannot. As we have already observed, scholarly articles and books offer an obvious example of *explicit* hypertextuality in nonelectronic form. Conversely, any work of literature—which for the sake of argument and economy I shall here confine in a most arbitrary way to mean "high" literature of the sort we read and teach in universities—offers an instance of *implicit* hypertext in nonelectronic form. Again, take Joyce's *Ulysses* for an example. If one looks, say, at the Nausicaa section, in which Bloom watches Gerty McDowell on the beach, one notes that Joyce's text here "alludes" or "refers" (the terms we usually employ) to many other texts or phenomena that one can treat as texts, including the Nausicaa section of the *Odyssey,* the advertisements and articles in the women's magazines that suffuse and inform Gerty's thoughts, facts about contemporary Dublin and the Catholic Church, and material that relates to other passages within the novel. Again, a hypertext presentation of the novel links this section not only to the kinds of materials mentioned but also to other works in Joyce's career, critical commentary, and textual variants. Hypertext here permits one to make explicit, though not necessarily intrusive, the linked materials that an educated reader perceives surrounding it.

Thaïs Morgan suggests that intertextuality, "as a structural analysis of texts in relation to the larger system of signifying practices or uses of signs in culture," shifts attention from the triad constituted by author/work/tradition to another constituted by text/discourse/culture. In so doing, "intertextuality replaces the evolutionary model of literary history with a structural or synchronic model of literature as a sign system. The most salient effect of this strategic change is to free the literary text from psychological, sociological, and historical determinisms, opening it up to an apparently infinite play of relationships" (1–2). Morgan well describes a major implication of hypertext (and hypermedia) intertextuality: such opening up, such freeing one to create and perceive interconnections, obviously occurs. Nonetheless, although hypertext intertextuality would seem to devalue any historic or other reductionism, it in no way prevents those interested in reading in terms of author and tradition from doing so. Experiments thus far with Intermedia, HyperCard, and other hypertext systems suggest that hypertext does not necessarily turn one's attention away from such approaches. What is perhaps most interesting about hypertext, though, is not that it may fulfill certain claims of structuralist and poststructuralist criticism but that it provides a rich means of testing them.

Hypertext and Multivocality

In attempting to imagine the experience of reading and writing with (or within) this new form of text, one would do well to pay heed to what Mikhail Bakhtin has written about the dialogic, polyphonic, multivocal novel, which he claims "is constructed not as the whole of a single consciousness, absorbing other consciousnesses as objects into itself, but as a whole formed by the interaction of several consciousnesses, none of which entirely becomes an object for the other" (18). Bakhtin's description of the polyphonic literary form presents the Dostoevskian novel as a hypertextual fiction in which the individual voices take the form of lexias.

If Derrida illuminates hypertextuality from the vantage point of the "bite" or "bit," Bakhtin illuminates it from the vantage point of its own life and force—the incarnation or instantiation of a voice, a point of view, a Rortyian conversation.[1] Thus, according to Bakhtin, "in the novel itself, nonparticipating 'third persons' are not represented in any way. There is no place for them, compositionally or in the larger meaning of the work" (18). In terms of hypertextuality this points to an important quality of this information medium: hypertext does not permit a tyrannical, univocal voice. Rather the voice is always that distilled from the combined experience of the momentary focus, the lexia one presently reads, and the continually forming narrative of one's reading path.

Hypertext and Decentering

As readers move through a web or network of texts, they continually shift the center—and hence the focus or organizing principle—of their investigation and experience. Hypertext, in other words, provides an infinitely recenterable system whose provisional point of focus depends upon the reader, who becomes a truly active reader in yet another sense. One of the fundamental characteristics of hypertext is that it is composed of bodies of linked texts that have no primary axis of organization. In other words, the metatext or document set—the entity that describes what in print technology is the book, work, or single text—has no center. Although this absence of a center can create problems for the reader and the writer, it also means that anyone who uses hypertext makes his or her own interests the de facto organizing principle (or center) for the investigation at the moment. One experiences hypertext as an infinitely decenterable and recenterable system, in part because hypertext transforms any document that has more than one link into a transient center, a directory document that one can employ to orient oneself and to decide where to go next.

Western culture imagined quasi-magical entrances to a networked reality long before the development of computing technology. Biblical typology, which played such a major role in English culture during the seventeenth and nineteenth centuries, conceived sacred history in terms of types and shadows of Christ and his dispensation. Thus, Moses, who existed in his own right, also existed as Christ, who fulfilled and completed the prophet's meaning. As countless seventeenth-century and Victorian sermons, tracts, and commentaries demonstrate, any particular person, event, or phenomenon could act as a magical window into the complex semiotic of the divine scheme for human salvation. Like the biblical type, which allows significant events and phenomena to participate simultaneously in many realities or levels of reality, the individual lexia inevitably provides a way into the network of connections. Given that evangelical Protestantism in America preserves and extends these traditions of biblical exegesis, one is not surprised to discover that some of the first applications of hypertext involved the Bible and its exegetical tradition.[2]

Not only do lexias work much in the manner of types, they also become Borgesian Alephs, points in space that contain all other points, because from the vantage point each provides one can see everything else—if not exactly simultaneously, then a short way distant, one or two jumps away, particularly in systems that have full text searching. Unlike Jorge Luis Borges's Aleph, one does not have to view it from a single site, neither does one have to sprawl in a cellar resting one's head on a canvas sack.[3] The hypertext document becomes a traveling Aleph.

As Derrida points out in "Structure, Sign, and Play in the Discourse of the Human Sciences," the process or procedure he calls "de-centering" has played an essential role in intellectual change. He says, for example, that "ethnology could have been born as a science only at the moment when a de-centering had come about: at the moment when European culture—and, in consequence, the history of metaphysics and of its concepts—had been dislocated, driven from its locus, and forced to stop considering itself as the culture of reference" (251). Derrida makes no claim that an intellectual or ideological center is in any way bad, for, as he explains in response to a query from Serge Doubrovsky, "I didn't say that there was no center, that we could get along without a center. I believe that the center is a function, not a being—a reality, but a function. And this function is absolutely indispensable" (271).

All hypertext systems permit the individual reader to choose his or her own center of investigation and experience. What this principle means in practice is that the reader is not locked into any kind of particular organization or hierarchy. Experiences with various hypertext systems reveal that, for those who organize their work in terms of authors—moving, say, from Keats to Tennyson—the system functions as an old-fashioned, traditional, and in many ways still useful author-centered approach. On the other hand, nothing constrains the reader to work in this manner, and readers who wish to investigate the validity of period generalizations can organize their hypertext sessions by using the Victorian and Romantic overviews as starting or midpoints, while yet others can begin with ideological or critical notions, such as feminism or the Victorian novel. In practice most readers who employ the materials developed at Brown University choose them because they form a text-centered system, since they tend to focus upon individual works; even if they enter the system looking for information about an individual author, they tend to spend most time with lexias devoted to specific texts, moving between poem and poem (Swinburne's "Laus Veneris" and Keats's "La Belle Dame Sans Merci" or works centering on Ulysses by Joyce, Tennyson, and Soyinka) and between poem and informational texts ("Laus Veneris" and files on chivalry, medieval revival, courtly love, Wagner, and so on).

Hypertext as Rhizome

Shortly after I began to teach hypertext and critical theory, Tom Meyer, a member of my first class, advised me that Gilles Deleuze and Félix Guattari's *A Thousand Plateaus* demanded a place in *Hypertext.* And he was clearly right. Anyone considering the subject of this book has to look closely at their discussion of rhizomes, plateaus, and nomadic thought for several obvious reasons, only the most obvious of which is that they present *A Thousand Plateaus* as a print proto-hypertext. Like Julio Cortázar's *Hopscotch,* their volume comes with instructions to read it in various reader-determined orders, so that, as Stuart Moulthrop explains, their "rhizome-book may itself be considered an incunabular hypertext . . . designed as a matrix of independent but cross-referential discourses which the reader is invited to enter more or less at random" and read in any order. "The reader's implicit task," Moulthrop explains, "is to build a network of virtual connections (which more than one reader of my acquaintance has suggested operationalizing as a web of hypertext links)" ("Rhizome and Resistance," 300–301).

Certainly, many of the qualities Deleuze and Guattari attribute to the rhizome require hypertext to find their first approximation if not their complete answer or fulfillment. Thus, Deleuze and Guattari's explanation of a plateau accurately describes the way both individual lexias and clusters of them participate in a web: "A plateau is always in the middle, not at the beginning or the end. A rhizome is made of plateaus. Gregory Bateson uses the word 'plateau' to designate something very special: a continuous, self-vibrating region of intensities whose development avoids any orientation toward a culmination point or external end" (21–22), such as orgasm, war, or other point of culmination. Deleuze and Guattari, who criticize the "Western mind" for relating "expressions and actions to exterior or transcendent ends, instead of evaluating them on a plane of consistency on the basis of their intrinsic value," take the printed book to exemplify such characteristic climactic thought, explaining that "a book composed of chapters has culmination and termination points" (22).

Like Derrida and like the inventors of hypertext, they propose a newer form of the book that might provide a truer, more efficient information technology, asking: "What takes place in a book composed instead of plateaus that communicate with one another across microfissures, as in a brain? We call a 'plateau' any multiplicity connected to other multiplicities by superficial underground stems in such a way as to form or extend a rhizome" (22). Such a description, I should add, perfectly matches the way clusters or subwebs organize themselves in large networked hypertext environments, such as the World Wide Web. In fact, reducing Deleuze and Guattari's grand prescription to relatively puny literal embodiment, one could take the sections concerning Gaskell and Trollope in *The Victorian Web,* or the individual student creations in *The Cyberspace Web,* as embodiments of plateaus. Indeed, one of the principles of reading and writing hypermedia—as in exploring a library of printed books—lies in the fact that one can begin anywhere and make connections, or, as Deleuze and Guattari put it, "each plateau can be read starting anywhere and can be related to any other plateau."

Such a characteristic organization (or lack of it) derives from the rhizome's fundamental opposition to hierarchy, a structural form whose embodiment Deleuze and Guattari find in the arborescent: "unlike trees or their roots, the rhizome connects any point to any other point, and its traits are not necessarily linked to traits of the same nature; it brings into play very different regimes of signs, and even nonsign states" (21). As Meyer explains in *Plateaus*, a Storyspace web that has since been published as part of *Writing at the Edge*, we generally rely upon "arborescent structures," such as binary thought, genealogies, and hierarchies, to divide the "seemingly endless stream of information about the world into more easily assimilable bits. And, for this purpose, these structures serve admirably." Unfortunately, these valuable "organizational tools end up becoming the only methods of understanding," and limit instead of enhancing or liberating our thought. "In contrast, Deleuze and Guattari propose the rhizome as a useful model for analysing structures—the potato, the strawberry plant, with their thickenings and shifting connections, with their network-like structure instead of a tree-like one" (*Plateaus*, "Tree/Rhizome").

This fundamental network structure, say Deleuze and Guattari, explains why

the rhizome is reducible neither to the One nor the multiple. . . . It has neither beginning nor end, but always a middle (milieu) from which it grows and which it overspills. . . . When a multiplicity of this kind changes dimension, it necessarily changes in nature as well, undergoes a metamorphosis. . . . . The rhizome is an antigenealogy. It is a short-term memory, or antimemory. The rhizome operates by variation, expansion, conquest, capture, offshoots. Unlike the graphic arts, drawing, or photography, unlike tracings, the rhizome pertains to a map that must be produced, constructed, a map that is always detachable, connectable, reversible, modifiable, and has multiple entryways and exits and its own lines of flight. . . . In contrast to centered (even polycentric) systems with hierarchical modes of communication and preestablished paths, the rhizome is an acentered, nonhierarchical, nonsignifying system without a General and without an organizing memory or central automaton, defined solely by a circulation of states. (21)

As we explore hypertext in the following pages, we shall repeatedly encounter the very qualities and characteristics Deleuze and Guattari here specify: Like the rhizome, hypertext, which has "multiple entryways and exits," embodies something closer to anarchy than to hierarchy, and it "connects any point to any other point," often joining fundamentally different kinds of information and often violating what we understand to be both discrete print texts and discrete genres and modes.

Any reader of hypertext who has experienced the way our own activities within the networked text produce multiple versions and approaches to a single lexia will see the parallel to hypertext in Deleuze and Guattari's point that "multiplicities are rhizomatic, and expose arborescent pseudomultiplicities for what they are. There is no unity to serve as a pivot in the object, or to divide in the subject" (8). Therefore, like hypertext considered in its most general sense, "a rhizome is not amenable to any structural or generative model. It is a stranger to any idea of genetic axis or deep structure" (12). As Deleuze and Guattari explain, a rhizome is "a map and not a tracing. Make a map, not a tracing. The orchid does not reproduce the tracing of the wasp; it forms a map with the wasp, in a rhizome. What distinguishes the map from the tracing is that it is entirely oriented toward an experimentation in contact with the real" (12). Maps and hypertexts both, in other words, relate directly to performance, to interaction.

Like some statements by Derrida, some of Deleuze and Guattari's more cryptic discussions of the rhizome often become clearer when considered from the vantage point of hypertext. For example, when they state that the rhizome is a "a short-term memory, or antimemory," something apparently in complete contrast with any information technology or technology of cultural memory, they nonetheless capture the provisional, temporary, changing quality in which readers make individual lexias the temporary center of their movement through an information space.

Perhaps one of the most difficult portions of *A Thousand Plateaus* involves the notion of nomadic thought, something, again, much easier to convey and experience in a fluid electronic environment than from within the world of print. According to Michael Joyce, the first important writer of hypertext fiction and one of the creators of Storyspace, Deleuze and Guattari reject "the word and world fully mapped as logos," proposing instead that "we write ourselves in the gap of nomos, the nomadic" (*Of Two Minds,* 207). They offer or propose, he explains, "being-for space against being-in space. We are in the water, inscribing and inscribed by the flow in our sailing. We write ourselves in oscillation between the smooth space of being for-time (what happens to us as we go as well as what happens to the space in which we do so) and the striated space of in-time (what happens outside the space and us)" (207).

Those who find the ruptures and seams as important to hypertext as the links that bridge such gaps find that the rhizome has yet another crucial aspect of hypertextuality. Moulthrop, for example, who "describes hypertexts as composed of nodes and links, local coherences and linearities broken across the gap or synapse of transition," takes this approach: "In describing the rhizome as a model of discourse, Deleuze and Guattari invoke the 'principle of asignifying rupture' (9), a fundamental tendency toward unpredictability and discontinuity. Perhaps then hypertext and hypermedia represent the expression of the rhizome in the social space of writing" ("Rhizome and Resistance," 304)

We must take care not to push the similarity too far and assume that their descriptions of rhizome, plateau, and nomadic thought map one to one onto hypertext, since many of their descriptions of the rhizome and rhizomatic thought appear impossible to fulfill in any information technology that uses words, images, or limits of any sort. Thus, when Deleuze and Guattari write that a rhizome "has neither beginning nor end, but always a middle (milieu) from which it grows and which it overspills," they describe something that has much in common with the kind of quasi-anarchic networked hypertext one encounters in the World Wide Web, but when in their next sentence they add that the rhizome "is composed not of units but of dimensions, or rather directions in motion" (21), the parallel seems harder to complete. The rhizome is essentially a counter paradigm, not something realizable in any time or culture; but it can serve as an ideal for hypertext, and hypertext, at least Nelsonian, ideal hypertext, approaches it as much as can any human creation.

The Nonlinear Model

of the Network

in Current Critical Theory

Discussions and designs of hypertext share with contemporary critical theory an emphasis upon the model or paradigm of the network. At least four meanings of *network* appear in descriptions of actual hypertext systems and plans for future ones. First, individual print works when transferred to hypertext take the form of blocks, nodes, or lexias joined by a network of links and paths. *Network,* in this sense, refers to one kind of electronically linked electronic equivalent to a printed text. Second, any gathering of lexias, whether assembled by the original author of the verbal text or by someone gathering together texts created by multiple authors, also takes the form of a network; thus document sets, whose shifting borders make them in some senses the hypertextual equivalent of a work, are called, in some present systems, a web.

Third, the term *network* refers to an electronic system involving additional computers as well as cables or wire connections that permit individual machines, workstations, and reading-and-writing-sites to share information. These networks can take the form of contemporary local area networks (LANs), such as Ethernet, which join sets of machines within an institution, department, or other administrative unit. Networks also take the form of wide area networks (WANs), which join multiple organizations in widely separated geographical locations. Early versions of wide area national and international networks include JANET (in the U.K.), ARPANET (in the U.S.A.), the proposed National Research and Education Network (NREN), and BITNET, which links universities, research centers, and laboratories in North America, Europe, Israel, and Japan.[4] Such networks, which until the arrival of the World Wide Web had been used chiefly for electronic mail and transfer of individual files, have also supported international electronic bulletin boards, like Humanist. More powerful networks that transfer large quantities of information at great speed will be necessary before such networks can fully support hypertext.

The fourth meaning of *network* in relation to hypertext comes close to matching the use of the term in critical theory. In this fullest sense, the word refers to the entirety of all those terms for which there is no term and for which other terms stand until something better comes along, or until one of them gathers fuller meanings and fuller acceptance to itself: *literature, infoworld, docuverse,* in fact, the concept of all writing in the alphanumeric as well as Derridean senses. The future wide area networks necessary for large scale, interinstitutional and intersite hypertext systems will instantiate and reify the current information worlds, including that of literature. To gain access to information, therefore, will require access to some portion of the network. To publish in a hypertextual world requires gaining access, however limited, to the network.

The analogy, model, or paradigm of the network so central to hypertext appears throughout structuralist and poststructuralist theoretical writings. Related to the model of the network and its components is a rejection of linearity in form and explanation, often in unexpected applications. One example of such antilinear thought will suffice. Although narratologists have almost always emphasized the essential linearity of narrative, critics have recently begun to find it to be nonlinear. Barbara Herrnstein Smith, for example, argues that, "by virtue of the very nature of discourse, nonlinearity is the rule rather than the exception in narrative accounts" ("Narrative Versions, Narrative Theories," 223). Since I shall return to the question of linear and nonlinear narrative in a later chapter, I wish here only to remark that, given nonlinearity's importance and fashionableness in contemporary critical thought, it was inevitable that someone would make this observation, whether accurate or not.

The general importance of non- or antilinear thought appears in the frequency and centrality with which Barthes and other critics employ the terms *link, network, web,* and *path.* More than almost any other contemporary theorist, Derrida uses the terms *link, web, network, matrix,* and *interweaving* associated with hypertextuality; and Bakhtin similarly employs *links* (9, 25), *linkage* (9), *interconnectedness* (19), and *interwoven* (72).

Like Barthes, Bakhtin, and Derrida, Foucault conceives of text in terms of the network, and he relies precisely upon this model to describe his project: "the archaeological analysis of knowledge itself." Arguing in *The Order of Things* that his project requires rejecting the "celebrated controversies" that occupied contemporaries, he claims that "one must reconstitute the general system of thought whose network, in its positivity, renders an interplay of simultaneous and apparently contradictory opinions possible. It is this network that defines the conditions that make a controversy or problem possible, and that bears the historicity of knowledge" (75). Order, for Foucault, is in part "the inner law, the hidden network" (xx); and according to him a "network" is the phenomenon "that is able to link together" (127) a wide range of often contradictory taxonomies, observations, interpretations, categories, and rules of observation.

Heinz Pagels' description of a network in *The Dreams of Reason* suggests why it has such appeal to those leery of hierarchical or linear models. According to Pagels, "a network has no 'top' or 'bottom.' Rather it has a plurality of connections that increase the possible interactions between the components of the network. There is no central executive authority that oversees the system" (20). Furthermore, as Pagels also explains, the network functions in various physical sciences as a powerful theoretical model capable of describing—and hence offering research agenda for—a range of phenomena at enormously different temporal and spatial scales. The model of the network has captured the imaginations of those working on subjects as apparently diverse as immunology, evolution, and the brain.

The immune system, like the evolutionary system, is thus a powerful pattern-recognition system, with capabilities of learning and memory. This feature of the immune system has suggested to a number of people that a dynamical computer model, simulating the immune system, could also learn and have memory. . . . The evolutionary system works on the time scale of hundreds of thousands of years, the immune system in a matter of days, and the brain in milliseconds. Hence if we understand how the immune system recognizes and kills antigens, perhaps it will teach us about how neural nets recognize and can kill ideas. After all, both the immune system and the neural network consist of billions of highly specialized cells that excite and inhibit one another, and they both learn and have memory. (134–35)

Terry Eagleton and other Marxist theorists who draw upon poststructuralism frequently employ the kind of network model or image to which the connectionists subscribe (see Eagleton, *Literary Theory,* 14, 33, 78, 104, 165,

169, 173, 201). In contrast, more orthodox Marxists, who have a vested interest (or sincere belief) in linear narrative and metanarrative, tend to use *network* and *web* chiefly to characterize error. Pierre Machery might therefore at first appear slightly unusual in following Barthes, Derrida, and Foucault in situating novels within a network of relations to other texts. According to Machery, "the novel is initially situated in a *network* of books which replaces the complexity of real relations by which a world is effectively constituted." Machery's next sentence, however, makes clear that, unlike most poststructuralists and postmodernists, who employ the network as a paradigm of an open-ended, non-confining situation, he perceives a network as something that confines and limits: "Locked within the totality of a corpus, within a complex system of relationships, the novel is, in its very letter, allusion, repetition, and resumption of an object which now begins to resemble an inexhaustible world" (268).

Frederic Jameson, who in *The Political Unconscious* attacks Louis Althusser for creating impressions of "facile totalization" and "a seamless web of phenomena" (27), himself more explicitly and more frequently makes these models the site of error. For example, when he criticizes the "anti-speculative bias" of the liberal tradition, in *Marxism and Form,* he notes "its emphasis on the individual fact or item at the expense of the network of relationships in which that item may be imbedded" as liberalism's means of keeping people from "drawing otherwise unavoidable conclusions at the political level" (x). The network model here represents a full, adequate contextualization, one suppressed by an other-than-Marxist form of thought, but it is still only necessary in describing pre-Marxian society. Jameson repeats this paradigm in his chapter on Herbert Marcuse when he explains that "genuine desire risks being dissolved and lost in the vast network of pseudosatisfactions which make up the market system" (*Marxism and Form,* 100–101). Once again, network provides a paradigm apparently necessary for describing the complexities of a fallen society. It does so again when in the Sartre chapter he discusses Marx's notion of fetishism, which, according to Jameson, presents "commodities and the 'objective' network of relationships which they entertain with each other" as the illusory appearance masking the "reality of social life," which "lies in the labor process itself" (296).

Cause or Convergence, Influence or Confluence?

What relation obtains between electronic computing, hypertext in particular, and the literary theory of the past three or four decades? J. Hillis Miller proposes that "the relation . . . is multiple, non-linear, non-causal, non-dialectical, and heavily overdetermined. It does not fit most traditional paradigms for defining 'relationship'" ("Literary Theory," 11). Miller himself provides a fine example of the convergence of critical theory and technology. Before he discovered computer hypertext, he wrote about text and (interpretative) text processing in ways that sound very familiar to anyone who has read or worked with hypertext. Here, for example, is the way, in *Fiction and Repetition,* he describes the way he reads a novel by Hardy, in terms of what I would term a Bakhtinian hypertextuality: "Each passage is a node, a point of intersection or focus, on which converge lines leading from many other passages in the novel and ultimately including them all." No passage has any particular priority over the others, in the sense of being more important or as being the "origin or end of the others" (58).

Similarly, in providing "an 'example' of the deconstructive strategy of interpretation," in "The Critic as Host," Miller describes the dispersed, linked text block whose paths one can follow to an ever-widening, enlarging metatext or universe. He applies deconstructive strategy "to the cited fragment of a critical essay containing within itself a citation from another essay, like a parasite within its host." Continuing the microbiological analogy, he next explains that "the 'example' is a fragment like those miniscule bits of some substance which are put into a tiny test tube and explored by certain techniques of analytical chemistry. [One gets] so far or so much out of a little piece of language, context after context widening out from these few phrases to include as their necessary milieux all the family of Indo-European languages, all the literature and conceptual thought within these languages, and all the permutations of our social structures of household economy, gift-giving and gift receiving" (223).

Miller does point out that Derrida's "*Glas* and the personal computer appeared at more or less the same time. Both work self-consciously and deliberately to make obsolete the traditional codex linear book and to replace it with the new multilinear multimedia hypertext that is rapidly becoming the characteristic mode of expression both in culture and in the study of cultural forms. The 'triumph of theory' in literary studies and their transformation by the digital revolution are aspects of the same sweeping change" ("Literary Theory," 20–21). This sweeping change has many components, to be sure, but one theme appears in both writings on hypertext (and the memex) and in contemporary critical theory—the limitations of print culture, the culture of the book. Bush and Barthes, Nelson and Derrida, like all theorists of these perhaps unexpectedly intertwined subjects, begin with the desire to enable us to escape the confinements of print. This common project requires that one first recognize the enormous power of the book, for only after we have made ourselves conscious of the ways it has formed and informed our lives can we seek to pry ourselves free from some of its limitations.

Looked at within this context, Claude Lévi-Strauss's explanations of pre-literate thought in *The Savage Mind* and in his treatises on mythology appear in part as attempts to decenter the culture of the book—to show the confinements of our literate culture by getting outside of it, however tenuously and however briefly. In emphasizing electronic, noncomputer media, such as radio, television, and film, Baudrillard, Derrida, Jean-François Lyotard, McLuhan, and others similarly argue against the future importance of print-based information technology, often from the vantage point of those who assume analogue media employing sound and motion as well as visual information will radically reconfigure our expectations of human nature and human culture.

Among major critics and critical theorists, Derrida stands out as the one who most realizes the importance of free-form information technology based upon digital, rather than analogue, systems. As he points out, "the development of *practical methods* of information retrieval extends the possibilities of the 'message' vastly, to the point where it is no longer the 'written' translation of a language, the transporting of a signified which could remain spoken in its integrity" (*Of Grammatology,* 10). Derrida, more than any other major theorist, understands that electronic computing and other changes in media have eroded the power of the linear model and the book as related culturally dominant paradigms. "The end of linear writing," Derrida declares, "is indeed the end of the book," even if, he continues, "it is within the form of a book that the new writings—literary or theoretical—allow themselves to be, for better or worse, encased" (86). Therefore, as Ulmer points out, "grammatological writing exemplifies the struggle to break with the investiture of the book" (13).

According to Derrida, "the form of the 'book' is now going through a period of general upheaval, and while that form appears less natural, and its history less transparent, than ever ... the book form alone can no longer settle ... the case of those writing processes which, in *practically* questioning that form, must also dismantle it." The problem, too, Derrida recognizes, is that "one cannot tamper" with the form of the book "without disturbing everything else" (*Dissemination,* 3) in Western thought. Always a tamperer, Derrida does not find that much of a reason for not tampering with the book. His questioning begins in the chain of terms that appears as a title, more-or-less, at the beginning pages of *Dissemination:* "Hors Livres: Outwork, Hors

D'Oeuvre, Extratext, Foreplay, Bookend, Facing, and Prefacing." He questions willingly, because, as he announced in *Of Grammatology*, "all appearances to the contrary, this death of the book undoubtedly announces (and in a certain sense always has announced) nothing but a death of speech (of a *so-called* full speech) and a new mutation in the history of writing, in history as writing. Announces it at a distance of a few centuries. It is on that scale that we must reckon it here" (8).

In conversation with me, Ulmer mentioned that since Derrida's gram equals link, grammatology is the art and science of linking—the art and science, therefore, of hypertext.[5] One may add that Derrida also describes dissemination as a description of hypertext: "Along with an ordered extension of the concept of text, dissemination inscribes a different law governing the effects of sense or reference (the interiority of the 'thing,' reality, objectivity, essentiality, existence, sensible or intelligible presence in general, etc.), a different relation between writing, in the metaphysical sense of the word, and its 'outside' (historical, political, economical, sexual, etc.)" (*Dissemination,* 42).

Reconfiguring
the Text

From Text to Hypertext

Although in some distant, or not-so-distant, future all individual texts will electronically link themselves to one another, thus creating metatexts and metametatexts of a kind only partly imaginable at present, less far-reaching forms of hypertextuality have already appeared. Translations into hypertextual form already exist of poetry, fiction, and other materials originally conceived for book technology. The simplest, most limited form of such translation preserves the linear text with its order and fixity and then appends various kinds of other texts to it, including critical commentary, textual variants, and chronologically anterior and later texts.[1] Hypertext corpora that employ a single text, originally created for print dissemination, as an unbroken axis off which to hang annotation and commentary appear in the by-now common educational and scholarly presentations of canonical literary texts (Figure 7). At Brown University my students and I first used Intermedia and Storyspace to provide annotated versions of stories by Kipling and Lawrence, and I have since created more elaborate World Wide Web presentations of Carlyle's "Hudson's Statue" and other texts. *The Dickens Web,* a corpus of materials focused on *Great Expectations* published in Intermedia (IRIS, 1990) and Storyspace (Eastgate, 1992), differs from these projects in excluding the primary text, as does Christiane Paul's *Unreal City: A Hypertext Guide to T. S. Eliot's "The Waste Land"* (1995).

A second case appears when one adapts for hypertextual presentation material originally conceived for book technology that divides into discrete lexias, particularly if it has multilinear elements that call for the kind of multisequential reading associated with hypertext. An example of this form of hypertext appears in Brian Thomas's early HyperCard version of *De Imitati-*

Axial structure characteristic of electronic books and scholarly books with foot- or endnotes

versus

Network structure of hypertext

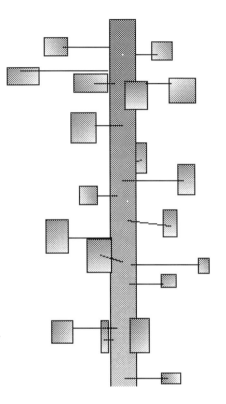

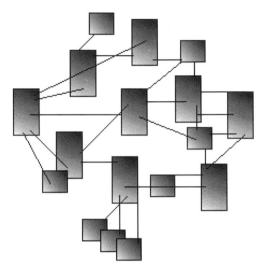

1. Where does the reader enter the text?

2. Where does the reader leave the text?

3. Where are the borders of the text?

Figure 7. Axial versus Network Structure in Hypertext

one Christi, and another is the electronic edition of the *New Oxford Annotated Bible* (1995), a hypertext presentation of the Revised Standard Version that uses AND Software's CompLex system. Like many commercially available electronic texts, the *New Oxford Annotated Bible* appears to be more a digitized book than a true hypertext, though it is no less valuable for that. Readers can supplement the biblical text with powerful search tools and various indices, including ones for Bible and annotation topics, and substantial essays, including those on approaches to Bible study, literary forms in the Gospels, and the characteristics of Hebrew poetry. The *New Oxford Annotated Bible*'s hypertextuality consists largely of variant readings (indicated by link icons in the form of red crosses) and the fact that readers can add both book-marks and their own annotations.

A more elaborate form of hypertextuality appears in the earlier *CD Word: The Interactive Bible Library,* which a team based at Dallas Theological Seminary created using an enhanced version of Guide. This hypertext Bible corpus, "intended for the student, theologian, pastor, or lay person" rather than for the historian of religion, includes the King James, New International, New American Standard, and Revised Standard versions of the Bible, as well as Greek texts for the New Testament and the Septuagint. These materials are supplemented by three Greek lexica, two Bible dictionaries, and three Bible commentaries (DeRose, *CD Word Tutorial,* 1, 117–26). Using this system, which stores the electronic texts on a compact disk, the Bible reader can juxtapose passages from different versions and compare variants, examine the original Greek, and receive rapid assistance on Greek grammar and vocabulary.

A similar kind of corpus that uses a more sophisticated hypertext system is Paul D. Kahn's *Chinese Literature* Intermedia web, which offers different versions of the poetry of Tu Fu (712–770), ranging from the Chinese text, pinyin transliterations, and literal translations to much freer ones by Kenneth Rexroth and others. *Chinese Literature* also includes abundant secondary materials interpreting Tu Fu's poetry. Like *CD Word,* Kahn's Intermedia corpus permits both beginning and advanced students to approach a canonical text in a foreign language through various versions; and like the hypertext Bible on compact disk, it situates its primary text within a network of links to both varying translations and reference materials.

Before considering other kinds of hypertext, we should note the implicit justifications or rationales for these two successful projects. A hypertext presentation of the Bible is particularly appropriate, because its readers habitually handle it in terms of brief passages—or, as writers on hypertext might put it, as if it had "fine granularity." Because the individual poems of Tu Fu are fairly brief, a body of them invites similar conversion to hypertext.

The "In Memoriam" Web

In contrast to the *CD Word* Bible and the *Chinese Literature Web,* which support study chiefly by electronically linking multiple parallel texts, *The "In Memoriam" Web* (Figure 8), another Intermedia corpus created at Brown University and since published in Storyspace (Figure 9) after an extensive expansion by Jon Lanestedt and me (Eastgate Systems, 1992), uses electronic links to map and hence reify a text's internal and external allusions and references—its inter- and *intra*textuality.[2]

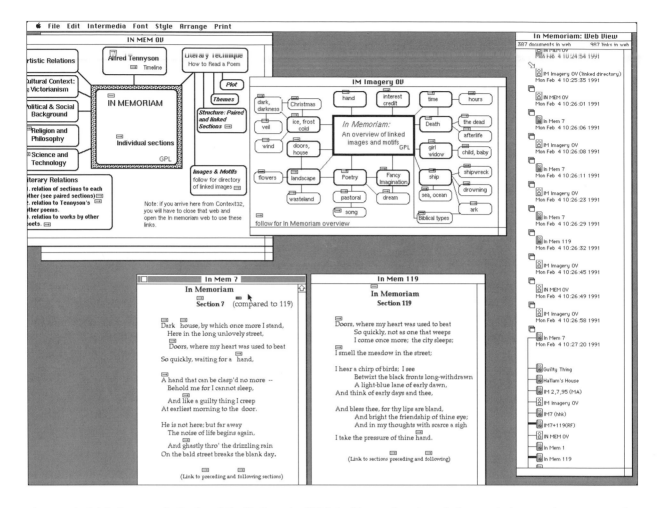

Figure 8. The Original Intermedia Version of *The "In Memoriam" Web*. In this snapshot of a typical screen during a session on Intermedia, the active document, *In Memoriam,* section 7 ("In Mem 7"), appears at the lower left center of the screen with a darkened strip across its top to indicate its status. Using the capacities of hypertext to navigate the poem easily, a reader has juxtaposed sections 119 and 7, which echo and complete each other. *In Memoriam* overview (IN MEM OV), which appears at the upper left, is a graphic document that serves as a directory: it organizes linked materials under generalized headings, such as "Cultural Context: Victorianism" or "Images and Motifs." The *In Memoriam* imagery overview (IM Imagery OV), a second visual index document, overlies the right border of the overview for the entire poem. On the right appears the Web View, which the system automatically creates for each document as the document becomes active either by being opened or, if it is already open on the desktop, by being clicked upon. In contrast to the hierarchically organized overviews the author creates, the Web View shows titled icons representing all documents connected electronically to the active document, here section 7 of the poem. Touching any link marker with the arrow-shaped cursor darkens the icons representing the documents linked to it; in this case, the reader has activated the marker above the phrase "compared to 119" and thereby darkened icons representing both the text of section 7 and a student essay comparing it to section 119.

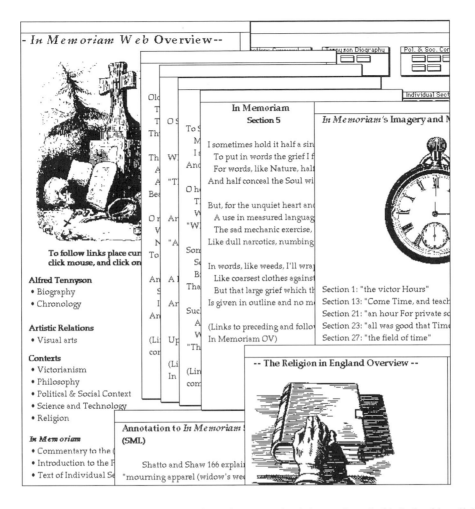

Figure 9. The Storyspace Version of *The "In Memoriam" Web*. **Readers can make their way through this body of interlinked documents in a number of ways. One can proceed by following links from principal overviews, such as that for the entire web (*at left*), religion in England (*lower right*), or individual motifs—in this case that for time (*middle right*). One can also explore the folderlike structure of the Storyspace View (*upper right*), which can contain a dozen or more layers, or one can follow links from individual sections of the poem. This screen shot indicates how multiwindow hypertext systems, such as Storyspace, Intermedia, and Microcosm, that enable authors to fix the location of windows thereby permit one to arrange the screen in ways that help orient the reader. Readers can easily move between parts of the poem and commentary upon it.**

Tennyson's radically experimental *In Memoriam* provides an exemplification of the truth of Walter Benjamin's remark that "the history of every art form shows critical epochs in which a certain art form aspires to effects which could be fully obtained only with a changed technical standard, that is to say, in a new art form" (237). Another manifestation of this principle appears in Victorian word painting, particularly in the hands of Ruskin and Tennyson, which anticipates in abundant detail the techniques of cinematography. Whereas word painting anticipates a future medium by using narrative to structure description, *In Memoriam* anticipates electronic hypertextuality precisely by challenging narrative and literary form based upon it. Convinced that the thrust of elegiac narrative, which drives the reader and the mourner relentlessly from grief to consolation, falsified his own experiences, the poet constructed a poem of 131 fragments to communicate the ebb and flow of emotion in mourning, particularly the way the aftershocks of grief irrationally intrude long after the mourner has supposedly recovered.

Arthur Henry Hallam's death in 1833 forced Tennyson to question his faith in nature, God, and poetry. *In Memoriam* reveals that Tennyson, who found that brief lyrics best embodied the transitory emotions that buffeted him after his loss, rejected conventional elegy and narrative because both presented the reader with a too unified—and hence too simplified—version of the experiences of grief and acceptance. Creating an antilinear poetry of fragments, Tennyson leads the reader of *In Memoriam* from grief and despair through doubt to hope and faith; but at each step, stubborn, contrary emotions intrude, and one encounters doubt in the midst of faith and pain in the midst of resolution. Instead of the elegiac plot of "Lycidas," "Adonais," and "Thyrsis," *In Memoriam* offers fragments interlaced by dozens of images and motifs and informed by an equal number of minor and major resolutions, the most famous of which is section 95's representation of Tennyson's climactic, if wonderfully ambiguous, mystical experience of contact with Hallam's spirit. In addition, individual sections, like 7 and 119 or 28, 78, and 104 variously resonate with one another.

The proto-hypertextuality of *In Memoriam* atomizes and disperses Tennyson the man. He is to be found nowhere, except possibly in the epilogue, which appears after and outside the poem itself. Tennyson, the real, once-existing man, with his actual beliefs and fears, cannot be extrapolated from within the poem's individual sections, for each presents Tennyson only at a particular moment. Traversing these individual sections, the reader experiences a somewhat idealized version of Tennyson's moments of grief and recovery. *In Memoriam* thus fulfills Paul Valéry's definition of poetry as a machine that reproduces an emotion. It also fulfills another of Benjamin's observations, one he makes in the course of contrasting painter and cameraman: "The painter maintains in his work a natural distance from reality, the cameraman penetrates deeply into its web. There is a tremendous difference between the pictures they obtain. That of the painter is a total one, that of the cameraman consists of multiple fragments which are assembled under a new law" ("Work of Art," 233–34). Although speaking of a different information medium, Benjamin here captures some sense of the way a hypertext, when compared to print, appears atomized; and in doing so, he also conveys one of the chief qualities of Tennyson's antilinear, multisequential poem.

The "In Memoriam" Web attempts to capture the multilinear organization of the poem by linking sections, such as 7 and 119, 2 and 39, or the Christmas poems, which echo across the poem to one another. More important, using the capacities of hypertext, the web permits the reader to trace from section to section several dozen leitmotifs that thread through the poem. Working with section 7, for example, readers who wish to move through the poem following a linear sequence can do so by using links to previous and succeeding sections, but they can also look up any word in a linked electronic dictionary or follow links to variant readings, critical commentary (including a comparison of this section and 119), and discussions of the poem's intertextual relations. Furthermore, activating indicated links near the words *dark, house, doors, hand,* and *guilty* produces a choice of several kinds of materials. Choosing *hand* instantly generates a menu that lists all the links to that word, and these include a graphic directory of *In Memoriam*'s major images, critical commentary on the image of the hand, and, most important, a concordancelike list of each use of the word in the poem and the phrase in which it appears; choosing any one item in the list produces the linked document, the graphic overview of imagery, a critical comment, or the full text of the section in which a particular use of hand appears.

Using the capacities of Intermedia and Storyspace to join an indefinite number of links to any passage (or block) of text, the reader moves through the poem along many different axes. Although, like the previously mentioned hypertext materials, *The "In Memoriam" Web* contains reference materials and variant readings, its major difference appears in its use of link paths that permit the reader to organize the poem by means of its network of leitmotifs and echoing sections. In addition, this hypertext presentation of Tennyson's poem also contains a heavily linked graphic overview of the poem's literary relations—its intertextual relations, sources, analogues, confluences, and influences—that permits one to read the poem along axes provided by sets of links relating to the Bible and to works by thirty-eight other writers, chiefly poets, including Vergil, Horace, Dante, Chaucer, Shakespeare, and Milton as well as the Romantics and Victorians. Although Lanestedt, various students, and I created these links, they represent a form of objective link that could have been created automatically by a full-text search in systems such as Microcosm. Here, as in other respects, this web represents an adaptive form of hypertext.

In contrast to adapting texts whose printed versions already divide into sections analogous to lexias, one may, in the manner of Barthes's treatment of Sarrasine in *S/Z*, impose one's own divisions upon a work. Obvious examples of possible projects of this sort include hypertext versions of either "Sarrasine" alone or of it and Barthes's *S/Z*. Stuart Moulthrop's version of *Forking Paths: An Interaction after Jorge Luis Borges* (1987) adapts Borges's "Forking Paths" in an electronic version that activates much of the work's potential for variation (see Moulthrop, "Reading from the Map"). Other fiction that obviously calls for translation into hypertext includes Julio Cortázar's *Hopscotch* and Robert Coover's "The Babysitter."

These instances of adaptive hypertext all exemplify forms of transition between textuality and hypertextuality. In addition, works originally conceived for hypertext already exist. These webs electronically link blocks of text, that is lexias, to one another and to various graphic supplements, such as illustrations, maps, diagrams, and visual directories and overviews. In the future there will be more metatexts formed by linking individual sections of individual works, although the notion of an individual, discrete work becomes increasingly undermined and untenable within this form of information technology, as it already has within much contemporary critical theory. Such metatexts include hypertextual poetry and fiction, which I shall discuss later in this volume, and the hypertextual equivalent of scholarly and critical work in print.

One of the first works in this new medium—certainly the first on Intermedia—was Barry J. Fishman's "The Works of Graham Swift: A Hypertext Thesis," a 1989 Brown University honors thesis on the contemporary British novelist. Fishman's thesis takes the form of sixty-two lexias, of which fifty-five are text documents and seven diagrams or digitized photographs. The fifty-five text documents he created, which range in length from one-half to three single-spaced pages, include discussions of Swift's six published book-length works, the reviews each received, correspondence with the novelist, and essays on themes, techniques, and intertextual relations of each individual book and of Swift's entire oeuvre. Although Fishman created his hypermedia corpus as a relatively self-contained set of documents, he linked his materials to several dozen documents already present on the Intermedia system, including materials by faculty members in at least three different departments and comments by other students. Since Fishman created his web, it has grown, as other students have added their own lexias, and it moved, first to Storyspace and, more recently, to the World Wide Web, where it constitutes an important part of a web containing materials on recent Anglophone postcolonial and postimperial literature.

Problems with Terminology:

What Is the Object We Read,

and What Is a Text in Hypertext?

Writing about hypertext in a print medium immediately produces terminological problems much like those Barthes, Derrida, and others encountered when trying to describe a textuality neither instantiated by the physical object of the printed book nor limited to it. Since hypertext radically changes the experiences that *reading, writing,* and *text* signify, how, without misleading, can one employ these terms, so burdened with the assumptions of print technology, when referring to electronic materials? We still read *according to* print technology, and we still direct almost all of what we write toward print modes of publication, but we can already glimpse the first appearances of hypertextuality and begin to ascertain some aspects of its possible futures. Terms so implicated with print technology necessarily confuse unless handled with great care. Two examples will suffice.

An instance of the kind of problem we face appears when we try to decide what to call the object at which or with which one reads. The object from which one reads the production of print technology is, of course, the book. In our culture the term *book* can refer to three very different entities—the object itself, the text, and the instantiation of a particular technology. Calling the machine by means of which one reads hypertext an "electronic book," however, would be misleading, since the machine at which one reads (and writes, and carries out other operations, including sending and receiving mail) does not itself constitute a book, a text: it does not coincide either with the virtual text or with a physical embodiment of it.

Additional problems arise when one considers that hypertext involves a more active reader, one who not only chooses her reading paths but also has the opportunity of reading as an author; at any time, the person reading can assume an authorial role by attaching links or adding material to the text being read. Therefore, a term like *reader,* which some computer systems employ for their electronic mailboxes or message spaces, does not seem appropriate either.[3]

One solution has been to call this reading-and-writing site a workstation, by analogy to the engineer's workstation. The term is assigned to relatively high-powered machines, often networked, that have far more computing power, memory, and graphic capacities than the personal computer. However, because *workstation* seems to suggest an object that will exist only in the work place and find application only for gainful labor or employment, this choice of terminology also misleads. Nonetheless, I shall employ it occasionally, if only because it seems closer to what hypertext demands than any of the other terms thus far suggested. This terminological problem arises, as has now become obvious, because the roles of reader and author change so much in hypermedia technology that our current vocabulary does not have much appropriate to offer.

Whatever one wishes to call the reading-and-writing site, one should think of the actual mechanism that one will use to work (and play) in hypertext not as a free-standing machine, like today's personal computer. Rather, the "object one reads" must be seen as the entrance, the magic doorway, into the docuverse, since it is the individual reader's and writer's means of participating in—of being linked to—the world of linked hypermedia documents.

A similar terminological problem is what to do with the term *text,* which I have already employed so many times thus far in this study. More than any other term crucial to this discussion, *text* has ceased to inhabit a single world. Existing in two very different worlds, it gathers contradictory meanings to itself, and one must find some way of avoiding confusion when using it. Frequently, in trying to explain certain points of difference, I have found myself forced to blur old and new definitions or have discovered myself using the old term in an essentially anachronistic sense. For example, in discussing that hypertext systems permit one to link a passage "in" the "text" to other passages "in" the "text" as well as to those "outside" it, one confronts precisely such anachronism. The kind of text that permits one to write, however incorrectly, of insides and outsides of text belongs to print, whereas we are here considering a form of electronic virtual textuality for which these already suspect terms have become even more problematic and misleading. One solution has been to use *text* as an anachronistic shorthand for the bracketed material in the following expression: "If one were to transfer a [complete printed] text (work), say, Milton's *Paradise Lost,* into electronic form, one could link passages within [what had been] the [original] text (Milton's poem) to each other; and one could also link passages to a wide range of materials outside the original text to it." Of course, as soon as one converts the printed text to an electronic one, it no longer possesses the same kind of textuality. In the following pages such references to text have to be understood, therefore, to mean "the electronic version of a printed text."

The question of what to call "text" in the medium of hypertext leads directly to the question, What should be included under that rubric in the first place? This question in turn immediately forces us to recognize that hypertext reconfigures the text in a fundamental way not immediately suggested by the fact of linking. Hypertextuality inevitably includes a far higher percentage of nonverbal information than does print; the comparative ease with which such material can be appended encourages its inclusion. Hypertext, in other words, implements Derrida's call for a new form of hieroglyphic writing that can avoid some of the problems implicit and therefore inevitable in Western writing systems and their printed versions. Derrida argues for the inclusion of pictographic elements in writing as a means of escaping the constraints of linearity. Commenting on this thrust in Derrida's argument, Gregory Ulmer explains that grammatology thereby "confronts" four millennia during which anything in language that "resisted linearization was suppressed. Briefly stated, this suppression amounts to the denial of the pluridimensional character of symbolic thought originally present in the 'mythogram' (Leroi-Gourhan's term), or nonlinear writing (pictographic and rebus writing)" (*Applied Grammatology,* 8). Derrida, who asks for a new pictographic writing as a way out of logocentrism, has to a large extent had his requests granted in hypertext.

Because hypertext systems link passages of verbal text and images as easily as they link two or more verbal passages, hypertext includes hypermedia. Moreover, since computing digitizes both alphanumeric symbols and pictorial images, electronic text in theory easily integrates the two. In practice, popular word-processing programs, such as Microsoft Word, have increasingly featured the capacity to include graphic materials in text documents. Linking, which permits an author to send the reader to an image from many different portions of the text, makes such integration of visual and verbal information even easier.

In addition to expanding the quantity and diversity of alphabetic and nonverbal information included in the text, hypertext provides visual elements not found in printed work. Perhaps the most basic of these is the cursor, the blinking arrow, line, or other graphic element that represents the reader-author's presence in the text. The cursor, which the user moves either from the keypad by pressing arrow-marked directional keys or with devices like a "mouse" or rollerball, provides a moving intrusive image of the reader's presence in the text. From this position, the reader can actually change the text: Using the mouse, one can position the cursor between the letters in a word, say, between *t* and *h* in *the*. Pressing a button on the mouse inserts a vertical blinking line at this point; pressing the backspace or delete key removes the *t*. Typing will insert characters at this point. In a book, one can always move one's finger or pencil across the printed page, but one's intrusion always remains physically separate from the text. One may make a mark on the page, but one's intrusion does not affect the text itself.

The cursor, which adds reader presence, activity, and movement, combines in most extant hypertext systems with another graphic element, a symbol that indicates the presence of linked material. To indicate the presence of one or more links, Intermedia places a link marker, which takes the form of a small horizontal rectangle containing an arrow, at the beginning of a passage. Apple's HyperCard permits a wide range of graphic symbols ("buttons") to indicate the unidirectional links that characterize this program. *CD Word,* which is based upon an amplification of Guide, employs an ingenious combination of cursor shapes to indicate linked material. For example, if one moves the cursor over a word and the cursor changes into an outline of a horizontal arrow, one knows the cursor is on a reference button, and clicking the mouse will produce the linked text. Following this procedure on the title page and clicking the cursor when it is on "Bibles" produces a list of abbreviations of included versions of the scriptures. Then, moving the cursor over RSV changes it to a crosshair shape, which indicates the presence of a replacement button; clicking the mouse button produces the phrase "Revised Standard Version." All these graphic devices remind readers that they are processing and manipulating a new kind of text, in which graphic elements play an important part.

Visual Elements in Print Text

This description of visual elements of hypertext reminds one that print employs a greater diversity of visual information than people usually take into account: visual information is not limited, as one might at first think, merely to the obvious instances, such as illustrations, maps, diagrams, flow charts, or graphs.[4] Even printed text without explicitly visual supplementary materials already contains a good bit of visual information in addition to alphanumeric code. The visual components of writing and print technology include spacing between words, paragraphing, changes of type style and size, formatting to indicate passages quoted from other works, assigning specific locations on the page or at the end of sections or of the entire document to indicate reference materials (foot- and endnotes).

Despite the considerable presence of visual elements in print text, they tend to go unnoticed when contemporary writers contemplate the nature of text in an electronic age. Like other forms of change, the expansion of writing from a system of verbal language to one that centrally involves nonverbal information—visual information in the form of symbols and representational elements as well as other forms of information, including sound—has encountered stiff resistance, often from those from whom one is least likely to expect it, namely, from those who already employ computers for writing. Even those who advocate a change frequently find the experience of advocacy and change so tiring that they resist the next stage, even if it appears implicit in changes they have themselves advocated.

This resistance appears particularly clearly in the frequently encountered remark that writers should not concern themselves with typesetting or desktop publishing but ought to leave those activities to the printer. Academics and other writers, we are told, do not design well; and even if they did, the argument continues, such activities are a waste of their time. Such advice, which has recently become an injunction, should make us ask why. After all, when told that one should not avail oneself of some aspect or form of empowerment, particularly as a writer, one should ask why. What if someone told us: "Here is a pencil. Although it has a rubber apparatus at the opposite end from that with which you write, you should not use it. Real writers don't use it"? At the very least we should wonder why anyone had included such capacities to do something; experimenting with it would show that it erases; and very likely, given human curiosity and perversity, which may be the same thing in certain circumstances, we would be tempted to try it out. Thus a capacity would evolve into a guilty pleasure!

Anyone with the slightest interest in design who has even casually surveyed the output of commercial and university presses has noticed a high percentage of appallingly designed or obviously undesigned books. Despite the exemplary work of designers like P. J. Conkwright, Richard Eckersley, and Glen Burris, many presses continue to produce nasty looking books with narrow margins and gutters, type too small or too coarse for a particular layout, and little sense of page design. Financial constraints are usually offered as the sole determinant of the situation, though good design does not have to produce a more costly final product, particularly in an age of computer typesetting. In several cases of which I am aware, publishers have assigned book design to beginning manuscript editors who confessed that they had no training or experience in graphic design. As one who has been fortunate enough to have benefited from the efforts of first-rate, talented designers far more than I have suffered from those of poor ones, I make these observations not as a complaint but as a preparation for inquiring why authors are told they should not concern themselves with the visual appearance of their texts and why authors readily accept such instruction.

They do so in part because this injunction clearly involves matters of status and power. In particular, it involves a particular interpretation—that is, a social construction—of the idea of writer and writing. According to this conception, the writer's role and function is just to write. Writing, in turn, is conceived solely as a matter of recording (or creating) ideas by means of language. On the surface, such an approach seems neutral and obvious enough, and that in itself should warn one that it has been so naturalized as to include cultural assumptions that might be worth one's while to examine.

The injunction "just to write," which is based upon this purely verbal conception of writing, obviously assumes the following: first, that only verbal information has value, at least for the writer as a writer and probably for the reader as reader;[5] second, that visual information has less value. Making use of such devalued or lesser-valued forms of information (or does visual material deserve the description "real information" at all?) in some way reduces the status of the writer, making him or her less of a real writer. This matter of status again raises its head when one considers another reason for the injunction "just to write," one tied more tightly to conceptions of division of labor, class, and status. In this view of things, it is thought that authors should not concern themselves with matters that belong to the printer. Although troubled by this exclusion, I accepted this argument until I learned that until recently (say, in the 1930s) authors routinely wandered around the typesetting shop at Oxford University Press while their books were being set and were permitted to render advice and judgment, something we are now told is none of our business, beneath us, and so on. The ostensible reason for instructing authors to refuse the power offered them by their writing implement also includes the idea that authors do not have the expertise, the sheer know-how to produce good design. Abundant papers by beginning undergraduates and beginning Macintosh users, cluttered with dissonant typefaces and font sizes, are thrust forward to support this argument, one that we receive too readily without additional information.

The fact that beginners in any field of endeavor do a fairly poor quality job at this new activity hardly argues forcefully for their abandoning that activity. If it did, we would similarly advise beginning students immediately to abandon their attempts at creative and discursive writing, at drawing and philosophy, and at mathematics and chemistry. One reason we do not offer such instructions is because we feel the skills involved in those endeavors are important—apparently in contrast to visual ones. Another reason, of course, is that teaching involves our livelihood and status. The question that arises, then, is Why is visual information less important? The very fact that people experiment with visual elements of text on their computers shows the obvious pleasure they receive in manipulating visual effects. This pleasure suggests in turn that by forbidding the writer visual resources, we deny an apparently innocent source of pleasure, something that apparently must be cast aside if one is to be a true writer and a correct reader.

Much of our prejudice against the inclusion of visual information in text derives from print technology. Looking at the history of writing, one sees that it has a long connection with visual information, not least the origin of many alphabetic systems in hieroglyphics and other originally visual forms of writing. Medieval manuscripts present some sort of hypertext combination of letter sizes, marginalia, illustrations, and visual embellishment, in the form of both calligraphy and pictorial additions.

This blindness to the crucial visual components of textuality not only threatens to hinder our attempts to learn how to write in electronic space but has also markedly distorted our understanding of earlier forms of writing. In particular, our habits of assuming that alphanumeric—linguistic—text is the only text that counts has led to often bizarre distortions in scholarly editing. As Jerome J. McGann reminds us in *The Textual Condition,* "literary works typically secure their effects by other than purely linguistic means" (77), always deploying various visual devices to do so. Hence leaving such aspects of the text out of consideration—or omitting them from scholarly editions— drastically reconfigures individual works. "All poetry, even in its most traditional forms, asks the reader to decipher the text in spatial as well as linear terms. Stanzaic and generic forms, rhyme schemes, metrical orders: all of these deploy spatial functions in scripted texts, as their roots in oral poetry's 'visual' arts of memory should remind us" (113). One cannot translate such nonprint and even antiprint works as those of Blake and Dickinson into print without radically reconfiguring them, without creating essentially new texts, texts a large portion of whose resources have been excised. Although "textual and editorial theory has heretofore concerned itself almost exclusively with the linguistic codes, the time has come," McGann urges, "when we have to take greater theoretical account of the other coding network which operates at the documentary and bibliographical level of literary works" (78). Once again, as with the scholarly editing of medieval manuscripts and nineteenth-century books, digital word and digital image provide lenses through which we can examine the preconceptions—the blinders—of what Michael Joyce calls "the late age of print" (*Of Two Minds,* 111).

The Fragmented Text

Hypertext linking, reader control, and variation not only militate against the modes of argumentation to which we have become accustomed but have other, far more general effects, one of which is to add what may be seen as a kind of randomness to the reader's text. Another is that the writer, as we shall see, loses certain basic controls over his text, particularly over its edges and borders. Yet a third is that the text appears to fragment, to atomize, into constituent elements (into lexias or blocks of text); and these reading units take on a life of their own as they become more self-contained, because they become less dependent on what comes before or after in a linear succession.

When compared to text as it exists in print technology, forms of hypertext evince varying combinations of atomization and dispersal. Unlike the spatial fixity of text reproduced by means of book technology, electronic text always has variation, for no one state or version is ever final; it can always be changed. Compared to a printed text, one in electronic form appears relatively dynamic, since it always permits correction, updating, and similar modification. Even without linking, therefore, electronic text abandons the fixity that characterizes print and that provides some of its most important effects on Western culture. Without fixity one cannot have a unitary text.

In linking, hypertext adds a second fundamental form of variation, further dispersing or atomizing text. Electronic links permit readers to take various paths through a given body of lexias. This quality of hypertext, which produces its characteristic avoidance of unilinearity, has obvious major effects upon conceptions of textuality and upon rhetorical structures. In explaining his procedure in *S/Z,* Barthes announces: "We shall therefore star the text, separating, in the manner of a minor earthquake, the blocks of signification of which reading grasps only the smooth surface, imperceptibly soldered by the movement of sentences, the flowing discourse of narration, the 'naturalness' of ordinary language. The tutor signifier will be cut up into a series of brief, contiguous fragments, which we shall call lexias, since they are units of reading" (*S/Z,* 13). However self-dramatizing and overheated Barthes's presentation of his method in *S/Z* might appear from the perspective of print, it accurately describes the way an attempt to move beyond print in the direction of hypertextuality disturbs the text and the reading experience as we know them. Text—or, more properly, passages of text—that had followed one another in an apparently inevitable seamless linear progression now fracture, break apart, assume more individual identities.

The Dispersed Text

While the individual hypertext lexia has looser, or less determining, bonds to other lexias from the same work (to use a terminology that now threatens to become obsolete), it also associates itself more readily with text created by other authors. In fact, it associates with whatever text links to it, thereby dissolving intellectual separation of texts as some chemicals destroy the cell membrane of an organism. Destroying the cell membrane destroys the cell; it kills. In contrast, similarly destroying now-conventional notions of textual separation may destroy certain attitudes associated with text, but it will not necessarily destroy text. It will, however, reconfigure it and our expectations of it.

In this effect of electronic linking—dispersal of "the" text into other texts—an individual lexia loses its physical and intellectual separation from others when linked electronically to them, it also finds itself dispersed into them. The necessary contextualization and intertextuality produced by situating individual reading units within a network of easily navigable pathways weaves texts, including those by different authors and those in nonverbal media, together. One effect is to weaken and perhaps destroy any sense of textual uniqueness.

Such notions are hardly novel to contemporary literary theory, but here, as in so many other cases, hypertext creates an almost embarrassingly literal reification or embodiment of a principle that had seemed particularly abstract and difficult when read from the vantage point of print. Since much of the appeal, even charm, of these theoretical insights lies in their difficulty and even preciousness, this more literal presentation promises to disturb theoreticians, in part, of course, because it greatly disturbs status and power relations within their field of expertise.

Hypertextual Translation of Scribal Culture. Hypertext fragments, disperses, or atomizes text in two related ways. First, by removing the linearity of print, it frees the individual passages from one ordering principle—sequence—and threatens to transform the text into chaos. Second, hypertext destroys the notion of a fixed unitary text. Considering the "entire" text in relation to its component parts produces the first form of fragmentation; considering it in relation to its variant readings and versions produces the second.

Loss of a belief in unitary textuality could produce many changes in

Western culture, many of them quite costly, when judged from the vantage point of our present print-based attitudes. Not all these changes would necessarily be costly or damaging, however, particularly to the world of scholarship, where this conceptual change would permit us to redress some of the distortions of naturalizing print culture. Accustomed to the standard scholarly edition of canonical texts, we conventionally suppress the fact that such twentieth-century print versions of works originally created within a manuscript culture are bizarrely fictional idealizations that produce a vastly changed experience of text. To begin with, the printed scholarly edition of Plato, Vergil, or Augustine provides a text far easier to negotiate and decipher than any that was available to contemporary readers. They encountered texts so different from ours that even to suggest that we share common experiences of reading misleads.

Contemporary readers of Plato, Vergil, or Augustine processed texts without interword spacing, capitalization, or punctuation. Had you read these last three sentences fifteen hundred years ago, they would have taken the following form:

theyencounteredtextssodifferentfromoursthateventosuggestthatwesharecommon experiencesofreadingmisleadscontemporaryreadersofplatovergiloraugustineprocessed textswithoutinterwordspacingcapitalizationorpunctuationhadyoureadtheselasttwo sentencesfifteenhundredyearsagotheywouldhavetakenthefollowingform

Such unbroken streams of alphabetic characters made even phonetic literacy a matter of great skill. Since deciphering such texts heavily favored reading aloud, almost all readers experienced texts not only as an occasion for strenuous acts of code breaking but also as a kind of public performance.

The very fact that the text we would have read fifteen hundred years ago appeared in a manuscript form also implies that to read it at all we would first have had to gain access to a rare, even unique object—assuming, that is, that we could have discovered the existence of the manuscript and made an inconvenient, expensive, and often dangerous trip to see it. Having gained access to this manuscript, we would also have approached it much differently from the way we today approach the everyday encounter with a printed book. We would probably have taken the encounter as a rare, privileged opportunity, and we would also have approached the experience of reading this unique object with a very different set of assumptions than would a modern scholar. As Elizabeth Eisenstein has shown, the first role of the scholar in a manuscript culture was simply to preserve the text, which was under a double threat of degradation: each time someone physically handled the fragile object, its longevity was reduced; and each time someone copied the manuscript to preserve and transmit its text, the copyist inevitably introduced textual drift.

Thus, even without taking into account the alien presence of pagination, indices, references, title pages, and other devices of book technology, the encounter and subsequent reading of a manuscript constituted a very different set of experiences from those which we take for granted. Equally significant, whereas the importance of scholarly editions lies precisely in their appearance in comparatively large numbers, each manuscript of a text by Plato, Vergil, or Augustine existed as a unique object. We do not know which particular version of a text by these authors any reader encountered. Presenting the history and relation of texts created within a manuscript culture in terms of the unitary text of modern scholarship certainly fictionalizes—and falsifies—their intertextual relations.

Modern scholarly editions combine uniqueness and multiplicity, as, in a different way, did preprint manuscripts. A modern edition of Plato, Vergil, or Augustine begins by assuming the existence of a unique, unitary text, but it is produced in the first place so it can disseminate that text in a number of identical copies. In contrast, each ancient or medieval manuscript, which embodied only one of many potential variations of a text, existed as a unique object. A new conception of text is needed by scholars, who should be trying to determine not some probably mythical and certainly long-lost master text but the ways individual readers actually encountered Plato, Vergil, or Augustine in a manuscript culture. In fact, we must abandon the notion of a unitary text and replace it with conceptions of a dispersed text. We must do, in other words, what some art historians working with analogous medieval problems have done—take the conception of a unique type embodied in a single object and replace it with a conception of a type as a complex set of variants. For example, trying to determine the thematic, iconological, and compositional antecedents of early fourteenth-century ivory Madonnas, Robert Suckale and other recent students of the Court Style have abandoned linear derivations and the notion of a unitary type. Instead, they emphasize that sculptors chose among several sets of fundamental forms or "groundplans" as points of departure. Some sort of change in basic attitudes toward the creations of manuscript culture seems necessary.

The capacity of hypertext to link all the versions or variants of a particular text might offer a means of somewhat redressing the balance between uniqueness and variation in preprint texts. Of course, even in hypertext presentations, both modern printing conventions and scholarly apparatus will still infringe upon attempts to recreate the experience of encountering these texts, and nothing can restore the uniqueness and corollary aura of the individual manuscript. Nonetheless, hypertext offers the possibility of presenting a text as a dispersed field of variants and not as a falsely unitary entity. High resolution screens and other technological capacities should some day also permit a means of presenting all the individual manuscripts. An acquaintance with hypertext systems might by itself sufficiently change assumptions about textuality and free students of preprint texts from some of their biases.

A Third Convergence:

Hypertext and Theories

of Scholarly Editing

All forms of hypertext, even the most rudimentary, change our conceptions of text and textuality. The dispersed textuality characteristic of this information technology therefore calls into question some of the most basic assumptions about the nature of text and scholarly textual editing. The appearance of the digital word has the major cultural effect of permitting us, for the first time in centuries, easily to perceive the degree to which we have become so accustomed to the qualities and cultural effects of the book that we unconsciously transfer them to the productions of oral and manuscript cultures. We so tend to take print and print-based culture for granted that, as the jargon has it, we have "naturalized" the book by assuming that habits of mind and manners of working associated with it have naturally and inevitably always existed. Eisenstein, McLuhan, Kernan, and other students of the cultural implications of print technology have demonstrated the ways in which the printed book formed and informed our intellectual history. They point out, for example, that a great part of these cultural effects derive from book technology's creation of multiple copies of essentially the same text. Multiple copies of a fixed text in turn produce scholarship and education as we know it by permitting readers in different times and places to consult and refer to the "same" text. Historians of print technology also point out that economic factors associated with book production led to the development of both copyright and related notions of creativity and originality. I am going over this familiar ground once again because these factors combine to reveal the singular unitary text as an almost unspoken cultural ideal. They provide, in other words, the cultural model and justification for scholarly textual editing as we have know it.

It is either particularly ironic or simple poetic justice—take your pick—that digital technology so calls into question the assumptions of print-associated editorial theory that it forces us to reconceive how we edit texts originally produced for print as well as those created within earlier information regimes. Print technology's emphasis on the unitary text prompted the notion of a single perfect version of all texts at precisely the cultural moment that the presence of multiple print editions undercut that emphasis—something not much recognized, if at all, until the arrival of digitality. As the works of James Thorpe, George Bornstein, Jerome McGann, and others have urged, any publication during an author's lifetime that in some manner received his or her approval—if only to the extent that the author later chose not to correct changes made by an editor or printer—is an authentic edition. Looking at the works of authors such as Ruskin and Yeats, who radically rewrote and rearranged their texts throughout their careers, one recognizes that the traditional scholarly edition generally makes reconstructing the version someone would have read at a particular date extremely difficult. Indeed, from one point of view a scholarly edition may radically distort our experience of an individual volume of poems by the very fact that it enforces a static, frozen model on what turns out to have been a continually shifting and changing entity.

This new conception, of a more fluid, dispersed text possibly truer than conventional editions, raises the issue of whether one can have a scholarly edition at all, or must we settle for what McGann terms an archive ("Complete Writings of Rossetti")—essentially a collection of textual fragments (or versions) from which we assemble, or have the computer assemble, any particular version that suits a certain reading strategy or scholarly question, such as "What version of *Modern Painters,* Volume 1, did William Morris read at a particular date and how did the text he read differ from what American Ruskinians read?"

One does not encounter many of these issues when producing print editions, because matters of scale and economy decide or foreclose them in advance. In general, physical and economic limitations shape the nature of the annotations one attaches to a print edition just as they shape the basic conception of that edition. So what can we expect to happen when these limitations disappear? Or, to phrase the question differently, what advantages and disadvantages, what new problems and new advantages, will we encounter with the digital word?

Hypertext, Scholarly Annotation, and the Electronic Scholarly Edition

One answer lies in what hypertext does to the concept of annotation. As I argue at length in the next chapter, this new information technology reconfigures not only our experience of textuality but also our conceptions of the author's relation to that text, for it inevitably produces several forms of asynchronous collaboration. The first, a limited one, inevitably appears when readers choose their own ways through a branching text. A second form appears only in a fully networked hypertext environment that permits readers to add links to texts they encounter. In such environments, which are exemplified by the World Wide Web, the editor, like the author, inevitably loses a certain amount of power and control. Or, as one of my friends who created the web site for a major computer company pointed out, "if you want to play this game, you have to give up control of your own text." Although one could envision a situation in which any reader could comment upon another editor's text, a far more interesting one arises when successive editors or commentators add to what in the print environment would be an existing edition. In fact, one can envisage a situation in which readers might ultimately encounter a range of annotations.

An example taken from my recent experience with having students create an annotated version—read "edition"—of Carlyle's "Hudson's Statue" on the World Wide Web illuminates some of the issues here. I intended the assignment in part to introduce undergraduates to various electronic resources available at my university, including the on-line versions of the *Oxford English Dictionary* and *Encyclopaedia Britannica*. I wished to habituate them to using electronic reference tools accessible outside the physical precincts of the library in order both to acquaint them with these new tools and to encourage them to move between the electronic resources and those presently available only in print form. For this project, students chose terms or phrases ranging from British political history ("Lord Ellenborough" and "People's League") to religion and myth ("Vishnu," "Vedas," "Loki"). They then defined or described the items chosen and briefly explained Carlyle's allusion and, where known, his uses of these items in other writings.

This simple undergraduate assignment immediately raised issues crucial to the electronic scholarly edition. First of all, the absence of limitations upon scale—or to be more accurate, the absence of the same limitations upon scale that one encounters with physical editions—permitted much longer, more substantial notes than might seem suitable in a print edition. To some extent a hypertext environment always reconfigures the relative status of main text and subsidiary annotation. Electronic linking makes information in a note easily available, and therefore these more substantial notes conveniently link to many more places both inside and outside the particular text under consideration than would be either possible or conveniently usable in a print edition. Taking our present example of "Hudson's Statue," for instance, we see that historical materials on, say, democratic movements like Chartism and the People's International League can shift positions in relation to the annotated text: unlike a print environment, an electronic one permits perceiving the relation of such materials in opposite manners. The historical materials can appear as annotations to the Carlyle text, or, conversely, "Hudson's Statue" can appear—be experienced as—an annotation to the historical materials. Both, in other words, exist in a networked textual field in which their relationship depends solely upon the reader's need and purpose.

Recognition of what happens to the scholarly text in wide-area-networked environments, such as those created by WWW and HyperG, only complicates matters by forcing us to confront the question What becomes of the concept and practice of scholarly annotation? Clearly, linking by itself is not enough, and neither is text retrieval. At first glance, it might seem that one could solve many issues of scholarly annotation in an electronic environment by using sophisticated text retrieval. In the case of my student-created annotated edition of "Hudson's Statue," one could just provide instructions for use of the available search tools, though this do-it-yourself approach would probably appeal only to the already-experienced researcher. Our textual experiment quickly turned up another, more basic problem when several bright, hard-working neophytes wrote elegant notes containing accurate, clearly attributed information that nonetheless referred to the wrong person, in two cases providing material about figures from the Renaissance rather than about the far-lesser-known nineteenth-century figures to whom Carlyle referred. What this simple-minded example suggests, of course, is nothing more radical than that for the foreseeable future scholarship will always be needed, or to phrase my point in terms relevant to the present inquiry, one cannot automate textual annotation. Text retrieval, however valuable, by itself can't do it all.

Fine, but what about hypertext? The problem, after all, with information retrieval is that active readers might obtain either nonsignificant information or information whose value they might not be able to determine. Hypertext, in contrast, can provide editorially approved connections in the form of links, which can move from a passage in the so-called main text—here "Hudson's Statue"—to other passages in the same text, explanatory materials relevant to it, and so on. Therefore, assuming that one had permission to create links to the various on-line resources, such as the *OED,* one could do so. If one did not have such permission, one could easily download copies of the materials from them, choose relevant sections, and put them back on-line within a web to which one had access; this second procedure is in essence the one many students chose to follow. Although providing slightly more convenience to the reader than the text-retrieval do-it-yourself model, this model still confronts the reader with passages (or notes) longer than he or she may wish to read

One solution lies in creating multilevel or linked progressive annotation. Looking at the valuable, if overly long, essay one student had written on Carlyle and Hindu deities, I realized that a better way of proceeding lay in taking the brief concluding section on Carlyle's satiric use of these materials and making that the first text or lexia the reader would encounter; the first mention of, say, Vedas or Vishnu, in that lexia would be linked to the longer essays, thereby providing conveniently accessible information on demand but not before it was required.

I have approached these questions about scholarly editions through the apparently unrelated matters of a student assignment and educational materials because they remind us that in anything like a fully linked electronic environment, all texts have variable applications and purposes. One consequence appears in the variable forms that annotation and editorial apparatus will almost certainly have to take: since everyone from the advanced scholar down to the beginning student or reader outside the setting of an educational institution might be able to read such texts, they will require various layers or levels of annotation, something particularly necessary when the ultimate linked text is not a scholarly note but another literary text.

Thus far I have written only as if the linked material in the hypertext scholarly edition consisted of textual apparatus, explanatory comment, and contextualization, but by now it should have become obvious that many of those comments inevitably lead to other so-called primary texts. Thus, in our putative edition of "Hudson's Statue" one can not only link it to reference works, such as the *OED,* the *Britannica,* and (possibly in future) the *Dictionary of National Biography,* but also to entire linguistic corpora and to other texts by the same author, including working drafts, letters, and other publications. Why stop there? Even in the relatively flat, primitive version of hypertext offered by the present WWW, the Carlylean text demands links to works upon which he draws, such as Jonathan Swift's *Tale of a Tub,* and to those that draw upon him, such as Ruskin's "Traffic," whose satiric image of the Goddess-of-Getting-on (or Britannia of the Market) derives rather obviously from Carlyle's ruminations on the never-completed statue of a stock swindler. Finally, one cannot restrict the text field to literary works, and "Hudson's Statue" inevitably links not only to the Bible and contemporary guides to its interpretation but also to a wide range of primary materials, including parliamentary documents and contemporary newspapers, to which Carlyle's text obviously relates.

Once again, though, linking, which reconfigures our experience and expectations of the text, is not enough, for the scholarly editor must decide *how* to link various texts. Once again, the need for some form of intermediary lexias seems obvious, the first, say, briefly pointing to a proposed connection between two texts, the next in sequence providing a summary of complex relations (the outline in fact of what might in the print environment have been a scholarly article or even book), the third an overview of relevant comparisons, and the last the actual full text by the second author. At each stage (or lexia), the reader should have the power not only to return to the so-called main text of "Hudson's Statue" but also to reach these linked materials out of sequence. Vannevar Bush, who invented the general notion of hypertext, thought that chains or trails of links might themselves constitute a new form of scholarly writing, and annotations in the form of such guided tours might conceivably become part of the future scholarly edition. We can be certain, however, that as constraints of scale lessen, increasing amounts of material will be summoned to illuminate individual texts and new forms of multiple annotation will develop as a way of turning availability into accessibility.

Hypertext and the Problem
of Text Structure

The fact that a single lexia can function in very different roles within a large networked hypertext raises fundamental questions about the applicability of Standard Generalized Markup Language (SGML) to electronic scholarly editions of the future, when they will increasingly appear in vast electronic information spaces rather than in the stand-alone versions we see today in CD-ROMs, such as Peter Robinson's Chaucer project and Anne McDermott's edition of Johnson's *Dictionary*. The relation of SGML and hypertext appears particularly crucial to scholarly editing, since so many large projects depend on SGML and its more specific scholarly forms, established by the Text Encoding Initiative (TEI).

One of the fundamental strengths of SGML lies in its creation of a single electronic text that can lend itself to many forms of both print and electronic presentation. In the medieval *scripta continua* we encountered text without any markup, not even spaces between words. Later manuscript and print text contains presentational markup—that is, the encoding takes the form of specific formatting decisions; one indicates a paragraph by skipping a line or indenting a few spaces. Although perfectly suited to physical texts, such forms of encoding appear particularly inefficient and even harmful in electronic environments, since they prevent easy transference and manipulation of texts. So-called procedural markup characterizes handwritten and printed text; to indicate a paragraph, authors and scribes, as we have seen, follow a certain procedure, such as those described above. Electronic text works better when one creates a generalized markup that simply indicates the presence of a text entity, such as a paragraph. These indicators are defined at the beginning of a document.

Once all aspects of any particular text have been indicated with the correct SGML tags, the text appears in a wonderfully generalized, potentially variable form. For example, after one has tagged (or "marked up") each instance of a text element, such as titles at the beginning of each chapter, by placing them between a particular set of tags—say, <chaptertitle> and </chaptertitle>—one can easily configure such text elements differently in different versions of a text. Thus, if printed on my university's mainframe printer, which permits only a single proportional font, chapter titles appear bolded in the larger of two available sizes. If printed with a typesetting device, however, the same chapter titles automatically appear in a very different font and size, say, 30-point Helvetica. If presented electronically, moreover, chapter titles can appear in a color different from that of the main text; in the first DynaText version of this volume, for example, they appear in green whereas the main text appears in black. My first point here is that once one has created such a generalized text, one can adapt it to different publication modes with a single instruction that indicates the specific appearance of all labeled text elements. My second point here is that such SGML-tagged text records its own abstract structure.

In "What Is Text Really?" their pioneering essay about SGML, James H. Coombs, Stephen J. DeRose, and David Durand argue that text consists of hierarchically organized context objects, such as sentences, paragraphs, sections, and chapters. Do hypertext and SGML therefore conceive of text in fundamentally opposed ways? At first glance, this seems to be the case, since hypertext produces nonhierarchical text structures whereas SGML records hierarchical book structures. To what extent do such visions of SGML and hypertext conflict? SGML fundamentally asserts structure, but does it assert a single essential structure, however reconfigurable? Hypertext fundamentally subverts hierarchy: in electronic space, an individual lexia may inhabit, or contribute to, several text structures simultaneously. At first consideration this fact might appear to suggest that SGML opposes hypertext, but such is hardly the case.

Once again, Ted Nelson provides assistance, for it is he who pointed out that the problem with classification systems is not that they are bad but that different people—and the same person at different times—require different ones. One of the great strengths of hypertext, after all, lies in its ability to provide access to materials regardless of how they are classified and (hence) how and where they are stored. From the Nelsonian point of view, hypertext does not so much violate classifications as supplement them, making up for their inevitable shortcomings. From the point of view of one considering either the relation of hypertext to SGML or the hypertextualization of SGML, the problem becomes one of finding some way to encode or signal multiple structures or multiple classifications of structure. If a scholarly annotation and main text can exchange roles, status, and nature, then one needs a device that permits an SGML-marked lexia to present a different appearance, if so required, on being entered or opened from different locations.

Returning to our examples from "Hudson's Statue," we realize that readers starting from Carlyle's text will experience linked materials on Chartism and the People's League as annotations to it, but readers starting with primary or secondary materials concerning these political movements will experience "Hudson's Statue" as an annotation to them. When discussing writing for electronic space in Chapter 5, I suggest ways in which both software designers and individual authors can assist readers. For the moment I shall point out only that one such means of orienting and hence empowering readers takes the form of clearly indicating the permeable borders of the provisional text to which any lexia belongs. Using such orientation rhetoric might require that materials by Carlyle have a different appearance from those of conceivably related materials, such as lexias about the English Revolution of the 1640s and Victorian political movements. In such a case, one needs a means of configuring the text according to the means from which it is accessed. This textual polymorphism in turn suggests that in such environments text is alive, changing, kinetic, open-ended in a new way.

The Living, Transient, Time-Bound Text: William J. Mitchell's *City of Bits* Project

Another effect of annotative linking in large electronic documents appears in William J. Mitchell's *City of Bits* project. When the MIT Press published *City of Bits: Space, Place, and the Infobahn* simultaneously as a printed book and as an HTML document on the World Wide Web, the two instantiations of the text immediately began to diverge. The chief importance of this pioneering project does not derive from the fact that the publisher decided to give away the electronic version while it marketed the print text. The University of Chicago had earlier made available the first chapter of Richard A. Lanham's *The Electronic Word* on the Web, and the Johns Hopkins University Press has offered the first chapter of the original edition of this book. The electronic versions of both Lanham's and my texts are simply HTML presentations of the print texts; Mitchell's, in contrast, takes the form of a living, growing text that has as its point of departure the print version of *City of Bits*. Once a week someone at MIT Press trolls the Internet, like a fisherman looking for value and sustenance, locates related materials that users of the document have created, decides which are appropriate to add, and links them to the document.

Several points demand remark here. First, Mitchell and his MIT Press co-authors have truly created a cyberbook, one that exists in process with its human helpers, assistants, or masters—however one wishes to describe the relationship. Second, the Web version of *City of Bits* has far more authors than does the print one, since it is now a production of Mitchell (the original author in the print-medium sense), someone at the press who has clearly an increasingly larger portion of the author function, and all those who created lexias to which the text now links.

One must observe that *City of Bits* also exists as a living and therefore necessarily time-bound text. After Mitchell had described the process or state of the WWW version of *City of Bits* at an MIT Communications Forum on the cyberbook, someone in the audience inquired what would happen when Mitchell, MIT Press, or both decided they no longer wished to maintain the HTML version. Mitchell responded that at that point *City of Bits* would freeze, become static, much like a print book in fact, and that in a sense the dynamic, living, in-process version would freeze—in fact, die. Mitchell pointed out that, being an architect, the idea that something had outlived its usefulness and might likely be removed or disappear did not disturb him as much as it might most print authors. Here we have a new paradigm, the information architect as hypertext author; and like the work of all architects, the digital *City of Bits* turns out to be not only a production by many hands but also one that, for however brief a time, lives in a changing relation with other works.

Argumentation, Organization, and Rhetoric

Electronic linking, which gives the reader a far more active role than is possible with books, has certain major effects. Considered from the vantage point of a literature intertwined with book technology, these effects appear harmful and dangerous, as indeed they must be to a cultural hegemony based, as ours is, on a different technology of cultural memory. In particular, the numerating linear rhetoric of "first, second, third" so well suited to print will continue to appear within individual blocks of text but cannot be used to structure arguments in a medium that encourages readers to choose different paths, rather than following a linear one. The shift away from linearization might seem a major change, and it is, but we should remind ourselves that it is not an abandon-ment of the natural.

"The structuring of books," Tom McArthur reminds us, "is anything but 'natural'—indeed, it is thoroughly unnatural and took all of 4,000 years to bring about. The achievement of the Scholastics, pre-eminently among the world's scribal elites, was to conventionalize the themes, plot and shapes of books in a truly rigorous way, as they also structured syllabuses, scripture and debate" (69). Their conventions of book structure, however, changed fundamentally with the advent of the printing press, which encouraged alpha-betic ordering, a procedure that had never before caught on. Why?

One reason must certainly be that people had already become accustomed over too many centuries to thematically ordered material. Such material bore a close resemblance to the "normal" organization of written work: . . . Alphabetization may also have been offensive to the global Scholastic view of things. It must have seemed a perverse, disjointed and ultimately meaningless way of ordering material to men who were interested in neat frames for containing all knowledge. Certainly, alphabetization poses problems of fragmentation that may be less immediately obvious with word lists but can become serious when dealing with subject lists. (76–77)

McArthur's salutary remarks, which remind us how we always naturalize the social constructions of our world, also suggest that from a point of view like the Scholastics', the movement from manuscript to print and then to hyper-text appears one of increasing fragmentation. As long as a thematic or other culturally coherent means of ordering is available to the reader, the fragmen-tation of the hypertext document does not imply the kind of entropy that such fragmentation would have in the world of print. Capacities such as full-text searching, automatic linking, agents, and conceptual filtering potentially have the power to retain the benefits of hypertextuality while insulating the reader from the ill effects of abandoning linearity.

Beginnings and Endings

in the Borderless Text

The concepts (and experiences) of beginning and ending im-ply linearity. What happens to them in a form of textuality not governed chiefly by linearity? If we regard hypertextuality as possessing multiple sequences rather than lacking linearity and sequence entirely, then one answer to this query must be that it provides multiple beginnings and endings rather than single ones. Drawing upon Ed-ward W. Said's work on origins and openings, one can suggest that, in con-trast to print, hypertext offers at least two different kinds of beginnings. The first concerns the individual lexia, the second a gathering of them into a metatext. Whenever one has a body of hypertext materials that stands alone—either because it occupies an entire system or because it exists, however transiently, within a frame, the reader has to begin reading at some point, and for the reader that point is a beginning. Writing of print, Said explains that "a work's beginning is, practically speaking, the main entrance to what it offers" (3). But what happens when a work offers many "main" entrances—in fact, offers as many entrances as there are linked passages by means of which one can arrive at the individual lexia (which, from one perspective, becomes equivalent to a work)? Said provides materials for an answer when he argues that a "'beginning' is designated in order to indicate, clarify, or define a *later* time, place, or action. In short, the designation of a beginning generally involves also the designation of a consequent *intention*" (5). In Said's terms, therefore, even atomized text can make a beginning when the link site, or point of departure, assumes the role of the beginning of a chain or path. According to Said, "we see that the beginning is the first point (in time, space, or action) of an accomplishment or process that has duration and meaning. *The beginning, then, is the first step in the intentional production of meaning*" (5).

Said's quasi-hypertextual definition of a beginning here suggests that "in retrospect we can regard a beginning as the point at which, in a given work, the writer departs from all other works; a beginning immediately establishes relationships with works already existing, relationships of either continuity or antagonism or some mixture of both" (3).

If hypertext makes determining the beginning of a text difficult because it both changes our conception of text and permits readers to "begin" at many different points, it similarly changes the sense of an ending. Readers can not only choose different points of ending, they can also continue to add to the text, to extend it, to make it more than it was when they began to read. As Nelson, one of the originators of hypertext, points out:

There is no Final Word. There can be no final version, no last thought. There is always a new view, a new idea, a reinterpretation. And literature, which we propose to electronify, is a system for preserving continuity in the face of this fact. . . . Remember the analogy between text and water. Water flows freely, ice does not. The free-flowing, live documents on the network are subject to constant new use and linkage, and those new links continually become interactively available. Any detached copy someone keeps is frozen and dead, lacking access to the new linkage. (*Literary Machines,* 2/61, 48)

Here, as in several other ways, Bakhtin's conception of textuality anticipates hypertext. Caryl Emerson, his translator and editor, explains that "for Bakhtin 'the whole' is not a finished entity; it is always a relationship. . . . Thus, the whole can never be finalized and set aside; when a whole is realized, it is by definition already open to change" (xxxix).

Conventional notions of completion and a finished product do not apply to hypertext, whose essential novelty makes difficult defining and describing it in older terms, since they derive from another educational and information technology and have hidden assumptions inappropriate to hypertext. Particularly inapplicable are the related notions of completion and a finished product. As Derrida recognizes, a form of textuality that goes beyond print "forces us to extend . . . the dominant notion of a 'text,'" so that it "is henceforth no longer a finished corpus of writing, some content enclosed in a book or its margins but a differential network, a fabric of traces referring endlessly to something other than itself, to other differential traces" ("Living On," 83–84).

Hypertextual materials, which by definition are open-ended, expandable, and incomplete, call such notions into question. If one put a work conventionally considered complete, such as *Ulysses,* into a hypertext format, it would immediately become "incomplete." Electronic linking, which emphasizes making connections, inherently expands a text, by providing large numbers of points to which other texts can attach themselves. The fixity and physical isolation of book technology, which permits standardization and relatively easy reproduction, necessarily closes off such possibilities. Hypertext opens them up.

Boundaries

of the Borderless Text

Hypertext redefines not only beginnings and endings of the text but also its borders—its sides, as it were. Hypertext thus provides us with a means to escape what Gérard Genette terms a "sort of idolatry, which is no less serious, and today more dangerous" than idealization of the author, "namely, the fetishism of the work—conceived of as a closed, complete, absolute object" (*Figures,* 147). When one moves from physical to virtual text, and from print to hypertext, boundaries blur—the blurring that Derrida works so hard to achieve in his print publications—and one therefore no longer can rely upon conceptions or assumptions of inside and out. As Derrida explains, "To keep the outside out . . . is the inaugural gesture of 'logic' itself, of good 'sense' insofar as it accords with the self-identity of *that which is:* being is what it is, the outside is outside and the inside inside. Writing must thus return to being what it *should never have ceased to be:* an accessory, an accident, an excess" (*Dissemination,* 128). Without linearity and sharp bounds between in and out, between absence and presence, and between self and other, philosophy will change. Working within the world of print, Derrida presciently argues, using

Platonic texts as an example, that "the textual chain we must set back in place is thus no longer simply 'internal' to Plato's lexicon. But in going beyond the bounds of that lexicon, we are less interested in breaking through certain limits, with or without cause, than in putting in doubt the right to posit such limits in the first place. In a word, we do not believe that there exists, in all rigor, a Platonic text, closed upon itself, complete with its inside and outside" (130).

Derrida furthermore explains, with a fine combination of patience and wit, that in noticing that texts really do not have insides and outsides, one does not reduce them to so much mush: "Not that one must then consider that it [the text] is leaking on all sides and can be drowned confusedly in the undifferentiated generality of the element. Rather, provided the articulations are rigorously and prudently recognized, one should simply be able to untangle the hidden forces of attraction linking a present word with an absent word in the text of Plato" (130).

Another sign of Derrida's awareness of the limitations and confinements of contemporary attitudes that arise in association with the technology of the printed book is his hypertextual approach to textuality and meaning, an approach that remains skeptical of "a fundamental or totalizing principle," since it recognizes that "the classical system's 'outside' can no longer take the form of the sort of extra-text which would arrest the concatenation of writing" (5).

Hypertext thus creates an open, open-bordered text, a text that cannot shut out other texts and therefore embodies the Derridean text, which blurs "all those boundaries that form the running border of what used to be called a text, of what we once thought this word could identify, i.e., the supposed end and beginning of a work, the unity of the corpus, the title, the margins, the signatures, the referential realm outside the frame, and so forth." Hypertext therefore undergoes what Derrida describes as "a sort of overrun [*débordement*] that spoils all these boundaries and divisions" ("Living On," 83).

In hypertext systems, links within and without a text—intratextual and intertextual connections between points of text (lexias, including images)—become equivalent, thus bringing texts closer together and weakening or reconfiguring the boundaries among them. Consider the case of intertextual links in Milton (Figure 10): Milton's various descriptions of himself as prophet or inspired poet in *Paradise Lost* and his citations of Genesis 3:15 provide obvious examples. Extratextual and intratextual links, in contrast, are exemplified by links between a particular passage in which Milton mentions prophecy and with his other writings in prose or poetry that make similar or obvi-

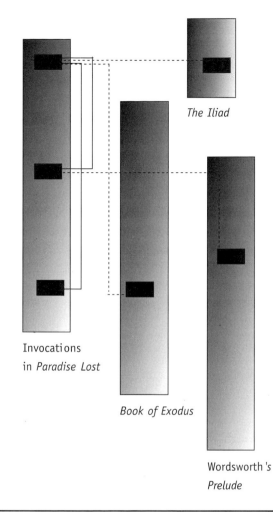

The Borderless Text

Linking changes the experience of text and authorship by rendering the borders of all text permeable:

By reifying allusions, echoes, references, and so on, linking

(1) makes them material,

(2) draws individual texts experientially closer together.

Consider, for example, a hypertext presentation (or "edition") of Milton's *Paradise Lost*.

The Iliad

Invocations
in *Paradise Lost*

Book of Exodus

Wordsworth 's
Prelude

Figure 10. The Borderless Electronic Text

ously relevant points, as well as with biblical texts, commentaries throughout the ages, comparable or contrasting poetic statements by others, and scholarly comment. Similarly, Miltonic citations of the biblical text about the heel of man crushing the serpent's head and being in turn bruised by the serpent link obviously to the biblical passage and its traditional interpretations as well as to other literary allusions and scholarly comment upon all these subjects. Hypertext linking simply allows one to speed up the usual process of making connections while providing a means of graphing such transactions, if one can apply the word *simply* to such a radically transformative procedure.

The speed with which one can move between passages and points in sets of texts changes both the way we read and the way we write, just as the high-speed number-crunching computing changed various scientific fields by making possible investigations that before had required too much time or risk. One change comes from this ability to move with equal facility to points within a text and to those outside it. If one can move as easily between the opening section of *Paradise Lost* and a passage in Book 12 thousands of lines "away" and between that opening section and a particular anterior French text or modern scholarly comment, then, in an important sense, the discreteness of texts, which print culture creates, has radically changed and possibly disappeared. One may argue that, in fact, all that the hypertext linking of texts does is embody the way one actually experiences texts in the act of reading; but if so, the act of reading has in some way gotten much closer to the electronic embodiment of text and in so doing has begun to change its nature.

These observations about hypertext suggest that computers bring us much closer to a culture some of whose qualities have more in common with those of preliterate man than even Walter J. Ong has been willing to admit. In *Orality and Literacy* he argues that computers have brought us into what he terms an age of "secondary orality" that has "striking resemblances" to the primary, preliterate orality "in its participatory mystique, its fostering of a communal sense, its concentration on the present moment, and even its use of formulas" (136). Nonetheless, although Ong finds interesting parallels between a computer culture and a purely oral one, he mistakenly insists: "The sequential processing and spatializing of the word, initiated by writing and raised to a new order of intensity by print, is further intensified by the computer, which maximizes commitment of the word to space and to (electronic) local motion and optimizes analytic sequentiality by making it virtually instantaneous" (*Orality and Literacy,* 136). In fact, hypertext systems, which insert every text into a web of relations, produce a very different effect, for they allow nonsequential reading and thinking.

One major effect of such multisequential reading, the weakening of the boundaries of the text, can be thought of either as correcting the artificial isolation of a text from its contexts or as violating one of the chief qualities of the book. According to Ong, writing and printing produce the effect of discrete, self-contained utterance: "By isolating thought on a written surface, detached from any interlocutor, making utterance in this sense autonomous and indifferent to attack, writing presents utterance and thought as uninvolved with all else, somehow self-contained, complete. Print in the same way situates utterance and thought on a surface disengaged from everything else, but it also goes farther in suggesting self-containment" (132).

We have already observed the way in which hypertext suggests integration rather than self-containment. Another possible result of such hypertext may also be disconcerting. As Ong also points out, books, unlike their authors, cannot really be challenged: "The author might be challenged if only he or she could be reached, but the author cannot be reached in any book. There is no way to refute a text. After absolutely total and devastating refutation, it says exactly the same thing as before. This is one reason why 'the book says' is popularly tantamount to 'it is true.' It is also one reason why books have been burnt. A text stating what the whole world knows is false will state falsehood forever, so long as the text exists" (79). The question arises, however, If hypertext situates texts in a field of other texts, can any individual work that has been addressed by another still speak so forcefully? One can imagine hypertext presentations of books (or the equivalent thereof) in which the reader can call up all the reviews and comments on that book, which would then inevitably exist as part of a complex dialogue rather than as the embodiment of a voice or thought that speaks unceasingly. Hypertext, which links one block of text to myriad others, destroys that physical isolation of the text, just as it also destroys the attitudes created by that isolation. Because hypertext systems permit a reader both to annotate an individual text and to link it to other, perhaps contradictory texts, it destroys one of the most basic characteristics of the printed text—its separation and univocality. Whenever one places a text within a network of other texts, one forces it to exist as part of a complex dialogue. Hypertext linking, which tends to change the roles of author and reader, also changes the limits of the individual text.

By changing a text's spatial and temporal relation to other texts, electronic linking radically changes the experience of the text. Reading a hypertext version of Dickens' *Great Expectations* or Eliot's *The Waste Land,* for example, one follows links to predecessor texts, variant readings, criticism, and so on. Following an electronic link to an image of, say, the desert or a wasteland in a poem by Tennyson, Browning, or Swinburne takes no more time than following one from a passage earlier in the poem to one near its end. Therefore, readers experience these other, earlier texts outside *The Waste Land* and the passage inside the work as existing equally distant from the first passage. Hypertext thereby blurs the distinction between what is "inside" and what is "outside" a text. It also makes all the texts connected to a block of text collaborate with that text.

The Status of the Text,

Status in the Text

Alvin Kernan claims that "Benjamin's general theory of the demystification of art through numerous reproductions explains precisely what happened when in the eighteenth century the printing press, with its logic of multiplicity, stripped the classical texts of the old literary order of their aura" (*Printing Technology,* 152), and it seems likely that hypertext will extend this process of demystification even further. Kernan convincingly argues that by Pope's time a "flood of books, in its accumulation both of different texts and identical copies of the same texts, threatened to obscure the few idealized classics, both ancient and modern, of polite letters, and to weaken their aura by making printed copies of them" (153). Any information medium that encourages rapid dissemination of texts and easy access to them will increasingly demystify individual texts. But hypertext has a second potentially demystifying effect: by making the borders of the text (now conceived as the individual lexia) permeable, it removes some of its independence and uniqueness.

Kernan further adds that, "since printed books were for the most part in the vernacular, they further desacralized letters by expanding its canon from a group of venerable texts written in ancient languages known only to an elite to include a body of contemporary writing in the natural language understood by all who read" (153–54). Will electronic versions of the Bible, like *CD Word,* that seem to be essentially democratizing similarly desacralize the Scriptures? They have the potential to do so in two ways. First by making some of the scholar's procedures easily available to almost any reader, this electronic Bible might demystify a text that possesses a talismanic power for many in its intended audience.

Second and more fundamental, the very fact that this hypertext Bible enforces the presence of multiple versions potentially undercuts belief in the possibility of a unique, unitary text. Certainly, the precedent of Victorian loss of belief in the doctrine of Verbal Inspiration of the Scriptures suggests that hypertext could have a potentially parallel effect (Landow, *Victorian Types,* 54–56). In Victorian England the wide-scale abandonment of belief that every word of the Bible was divinely inspired, even in its English translation, followed from a variety of causes, including influence of the German Higher Criticism, independent British applications of rational approaches like those by Bishop Colenso, and the discoveries of geology, philology, and (later) biology. The discovery, for instance, that Hebrew did not possess the uniqueness as a language that some believers, particularly Evangelicals, long assumed it did, eroded faith, in large part because believers became aware of unexpected multiplicity where they had assumed only unity. The discovery of mul-

tiple manuscripts of scripture had parallel effects. Hypertext, which emphasizes multiplicity, may cause similar crises in belief.

Although the fundamental drive of the printed page is a linear, straight-
ahead thrust that captures readers and forces them to read along if they are
to read at all, specialized forms of text have developed that use secondary
codes to present information difficult or impossible to include in linear text.
The foot- or endnote, which is one of the prime ways that books create an
additional space, requires some code, such as a superscript number or one
within parentheses, that signals readers to stop reading what is conventionally termed the *main* text or the body of the text and begin reading some
peripheral or appended patch of text that hangs off that part of the main text.

In both scholarly editing and in scholarly prose such divisions of text
partake of fixed hierarchies of status and power. The smaller size type that
presents footnote and endnote text, like the placement of that text away from
the normal center of the reader's attention, makes clear that such material is
subsidiary, dependent, less important. In scholarly editing, such typographic
and other encoding makes clear that the editor's efforts, no matter how lavish
or long suffering, are obviously less important than the words being edited,
for these appear in the main text. In scholarly and critical discourse that
employs annotation, these conventions also establish the importance of the
dominant argument in opposition to the author's sources, scholarly allies and
opponents, and even the work of fiction or poetry upon which the critical
text focuses.

One experiences hypertext annotation of a text very differently. In the
first place, electronic linking immediately destroys the simple binary opposition of text and note that founds the status relations that inhabit the printed
book. Following a link can bring the reader to a later portion of the text or to
a text to which the first one alludes. It may also lead to other works by the
same author, or to a range of critical commentary, textual variants, and the
like. The assignment of text and annotation to what Tom Wolfe calls different
"statuspheres" therefore becomes very difficult, and such text hierarchies
tend quickly to collapse.

Hypertext linking situates the present text at the center of the textual
universe, thus creating a new kind of hierarchy, in which the power of the
center dominates that of the infinite periphery. But because in hypertext that
center is always a transient, decenterable virtual center—one created, in
other words, only by one's act of reading that particular text—it never tyran-
nizes other aspects of the network in the way a printed text does.

Barthes, well aware of the political constraints of a text that makes a reader read in a particular way, himself manipulates the political relations of text in interesting ways. The entire procedure or construction of *S/Z*, for example, serves as a commentary on the political relationships among portions of the standard scholarly text, the problem of hierarchy. Barthes playfully creates his own version of complex footnote systems. Like Derrida in *Glas,* he creates a work or metatext that the reader accustomed to reading books finds either abrasively different or, on rare occasion, a wittily powerful commentary on the way books work—that is, on the way they force readers to see relationships between sections and thereby endow certain assemblages of words with power and value because they appear in certain formats rather than others.

Barthes, in others words, comments upon the footnote, and all of *S/Z* turns out to be a criticism of the power relations between portions of text. In a foot- or endnote, we recall, that portion of the text conventionally known as the main text has a value for both reader and writer that surpasses any of its supplementary portions, which include notes, prefaces, dedications, and so on, most of which supplements take the form of apparatuses designed to aid information retrieval. These devices, almost all of which derive directly from print technology, can function only when one has fixed, repeatable, physically isolated texts. They have great advantages and permit certain kinds of reading: one need not, for example, memorize the location of a particular passage if one has system features such as chapter titles, tables of contents, and indices. So the reference device has enormous value as a means of reader orientation, navigation, and information retrieval.

It comes at certain costs, costs that, like most paid by the reader of text, have become so much a part of our experience of reading that we do not notice them at all. Barthes makes us notice them. Barthes, like most late-twentieth-century critical theorists, is at his best when seeing the invisible, breathing on it in hopes that the condensate will illuminate the shadows of what others have long missed and taken to be not there. What then does the footnote imply, and how does Barthes manipulate or avoid it? Combined with the physical isolation of each text, the division between main text and footnote establishes the primary importance of main text in its relation to other texts even when thinking about the subject instantly reveals that such relationship cannot in fact exist.

Take the scholarly article, the kind of articles we academics all write. One wishes to write an article on some aspect of the Nausicaa section of Joyce's *Ulysses,* a text that by even the crudest quantitative measures appears to be more important, more powerful than our note that, say, identifies one of the sources of Gerty McDowell's phrasing as a contemporary women's magazine. Joyce's novel exists in more copies than our article can or will, and it therefore has an enormously larger readership and reputation—all problematic notions, I admit, all relying on certain ideologies; and yet most of us, I expect, will accede to them, for they are the values by which we work. Ostensibly, that is. Even deconstructionists privilege the text, the great work.

Once one begins to write one's article, however, the conventions of print quickly call those assumptions into question, since anything in the main text is clearly more important than anything outside it. The physically isolated discrete text is very discreet indeed, for as Ong makes clear, it hides obvious connections of indebtedness and qualification. When one introduces other authors into the text, they appear as attenuated, often highly distorted shadows of themselves. Part of this is necessary, since one cannot, after all, reproduce an entire article or book by another author in one's own. Part of this attenuation comes from authorial inaccuracy, slovenliness, or outright dishonesty. Nonetheless, such attenuation is part of the message of print, an implication one cannot avoid, or at least one cannot avoid since the advent of hypertext, which by providing an alternative textual mode reveals differences that turn out to be, no longer, inevitabilities and invisibilities.

In print, when I provide the page number of an indicated or cited passage from Joyce, or even include that passage in text or note, the passage—which is the occasion for my article—clearly exists in a subsidiary, comparatively minor position in relation to my words, which appear, after all, in the so-called main text. What would happen, though, if I wrote my article in hypertext? Assuming I was working in a fully implemented hypertextual environment, I would begin by calling up Joyce's novel and, on one side of the video screen, opening the passage or passages involved. Next, I would write my comment, but instead of citing Joyce, I would create an electronic link between my own text and one or more sections of the Joycean text. At the same time, I would also link my text to other aspects of my present text, text by others, and texts I had written earlier. Several things have happened, things that violate our expectations. First, attaching my commentary to the passage from Joyce makes it exist in a far different, far less powerful relation to Joyce, the so-called original text, than it would in the world of physically isolated texts. Second, as soon as one attaches more than one text block or lexia to a single anchor (or block, or link marker), one destroys all possibility of the bipartite hierarchy of footnote and main text. In hypertext, the main text is that which one is presently reading. So one has a multiple revaluation:

with the dissolution of this hierarchy, all attached texts gain an importance they might not have had before.

In Bakhtin's terms, the scholarly article, which quotes or cites statements by others—"some for refutation and others for confirmation and supplementation—is one instance of a dialogic interrelationship among directly signifying discourses within the limits of a single context. . . . This is not a clash of two ultimate semantic authorities, but rather an objectified (plotted) clash of two represented positions, subordinated wholly to the higher, ultimate authority of the author. The monologic context, under these circumstances, is neither broken nor weakened" (188). Trying to evade the constraints, the logic, of print scholarship, Bakhtin himself takes an approach to quoting other authors that is characteristic of postbook technology, especially hypertext. In the Introduction to *Problems of Dostoevsky's Poetics,* Bakhtin's editor and translator, Caryl Emerson, explains that when Bakhtin quotes other critics, "he does so at length, and lets each voice sound fully. He understands that the frame is always in the power of the framer, and that there is an outrageous privilege in the power to cite others. Thus Bakhtin's footnotes rarely serve to narrow down debate by discrediting totally, or (on the other hand) by conferring exclusive authority. They might identify, expand, illustrate, but they do not pull rank on the body of the text—and are thus more in the nature of a marginal gloss than an authoritative footnote" (xxxvii).

Derrida also comments upon the status relations that cut and divide texts, but unlike Barthes in *S/Z,* he concerns himself with oppositions between preface and main text and main text and other texts. Recognizing that status that accrues to different portions of a text, Derrida examines the way each takes on associations with power or importance. In discussing Hegel's introduction to *The Science of Logic,* Derrida points out, for example, that the Preface must be distinguished from the Introduction. They did not have the same function, nor even the same dignity, in Hegel's eyes (*Dissemination,* 17). Derrida's new textuality, or true textuality (which I have continually likened to hypertextuality), represents "an entirely other typology where the outlines of the preface and the 'main' text are blurred" (39).

Hypertext and Decentrality: The Philosophical Grounding

Accustomed to reading pages of print on paper, we tend to conceive of text from the vantage point of the reader experiencing that page or passage, and that portion of text assumes a centrality. Hypertext, however, makes such assumptions of centrality fundamentally problematic. In fact, hypertext thrives on marginality. In hypertext, any linked text can serve as annotation, commentary, or appended text; and each linked text exists as the *other* text, which leads to a conception (and experience) of text as Other. Therefore, the position of any lexia in hypertext resembles that of the Victorian sage, for, like the sage—Carlyle, Thoreau, Ruskin—the lexia stands outside, off center, and challenges. From that essential marginality, to which he stakes his claim by his skillful, aggressive use of pronouns to oppose his interests and views to those of the reader, he defines his discursive position or vantage point.

Hypertext similarly emphasizes that the marginal has as much to offer as does the central, in part because hypertext does more than redefine the central by refusing to grant centrality to anything, to any lexia, for more than the time a gaze rests upon it. In hypertext, centrality, like beauty and relevance, resides in the mind of the beholder. Like Andy Warhol's modern person's fifteen minutes of fame, centrality in hypertext exists only as a matter of evanescence. As one might expect from an information medium that changes our relations to data, thoughts, and selves so dramatically, that evanescence of this (ever-migrating) centrality is merely a given—that's the way things are—rather than an occasion for complaint or satire. It is simply the condition under which—or within which—we think, communicate, or record these thoughts and communications in the hypertextual docuverse.

This hypertextual dissolution of centrality, which makes the medium such a potentially democratic one, also makes it a model of a society of conversations in which no one conversation, no one discipline or ideology, dominates or founds the others. It is thus the instantiation of what Richard Rorty terms "edifying philosophy," the point of which "is to keep the conversation going rather than to find objective truth." It is a form of philosophy

having sense only as a protest against attempts to close off conversation by proposals for universal commensuration through the hypostatization of some privileged set of descriptions. The danger which edifying discourse tries to avert is that some given vocabulary, some way in which people might come to think of themselves, will deceive them into thinking that from now on all discourse could be, or should be, normal discourse. The resulting freezing-over of culture would be, in the eyes of edifying philosophers, the dehumanization of human beings. (377)

Hypertext, which has a built-in bias against "hypostatization" and probably against privileged descriptions as well, therefore embodies the approach to philosophy that Rorty urges. The basic hypertext experience of text, information, and control, which moves the boundary of power away from the author in the direction of the reader, models such a postmodern, antihierarchical medium of information, text, philosophy, and society.

Reconfiguring

the Author

Erosion of the Self

Like contemporary critical theory, hypertext reconfigures—rewrites—the author in several obvious ways. First of all, the figure of the hypertext author approaches, even if it does not entirely merge with, that of the reader; the functions of reader and writer become more deeply entwined with each other than ever before. This transformation and near merging of roles is but the latest stage in the convergence of what had once been two very different activities. Although today we assume that anyone who reads can also write, such was long not the case, and historians of reading point out that for millennia many people capable of reading could not even sign their own names. Today when we consider reading and writing, we probably think of them as serial processes or as procedures carried out intermittently by the same person: first one reads, then one writes, and then one reads some more. Hypertext, which creates an active, even intrusive reader, carries this convergence of activities one step closer to completion; but in so doing, it infringes upon the power of the writer, removing some of it and granting that portion to the reader.

One clear sign of such transference of authorial power appears in the reader's abilities to choose his or her way through the metatext, to annotate text written by others, and to create links between documents written by others. Hypertext does not permit the active reader to change the text produced by another person, but it does narrow the phenomenological distance that separates individual documents from one another in the worlds of print and manuscript. In reducing the autonomy of the text, hypertext reduces the autonomy of the author. In the words of Michael Heim, "as the authoritativeness of text diminishes, so too does the recognition of the private self of the creative author" (*Electric Language,* 221). Granted, much of that so-called autonomy had been illusory and had existed as little more than the readers' difficulty in perceiving connections between documents. Nonetheless, hypertext—which I am here taking as the convergence of poststructuralist conceptions of textuality and electronic embodiments of it—does do away with certain aspects of the authoritativeness and autonomy of the text, and in so doing it does reconceive the figure and function of authorship.

William R. Paulson, who examines literature from the vantage point of information theory, arrives at much the same position when he argues that "to characterize texts as artificially and imperfectly autonomous is not to eliminate the role of the author but to deny the reader's or critic's submission to any instance of authority. This perspective leaves room neither for authorial mastery of a communicative object nor for the authority of a textual coherence so complete that the reader's (infinite) task would be merely to receive its rich and multilayered meaning." Beginning from the position of information theory, Paulson finds that in "literary communication," as in all communication, "there is an irreducible element of noise," and therefore "the reader's task does not end with reception, for reception is inherently flawed. What literature solicits of the reader is not simply receptive but the active, independent, autonomous construction of meaning" (139). Finding no reason to exile the author from the text, Paulson nonetheless ends up by assigning to the reader power that, in earlier views, had been the prerogative of the writer.

Hypertext and contemporary theory reconceive the author in a second way. As we shall observe when we examine the notion of collaborative writing, both agree in configuring the author of the text as a text. As Barthes explains in his famous exposition of the idea, "this 'I' which approaches the text is already itself a plurality of other texts, of codes which are infinite" (*S/Z,* 10). Barthes's point, which should seem both familiar and unexceptional to anyone who has encountered Joyce's weaving of Gerty McDowell out of the texts of her class and culture, appears much clearer and more obvious from the vantage point of intertextuality. In this case, as in others at which we have already looked, contemporary theory proposes and hypertext disposes; or, to be less theologically aphoristic, hypertext embodies many of the ideas and attitudes proposed by Barthes, Derrida, Foucault, and others.

One of the most important of these ideas involves treating the self of author and reader not simply as (print) text but as a hypertext. For all these authors, the self takes the form of a decentered (or centerless) network of codes that, on another level, also serves as a node within another centerless network. Jean-François Lyotard, for example, rejects nineteenth-century Romantic paradigms of an islanded self in favor of a model of the self as a node in an information network: "A self does not amount to much," he assures us with fashionable nonchalance, "but no self is an island; each exists in a fabric of relations that is now more complex and mobile than ever before. Young or old, man or woman, rich or poor, a person is always located at 'nodal points' of specific communication circuits, however tiny these may be. Or better: one is always located at a post through which various kinds of messages pass" (*Postmodern Condition,* 15). Lyotard's analogy becomes even stronger if one realizes that by "post" he most likely means the modern European post office, which is a telecommunications center containing telephones and other networked devices.

Some theorists find the idea of participating in a network to be demeaning and depressing, particularly since contemporary conceptions of textuality de-emphasize autonomy in favor of participation. Before succumbing to posthumanist depression, however, one should place Foucault's statements about "the author's disappearance" in the context of recent discussions of "machine intelligence" (Foucault, "What Is an Author?" 119). According to Heinz Pagels, machines capable of complex intellectual processing will "put an end to much discussion about the mind-body problem, because it will be very hard not to attribute a conscious mind to them without failing to do so for more human beings. Gradually the popular view will become that consciousness is simply 'what happens' when electronic components are put together the right way" (92). Pagels' thoughts on the eventual electronic solution to the mind-body problem recall Foucault's discussion of "the singular relationship that holds between an author and a text [as] the manner in which a text apparently points to this figure who is outside and precedes it" ("What Is an Author?" 115). This point of view makes apparent that literature generates precisely such appearance of a self, and that, moreover, we have long read a self "out" of texts as evidence that a unified self exists "behind" or "within" or "implicit in" it. The problem for anyone who yearns to retain older conceptions of authorship or the author function lies in the fact that radical changes in textuality produce radical changes in the author figure derived from that textuality. Lack of textual autonomy, like lack of textual centeredness, immediately reverberates through conceptions of authorship as well. Similarly, the unboundedness of the new textuality disperses the author as well. Foucault opens this side of the question when he raises what, in another context, might be a standard problem in a graduate course on the methodology of scholarship:

If we wish to publish the complete works of Nietzsche, for example, where do we draw the line? Certainly, everything must be published, but can we agree on what "everything" means? We will, of course, include everything that Nietzsche himself published, along with the drafts of his works, his plans for aphorisms, his marginalia; notations and corrections. But what if, in a notebook filled with aphorisms, we find a reference, a reminder of an appointment, an address, or a laundry bill, should this be included in his works? Why not? . . . If some have found it convenient to bypass the individuality of the writer or his status as an author to concentrate on a work, they have failed to appreciate the equally problematic nature of the word "work" and the unity it designates. (119)

Within the context of Foucault's discussion of "the author's disappearance" (119), the illimitable plenitude of Nietzsche's oeuvre demonstrates that there's more than one way to kill an author. One can destroy (what we mean by) the author, which includes the notion of sole authorship, by removing the autonomy of text. One can also achieve the same end by decentering text or by transforming text into a network. Finally, one can remove limits on textuality, permitting it to expand, until Nietzsche, the edifying philosopher, becomes equally the author of *The Gay Science* and laundry lists and other such trivia—as indeed he was. Such illimitable plenitude has truly "transformed" the author, or at least the older conception of him, into "a victim of his own writing" (117).

Fears about the death of the author, whether in complaint or celebration, derive from Claude Lévi-Strauss, whose mythological works demonstrated for a generation of critics that works of powerful imagination take form without an author. In *The Raw and the Cooked* (1964), for example, where he showed, "not how men think in myths, but how myths operate in men's minds without their being aware of the fact," he also suggests "it would perhaps be better to go still further and, disregarding the thinking subject completely, proceed as if the thinking process were taking place in the myths, in the reflection upon themselves and their interrelation" (12).[1] Lévi-Strauss's presentation of mythological thought as a complex system of transformations without a center turns it into a networked text—not surprising, since the network serves as one of the main paradigms of synchronous structure.[2] Edward Said claims that the "two principal forces that have eroded the authority of the human subject in contemporary reflection are, on the one hand, the host of problems that arise in defining the subject's authenticity and, on the other, the development of disciplines like linguistics and ethnology that dramatize the subject's anomalous and unprivileged, even untenable, position in thought" (293). One may add to this observation that these disciplines' network paradigms also contribute importantly to this sense of the attenuated, depleted, eroding, or even vanishing subject.

Some authors, such as Said and Heim, derive the erosion of the thinking subject directly from electronic information technology. Said, for example, claims it is quite possible to argue "that the proliferation of information (and what is still more remarkable, a proliferation of the hardware for disseminating and preserving this information) has hopelessly diminished the role apparently played by the individual" (51).[3] Michael Heim, who believes loss of authorial power to be implicit in all electronic text, complains: "Fragments, reused material, the trails and intricate pathways of 'hypertext,' as Ted Nelson terms it, all these advance the disintegration of the centering voice of contemplative thought. The arbitrariness and availability of database searching decreases the felt sense of an authorial control over what is written" (*Electric Language,* 220). A data base search, in other words, permits the active reader to enter the author's text at any point and not at the point the author chose as the beginning. Of course, as long as we have had indices, scholarly readers have dipped into specialist publications before or (shame!) instead of reading them through from beginning to end. In fact, recent studies of the way specialists read periodicals in their areas of expertise confirm that the linear model of reading is often little more than a pious fiction for many expert readers (McKnight, Richardson, and Dillon, "Journal Articles").

Although Heim here mentions hypertext in relation to the erosion of authorial prerogative, the chief problem, he argues elsewhere, lies in the way "digital writing turns the private solitude of reflective reading and writing into a public network where the personal symbolic framework needed for original authorship is threatened by linkage with the total textuality of human expressions." Unlike most writers on hypertext, he finds participation in a network a matter for worry rather than celebration, but he describes the same world they do, though with a strange combination of prophecy and myopia. Heim, who sees this loss of authorial control in terms of a corollary loss of privacy, argues that "anyone writing on a fully equipped computer is, in a sense, directly linked with the totality of symbolic expressions—more so and essentially so than in any previous writing element." Pointing out that word processing redefines the related notions of publishing, making public, and privacy, Heim argues that anyone who writes with a word processor cannot escape the electronic network: "Digital writing, because it consists of electronic signals, puts one willy-nilly on a network where everything is constantly published. Privacy becomes an increasingly fragile notion. Word processing manifests a world in which the public itself and its publicity have become omnivorous; to make public has therefore a different meaning than ever before" (*Electric Language,* 215).

The key phrase here, of course, is "in a sense," for as a famous Princeton philosopher used to say when a student used that phrase, "Yes, yes, in a sense a cow and a pig are the same animal, but in what sense?" The answer must be in some bizarrely inefficient dystopic future sense—"future" because today few people writing with word processors participate very frequently in the lesser versions of such information networks that already exist, and "bizarrely inefficient" because one would have to assume that the billions and billions of words we would write would all have equal ability to clutter the major resource that such networks will be. Nonetheless, although Heim may much overstate the case for universal loss of privacy, particularly in relation to decentered networks, he has accurately presented both some implications of hypertext for writers and the reactions against them by the print author accustomed to the fiction of the autonomous text.

The third form of reconfiguration of self and author shared by theory and hypertext concerns the decentered self, an obvious corollary to the network paradigm. As Said points out, major contemporary theorists reject "the human subject as grounding center for human knowledge. Derrida, Foucault, and Deleuze . . . have spoken of contemporary knowledge (*savoir*) as decentered; Deleuze's formulation is that knowledge, insofar as it is intelligible, is apprehensible in terms of *nomadic centers,* provisional structures that are never permanent, always straying from one set of information to another" (376). These three contemporary thinkers advance a conceptualization of thought best understood, like their views of text, in an electronic, virtual, hypertextual environment.

Before mourning too readily for this vanished or much diminished self, we would do well to remind ourselves that, although Western thought long held such notions of the unitary self in a privileged position, texts from Homer to Freud have steadily argued the contrary position. Divine or demonic possession, inspiration, humors, moods, dreams, the unconscious— all these devices that serve to explain how human beings act better, worse, or just different from their usual behavior argue against the unitary conception of the self so central to moral, criminal, and copyright law. J. H. Hertz, the editor of the Soncino edition of the Hebrew Bible, reminds us that

Balaam's personality is an old enigma, which has baffled the skill of commentators. . . . He is represented in Scripture as at the same time heathen sorcerer, true Prophet, and the perverter who suggested a peculiarly abhorrent means of bringing about the ruin of Israel.

Because of these fundamental contradictions in character, Bible Critics assume that the Scriptural account of Balaam is a combination of two or three varying traditions belonging to different periods. . . . Such a view betrays a slight knowledge of the fearful complexity of the mind and soul of man. It is only in the realm of Fable that men and women display, as it were in a single flash of light, some one aspect of human nature. It is otherwise in real life. (668)

Given such long-observed multiplicities of the self, we are forced to realize that notions of the unitary author or self cannot authenticate the unity of a text. The instance of Balaam also reminds us that we have access to him only in Scriptures and that it is the biblical text, after all, which figures the unwilling prophet as a fractured self.

How I Am Writing This Book

Let me tell you how I am writing—which is to say, composing or putting together—the book version of this text, after which I shall compare this form of composition to that practiced within a hypertext environment. During my undergraduate years, I used to take preliminary preparatory notes, make outlines, and begin rough drafts directly on a typewriter. The same procedures continued when I shifted to a word-processing program on the university's mainframe computer, which I used by means of a terminal first across campus in the English Department or in the Computer Center and then on one in my home that connected to the university by a telephone line. Increasingly, the virtuality and manipulability of computer text processing changed my work habits. My usual manner of proceeding now entails taking reading notes, usually in the form of selected passages to which I append preliminary commentary, directly on the computer. I have long taken a few such notes, particularly in preparation for complex projects, but the movement first to a mainframe computer and then to an Apple Macintosh (and later a Macintosh II, a Quadra 950, and other machines) made taking such notes both easier to carry out and potentially more valuable, since the ability to copy and paste electronic text encourages one to expend effort, knowing that it need not be duplicated by the later need to retype or recopy.

Two things about working with a word processor first attracted me to carrying out writing projects on a computer. First, there was the ease with which the writer can make changes and corrections, both the direct result of the virtuality of electronic text. Second, working with a word processor permits one to segment one's work, carrying out certain tasks, particularly less creative ones, as one's time, energy, and disposition permit. Thus, instead of having to complete one's writing before adding footnotes, or adding foot- or endnotes in the text of drafts before the last, one can take advantage of the automatic numbering (and renumbering) of notes to complete them ahead of time. Relying on this capacity of computing, I discovered early on that one could accomplish major projects in far less time than they took with typewriters and with fewer of the inevitable errors of retyping.

The present work (which is to this point not one "work" but still a fragmentary set of separate documents or computer files in Microsoft Word) is taking form as a series of fragments that are imported and, when necessary, rearranged under the headings of a continually changing outline. Most of the text thus far has been written in this manner, but those sections that discuss Vannevar Bush take advantage of the availability of digitized text. When I was about to start the section discussing the memex, I mentioned to Paul Kahn, who was working on a book on Bush, that I wanted to borrow from him several of Bush's books in order to make photocopies on which I could then mark passages and prepare them for entry into my word processor. Paul replied, "Why would you want to do that? I have digitized copies of four of his most important articles and placed them on Intermedia and can easily export them from it into MS Word." True to his word, he made copies of Bush's essays for me, which he placed on a disk, after which, using the large two-page graphics monitor on which I work, I opened both the developing draft of the introduction and Bush's "As We May Think" and placed them side by side. Having decided which passages I wished to quote, I first copied and then pasted them as needed into the appropriate place in the text I was "writing." In some cases, I wrote the introductory passages, concluding discussion, and transitions in the Bush document and then transferred these blocks to their new context; in others, I first copied the passages from Bush and only later worked them into my text.

This scenario began with my remarking upon the frustrations experienced by one who has written within a hypertext environment then returns to the linear world of the printed book. Such frustrations derive from repeated recognitions that effective argument requires closing off connections and abandoning lines of investigation that hypertextuality would have made available. Here are two examples of what I mean.

Earlier in this chapter, in the midst of discussing the importance of Lévi-Strauss to recent discussions of authorship, I made the following statement: "Lévi-Strauss's presentation of mythological thought as a complex system of transformations without a center turns it into a networked text—not surprising, since the network serves as one of the main paradigms of synchronous structure"; and to this text I appended a note, pointing out that in *The Scope of Anthropology* "Lévi-Strauss also employs this model for societies as a whole: 'Our society, a particular instance in a much vaster family of societies, depends, like all others, for its coherence and its very existence on a network—grown infinitely unstable and complicated among us—of ties between consanguineal families.'" At this point in the main text, I had originally planned to place Foucault's remark that "we can easily imagine a culture where discourse would circulate without any need for an author" ("What Is an Author," 138), and to this remark I had considered adding the observation that, yes, we can easily "imagine" such a culture, but we do not have to do so, since Lévi-Strauss's mythographic works have provided abundant examples of it. Although the diachronic relationship between these two influential thinkers seemed worthy of notice, I could not add the passage from Foucault and my comment, because it disturbed my planned line of argument, which next required Said's relation of ethnology and linguistics to the erosion of "the authority of the human subject in contemporary reflection," and I did not want to veer off in yet another direction. I then considered putting this observation into an endnote that fell at that point, but it also seemed out of place there.

Had I written this chapter within a hypertext environment, the need to maintain a linear thrust would not have required this kind of choice; it would have required choices, but not this kind. And I could have linked two or more passages to this point in the main text, thereby creating multiple contexts both for my argument and for the quoted passage that served as my point of departure. I am not urging, of course, that in its print form this chapter has lost something of major importance because I could not easily append multiple connections without confusing the reader. (Had my abandoned remark seemed important enough to my overall argument, I could have managed to include it in several obvious ways, such as adding another paragraph or rewriting the main text to provide a point from which to hang another note.) No, I make this point to remind us that, as Derrida emphasizes, the linear habits of thought associated with print technology often force us to think in particular ways that require narrowness, decontextualization, and intellectual attenuation, if not downright impoverishment. Linear argument, in other words, forces one to cut off a quoted passage from other, apparently irrelevant contexts that in fact contribute to its meaning. The linearity of print also provides the passage with an illusory center, whose force is intensified by such selection.

A second example points to another kind of exclusion associated with linear writing. During the course of composing these first three chapters, several passages, such as Barthes's description of the writerly text and Derrida's exposition of borders, boundaries, and *débordement,* forced themselves into the line of argument and hence deserved inclusion seven or eight times. One can repeatedly refer to a particular passage, of course, by combining full quotation, selections, and skillful paraphrase; but in general the writer can concentrate on a quoted section of text in this manner only when it serves as the center, or one of the centers, of the argument. If I wished to write a chapter or an entire book about Derridean *débordement,* I could return repeatedly to it in different contexts, thereby revealing its richness of implication; but that is not the book I wish to write now, that is not the argument I wish to pursue here, and so I suppress that text and argument, which henceforth exist only *in potentia.* After careful consideration, I decide which of the many places in the text would most benefit from introduction of the quotation; and then, at the appropriate moment, I trundle it forward. As a result, I necessarily close off all but a few of its obvious points of connection.

As an experienced writer accustomed to making such choices, I realize that selection is one of the principles of effective argument. But why does one have to write texts in this way? If I were writing a hypertext version of my text—and the versions would exist so differently that one has to place quotation marks around "version" and "text"—and probably "my" as well—I would not have to choose to write a single text. I could, instead, produce one that contained a plurality of ways through it. For example, after preparing the reader for Derrida's discussion of *débordement,* I could then link my preparatory remarks either to the passage itself or to the entire text of "Living On," and I could provide temporary markings that would indicate the beginning and end of the passage I wished to emphasize. At the same time, my hypertext would link the same passage to other points in my argument. How would I go about creating such links?

To answer this question, let me return to my first and simpler example, which involved linking passages from Lévi-Strauss's *Scope of Anthropology* and Foucault's "What Is an Author" to a remark about the anthropologist's use of the network model. Linking in Microcosm, Storyspace, Intermedia, and other systems follows the now common cut-and-paste procedure found in word processors, graphics editors, and spread sheets (Figures 11 and 12). Using the mouse or moving the cursor, one highlights the passage one wishes to link. With the text highlighted, one selects "Intermedia" from the horizontal "menu" of words at the top of the screen ("File," "Edit," "Intermedia," and so on), by placing the mouse-controlled pointer on it and clicking the

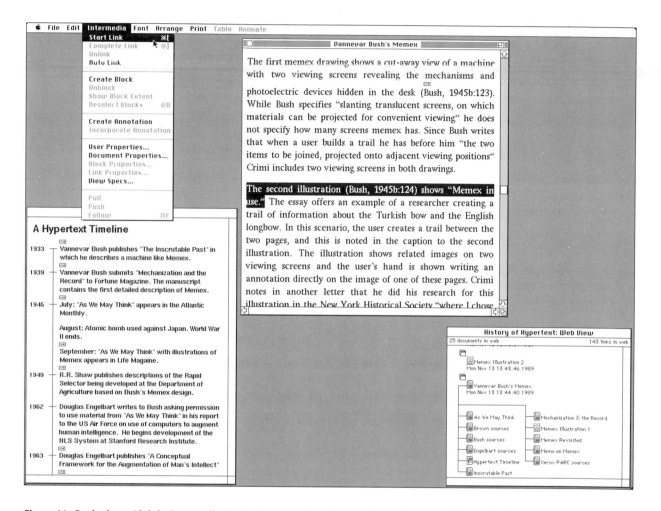

Figure 11. Beginning a Link in Intermedia. To create a new link, the user first selects a portion of the document as an anchor and chooses the "Start Link" command from the Intermedia menu. In this example, the reader-author has selected the sentence beginning "The second illustration." Link creation in Intermedia follows the standard cut-and-paste paradigm. Once the "Start Link" command is chosen, the selection which will become one anchor for the bidirectional link is saved in an invisible link board. One can perform any number of actions, including creating new documents or editing old ones, before completing the pending link. Using selections as anchors for links allows users to create fine-grained endpoints for their links. Anchors (or blocks) can range in size from an insertion point to the contents of an entire document. (Image copyright 1989 by Brown University. Used by permission.)

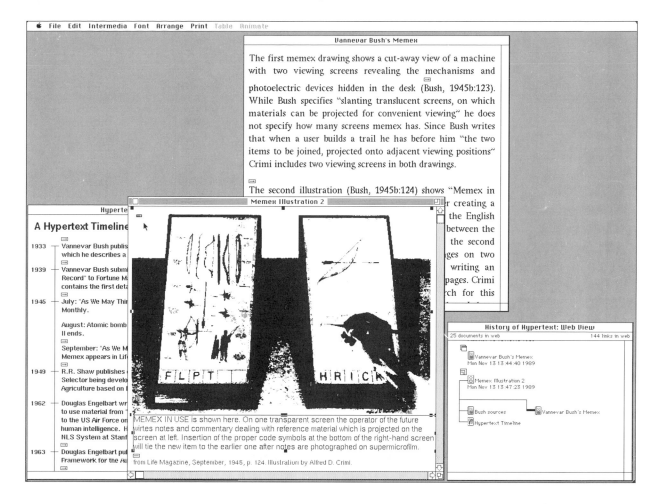

Figure 12. Completing a Link in Intermedia. Choosing the "Complete Link" command from the Intermedia menu places link icons at the source and destination of the link. The Web View reflects the new connection. (Image copyright 1989 Brown University. Used by permission.)

mouse button. Holding down the mouse button, one draws down the Intermedia menu, which contains choices. Placing the pointer over "Start Link," one releases the mouse button.

Proceeding to the second text, one carries out the same operation but in the Intermedia menu chooses "Complete Link." The system then produces a panel containing places to type any desired labels for the linked passages; it automatically ads the title of the entire text, and the writer can describe the linked passage within that text. For example, if I created a link between the hypermedia equivalent of my text for the previous section of this chapter and a passage in *The Scope of Anthropology,* Intermedia and similar systems would automatically add the title of that text, "The Erosion of the Author," to which I would add a phrase, say, "Lévi-Strauss & myth as network." At the other end of the link, the system would furnish "Claude Lévi-Strauss, *The Scope of Anthropology,*" and I would add something like "Lévi-Strauss & society as network." When a reader activates the link marker in the main text, the new entry appears as an option: "Claude Lévi-Strauss, *The Scope of Anthropology*: (Lévi-Strauss & society as network)."

To link a second text, in my case the passage from Foucault, one follows the identical procedure, with the single exception that one no longer has to provide a label for the lexia in the main text, since it already has one. If instead of linking these two brief passages of quotation, documentation, and commentary, I created a more complex document set, focused upon Derridean *débordement,* I would follow the same procedure to create links.

One can also create kinds of documents not found in printed text, some of which would be primarily visual or hieroglyphic. One, for example, might take the form of a concept map showing, among other things, uses of the term *débordement* in "Living On," other works by Derrida in which it appears, and its relation to a range of contexts and disciplines from cartography and histology to etymology and French military history. Current hypermedia systems, including popular WWW viewers, permit one to link to interactive video, music, and animation as well as dictionaries, text, time lines, and static graphics. In the future these links will take more dynamic forms, and following them will animate some procedure, say, a search through a French thesaurus or a reader-determined tracking of *débordement* through various Indo-European languages. Other forms of linking will permit automatic data gathering, so that lists of relevant publications or current statements about *débordement* created after I had completed my document would automatically become available.

My brief description of how I would go about producing this text were I writing it in something like a complete hypertext environment will probably strike most readers as simultaneously terrifying and bizarrely celebratory. One reason lies in the fact that a certain aspect of authorial control has vanished, or rather been ceded to the reader, another in that writing becomes different. Electronic hypertext and contemporary discussions of critical theory, particularly those of the poststructuralists, display many points of convergence, but one point on which they differ is tone. Whereas most writings on theory, with the notable exception of Derrida, are models of scholarly solemnity, records of disillusionment and brave sacrifice of humanistic positions, writers on hypertext are downright celebratory. Whereas terms like *death, vanish, loss,* and expressions of depletion and impoverishment color critical theory, the vocabulary of freedom, energy, and empowerment marks writings on hypertextuality. One reason for these different tones may lie in the different intellectual traditions, national and disciplinary, from which they spring. A more important reason, I propose, is that critical theorists, as I have tried to show, continually confront the limitation—indeed, the exhaustion—of the culture of print. They write from an awareness of limitation and shortcoming, and from a moody nostalgia, often before the fact, over the losses their disillusionment has brought and will bring. Writers on hypertext, in contrast, glory in possibility, excited by the future of textuality, knowledge, and writing. Another way of putting this opposing tone and mood is that most writers on critical theory, however brilliantly they may theorize a much-desired new textuality, nonetheless write from within daily experience of the old, and only the old. Many writers on hypertext, on the other hand, have already had some experience, however merely proleptic and partial, of hypertext systems, and they therefore write from a different experiential vantage point. Most poststructuralists write from within the twilight of a wished-for coming day; most writers of hypertext, even when addressing the same subjects, write from within the dawn.

Virtual Presence

Many features of hypermedia derive from its creating the virtual presence of all the authors who contribute to its materials. Computer scientists draw upon optics for an analogy when they speak of "virtual machines" created by an operating system that provides individual users sharing a system with the sense of working on their own individual machines. In the first chapter, when discussing electronic textuality, I pointed to another kind of "virtual" existence, the virtual text: all texts that one encounters on the computer screen are virtual, rather than real. In a similar manner, the reader experiences the virtual presence of other contributors.

Such virtual presence is of course a characteristic of all technology of cultural memory based on writing and symbol systems. Since we all manipulate cultural codes—particularly language but also mathematics and other symbols—in slightly different ways, each record of an utterance conveys a sense of the one who makes that utterance. Hypermedia differs from print technology, however, in several crucial ways that amplify this notion of virtual presence. Because the essential connectivity of hypermedia removes the physical isolation of individual texts characteristic of print technology, the presence of individual authors becomes both more available and more important. The characteristic flexibility of this reader-centered information technology means, quite simply, that writers have a much greater presence in the system, as potential contributors and collaborative participants but also as readers who chose their own paths through the materials.

Collaborative Writing, Collaborative Authorship

The virtual presence of other texts and other authors contributes importantly to the radical reconception of authorship, authorial property, and collaboration associated with hypertext. Within a hypertext environment all writing becomes collaborative writing, doubly so. The first element of collaboration appears when one compares the roles of writer and reader, since the active reader necessarily collaborates with the author in producing a text by the choices she makes. The second aspect of collaboration appears when one compares the writer with other writers—that is, the author who is writing now with the virtual presence of all writers "on the system" who wrote at another moment but whose writings are still present.

The word *collaboration,* which derives from the Latin for working plus that for *with* or *together,* conveys the suggestion, among others, of working side by side on the same endeavor. Most people's conceptions of collaborative work take the form of two or more scientists, songwriters, or the like continually conferring as they pursue a project in the same place at the same time. I have worked on an essay with a fellow scholar in this manner. One of us would a type a sentence, at which point the other would approve, qualify, or rewrite it, and then we would proceed to the next sentence. Far more common a form of collaboration, I suspect, is that second mode, described as "versioning," in which one worker produces a draft that another person then edits by modifying and adding. The first and the second forms of collaborative authorship tend to blur, but the distinguishing factor here is that versioning takes place out of the presence of the other collaborator and at a later time.

Both of these models require considerable ability to work productively with other people, and evidence suggests that many people either do not have such ability or do not enjoy putting it into practice. In fact, according to those who have carried out experiments in collaborative work, a third form proves more common than the first two—the assembly-line or segmentation model of working together, according to which individual workers divide the overall task and work entirely independently. This last mode is the form that most people engaged in collaborative work choose when they work on projects ranging from programming to art exhibitions.

Networked hypertext systems like WWW, Hyper-G, Sepia, and Intermedia offer a fourth model of collaborative work that combines aspects of the previous ones. By emphasizing the presence of other texts (the virtual presence of other writers) and their cooperative interaction, networked hypertext makes all additions to a system simultaneously a matter of versioning and of the assembly-line model. Once ensconced within a network of electronic links, a document no longer exists by itself. It always exists in relation to other documents in a way that a book or printed document never does and never can. From this crucial shift in the way texts exist in relation to others derive two principles that, in turn, produce this fourth form of collaboration: first, any document placed on any networked system that supports electronically linked materials potentially exists in collaboration with any and all other documents on that system; second, any document electronically linked to any other document collaborates with it.

According to the *American Heritage Dictionary of the English Language,* the verb *to collaborate* can mean either "to work together, especially in a joint intellectual effort" or "to cooperate treasonably, as with an enemy occupying one's country." The combination of labor, political power, and aggressiveness that appears in this dictionary definition well indicates some of the problems that arise when one discusses collaborative work. On the one hand, the notion of collaboration embraces notions of working together with others, of forming a community of action. This meaning recognizes, as it were, that we all exist within social groups, and it obviously places value on contributions to that group. On the other hand, collaboration also includes a deep suspicion of working with others, something aesthetically as well as emotionally engrained since the advent of Romanticism, which exalts the idea of individual effort to such a degree that it often fails to recognize, or even suppresses, the fact that artists and writers work collaboratively with texts created by others.

Most of our intellectual endeavors involve collaboration, but we do not always recognize the fact for two reasons. The rules of our intellectual culture, particularly those that define intellectual property and authorship, do not encourage such recognitions; and furthermore, information technology from Gutenberg to the present—the technology of the book—systematically has hindered full recognition of collaborative authorship.

Throughout this century the physical and biological sciences have increasingly conceived of scientific research, authorship, and publication as group endeavors. The conditions of scientific research, according to which many research projects require the cooperating services of a number of specialists in the same or (often) different fields, bear some resemblances to the medieval guild system in which apprentices, journeymen, and masters all worked on a single complex project. Nonetheless, "collaborations differ depending on whether the substance of the research involves a theoretical science, such as mathematics, or an empirical science, such as biology or psychology. The former are characterized by collaborations among equals, with little division of labor, whereas the latter are characterized by more explicit exchange of services, and more substantial division of labor" (Galegher, Egido, and Kraut, *Intellectual Teamwork,* 151). The financing of scientific research, which supports the individual project, the institution at which it is carried out, and the costs of educating new members of the discipline all nurture such group endeavors and consequent conceptions of group authorship.[4]

In general, the scientific disciplines rely upon an inclusive conception of authorship: anyone who has made a major contribution to finding particular results, occasionally including specialized technicians and those who develop techniques necessary to carry out a course of research, can appear as authors of scientific papers, and similarly, those in whose laboratories a project is carried out may receive authorial credit if an individual project and the publication of its results depend intimately upon their general research. In the course of a graduate student's research for his dissertation, he or she may receive continual advice and evaluation. When the student's project bears fruit and appears in the form of one or more publications, the advisor's name often appears as co-author.

Not so in the humanities, where graduate student research is supported largely by teaching assistantships and not, as in the sciences, by research funding. Although an advisor of a student in English or art history often acts in ways closely paralleling the advisor of the student in physics, chemistry, or biology, explicit acknowledgments of cooperative work rarely appear.

Even when a senior scholar provides the student with a fairly precise research project, continual guidance, and access to crucial materials that the senior scholar has discovered or assembled, the student does not include the advisor as co-author.

The marked differences between conceptions of authorship in the sciences and the humanities demonstrate the validity of Michel Foucault's observation that "the 'author-function' is tied to the legal and institutional systems that circumscribe, determine, and articulate the realm of discourses; it does not operate in a uniform manner in all discourses, at all times, and in any given culture it is not defined by the spontaneous attribution of a text to its creator, but through a series of precise and complex procedures; it does not refer, purely and simply, to an actual individual" ("What Is an Author," 131). One reason for the different conceptions of authorship and authorial property in the humanities and the sciences lies in the different conditions of funding and the different discipline-politics that result.

Another corollary reason is that the humanistic disciplines, which traditionally apply historical approaches to the areas they study, consider their own assumptions about authorship, authorial ownership, creativity, and originality to be eternal verities.[5] In particular, literary studies and literary institutions, such as departments of English, which still bathe themselves in the afterglow of Romanticism, uncritically inflate Romantic notions of creativity and originality to the point of absurdity. An example comes readily to hand from the preface of Lisa Ede and Andrea Lunsford's recent study of collaborative writing, the production of which they discovered to have involved "acts of subversion and of liberatory significance": "We began collaborating in spite of concerned warnings of friends and colleagues, including those of Edward P. J. Corbett, the person in whose honor we first wrote collaboratively. We knew that our collaboration represented a challenge to traditional research conventions in the humanities. Andrea's colleagues (at the University of British Columbia) said so when they declined to consider any of her coauthored or coedited works as part of a review for promotion" (ix–x).

Ede and Lunsford, whose interest in their subject grew out of the "difference between our personal experience as coauthors and the responses of many of our friends and colleagues" (5), set the issue of collaborative writing within the contexts of actual practice in the worlds of business and academia, the history of theories of creative individualism and copyright in recent Western culture, and contemporary and feminist analyses of many of these other contexts. They produce a wide range of evidence and convincingly argue that "the pervasive commonsense assumption that writing is inherently and necessarily a solitary, individual act" supports a traditional patriarchal construction of authorship and authority (5). After arguing against "univocal psychological theories of the self" and associated notions of an isolated individualism, Ede and Lunsford call for a more Bakhtinian reconception of the self and for what they term a dialogic, rather than a hierarchical, mode of collaboration (132).

I shall return to their ideas when I discuss the role of hypertext in collaborative learning, but now I wish to point out that, as scholars from McLuhan and Eisenstein to Ede and Lunsford have long argued, book technology and the attitudes it supports are the institutions most responsible for maintaining exaggerated notions of authorial individuality, uniqueness, and ownership that often drastically falsify the conception of original contributions in the humanities and convey distorted pictures of research. The sciences take a relatively expansive, inclusive view of authorship and consequently of text ownership.[6] The humanities take a far more restricted view that emphasizes individuality, separation, and uniqueness—often creating a vastly distorted view of the connection of a particular text to those that preceded it. Neither view possesses an obvious rightness. Each is obviously a social construction, and each has on occasion proved to distort actual conditions of intellectual work carried out in a particular field.

Whatever the political, economic, and other discipline-specific factors that maintain the conception of noncooperative authorship in the humanities, print technology has also contributed to the sense of a separate, unique text that is the product—and hence the property—of one person, the author. Hypertext changes all this, in large part because it does away with the isolation of the individual text that characterizes the book. As McLuhan and other students of the cultural influence of print technology have pointed out, modern conceptions of intellectual property derive both from the organization and financing of book production and from the uniformity and fixity of text that characterizes the printed book. J. David Bolter explains that book technology itself created new conceptions of authorship and publication:

Because printing a book is a costly and laborious task, few readers have the opportunity to become published authors. An author is a person whose words are faithfully copied and sent round the literary world, whereas readers are merely the audience for those words. The distinction meant less in the age of manuscripts, when "publication" was less of an event and when the reader's own notes and glosses had the same status as the text itself. Any reader could decide to cross over and become an author: one simply sat down and wrote a treatise or put one's notes in a form for others to read. Once the treatise was written, there was no difference between it and the works of other "published" writers, except that the more famous works existed in more copies. (*Writing Space,* 148–49)

Printing a book requires a considerable expenditure of capital and labor, and the need to protect that investment contributes to notions of intellectual property. But these notions would not be possible in the first place without the physically separate, fixed text of the printed book. Just as the need to finance printing of books led to a search for the large audiences that in turn stimulated the ultimate triumph of the vernacular and fixed spelling, so, too, the fixed nature of the individual text made possible the idea that each author produces something unique and identifiable as property.

The needs of the marketplace, at least as they are perceived by editors and publishing houses, reinforce all the worst effects of these conceptions of authorship in both academic and popular books. Alleen Pace Nilsen reports that Jessica Mitford and her husband wrote the best-selling *American Way of Death* together, but only her name appears as author, because the publisher urged that multiple authors would cut sales. In another case, to make a book more marketable a publisher replaced the chief editor of a major psychiatric textbook with the name of a prestigious contributor who had not edited the volume at all (cited by Ede and Lunsford, 3–4). I am sure all authors have examples of such distortion of authorial identity for the sake of what a publisher believes to be good business. I have mine: a number of years ago after an exercise in collaborative work and writing with three graduate students produced a publishable manuscript, we decided by mutual agreement upon the ordering of our names on the title page. By the time the volume appeared, the three former graduate students all held teaching positions; and the book's appearance, one expects, might have helped them professionally. Unfortunately, the publisher insisted upon including only the first editor's name in all notices, advertisements, and catalogues. Such an action, of course, does not have so serious an effect as removing the editors' names from the title page, but it certainly discriminates unfairly between the first two editors, who did equal amounts of work, and it certainly conveys a strong message to beginning humanists about the culturally assigned value of cooperation and collaboration.

Even though print technology is not entirely or even largely responsible for current attitudes in the humanities toward authorship and collaboration, a shift to hypertext systems would change them, by emphasizing elements of collaboration. As Tora K. Bikson and J. D. Eveland point out in relation to nonhumanities work, "the electronic environment is a rich context in which doing work and sharing work becomes virtually indistinguishable" (286). If we can make ourselves aware of the new possibilities created by these changes, we can at the very least take advantage of the characteristic qualities of this new form of information technology.

One relevant characteristic quality of networked hypertext systems is that they produce a sense of authorship, authorial property, and creativity that differs markedly from that associated with book technology. Hypertext changes our sense of authorship and creativity (or originality) by moving away from the constrictions of page-bound technology. In so doing, it promises to have an effect on cultural and intellectual disciplines as important as those produced by the earlier shifts in the technology of cultural memory that followed the invention of writing and printing (see works by Bolter, McLuhan, and Eisenstein).

Examples of Collaboration in Hypertext. Collaborative work in hypertext takes many forms, one of the most interesting of which illustrates the principle that one almost inevitably works collaboratively whenever creating documents on a multiauthor hypertext system. Let me cite an example from the old Intermedia days: While linking materials to the overview (or directory) file for Graham Swift's *Waterland* (1983), I observed Nicole Yankelovich, project coordinator of the Intermedia project at the Institute for Research in Information and Scholarship (IRIS), working on materials for a course in arms control and disarmament offered by Richard Smoke of Brown University's Center for Foreign Policy Development. Those materials, which were created by someone from a discipline very different from mine for a very different kind of course, filled a major gap in a project I was working on. Although my coauthors and I had created materials about technology, including graphic and text documents on canals and railroads, to attach to the science and technology section of the *Waterland* overview, we did not have the expertise to create parallel documents about nuclear technology and the antinuclear movement, two subjects that play a significant part in Swift's novel. Creating a brief introduction to the subject of *Waterland* and nuclear disarmament, I linked it first to the science and technology section in the *Waterland* overview and then to the time line that the nuclear arms course materials employ as a directory file. A brief document and a few links enable students in the introductory survey of English literature to explore the materials created for a course in another discipline. Similarly, students from that course can now encounter materials showing the effects on contemporary fiction of the concerns covered in their political science course. Hypertext thus allows and encourages collaborative work, and at the same time it encourages interdisciplinary approaches, by making materials created by specialists in different disciplines work together—collaborate.

The important point here is that hypermedia linking automatically produces collaboration. Looking at the way the arms control materials were joined to those supporting the four English courses, one encounters a typical example of how the connectivity that characterizes hypertext transforms independently produced documents into collaborative ones and authors working alone into collaborative authors. When one considers the arms control materials from the point of view of their originator, they exist as part of a discrete body of materials. When one considers them from the vantage point of a reader, their status changes: as soon as they appear within a hypertext environment, these and all other documents then exist as part of a larger system and in relation therefore to other materials on that system. By forming electronic pathways between blocks of texts, Intermedia links actualize the potential relations between them.

The Dickens Web, a sample Intermedia document set published by IRIS in 1990, exemplifies the kinds of collaborative authorship characteristic of hypertext. The web, which contains 245 documents and almost 680 links, takes the form of "a collection of materials about Charles Dickens, his novel *Great Expectations,* and many related subjects, such as Victorian history, public health issues, and religion" (5). Creating *The Dickens Web* involved dozens of "authors" and almost that many kinds of collaboration.

I created sixty-four text documents, three time lines, the original versions of ten graphic concept maps (more on this subject later), and provided captions, some elaborate enough to be brief essays, for thirty-odd reproductions of art works, mostly Victorian woodblock illustrations, and a few maps. David Cody, the most prolific of the four graduate and postdoctoral assistants on the part of the Intermedia project funded by the Annenberg/CPB Project, produced forty-four text documents, one or two time lines, and a number of concept maps; he also selected and digitized many of the illustrations, all of which were later redigitized by Paul D. Kahn, the IRIS project coordinator, and Julie Launhardt, assistant project coordinator, both of whom also copyedited the verbal and graphic content of all the documents.

Working with his permission, I produced thirty documents from published and unpublished works by Anthony S. Wohl, professor of history, Vassar College, on the subjects of Victorian public health and race and class in Victorian Britain. Since my work here consisted of little more than dividing Wohl's text into appropriate lexias, and since he then gave final approval to the resultant hypertext translations of his writing, the documents bear his name alone. Twenty documents created by undergraduates at Brown University were included after obtaining their written permission, and approximately the same number of documents take the form of brief one- or two-paragraph quotations by critics of Dickens; these quotations, which are often preceded by introductory remarks and followed by questions, act as hypertext versions of standard scholarly quotation and are quoted without specific permission under the fair use doctrine. Kathryn B. Stockton, the sole graduate assistant during the third year of the project, created an additional fifteen text and graphic documents, to some of which materials have since been added another dozen or so lexias by additional graduate and undergraduate research assistants or students working on independent projects.

Five faculty members from several universities provided additional materials: Linda H. Peterson, associate professor of English, Yale University, contributed bibliographies on Victorian religion, art, and literature; and Joan D. Richardson, associate professor of history, Brown University, provided a bibliography for Victorian science. Peter Heywood, associate professor of biology, one of two original Intermedia teachers, allowed us to incorporate essays on Darwinism he had created for an upper-division course in plant cell biology; Walter L. Arnstein, professor of history, University of Illinois, contributed a bibliography of materials on religion in Victorian Britain; and Michel-André Bossy, professor of French and comparative literature, Brown University, kindly permitted the inclusion of his brief discussion of detective fiction.

Bossy's contribution exemplifies how complex decisions about authorship can be in a hypertext environment. Bossy's document, which he had developed as a handout for one of his courses in comparative literature, became part of the Intermedia materials after Barry J. Fishman, a student in that course, perceived the essay's connection to Dickens and to other authors he had read a year earlier in my course. Receiving permission from Professor Bossy, he placed it on the Intermedia system and made links, so students in other courses could benefit from it. Now the question arises, Who is "author" of this valuable summary? Bossy, obviously, because he summed up other experts "in his own words." But what about those critics on whom he drew? In print they would not appear worthy of inclusion as authors, but in hypertext the situation might change. Then, what about Fishman, who initially perceived the possible connection, gained permission from both Bossy and myself to include it, and then made the necessary links? To my mind, he obviously deserves to share some part of the hypertext document's authorship, as perhaps should those people who created the lexias to which it links.

An even more complex problem of authorship arises in relation to the many graphic overviews in *The Dickens Web.* After Nicole Yankelovich handed me a copy of Joseph D. Novak and D. Bob Gowin's *Learning How to Learn,* which urges the use of concept mapping in support of its constructionist view of knowledge, I drew crude initial versions of graphic directories in which various phenomena, such as religion and philosophy, biography, and cultural context, surrounded an entity (say, Robert Browning, "My Last Duchess," or Victorianism) and were connected to it by lines radiating from it. Since my then-twelve-year-old son had far more facility with the graphics program MacDraw than I did, he ended up creating computer versions of my concept map, which I then took to the development team at IRIS (where for a while it became known, only partly in jest, as "the Noah Landow paradigm"). Helen deAndrade, the IRIS graphic designer, then produced elegant versions of these concept maps on the IBM equipment that first supported our hypermedia environment. Using her work as a template, David Cody modified it in creating the Dickens overview; and more than a year later, I created an additional one, for *Great Expectations,* and added many more, including those for religion in England, public health, and Victorianism. When IRIS transferred ("ported") the Intermedia system to Apple Macintosh IIs, Shoshana M. Landow, an undergraduate summer research assistant, recreated all the overviews, making them smaller, clearer, and more efficient. Then, after IRIS decided to publish a small selection of these materials supporting humanities teaching in the form of *The Dickens Web,* Ronnie Peters of the Rhode Island School of Design undertook a major reconception of the graphic presentation of all materials included. He provided design principles, a graphics style sheet, and specific examples, but most of the overviews were actually designed by Paul D. Kahn. Who, then, is the "author" of the Dickens, *Great Expectations,* and "Religion in England" overviews? Going over my preceding narrative of origins, I count at least ten individuals who partook of authorship in one important way or another—and I have not even mentioned those who linked these overviews to hundreds of other lexias. Some of those people who created links appear in the account above, but there was a host of others, the most important of whom were Suzanne Keene, now an assistant professor at Washington and Lee, and David Cody, associate professor, Hartwick College, who created the first extensive linking on Intermedia.

In the published version, IRIS chose to append sets of initials to these overviews. The *Great Expectations* and "Religion in England" overviews, for example, list "GPL, RP" to indicate authorship, and the preceding account should indicate how misleading is such a limited attribution. "Dickens Literary Relations," which Kahn entirely reconceived following a design of his own, bears the initials "DC, SML, PDK," thus indicating its line of descent more than its direct parentage; and the graphic directory for "Victorian Bibliography," which replaces my standard, rather crude radiating design with a beautiful illustration of an ornate Victorian book, lists only "GPL," despite the fact that the conception was Kahn's. The rationale seems to be that the person who first thought of the need for a particular document and mapped out its intellectual contents, in this case merely eight subject headings, receives credit. More important, part of the credit here arises in the generosity of colleagues, and part then in turn derives as a kind of reward for earlier, preparatory work.

As this account should make clear, "authorship" of individual texts in a hypermedia environment becomes even more problematic than in the world of print. The concept of "authorship" moves beyond quotation marks when one attempts to account for *The Dickens Web* as a whole: the title page of the user's manual fittingly reads only "IRIS Intermedia / The Dickens Web / User's and Installation Guide." The reverse, which makes required copyright announcements and prohibitions against unauthorized copying, credits the Henry W. and Albert A. Berg Collection of the New York Public Library for permission to publish Frederic W. Pailthorpe's illustrations for *Great Expectations*. The copyright page lists no authors. Instead, it states the following: "Developed by George P. Landow / Edited by Julie Launhardt and Paul Kahn / Graphic design by Ronnie Peters." This solution, which Launhardt and Kahn arrived at after consulting with others at IRIS, contains an important truth about writing within a hypertext environment: hypertext has no authors in the conventional sense. Just as hypertext as an educational medium transforms the teacher from a leader into a kind of coach or companion, hypertext as a writing medium metamorphoses the author into an editor or developer. Hypermedia, like cinema and video or opera, is a team production.

Reconfiguring

Writing

The Problematic Concept of Disorientation

Since writing hypermedia successfully involves finding ways to prevent readers from becoming confused and discouraged when they encounter text in e-space, let us examine this notion of disorientation before considering some of the methods used to prevent it. Crucial as disorientation might seem to discussions of hypertext authoring, this term remains unexamined and inadequately defined. Such a claim might appear particularly odd because writers on the subject since Jeff Conklin have apparently provided fairly precise statements of what they mean by what Conklin himself termed the *disorientation problem*. According to his initial statement of the issue, disorientation seems to inhere in the medium itself: "Along with the power of being able to organize information much more complexly comes the problem of having to know (1) where you are in the network and (2) how to get to some other place that you know (or think) exists in the network. I call this the *disorientation problem*. Of course, one has a disorientation in traditional linear text documents, but in a linear text the reader has only two options: He can search for the desired text earlier in the text or later in the text" (38). Kenneth Utting and Nicole Yankelovich, who similarly point out that hypermedia "has the potential to dramatically confuse and confound readers, writers, teachers, and learners," quote Conklin's definition of disorientation as "the tendency to lose one's sense of location and direction in a nonlinear document" (58). In their example of three aspects of disorientation, they mention "confusion about where to go or, having decided on a destination, how to get there" and also disorientation in the sense of not knowing "the boundaries of the information space" (61) one is exploring.

Three points here demand notice: First, the concept of disorientation relates closely to the tendency to use spatial, geographical, and travel metaphors to describe the way users experience hypertext. Such uses are obviously appropriate to dictionary definitions of *disorient*. According to *The American Heritage Dictionary,* to disorient is "to cause to lose one's sense of direction or location, as by removing from a familiar environment," and *Webster's Collegiate Dictionary* offers three definitions of *disorient:* (1) "to cause to lose one's bearings: displace from normal position or relationship"; (2) "to cause to lose the sense of time, place, or identity"; and (3) "to confuse."

In general, authors writing about hypertext seem to mean *confuse* and specifically *lose bearings* when they use the term, and this usage derives from commonplace application of spatial metaphors to describe the reader's behavior in a hypertext environment. Thus, in "The Art of Navigating through Hypertext," Jakob Nielsen points out in the usual formulation that "one of the major usability problems with hypertext is the user's risk of disorientation while navigating the information space. For example, our studies showed that 56 percent of the readers of a document written in one of the most popular commercial hypertext systems agreed fully or partially with the statement *I was often confused about where I was.*" Nielsen believes that "true hypertext should also make users *feel* that they can move freely through the information according to their own needs" (298).

Second, as Conklin and others writing in this field state the problem of disorientation, it obviously concerns the design of the information technology alone. In other words, the related concepts of disorientation and confusion appear, in their terms, to have nothing to do with the materials, the content, on the hypertext system. Nonetheless, we all know that readers often experience confusion and disorientation simply because they fail to grasp the logic or even meaning of a particular argument. Even if the works of Kant, Einstein, and Heidegger were to appear on the finest hypertext and information retrieval system in the world, they would still disorient many readers. Although Conklin and other students of hypertext have not naively or incompletely defined what they mean by disorientation, their restriction of this term to system-generated disorientation in practice does not take into account a large portion of the actual reading experience—and its implications for hypertext authors. The issue has a bearing upon a third point about the notion of disorientation.

Third, disorientation, as these comments make clear, is conceived by these authors as crippling and dis-enabling, as something, in other words, that blocks completion of a task one has set for oneself or that has been set for one by others. Disorientation, furthermore, is presented as such a massive, monolithic problem that these authors pay little or no attention to how people actually cope with this experience. Is it, in fact, crippling, and do users of hypertext systems simply give up or fail in their tasks when they meet disorientation? As we shall see, expert users of hypertext do not always find the experience of disorientation to be particularly stressful, much less paralyzing.

The role of disorientation in literature suggests some reasons why this might be the case. Readers of literature in fact often describe the experience here presented as disorientation as pleasurable, even exciting, and some forms of literature, particularly those that emphasize either allegory or stylistic and narrative experimentation, rely on disorienting the reader as a primary effect. Although the kind of pleasurable disorientation that one finds in Dante's *Divine Comedy,* Browning's *Ring and the Book,* and Eliot's *Waste Land* derives from what we have termed the content and not from the information technology that presents it, this effect has one important parallel to that encountered in some forms of hypertext: in each case the neophyte or inexperienced reader finds unpleasantly confusing materials that more expert readers find a source of pleasure.

The Concept of Disorientation in the Humanities. The reasons for the radically different ways people in the humanities and in technological disciplines regard disorientation become particularly clear in three areas—aesthetic theories of disorientation, conceptions of modernism and postmodernism as cultural movements, and the related conceptions of hypertext fiction.

The classic statement of the positive value of cognitive and other disorientation in aesthetic works appears in Morse Peckham's *Man's Rage for Chaos: Biology, Behavior, and the Arts,* which argues that "art offers not order but the opportunity to experience more disorder than any other human artifact, and . . . artistic experience, therefore, is characterized . . . by disorientation" (41). According to him, "the artist's role is to create occasions for disorientation, and . . . the perceiver's role to experience it. The distinguishing mark of the perceiver's transaction with the work of art is discontinuity of experience, not continuity; disorder, not order; emotional disturbance, not emotional catharsis, even though some works have a cadential close" (254). Human beings so "passionately" want "a predictable and ordered world" that "only in protected situations, characterized by high walls of psychic insulation," can they permit themselves to perceive the gap between "expectancy or set or orientation, and the data ... interaction with the environment actually produces. . . . Art offers precisely this kind of experience" (313).

Peckham argues finally that art is "an adaptational mechanism" that reinforces our ability to survive:

Art is rehearsal for those real situations in which it is vital for our survival to endure cognitive tension, to refuse the comforts of validation by affective congruence when such validation is inappropriate because too vital interests are at stake; art is the reinforcement of the capacity to endure *disorientation* so that a real and significant problem can emerge. Art is the exposure to the tensions and problems of a false world so that man can endure exposing himself to the tensions and problems of a real world. (314)

Peckham's positive views of aesthetic disorientation, which seem to grow out of the arts and literature of modernism, clearly present it as a matter of freedom and human development.

Students of literature and the arts have long emphasized the role of disorientation in both modernism and postmodernism. Like the works of the Cubists, Expressionists, and other movements of twentieth-century art, James Joyce's *Ulysses,* T. S. Eliot's *Waste Land,* and William Faulkner's *The Sound and the Fury*—to cite three classics of literary modernism—all make disorientation a central aesthetic experience. Similarly, as recent writers on postmodernist fiction point out, it is characterized by a range of qualities that produce cognitive disorientation: "contradiction, discontinuity, randomness," "intractable epistemological uncertainty," and "cognitive estrangement" (McHale, 7, 11, 59).

These attitudes, which students of this century's culture almost universally view positively, appear throughout discussions of hypertext fiction as well. Robert Coover, for example, makes quite clear the relations between disorientation, hypertext, and the traditions of the avant-garde when he describes the way hypertext fiction promises to fulfill the liberating functions of the experimental tradition in fiction:

For all its passing charm, the traditional novel, which took centerstage at the same time the industrial mercantile democracies arose—Hegel called it "the epic of the middle class world"—is perceived by its would-be executioners as being the virulent carrier of patriarchal, colonial, canonical, proprietary, hierarchical, and authoritarian values of a past which is no longer with us.

Much of the novel's alleged power is imbedded in *the line,* that compulsory author-directed movement from the beginning of a sentence to its period, from the top of the page to the bottom, from the first page to the last. Of course, through print's long history, there have been countless counter-strategies to the line's power, from marginalia and footnoting to the creative innovations of novelists like Sterne, Joyce, Queneau, Cortázar, Calvino, and Pavič, and not excluding the form's father Cervantes himself, but true freedom from the tyranny of the line is perceived as only really possible now at last with the advent of *hypertext,* where the line in fact does not exist unless one invents and implants it. ("End of Books," 1, 11)

Coover particularly emphasizes the effect on writers of this disorienting freedom. Discussing the conservatism of writing students, he claims,

Getting them to consider trying out alternative or innovative forms is harder than talking them into chastity as a life-style. But suddenly, confronted with hyperspace, they have no choice: all the comforting structures have been erased. It's improvise or go home. Some frantically rebuild those old structures, some just get lost and drift out of sight, most leap in fearlessly without even asking how deep it is (*infinitely* deep), admitting, even as they continue to paddle for dear life, that this new arena is indeed an exciting, provocative, if frequently frustrating medium for the creation of new narratives, a potentially revolutionary space, empowered, exactly as advertised, to transform the very art of fiction. (24)

Michael Joyce describes potentially disorienting qualities of hypertext fiction in terms that praise the necessary activism required of readers: "Constructive hypertexts require a capability to act: to create, to change and to recover particular encounters within the developing body of knowledge. These encounters . . . are maintained as versions, i.e., trails, paths, webs, notebooks, etc.; but they are versions of what they are becoming, a structure for what does not yet exist" (*Of Two Minds,* 42). In much the same vein Stuart Moulthrop, like Coover, relates the experience of encountering the gaps and disorientation that characterize the reader's experience in hypertext as potentially liberating. "In a world where the 'global variables' of power and knowledge tend to orient themselves toward singular, hegemonic world orders, it becomes increasingly difficult to jump outside 'the system.' And as Thomas Pynchon reminds us: 'Living inside the System is like riding across the country in a bus driven by a maniac bent on suicide' (*Gravity's Rainbow,* 412)" ("Toward a Paradigm," 76). Given the fact that many humanities users of hypertext, like those specifically concerned with hypertext fiction, associate the general experience of disorientation with avant-garde, liberating, and culturally approved aesthetic experience, it should be no surprise that they treat the issue of disorientation far differently than do almost all who consider it in the technical disciplines.

This delight in disorientation as an aesthetic effect particularly characterizes that group of young writers, like Mark Amerika, Shelley Jackson, and Michael Joyce, who see hypertext as the latest embodiment of the literary avant-garde. Amerika, the founder and editor of *Alt-X,* a much-acclaimed avant garde literary web site, sees the disorienting effect in hypertext environments as signaling "the radical becoming of a new, more fluid subjectivity, one that is digital, intuitive, nomadic, and desperately trying to break free from the materiality of a fettered culture" (personal communication). *The Kafka Chronicles* and Amerika's other print works use a proto-hypertextual style to challenge the linear plot of conventional books, and his interest in disorientation as aesthetic effect reappears amplified in two large hypertext fictions, *Hypertextual Consciousness* and *Grammatron,* both of which began as Storyspace webs and then migrated to HTML. Both works represent what Amerika, following Larry McCaffrey, calls the "Avant Pop," a blend of experimental technique with high, low, and pop culture (see McCaffrey; Amerika and Olsen). Genres and modes blur as a manifesto, fiction, poem, personal essay, and critical and cultural theory come together in a new collage-like literary form.

The Love of Possibilities. In experiments that Paul Kahn and I conducted in 1991, experienced student users of hypertext showed a love of browsing and of the serendipity it occasions that was very much at odds with by-now conventional attitudes towards disorientation in hypertext. For example, one user explained that by "accidentally clicking" on a particular link he found that he had made a "delightful detour," which led to an answer to one of the assigned problems. "Although I guess this mistake has an analog in book technology, it would be the improbable act of being in the wrong section of the library, the wrong row of books, the wrong shelf, picking up the wrong book, and opening up magically to the correct page."

Some of the students' responses during these experiments were disconcertingly unexpected and for that reason potentially quite valuable to anyone considering the design, implementation, and educational application of hypertext. In two cases very experienced programmers had more difficulties with certain aspects of information retrieval tasks than did comparative neophytes. It would appear that their expectations of systems and retrieval mechanisms served to hinder rather than assist their explorations. Accustomed to using full-text search mechanisms in other kinds of computer systems, one of these students spent fifteen minutes searching for such an aid in Intermedia (the version used did not have the system's later search tools) and then gave up on the assignment, assuming that no other methods of locating the information existed.

In contrast, a relatively unsophisticated user solved the first problem—

locating works by a single scholar—in a matter of moments. As he explained: "I found these references by opening the Critics Quoted Document in the Bibliographical Folder in the Dickens Folder. . . . Total Time: 6 min." Another similarly responded:

I answered the first question of the assignment using [the Intermedia folder system]. Since the folders were labeled well, I found it quick and easy to first find the "Bibliography" folder, and then open the "Critics Quoted" document. There I found the names of the three authors in the question. Since the web was already engaged, I could activate the link markers and see all the destination documents connected to a particular author (if in fact the web was well linked). Thus, I approached the web from an odd angle, from the actual document folders, but it was the one which I felt to be the easiest and quickest for this question. This same information could be found in the Bibliography Overview. . . . If I had never come across the Victorianism Overview, for whatever reason, I might never have come across the sought after bibliographic information. But I did find the information, outside the system's (few) attempts at organization.

This student's narrative forcefully restates the truism that people who want to find information will find it as much by what they know about that information as by system features alone. In other words, orientation by content seems able to solve potential problems of disorientation caused by the system design considered in isolation. In this case, some experienced users of computers tended to conceive the assignment as a means of testing system capacities, whereas the person who was more of a content expert, or who *took the approach of a content expert,* conceived the task in terms that made the desired information the center of the task.

One important lesson for both designers of hypertext software and those who teach or write with hypertext appears in the problems encountered by the students with more computer skills. In relying too heavily upon system features, they implicitly made the assumption that the system, rather than the author, does most of the work. In doing so, they tended to ignore the stylistic and other author-created devices that made the search quick and easy for a majority of users.

We should also note that a preference for browsing, up to and including the sense of "disorientation," can create disconcerting results for hypertext designers, despite the fact that hypertext theorists often praise this approach to wandering through a database. For example, one user criticized one of the systems precisely because it proved "more difficult to become disoriented in the good way that Intermedia and Storyspace tend to facilitate. I found that links continually brought me back to crossroads or overviews, rather than to other documents. For this reason I felt less like an active reader. Orientation devices such as these explained and categorized links rather than allowing me to make my own connections and categories." To those who find disorientation a negative quality, these comments might puzzle, because apparently negative qualities here come in for praise. In fact, this student specifically mentions "the good way" Intermedia and Storyspace create a sense of disorientation, which she takes to be a condition that empowers hypertext users, because it places them in an active role—one particularly appropriate to this new information medium.

The reactions of these student evaluators suggest six points about reader disorientation, the first of which is that although it represents a potentially significant problem in some systems, a priori concerns about it may well arise from lack of experience with hypertext systems, specifically from attempting to apply reading and information retrieval protocols appropriate to book technology to this new medium.

Second, what one reader experiences as unwanted disorientation, another may find pleasurable.

Third, disorientation has quite different connotations in the writings of those based in technological as opposed to literary disciplines. The technologically based notion of disorientation relates to a conception of education as being essentially limited to factual information. Literary or humanistic assumptions about disorientation seem related to a conception of education in which students learn to deal with complex matters of interpretation.

Fourth, disorientation—let me emphasize this point yet again—arises both in the normal act of reading difficult material *and* in poorly designed systems. Knowledge of content, as some of our evaluators demonstrated, has to be considered as part of any solution to issues of system-generated or system-permitted disorientation.

Fifth, since for the foreseeable future, book and electronic technologies will exist together, in some applications supplementing and in others competing with each other, designers of hypertext systems will continue to find themselves in a terribly difficult situation. Systems they design will almost certainly encounter a heterogeneous pool of users, some still trying to read according to the rules of books, others, increasingly sophisticated in electronic media, who find the specific qualities of hypertext reading and exploration, including occasional "disorientation," to be pleasurable, desirable qualities.

Sixth—and most important—the way we write, as much as system design, as much as software design, can prevent the less pleasant forms of disorientation. We must therefore develop a rhetoric and stylistics of hypertext writing.

The Rhetoric and Stylistics of Writing for E-Space; or, How Should We Write Hypertext?

General Observations. One thing seems clear even from the limited experience of reading and writing hypertext already gathered: Linking, by itself, is not enough. The hypermedia author cannot realize the enormous potential of the medium simply by linking one passage or image to others. The act of connecting one text to another fails to achieve all the expected benefits of hypermedia and can even alienate the user. On the briefest consideration, such a recognition will hardly surprise, since authors of print essays, poems, narratives, and books do not expect to *write* merely by stringing together sentences and paragraphs without the assistance of stylistic devices and rhetorical conventions. If to communicate effectively, hypermedia authors must employ devices suited to their medium, two questions arise. First, what are the defining characteristics or qualities of hypertext as a reading and writing medium? Second, to what extent do they depend upon specific hardware and software? What effect, for example, does the presence or absence of color, the size of one's monitor, or the speed of one's computer affect reading hypertext?

Then there are questions less immediately derived from the hardware. Assuming that writing at the level of phrase, sentence, and paragraph will not change in some fundamental way—and this, I admit, may be too large an assumption to make at this stage—what new forms of organization, rhetoric, and structure must we develop to communicate effectively in electronic space? In other words, if hypertext demands a new rhetoric and a new stylistics, of what do they consist, and how, if at all, do they relate to issues such as system speed and the like?

To begin, let us look once again at the nature of the medium. Hypertext changes the way texts exist and the way we read them, and in earlier chapters we have observed many examples of such difference from chirographic and print textuality. Whether or not it is true that the digital word produces a secondary or new kind of orality, many of the devices required by hypertext appear in oral speech, just as they do in its written versions or dialects. Many of these devices to which I wish to direct our attention fall into a single category: they announce a change of direction and often also provide some indication of what that new direction will be. For example, words and phrases like "in contrast," "nevertheless," and "on the other hand" give advance notice to listeners and readers that something, say an instance or assertion, is coming that is contrary to what has come before. "For example" announces a category shift as the discourse switches, most likely from general or abstract statement to proposed instances of it. Causal or temporal terms, such as "because" or "after," similarly ready listeners for changes of intellectual direction. In both print and oral communication, they are means of preparing us for breaks in a linear stream of language. One must take care in using this term *linear,* since, as we have already seen when looking at hypertext narrative, all experiences of listening or reading in whatever medium are in an important sense linear, unidirectional. Thus, although readers—or, to be precise, *readings*—take different paths through a work, each experience of reading takes the form of a sequence. It is the text that is multisequential not a particular reading path through it. I emphasize this point because the problem of preparing for change of direction (and openings and closings are also such changes) has been with us since the beginnings of human language.

Since hypertext and hypermedia are chiefly defined by the link, a writing device that offers potential changes of direction, the rhetoric and stylistics of this new information technology generally involve such change—potential or actual change of place, relation, or direction. Before determining which techniques best accommodate such change, we must realize that, together, they attempt to answer several related questions: First, what must one do to orient readers and help them read efficiently and with pleasure? Second, how can one help readers retrace the steps in their reading path? Third, how can one inform those reading a document where the links in that document lead? Finally, how can one assist readers who have just entered a new document to feel at home there?

Drawing upon the analogy of travel, we can say that the first problem concerns *orientation* information, necessary for finding one's place within a body of interlinked texts. The second concerns *navigation* information, necessary for making one's way through the materials. The third concerns *exit* or *departure* information and the fourth *arrival* or *entrance* information. In each case, creators of hypermedia materials must decide what readers need to know at either end of a hypermedia link in order to make use of what they find there. The general issue here is one of interpretation. More specifically, to enable visitors to this new kind of text to read it pleasurably, comfortably, and efficiently, how much interpretation must the designer-author attach to the system as a whole, to link pathways, and to documents at the end of links?

Unfortunately, no analogy maps reality with complete accuracy. Navigation, the art of controlling the course of a plane or ship, presupposes a spatial world, but one does not experience hypertext *entirely* as such. In navigation, we remember, one must determine one's spatial position in relation to landmarks or astral locations and then decide upon a means of moving toward one's goal, which lies out of sight at some spatial distance from one. Because it takes time to move across the separating distance, one also experiences that distance as time: one's ship lies so many nautical miles, and therefore so many days and hours, from one's goal. The reader, however, does not experience hypertext in this way. The reader of *Paradise Lost,* for example, experiences as equally close the linked parts of Homer and Vergil to which the poem's opening section alludes and linked lines on the next page or in the next book (see Figure 10, in Chapter 3). Because hypertext linking takes relatively the same amount of time to traverse, all linked texts are experienced as lying at the same "distance" from the point of departure. Thus, whereas navigation presupposes that one finds oneself at the center of a spatial world in which desired items lie at varying distances from one's own location, hypertext (and other forms of addressable, digital textuality) presupposes an experiential world in which the goal is always potentially but one jump or link away.

I propose to approach these questions by looking at problems and solutions in a range of systems that have seen extensive use. Although Intermedia, the first hypertext system about which I wrote some years back, is now used only at a few computer museums and archives, I shall refer to it in the following pages for two reasons, the first of which is that in some ways it remains the finest system yet developed. Any really workable hypermedia system that can realize the potential of this new form of information technology—and by this I certainly include the future developments of the World Wide Web—must have *at least* the features of Intermedia. Second, despite possessing a range of features that made writing hypertext comparatively easy, Intermedia still required authors to employ a rhetoric of linking. It therefore provides a good point of departure for discussing general issues of hypermedia rhetoric and stylistics.

Hypermedia as a medium conveys the strong impression that its links signify coherent, purposeful, and above all *useful* relationships, from which it follows that the very existence of links conditions the reader to expect purposeful, important relationships between linked materials. One of the presuppositions in hypertext, particularly when applied to education, is that linking materials encourages habits of relational thinking in the reader. Such intrinsic hypermedia emphasis upon interconnectedness (or connectivity) provides a powerful means of teaching sophisticated critical thinking, particularly that which builds upon multicausal analyses and relates different kinds of data. But since hypermedia systems predispose users to expect significant relationships among lexias, those that disappoint these expectations tend to appear particularly incoherent and nonsignificant. When users follow links and encounter materials that do not appear to possess a significant relation to the document from which the link pathway originated, readers feel confused and resentful. In reading materials on the Web, just as in reading Intermedia documents during its earliest stages, the delays encountered by users tend to exaggerate this effect, thus providing a reason for avoiding time-consuming graphic or other elements whenever possible.

System-Generated Means of Reader Orientation. Devices of orientation permit readers to (1) determine their present location, (2) have some idea of that location's relation to other materials, (3) return to their starting point, and (4) explore materials not directly linked to those in which they presently find themselves. Before examining the range of techniques that we as writers might employ, let us look at some of the means individual hypertext systems offer, in part because they might prove worth manually recreating in those in which they are unavailable.

Folder systems permit one to use an easily comprehensible visual metaphor both to begin reading and, later, to discern one's location within a complex information space. Although readers use links as their primary means of moving throughout well-organized hypertext webs, in some systems they first confront a folder arrangement, which can take various forms. In the old Intermedia system, readers began each session by confronting a Macintosh-style desktop (even on the first version, an IBM system). The user first started up Intermedia and then opened individual webs; as in Microcosm, multiple webs or link sets could knit together the same documents. The webs' icons appeared both on the desktop and within individual subject folders. Readers wanting information about, say, Dickens' novel *Great Expectations* began by starting up the relevant web, opening the English folder labeled "Dickens," and then the Dickens overview or that for "novel." From this point onward in a session, readers generally used links and Intermedia's other features to navigate through the materials. The folder system, reassuring in its familiarity, provided a clear point of departure while also offering an alternate, if not particularly efficient, means of browsing. Nonetheless, the desktop and folder system efficiently oriented readers by making movement back to documents opened previously a quick and easy matter.

In Storyspace's author environment and in the Storyspace Reader, users also confront a folder mechanism, though one can arrange an opening screen to keep them from encountering it initially. Users, however, can easily obtain the folderlike structure at any time from the menu at the top of the screen. Storyspace folders differ from those in Intermedia in several ways, the most important for our present purposes being, as we have already observed, that authors can arrange them in various patterns and orders. Storyspace authors, particular writers of experimental fiction, often take advantage of the fact that such a folder system takes some of the burden off linking: One doesn't have to worry as much about dead-ended links—that is, lexias with no links out—since readers who have folders available can easily jump to another subject. Some Storyspace fiction, like Carolyn Guyer's *Quibbling* and Shelley Jackson's *Patchwork Girl,* emphasizes this capacity, urging aggressive reading by inviting us to probe the work's structure, just as do some CD-ROM storyworlds, such as *Freak Show,* or similar games, like *Myst.* (A sample screen from *Patchwork Girl* appears as Figure 26 in Chapter 6.)

Microcosm, which runs on Windows machines, offers yet another variation on folder organization, for rather than appearing within a desktop metaphor, its folders take the form of a vertically arrayed outline. Although Microcosm does not offer some of the capacities for experimentation and visual writing that have so appealed to some writers of fiction and poetry, it offers something that neither of the two previous systems have—virtual folders, a device that permits icons representing the same lexia to appear in multiple folders. Such an arrangement allows readers both to orient themselves and to find materials easily at the beginning of a session. In one sense the Microcosm virtual folder might appear to go against one important strain in thinking about hypertext. After all, in hypertext, by definition, it does not matter very much which folder or class holds a lexia, since linking permits multiple orderings and multiple ways of traversing classification systems. As Nelson emphasized so many years ago, hypertext solves the basic problem with taxonomy and classification, namely, that whereas all classifications and categories derive from limited purposes and hence limited points of view, information bursts these limits—and thus we need linking. However, I believe that redundancy in hypertext systems and documents provides additional power and flexibility and only helps readers and writers.

The graphic presentation of information embodied in the useful, if limited, desktop metaphor has proved an especially effective means of reader orientation in the systems that use it; but WWW viewers, which carry particularly grave risks of disorientation, do not use this visual metaphor. Of course, the "Show Location" window in Mosaic, Netscape, and other HTML viewers does provide the exact address of a lexia; a link to one student's essay on *Patchwork Girl*, say, Lars Hubrich's "Stitched Identity"—would produce the following information in the location window: "http://www.stg.brown. edu/projects/hypertext/landow/cpace/ht/pg/lhpatch.html." Such an address is daunting to most readers; it fails to be very helpful on two other counts: first, the need to create economically brief directory names often renders the file name incomprehensible to all but the person who maintains the web site, and second, it provides very little information about the relation of this particular lexia to the information space it inhabits.

A particularly elegant and effective use of graphic presentations of folder structure appears in Dynamic Diagrams' MAPA™ software for the Web (see example in Figure 13). "Composed of a Java applet, a Web walker, and a database," MAPA first automatically creates hierarchical relationships among all the documents on a web site and then visualizes them in two ways, first "as an animated three-dimensional site map" and then as a list of all links into and out of a particular lexia (Dynamic Diagrams, "Introducing MAPA"). Moving one's mouse over the icons representing individual documents on the site map reveals both their URLs (uniform resource locators) and their titles in a pop-up window. Clicking once on any icon representing a lexia in the site map makes that document the center of a newly generated site map. Clicking twice opens the lexia represented by the icon, thereby permitting users to obtain lexias that exist several or even dozens of links away from the current one. By permitting readers first to gain an idea of the overall organization of an entire web site and then to move rapidly between distant portions of it, MAPA fulfills much of hypertext's potential to reconfigure our experience of distance and separation in information space. By permitting users to locate and then open lexias widely separated in the document or file structure, this software places needed information just one jump away.

Where such software solutions are not available, authors have employed two solutions. One involves organizing an entire site according to what is essentially a folder structure and then making that organization clear. Thus, Susan Farrell's *Art-Crimes,* a site containing graffiti from around the world, presents its information in terms of country, city, and additional collections for each city. Of course, this beautiful site, which provides a visual archive, has little intrinsically hypertextual about it and therefore cannot serve as an example for other kinds of webs.

A second approach involves providing readers a manually created graphic presentation, such as a concept map or screen shot of the organiza-

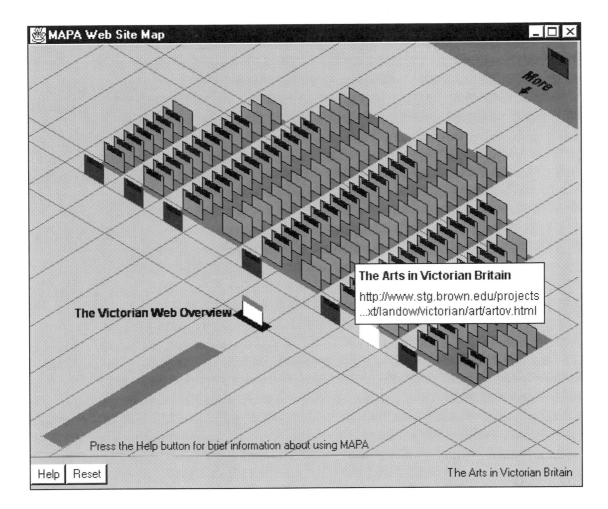

Figure 13. A View of *The Victorian Web*. This map was created by Dynamic Diagram's MAPA™ from the vantage point of this web's homepage (or chief overview). In this screen shot, a user has activated a pop-up window displaying the URL and title of "The Arts in Victorian Britain," a second-level overview. By using a computer mouse to move the cursor farther away from the top level, users can also learn the titles of lexias linked to this and other overviews. Double clicking upon the icon for any lexia opens it. (Copyright 1996 Dynamic Diagrams. Used by permission.)

tional structure. When Jay Dillemuth translated his *Omphaloskepsis* from Storyspace to HTML, he included several screenshots so that readers of the WWW version could have some idea of the work's conceptual organization (Figure 14). The next stage, which Rosemarie Simpson has followed in creating WWW materials for an engineering course at the University of Colorado,

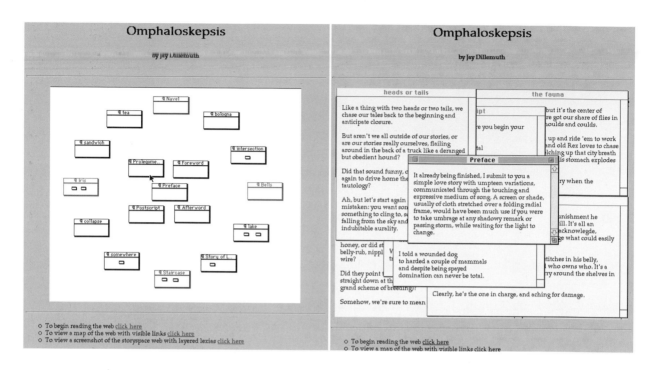

Figure 14. Jay Dillemuth's *Omphaloskepsis*. In this translation of his Storyspace web into HTML, Dillemuth offers readers alternate opening screens that suggest the web's original organization and collage effects. To do so he uses screen shots of both the original web's Storyspace View and the tiled lexias at one point in a reading.

takes such a snapshot of the Storyspace View and transforms it into an image map, thereby permitting readers to use it as an overview.

Keeping Track: Where Have I Been, What Did I Read? In addition to helping readers discern their general location within an information space at any moment, hypertext systems also have to provide both some means of informing them whence they came and also a means of allowing them to return there. As one of its functions, the Roadmap in Storyspace constructs a sequential list of lexias one has visited and provides a slightly cumbersome means of returning to any one. The Intermedia Web View (which we shall examine more closely below) also offered a record of the documents at which one had looked during one's present or an earlier session. This record took the form of a vertical series of labeled icons. Clicking upon any one reopened the document to which it referred or, if already open, activated it and brought it to the top surface of the desktop.

Web viewers also have means of obtaining current reading history, though it assumes much less useful form than did Intermedia's. In Netscape, for example, mousing down the "Go" menu at the top of the screen produces a chronologically ordered list of lexias one has opened. Unfortunately, when one returns to one of them, Netscape deletes the intervening document titles, thereby turning what been Ariadne's thread into Hansel and Gretel's bread-crumbs. Furthermore, Netscape and similar Web viewers not only do not retain records of the complete reading path when one backtracks but also delete it entirely both after each session and when one closes the viewer window, even if one has not quit the application.

Bookmarks. One partial replacement for this lack of complete reading history appears in the ability to make permanent bookmarks in WWW and various HyperCard-based systems, like Voyager Expanded Book, Keyboard, and Toolbook. A bookmark function permits readers to record places to which they might like to return at some future time. When designing a large web site, most of whose links are internal, authors can advise readers to use the bookmark facility before following links to materials offsite, thus making re-turn easier, particularly in a complex session. In Netscape and Mosaic, one activates a bookmark simply by choosing it from a list available at the top of the screen. Voyager's system, which relies heavily on the book metaphor, indicates the existence of such placeholders with tabs in the margins of pages in a virtual book. Although these devices allow readers to customize their own reading experiences, they do not compensate for the absence of long-term reading histories in very large, complex corpora, such as one finds on the Web.

Dynamic and Static Tables of Contents. In hypertext, one often encounters the table of contents, a device directly transferred from book design, often to very good effect. Readers of materials on the Web will frequently have en-countered it, since a good many homepages and title screens consist essen-tially of linked tables of contents. I have used the device myself, particularly when creating hypertext versions of print materials, a subject I shall discuss at greater length in a separate section below. The WWW version of the first edition of this book, for instance, employs two such contents screens, one for the entire volume and a second for the first chapter, the only chapter available on the Web. Although such a table provides a familiar, often effective means of presenting a work's organization, in its static form it often overemphasizes the booklike quality of an electronic document to the detriment of its hyper-textuality.

132

Electronic Book Technologies' DynaText, which features a dynamic, automatically generated contents screen, offers a much more powerful version of this device. DynaText uses text in the form of Standard Generalized Markup Language (SGML), a far richer, more powerful older relation of the Web's HTML. Since SGML requires that one begin and end every chapter title, section heading, and all other text structures with specific tags (mark up), DynaText employs this information to produce an automatically generated contents screen, which authors and designers can arrange to appear at particular places on the screen. In *Hypertext in Hypertext,* the electronic version of this book's first edition, this contents section appears to the left of the main text.

This electronic table of contents differs in several ways from the static versions one encounters in the printed book and on the Web. First, clicking upon an icon near the title of a chapter immediately causes the first level of chapter subheads to appear, and clicking upon them in turn displays the next level of subheadings, and so on. Since I had added additional subdivisions to almost every section, to facilitate reading in an electronic environment, this feature permitted *Hypertext in Hypertext* to display both the book's original organization and the added elements as readers needed them.

The second point at which DynaText's dynamic contents screen differs from static ones is that clicking upon any section immediately brings up the relevant section in the text window to the right of the section title (see Figure 15). Finally, because the designers of this system have combined this feature with its full-text search engine, the results of a search appear in the contents screen as well as in the text itself. Searching for "Derrida," one learns that this name appears 74 times in the entire book, 41 times in the first chapter, and 5 times in the first section of that chapter. This dynamic listing proves particularly valuable when a DynaText web is configured as an electronic book, for then, following a link from one point in the text to another causes the destination text to replace the departure one. The system works so quickly—near instantaneously—that without the contents listing at the side, readers might well become disoriented.

Tables of contents, whether static or dynamic, certainly have their uses, particularly when one is hypertextualizing material originally conceived for print presentation. Linked static tables are already common in HTML, but one can also create some of the effects of the DynaText form by using Netscape frames, placing the contents at the left and text at the right.

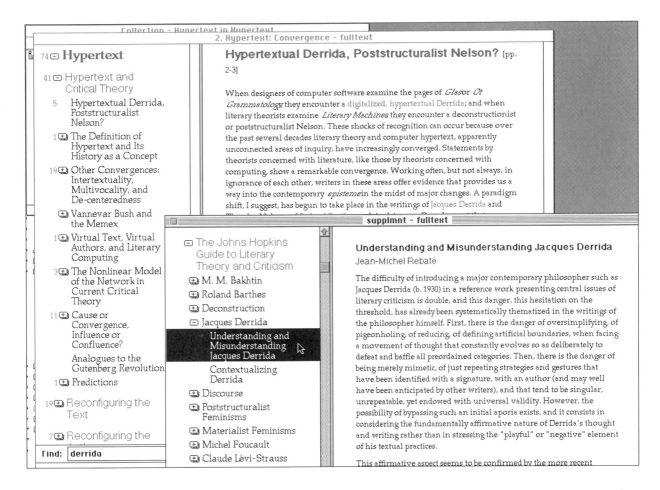

Figure 15. The Dynamic Table of Contents in Electronic Book Technologies' DynaText. This system, which combines the features of an electronic book with hypertext linking, automatically generates a reconfigurable, linked table of contents from the SGML codes used to mark elements of a text, such as chapter and section titles. In this example from *Hypertext in Hypertext,* mousing down on the plus signs to the left of items in the table of contents immediately displays titles of subsections. Clicking on the subsection title immediately brings up the relevant section in the right-hand panel. The table of contents also reinforces DynaText's full-text retrieval functions: in this case, after a reader has typed in "derrida" (the system is not case sensitive), DynaText both highlights all occurrences of the word throughout the text (*top center*) and lists the number of occurrences next to each chapter and section heading (*left*). Having observed that "Derrida" occurs five times in the book's opening section, the reader has moved that section into view; noticing that "Derrida" appears in red type, the sign of a link, the reader has then clicked once upon that link and opened a second DynaText "book" at Jean-Michel Rabaté's "Understanding and Misunderstanding Derrida" from *The Johns Hopkins Guide to Literary Theory and Criticism.*

Suppose You Could Have Everything?: The Intermedia Web View and Some Partial Analogues. The most important Intermedia feature that current systems, particularly Web viewers, lack is its system-generated dynamic tracking map, whose basic idea evolved through three stages. The first, the Global Tracking Map, provided graphic information about all links and documents in a particular body of linked documents. Clicking twice upon the icon for a particular hypertext corpus, such as *Context32, Nuclear Arms,* or *Biology,* simultaneously activated—that is, opened—that hypertext web and generated a document in which icons representing each document in the web were joined by lines representing all links between documents. This Global Tracking Map, which functioned only during early stages of Intermedia's development, immediately demonstrated that such a device was virtually useless for all but the smallest document sets or webs. (Although pictures of it have appeared in articles on hypertext, the Global Tracking Map was never used educationally and was never part of any released version of Intermedia.)

IRIS next developed the Local Tracking Map, which presented icons for all documents linked to whichever one was currently active. As before, readers chose a particular web and opened it, either by double clicking upon its icon or by first activating it and then choosing "open" from the Intermedia menu. Readers then moved the Local Tracking Map to one side of the screen, permitting them to work with an individual document while keeping the tracking map it generated open beside it. Each time the reader opened a new document or activated a previously opened one, the Local Tracking Map transformed itself, thus informing readers where they could go next. This information alone served to remove much potential disorientation from the reader's experience.

In its third instantiation, the Local Tracking Map, whose name then changed to Web View, added two chief features that I would very much like to see in WWW viewers, such as Netscape: First, double clicking on any icon in the Web View opened the document represented by that icon, thereby adding another way of making one's way through webs. Second, the Web View presented a history of the reader's path by means of a vertical array of icons that indicated the titles of documents previously opened; additional smaller icons showed that the document was opened from a folder, by following a link, or by reactivating a document previously opened on the desktop (for illustrations, see Utting and Yankelovich).

Although this feature succeeded well in orienting the reader, it worked even better when combined with author-generated concept maps, such as the overviews I have employed on systems (Intermedia, Interleaf World

View, Storyspace, Microcosm, MacWeb, and World Wide Web) that surround a single concept (Victorianism, Darwinism, gender matters) or entity (Gaskell's *North and South,* Dickens) with a series of other concepts (literary relations, cultural context, economic background), to each of which many documents link. Whereas the Web View presented all documents attached to the entire overview, the overview has a hierarchical organization but does not reveal the nature or number of documents linked to each block. Intermedia provided two ways of obtaining this information—a menu, which followed links from a particular link marker, and the Web View. Clicking upon a particular link and thus activating it darkened all the links attached to that block in the Web View. Thus, working together, individual documents and the Web View continually informed the reader what information lay one jump away from the current text. This combination of materials generated by authors and materials generated by Intermedia well exemplifies the way hypertext authors employ what are essentially stylistic and rhetorical devices to supplement system design and work synergistically with it.

These features of this no-longer-available system solved the basic problem of orienting readers. Unfortunately, most current WWW viewers, like early HyperCard, permit readers to see only a single window or document at a time, and one easily becomes disoriented. Designers have made use of homecards and homepages that return one to the first screen of a web or document set. These systems, however, are essentially disorienting, because they provide no overall view of materials and do not indicate to readers enough about where links will take them. Disorientation, then, arises when readers find themselves within a hypermedia system and feel that they do not know "where" they are, and also when they are within a particular document and do not know how to return to a document read earlier or how to find one they suspect exists or hope exists.

Various research and commercially available systems have had partial analogues to the Intermedia Web View. One research version of the University of Southampton Microcosm system, for example, had something very like the Local Tracking Map, but it was not implemented in the released version; and Storyspace, a commercially available system, has its Roadmap, which has many of the Web View's functions (Figure 16). Like the Web View, the Roadmap records one's reading path, shows linked lexias, and permits one to open them; unlike it, the Storyspace device also lists all links coming into the current lexia. Unfortunately, the Roadmap, which takes the form of a menu containing scrollable lists, lacks the Web View's dynamic quality, for

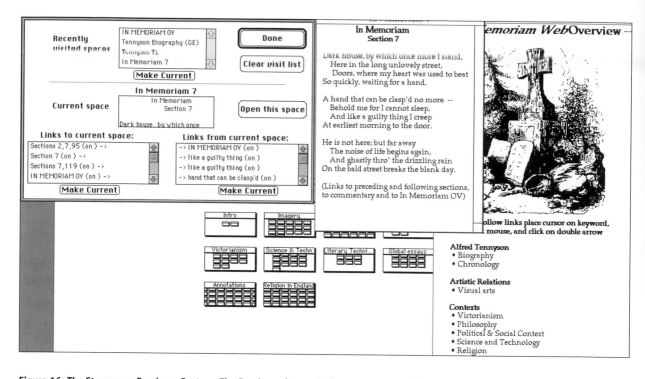

Figure 16. The Storyspace Roadmap Feature. The Roadmap (*upper left*) represents a static analogue to the Intermedia Web View. At the top center of the Roadmap appears one's reading history and, immediately below it, the first few lines of the currently active lexia. Like the Web View, the Roadmap informs readers of possible destination lexias and permits readers to open them directly, but unlike the Intermedia tool, which displayed only destination lexias, the Roadmap displays all links in and out of the current lexia. Unfortunately, whereas the Web View always remained in sight and automatically reconfigured itself as each new document opened, the Roadmap appears only upon demand and has to be opened separately for each document.

it does not run continuously and has to be opened from a menu or by means of a key combination for each individual document.

Intermedia's dynamic hypergraph proved so valuable as a means of orientation and navigation that I hope someone will develop an equivalent application either as part of widely used WWW viewers or as an add-on that will function with them. Certain halting steps have already begun in that direction. The University of Heidelburg's Hyper-Tree, for example, offers graphic representations of the file structure of individual servers; but, unfortunately, like the original Intermedia attempt to graph links, it provides too much information, thus rendering it of little practical use.

As the Web View and Roadmap show, readers need effectively organized preview functions—what Mark Bernstein terms "airlocks"—that show them what lexias exist one jump away. In the next section I shall suggest stylistic, rhetorical techniques that hypertext authors can employ in the absence of such software tools.

Author-Created Orientation Devices: Overviews. Some hypertext systems like Microcosm, Storyspace, and Intermedia provide several means of helping orient the reader; others provide little built-in assistance in solving basic problems of orientation. But whatever system authors employ, they should use overview and gateway documents, which are devices entirely under their own control. Overviews, which can take many forms, are author-created (as opposed to system-generated) documents that serve as directories to aid in navigating the materials. Overviews assist readers to gain convenient access to all the materials in many documents or to a broad topic that cuts across several disciplines.

Furthermore, when so many links attach to a single anchor in a general overview that the reader will not be able to evaluate them conveniently, one should consider using some form of suboverview or what my colleague Paul Kahn has termed a crossroads document. Unlike hypermedia systems that permit only one link per block or screen, Microcosm, Storyspace, and Intermedia permit an indefinite number of links to attach to each link marker. Overusing this feature, which supports the capacity of hypermedia to model complex relationships, can create too many linked documents. A variety of factors makes defining "too many" difficult to do. In some unusual cases more than 100 documents can conveniently link to a single block and be conveniently accessed from a single link marker. The *In Memoriam* overview has the text "individual sections" to which all 133 sections of the poem link, and since the menu that appears when readers follow that link simply lists the sections in numerical order, this large number of linked documents creates no problems. Similarly, another part of this same document links to several dozen uses of several words or phrases found throughout the poem. Because, like the linking of individual sections, this linking of terms takes the form of a list, a menu containing many items works well.

Most of the time, however, authors link different kinds of documents on different subjects, and long lists here confuse. When planning to link more than five or six documents on the same subject, particularly when these appear in a list with documents on different subjects, one should consider organizing materials in one subject by an overview and linking that overview instead. For example, rather than link several dozen documents about a range of subjects to a text "Social and Political History" in the Victorian overview, one does better to organize them with overviews for public health, the British Empire, and political history and then link these overviews. Since a body of hypermedia materials has the capacity to grow and change, adding both links and documents, one can expect that the nature and number of such overviews will change as the other materials do.

Subject overviews, like other overviews, take one of six forms, the most important of which is a graphic concept map that suggests visually that various ideas relate to some central phenomenon or impinge upon it. This center, the subject of the overview, can be an author (Tennyson, Darwin), chronological or period term (eighteenth century, Victorian), idea or movement (realism, feminism), or other concept (biblical typology, cyborg). The implied and often reinforced message of such arrangements is simply that any idea that the reader makes the center of his or her investigations exists within a field of other phenomena, which may or may not relate to it causally. Such graphic presentation of materials depicts one informing idea or hidden agenda of hypermedia materials, namely, that one proceeds in understanding any particular phenomenon by relating it to other contexts.

These kinds of overview lexias, which I have used since the first days of Intermedia, have particular value for the World Wide Web, the present limitations of which tend towards a flattened form of hypertext. The emphasis of overviews upon multiple approaches simultaneously provides a way of breaking out of the implied page format that confines the Web and also of creating a crossroads document, to which the reader can return repeatedly and before departing in new directions. The various web sites I maintain use various kinds of overviews. *The Victorian Web,* which attempts to emulate designs used by its predecessors in Intermedia, Storyspace, and Microcosm, surrounds a central image with a range of related topics. In the web for Elizabeth Gaskell's *North and South,* for example, a linked icon for political and social context appears at the top center, and immediately beneath come those for biography, other works by the same author, Victorianism, and women's lives (see Figure 17). The icons for literary relations and visual arts flank the image representing the novel. In the line below are five icons representing aspects of technique—setting, symbolism, characterization, narration, and genre; centered beneath them appears that for religion and philosophy.

Although one could use a single image map for such an overview in Netscape, using separate icons has three distinct advantages, the first of which is that thus employing separate tiny images created in one of the popular image formats produces documents that load much faster than do image maps, which take considerably more processing time. Second, by using the

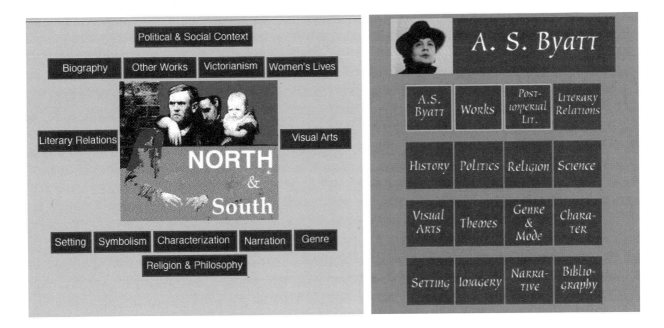

Figure 17. Two World Wide Web Overviews. These examples show two different approaches to creating overview lexias for the World Wide Web. That on the left, the overview for Elizabeth Gaskell's *North and South* in *The Victorian Web,* represents the latest version of the original Intermedia-style overviews, which emphasize that readers can approach a subject from multiple points of view. The A. S. Byatt overview, in contrast, presents a similarly nonhierarchical approach to organizing information, by arranging its linked headings in a series of horizontal rows. This approach to creating overviews with HTML (text) documents has several advantages over image maps: (1) this text-based overview loads (opens) approximately three times faster than do image maps, (2) since Netscape and other WWW viewers retain images in a cache, building different overviews with the same elements creates documents that load very quickly, (3) such overviews are easily modified by adding, subtracting, or otherwise changing individual icon-and-link combinations. The kind of overview represented by that for Byatt has the added advantage of employing the same files for both overviews and footer icons, thus reducing storage space and access time.

"alt" option in HTML that permits one to include a text label, these kinds of overviews will work with viewers that do not have graphics capacities—an important consideration when portions of one's intended audience may not have the kind of computer access or equipment needed to handle large images. Third, one may create standard templates for all the overviews in a particular web, thus producing a kind of visual consistency, and yet one can easily modify appropriate elements. In the *North and South* overview, for instance, the icon "Other Works" replaces the "Works" icon that appears in the Gaskell overview.

The circular or daisy arrangement of linked icons shown in Figure 17 appears widely used, and many examples of it organize stand-alone hypertexts and those on CD-ROMs. Christine Tamblyn's *She Loves It, She Loves It Not: Women and Technology* employs a particularly effective form of this design. In keeping with its title, this CD-ROM arrays a dozen petal-shaped icons, each bearing an image, around a central point. Text labels for each move in a circular path, appearing and disappearing on each one. Gunnar Liestøl's *Kon-Tiki Interactive,* which I shall discuss in more detail below, surrounds an image of the globe with seven circular images, each of which animates in turn, representing Thor Heyerdahl and six of his expeditions (Figure 18).

Not all the overviews designed to avoid hierarchy or linearity need to have a circular format. Unlike the Tamblyn, Liestøl, and *Victorian Web* overviews, those for the hypertext section of the *Cyberspace, Hypertext, and Critical Theory Web* and all materials in the *Postcolonial and Postimperial Literature in English* web do not so emphasize centrality. Taking the A. S. Byatt overview shown in Figure 17 as an example, we find the topic of the document above four rows of four square icons each. This arrangement, which also avoids the linearity of a table of contexts, has the advantage for the designer of permitting one to employ some of the same icons both in overviews and at the foot of each screen.

Another kind of graphic concept overview, the flow chart suggesting vector forces, uses arrows to show lines of influence or causal connection. "Dickens's Literary Relations" (Figure 19), for example, uses arrows to show his relation to authors who influenced him, those he influenced, and those with whom he existed in terms of mutual influence. This form of graphic overview proves particularly useful in presenting obviously diachronic or chronological relationships.

Timelines represent a third kind of graphic overview. Intermedia had InterVal, an elegant timeline editor, but one can easily create similar documents using any text editor, as we have done when translating the Intermedia webs to a range of environments. Timelines offer a means of clearly organizing materials or even entire courses that have a strong chronological orientation. In fact, any timeline with links serves as an overview for the materials it joins. Although timelines provide a means of organization particularly convenient to authors, remember that they may simplify complex relationships and have little to compel the interest of a reader unacquainted with their subject.

Images that represent natural objects, like a photograph of a cell or maps, provide a kind of familiar basis on which authors can construct concept

Figure 18. Gunnar Liestøl's *Kon-Tiki Interactive:* the introductory overview. This interactive overview surrounds an image of the globe with seven circular images, representing Thor Heyerdahl and six of his expeditions. These images serve as icons, previews, and conceptual overviews. Clicking upon any one of them halts sound and animation and opens an overview for the subject it represents. (Used by permission of Gyldendal Publishers.)

maps. Attaching links to labels in technical diagrams similarly provides an obvious way of enriching conventional information technology. These kinds of overviews, incidentally, exemplify a perfect use for WWW image maps. Perhaps my favorite is a map of Italy showing major Italian web sites: click on the tiny square representing a particular city, and a link takes you to its web site.

Outlines add a graphic component to text by breaking up the flow that

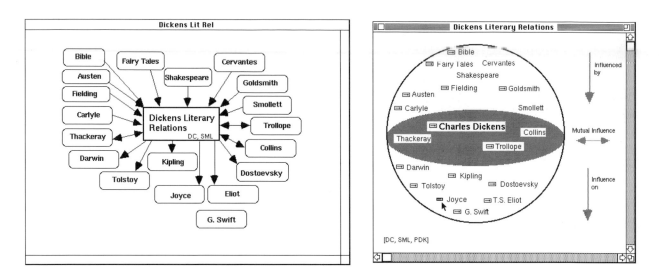

Figure 19. Two Versions of "Dickens Literary Relations." The original form of this kind of visual directory appears at the left and Paul D. Kahn's more recent one at the right.

characterizes discursive prose. By abandoning the table-of-contents or list mode that characterizes page-bound, printed text, one liberates hypermedia from the restrictions of print and enables it to do what it does best—present networks of relationships while also enabling the reader easily to traverse those relationships, establishing connections between paired sets of data among larger groupings of material. If hypermedia is characterized by connectivity, to realize its potential one must employ devices that emphasize that quality. Lists, tables of contents, and indices, though still of significant use, do not work in this manner; but one may wish to use them in addition to other kinds of graphic organizing devices, as does the elegant *Kon-Tiki Interactive* CD-ROM, which parallels its circular overview with an interactive outline (Figure 20). Selecting one of its individual elements, say, that for the Kon-Tiki itself, produces a list of eleven items.

When converting for presentation in hypermedia text documents originally created for book technology, one may occasionally use the document itself as its own overview. Any hypermedia document with more than a few links in essence serves as a directory, since, once opened, it provides the immediate center and reference point for the reader's next act of exploration. The author of educational materials, particularly those involving literary texts or those that place primary emphasis on the details of a text, may therefore wish to take advantage of this quality of hypermedia. Section 7 of *In Memo-*

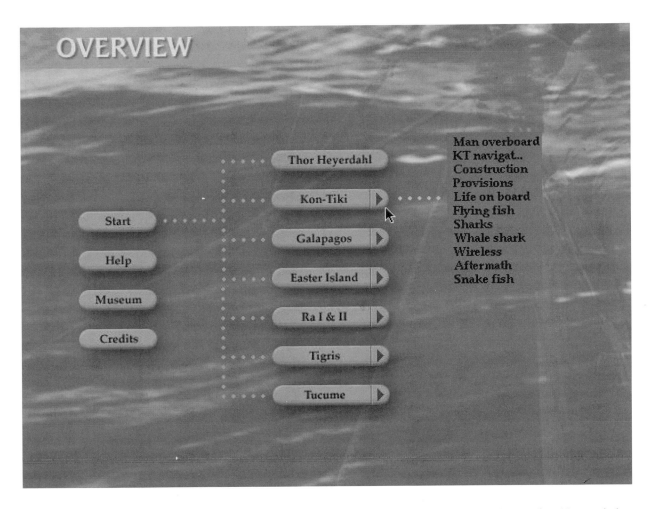

Figure 20. Kon-Tiki Overview. Selecting any item in this interactive outline overview produces a sublist of items. (Used by permission of Gyldendal Publishers.)

riam (lower left window in Figure 8) exemplifies a brief text document that functions as its own overview in a Storyspace web. One must take care not to overdo this kind of heavy linking in text documents on the Web, which has few orienting devices; linked text alone does not always provide very clear indications of where its links will take the reader. In a scholarly or critical presentation of a text, however, in which the links clearly take one to annotations and commentary, heavily linked lexias can function as an orientation aid, in large part because the nature of the document indicates the kind of links that will attach to it. In contrast, some heavily linked personal pages on the Web, though occasionally amusing, often appear completely chaotic.

Whatever kind of overviews one chooses, one should accommodate—and encourage—different styles of hypertext reading by providing as many as is convenient for each subject; and one should also expect that individual lexias, particularly in information hypertexts, will link to multiple overviews. Thus, an essay comparing women's issues in Graham Swift's *Waterland* and A. S. Byatt's *Possession* would link to the literary relations document for each work but also to those for themes, gender matters, and techniques as well.

Closely related to overviews and directories are those documents that serve as gateways between academic courses or bodies of materials in separate disciplines. One such gateway document, mentioned earlier, joins the materials that supported several English courses and those for the nuclear arms and arms control course offered by Richard Smoke of Brown University's Center for Foreign Policy Development. The literary materials discuss Victorian technology, canals, and railroads but contain no parallel documents about nuclear technology and the antinuclear movement, two subjects that play a significant part in Graham Swift's *Waterland* (1983), a novel read in one of the literature courses. Therefore, a brief document that announces the connections between *Waterland* and the subject of nuclear disarmament links to the science and technology section in *Waterland* OV and also to the timeline that the nuclear arms course materials employ as a directory. This brief document enabled students in the introductory survey of English literature to explore the materials created for a course in another discipline. Similarly, students from that other discipline could encounter materials showing the effects on contemporary fiction of the concerns covered in their political science course.

Author-Created Orientation Devices: Marking the Edges. What kinds of techniques can one use to assist readers? One device especially important to those creating materials for the World Wide Web uses visual indications of a lexia's identity, location, and relation to others. These signals can take the form of header icons, color schemes, background textures, linked icons that appear at the foot of lexias, or all of these in combination. Such devices play a crucial role on the Web, where readers may arrive at any document via a search engine, entering at what could be the middle of a planned sequence or set of documents. Without some such device, even readers who find that a particular lexia meets their needs and taste become frustrated when they cannot conveniently determine whether it forms part of a larger structure.

One of the most commonly used of such orientation devices is the header icon, which immediately informs the reader that a lexia belongs to a particular web or subweb. For example, in *The Victorian Web* a blue and white header element appears immediately following the lines providing title and author. At the left of this icon, which is a third of an inch high and seven wide, appears a black-and-white image of Queen Victoria, followed by the words "The Victorian Web" and a white line extending the remaining length of the header. Editing programs that permit one to perform global changes easily—throughout an entire set of documents, not just one document at a time—make inserting such elements extremely easy to do. Whereas *The Victorian Web* employs a single header icon, some of the other web sites I maintain, such as that on recent postcolonial literature, use a different icon for each major division or subweb.

The *Postcolonial Literature* web has separate sections for anglophone literature of Great Britain, the Indian subcontinent, Africa, and Australia and New Zealand, and employs not only different headers for each section but other devices as well. These other devices include variations in color scheme and background texture, and combined with footer icons they make an effective means of simultaneously orienting the reader while indicating the permeable borders of both the lexia and the larger units to which it belongs. For example, an essay from *The Victorian Web* that compares the railway swindlers in Trollope's *The Way We Live Now* and Carlyle's "Hudson's Statue" has five icons, one for the main Victorian overview followed by one each for Trollope, his novel, Carlyle, and his text (at top in Figure 21). The first three icons denote increasing specificity, indicating that the document contributes to the web as a whole, to those materials concerning Trollope, and to those about this particular novel. In contrast, the five icons, taken together, indicate that the lexia in question simultaneously participates in two subwebs or directories. These icons thus serve to orient readers by clearly showing how the lexia being explored relates to one or more larger categories—in this example five separate ones.

Furthermore, because links attach to each of these icons, clicking upon them brings readers to an overview for these larger categories. Attaching links to the icons, in other words, makes them devices of navigation as well as orientation. In one sense these devices mark the edges of one or more groups or structures to which the lexia belongs or with which it associates, but the most important function involves not so much delimiting an edge or border of a document as indicating its relation to, or membership in, one or more subwebs. The effect of this congeries of devices, therefore, is to orient readers who find themselves in a particular lexia, by clearly indicating its relation to others, its (intellectual) place within a web.

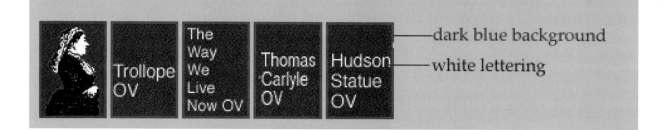

In contrast, Carlyle focuses on the English public's blind admiration for Hudson, the powerful railway king. He criticizes them for allowing a corrupt financier to be "[mounted] on the highest place you can discover in the most crowded thoroughfare." Carlyle argues the people's desire to erect a statue to Hudson is itself lamentable.

Trollope OV · The Way We Live Now OV · Thomas Carlyle OV · Hudson Statue OV

———dark blue background
———white lettering

1. First three icons indicate increasing specificity: As one moves from left to right, one moves down directory structure.

2. In contrast, the five icons indicate that the present document simultaneously participates in two subwebs or directories.

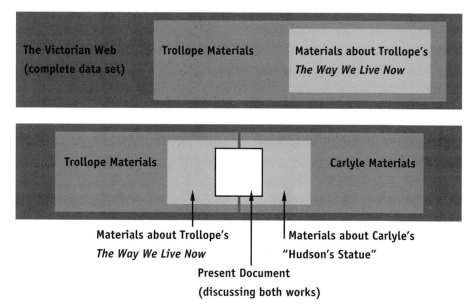

The Victorian Web (complete data set) · Trollope Materials · Materials about Trollope's *The Way We Live Now*

Trollope Materials · Carlyle Materials

Materials about Trollope's *The Way We Live Now* · Materials about Carlyle's "Hudson's Statue"

Present Document (discussing both works)

Figure 21. Footer Icons in World Wide Web Documents. This example from *The Victorian Web* shows how linked icons at the bottom of a lexia can indicate its simultaneous participation in several subwebs or document sets, thereby orienting the reader.

This combination of headers, color schemes, and linked footer icons works particularly well for large or complex collections of interlinked lexias, such as those created by participants in courses or departments. The *Cyberspace, Hypertext, and Critical Theory Web,* created at Brown University, contains not only course materials and links to many web sites external to Brown but also to a collection of elaborate individual student projects, some consisting of more than one hundred lexias and graphic elements. In this sort of situation, identification and bordering schemes prove especially useful by informing readers that they have arrived at a discrete document set. Following a link from the section about print technology of the information technology overview brings one to Amanda Griscom's *Trends of Anarchy and Hierarchy: Comparing the Cultural Repercussions of Print and Digital Media,* her WWW translation of a substantial honors thesis comparing the seventeenth-century pamphlet wars in England and the periodical press that succeeded them with the situation on the Internet today. Like many student contributions to the *Cyberspace* web, this one contains a link to the web overview only on its contents page; the other lexias contain only footer icons to the contents, next page, and works cited. Since the reader can enter portions of this subweb from various overview headings that indicate discussions of McLuhan, scribal culture, media in the seventeenth century, and so on, the reader needs to know the separateness—as well as the entire scope—of this subweb.

Other student subwebs extend such schemes even further, using individual subwebs for separate portions, an approach we see exemplified in Michael DiBianco's *Is the Novel Dead Yet? Of Course Not. But It's Sick Isn't It?* An opening screen on which green bold type appears against a light gray crinkled paper surface leads to three subwebs, one of which, a discussion of Victor Nell's *Lost in a Book,* looks like a spiral-bound white notebook, whereas another, "Hypertext Notes," appears as a slightly different-looking notebook.

An even more elaborate use of graphic devices to indicate a complex organization informs Leni Zumas's *Semio-Surf,* a web originally created in Storyspace that combines fiction, an Ulmerian mystory, and literary theory. When I decided to translate *Semio-Surf,* which its author created in the days before the Web, I had two goals. First, I had to find a means of indicating its relation to the rest of the course web, and second, I also needed to create a way of communicating the clear organization the author had created in the original software. Color schemes proved an obvious, workable solution. Since the opening screen employs the medium gray background color and red and yellow icons of the hypertext materials rather than the more general one used throughout most of the *Cyberspace* web, the reader easily perceives *Semio-Surf's* principal axis or place in the organization of this miniature docuverse.

This use of backgrounds continues with all nine of the subsections of *Semio-Surf.* The opening screen has seven points of departure, four internal ones presented in a contents list and three links out presented by three footer icons, each of which takes the reader to a different point in the *Cyberspace Web*—the *Cyberspace* or principal overview and those for critical theory and hypertext.

One can enter Zumas's cluster of interlinked satirical narratives with "La Vie Construite de Rita," the story involving her protagonist, or through "TV Guide," which lists one tale for each of eight channels: local Providence news on a fictional Channel One, MTV, the Maury Povich show, *Jeopardy!, As the Channel Changes,* the Reid and Rita sitcom, the NCAA Basketball championship, and *Murder, She Filmed.* Each of these sections, like "La Vie Construite de Rita," has its own distinguishing background, text, and link colors, as do two other main sections of the web—one composed of materials from Rick Altman's "Television/Sound" and another of those from Gregory Ulmer's *Teletheory.*

I have to emphasize that on the World Wide Web the borders and limits of these hypertext documents, their edges, as it were, clearly have to be understood only as fictions, as agreed-upon convention, since both links and search engines easily cross these proposed margins. The header graphic, for example, indicates the existence of an entire web, which is also essentially a fiction, an assertion of class or category, which, we know, on the web cannot finally be a factual claim, and as such it remains something like a gesture or wish or hope, particularly when, as in any large and complex web (site), the documents do not possess the kinship endowed by author function, for they have been produced by more than one author or entity. In sets of lexias created by a single author one can posit limits—that is, pretend they exist—more easily than one can for webs that both draw extensively upon quoted passages and images created by others and also link to other sites. Nonetheless, we need such classifications in order to read. But the crossing of such textual (non)borders is one of the characteristics of hypertextuality, one completely analogous to the way links both permit one to employ a folder structure and yet not be confined by it.

Gleamware. Permit me to propose something like a wish list. Computer users often refer to certain projects as "so much vaporware," meaning that a product or research project that someone has presented as already existing is in fact little closer to reality than a plan or a promise. Let's go even far-ther back—from promise to desire. Playing on the old expression, "when you were just a gleam in your parents' eyes," let us consider gleamware—wishware.

An example of gleamware would be semiautomatically generated over-view and crossroads documents in HTML that would permit reader-authors on the Web to produce such intermediary documents by combining complex searches with elegant templates. At the moment of this writing, no WWW viewer offers the one-to-many linking that I believe so crucial to creating a fully multiple hypertext. To translate materials originally created in systems that have this sort of linking, such as Microcosm, Storyspace, and Intermedia, authors find themselves forced to recreate, with an enormous expenditure of time and effort, their automatically generated link menus. The multiple links that require 20 to 30 minutes to create for an Intermedia or Storyspace over-view—and less than half that time for Microcosm, using its more sophisti-cated generic link options—can take several days to translate for the Web: one must go through the subset of documents that will link to the overview and manually create separate ones for literary relations, themes, biographical materials, and so on. Even if an earlier version of the material in another software environment is available to remind one of possible links, it still takes hours of repetitive work—with the result that authors inevitably tend to avoid as much of it as possible and thereby produce a relatively flattened hyper-text document.

So here are my first two gleamware proposals, the first of which may already exist as a proprietary research tool in some large corporations in the computer industry. Imagine combining a commercially available search tool, such as On Location, with a popular programming language and a set of templates that would permit one to generate, with minimal expenditure of time and effort, a suboverview entitled, say, "Political Themes in Dickens" simply by calling up a menu and typing "Dickens," "themes," and "politics." An even better version—one that I have spoken about longingly since the last few years of the Intermedia project—would involve automatically gener-ated graphic representations of literary and other complex relations. In this example of gleamware, one would simply choose from a menu a thematic option (literary relations, for instance), and one's authoring (reading?) system would combine a graphics engine, search tools, resulting indices, glossaries, chronologies, and synonym lists and would produce automatically the kind of concept maps Paul Kahn created in the early Dickens Web (Figure 19). Using synonym lists and chronologies, this Relations Map Generator—let's

give it a properly stuffy name—would place the chronologically earlier authors or texts towards one end of a chosen axis; earlier ones could appear,
for example, at the left, top, or, if one could represent a third dimension,
farther away. Authors or texts that I considered more important—for reasons
of some cultural standard (Shakespeare), relation to the author in question
(Hallam to Tennyson, the Brownings to each other), or quantity of available
commentary—could be made to appear larger or in brighter colors. You get
the idea. Let's take the gleam one step farther: if one could produce such
documents quickly enough—something that would probably assume pre-
existent indices—they could exist only dynamically, created each time one
followed a link from an overview, and would hence be always current, always
up-to-date.

This Text Is Hot. Readers of hypermedia need some indication of where they
can find links and then, after they have found them, where those links lead;
finally, after they have arrived at a new lexia, they need some justification for
why they have been led there. All three of these issues raise the question of
the degree to which specific systems, authors, or both working together require an active, even aggressive reader. In examining a range of solutions to
the first problem—how to indicate the presence of hot (or linked) text—I
shall follow my usual procedure and begin by surveying the means thus far
employed to do so and then suggest ways authors can write with and against
their systems. As always, a major theme will be to suggest how WWW authors can benefit from lessons provided by other forms of hypermedia.

In examining some ways existing hypertext systems signal the presence
of linked text or images, I shall begin with least successful examples and
proceed to better ones. Let me again begin with Intermedia, this time because its solution, though clear, unambiguous, and furnishing ancillary information, proved too visually intrusive. All versions of this system employed a
link marker in the form of a small horizontal rectangle within which appeared
an arrow. The system automatically placed this icon above and to the left
of any section of linked text, and the author could not move it; in graphics
documents, however, the authors could place it wherever they wished. Like
many elements in Intermedia, the link marker worked synergistically with
other system features. Clicking once upon it, for example, highlighted the
icons representing destination lexias in the Web View, and by going to the
main menu, readers could learn both anchor extent (the extent of the linked
text) and anchor description (the label the author attached to it). Unfortunately, placing the icon above linked text proved too intrusive, for it distorted

the document's leading—the spacing between lines—a particularly annoying effect when one hypertextualized a print text, say, a poem by Tennyson.

Mosaic, Netscape, and other WWW viewers offer a slightly better solution to the problem of how to inform readers about the location of links. World Wide Web viewers conventionally indicate the presence of links with color and underscored text: in Netscape, for example, unlinked text appears in black against a light gray background, and blue, underlined text indicates the presence of a link, magenta underlined text a link that one has previously followed. I am of course describing the default version—that which one receives if neither reader nor author customizes these elements; authors can choose entirely different color schemes or choose to make regular and linked text the same color, thus employing only underlining to indicate link presence.

Although this HTML approach seems like it would be less visually intrusive than Intermedia's link marker, its manner of signaling link presence, like that of the earlier system, produces a visual hodgepodge in alphanumeric text. Although annoying in written text, such permanently displayed link markings work quite well with graphic elements, since a colored outline does not intrude upon an icon the way a combination of color and underlining do upon text.

In contrast to HTML and Intermedia, Microcosm, like several other hypertext systems, does not permanently display indications of links but makes them visible on call. This removes any possibility of visually marring the appearance of literary texts. As we have already observed when examining Microcosm's rich assortment of link types, this system invites active, even aggressive readers who interrogate the text they encounter (see pages 17–20). In keeping with Microcosm's encouragement of the active reader, users who come upon a word or phrase that they believe likely to serve as a link anchor have several choices: they can double click upon it, perform the equivalent action by choosing "Follow Link" from a menu, ask about link extent from a menu, or create their own links with the "Compute Links" function. For many applications, particularly educational and informational ones, the Microcosm approach strikes me as wonderfully appropriate to the medium of hypertext. I would suggest that Microcosm follow HyperCard and Storyspace and make a simple key combination show both the presence and extent of author-created links. And Storyspace's use of frames that surround hot text when readers hold down option and apple keys simultaneously has proved a particularly valuable feature and one that I would like to see both Microcosm and HTML viewers emulate.

Airlocks, Preview Functions, and the Rhetoric of Departure. All these system-based devices that we have just observed constitute the first, and simplest, part of any rhetoric of departure, for they inform readers that they can leave a text stream for somewhere or something else. Not surprisingly, most readers do not feel comfortable jumping off into limbo. Although much hypertext fiction and poetry plays with surprise and disorientation as desired aesthetic effects, other kinds of hypertext writing require some way of giving readers an idea of what links will do.

Such preview functions—what Mark Bernstein has called an "airlock"— serve to both inform and reassure readers; and when systems do not provide adequate preview information, authors must find their own ways to do so. The HTML feature of changing the color (usually from blue to red or magenta) of anchors to indicate that they have already been followed exemplifies one kind of valuable system support. When one mouses over an anchor, most Web viewers also show the destination URL, though unfortunately not the title of the linked lexia, in a panel at the bottom of the viewer window; this feature does not seem to work with some versions of Netscape frames.

Intermedia provided two forms of preview information. First, as we have already observed, its Web View announced destinations of all links from the current lexia; activating a link marker with a single mouse click darkened the icons for all the lexias linked to it; clicking twice followed the link. Intermedia also permitted authors to attach descriptions to each anchor, and these descriptions appeared in menus automatically generated when one followed a link leading to two or more lexias. In contrast to Intermedia, Storyspace allows authors to attach descriptions to the links themselves rather than to anchors, though the reader perceives the result as much the same. As useful as these features were and are, writers in hypertext still have to assist readers by employing various techniques that constitute a rhetoric of departure.

The point is that readers need a general idea of what to expect before they set out on their explorations. Authors can help them by making the text serve as its own preview: Phrase statements or pose questions that provide obvious occasions for following links. For example, when an essay on Graham Swift or Salman Rushdie uses phrases like "World War I" or "self-reflexive narrators," readers will know that links attached to those phrases will lead to material on those subjects.

In addition, when possible provide specific information about a link destination by directly drawing attention to it, such as one does by creating text- or icon-based footer links. Another precise use of text to specify a link destination takes the form of specific directions. For example, in *The Victorian*

Web, to which student authors contributed differing interpretations of the same topic—say, labor unrest in *North and South* or gender issues in *Great Expectations*—functioning as an editor, I added notifications of these contributions. Thus, at the close of essays quoting and summarizing different contemporary opinions about strikes and labor unrest, I added, "Follow for another contemporary view." This device, which must be used sparingly, is particularly useful when indicating bibliographical information, definitions of key terms, and the presence of opposing points of view.

Such careful linking becomes especially important in writing hypertext for WWW, since current Web viewers lack one-to-many-linking (Figure 2). This apparently minor lack has devastating consequences for authors, who have to create manually the link menus that other systems generate automatically. Without one-to-many links, readers and writers lose the crucial preview function they provide. I find that the effect of being reminded of branching possibilities produces a different way of thinking about text and reading than does encountering a series of one-to-one links sprinkled through a text.

The Rhetoric of Arrival. Systems like Intermedia, Storyspace, and Microcosm use various means to highlight the reader's point of arrival. Intermedia, for example, surrounded the destination anchor with a marquee-like moving dotted line that traversed a rectangular path around the intended point of arrival; a single mouse click turned off the marquee. Storyspace employs a rectangular block of reverse video around arrival anchors. Unfortunately, thus far, although WWW authors can use the anchor feature to bring the reader to a particular portion of a document, no viewer I've used shows the exact extent of the arrival anchor. Instead, HTML just opens the document with the beginning of the anchor appearing as the very top of the screen window, something extremely useful for certain applications, such as bibliographical citations, since when arriving at bibliographies readers easily recognize an obvious—and obviously limited—point of arrival like a single bibliographic citation.

The difficulty in WWW is exacerbated by the fact that one often links to documents over which one has no control. If one can obtain permission from the document's author or owner, one can place an anchor in that document. Similarly, if one can obtain permission to do so, one can copy and incorporate the arrival lexia within one's own web. Although such an approach, which I have used in *The Victorian Web,* occasionally proves useful, it strikes me as basically inefficient and against the spirit of WWW's dispersed textuality.

Converting Print Texts to Hypertext. Before considering the best ways to hyper-textualize printed matter, we might wish to ask why one would want to bother. After all, a somewhat sympathetic devil's advocate might begin, it's one thing to expend time and effort developing new modes of reading and writing, but why modify the book, which is in so many ways a perfectly good text-delivery machine? For many nonliterary uses, the answer seems obvious, since linked digital text permits an adaptability, speed of dissemination, and economy of scale simply not possible with print. Maintenance manuals for large, complex machines, like airplanes, parts catalogues, and many other uses of the codex form of text presentation seem better served by electronic form. For these reasons, in some scholarly or scientific fields, such as high-energy physics, the digital word has increasingly replaced the physical.

But why in literature and in humanities education, our devil's advocate might continue, would we want to take works originally conceived for print and translate them into hypertext? Particularly given the primitive state of commonly available screen technology and on-screen typography, why take a high-resolution object like a book and transform it into blurrier words on flickering screens? Now that the World Wide Web promises to make all of us self-publishers, these questions become particularly important. I would answer that we translate print into digital text and then hypertextualize it for several reasons: for accessibility, for convenience, and for intellectual, experiential, or aesthetic enrichment impractical or impossible with print.

When I began to work with Intermedia a decade ago, the combination of a desire to create materials best suited for reading in an electronic environment and the need to avoid possible copyright infringement led my team to create all our materials from scratch, but soon enough teaching needs drove us to include hypertext translations of printed works. One need will be familiar to anyone teaching today: works around which I had planned portions of a course suddenly went out of print. Placing these otherwise unavailable documents within a hypertext environment allowed us to create an economical, convenient electronic version of a reserve reading room, one that never closes and in which all materials always remain available to all readers who need them.

Now that the World Wide Web has created the rudiments of a hypertext system that can link together lexias whose source code resides on different continents, such accessibility provides an even stronger impetus to hypertextualize otherwise unavailable materials. This ease of accessibility from a great distance means that more readers can use one's text and one can hope to find texts translated by others for one's own use. As some of my books on

Victorian art, literature, and religion have gone out of print, I have retrieved the copyright from my publishers, translated them into HTML, and placed them on the Web. As I did so, I began to take advantage of characteristics of hypertext that justify translating a book into a web document, the most basic of which is the synergy that derives from linking materials together. Once I had created web versions of my edition of the letters of John Ruskin and the Victorian artist, W. Holman Hunt, my book on that artist, and articles from *Art Bulletin* and other journals, I found that these texts all worked better together than they had alone. A footnote providing the source of a letter could now, for example, lead to the text of the letter itself. Even more important, if an illustration was available in any of the texts, it became available everywhere. Texts needing illustrations particularly benefit from electronic presentation, since a digital image is a matter of codes rather than physical marks on physical surfaces. Using an image fifty times within one text or set of texts requires no more storage space or other resources than does using it once, so digitization thus permits the reuse of the image at several fixed places in a text. Hypertextualization permits the image to be called up from numerous points as the reader finds its presence of use. In WWW viewers, which temporarily store images downloaded from a network in a cache, reusing the same image takes much less time than did obtaining it in the first place.

Finally, translating a book into an electronic environment adds capacities not possible in print. Already available are hypermedia translations of print texts in mathematics, the sciences, music, history, and the arts using sound, animation, video, and simulation environments. Let us look at some instances of these while proposing some general rules for the use of sound and motion within alphanumeric text.

Assuming that you have a text that demands hypertextualization, how should you proceed? My experience converting several books and a dozen articles into various hypermedia systems may be instructive, and we can draw on it to create some general guidelines. Furthermore, since all these electronified books exist in two or more different hypertext environments, my experience can illustrate the degree to which minor differences in hard- and software influence hypertextualization.

First, one has to obtain an accurate digital version of the text to be converted. For my earlier books and articles, written before I began to work with computing, I used OminPage Professional, software for scanning text and then interpreting the resultant image into alphabetic characters—an often time-consuming process. Since I had written the first version of this book in Microsoft Word, working with it proved much easier. Converting the text for Intermedia required only saving it in a particular format (RTF—rich text format) and then creating links within Intermedia. Working in Storyspace proved even easier, because when it imports Word documents it automatically translates footnotes into linked lexias; the one chapter translated in HTML used the Storyspace export function to create a basic linked working text to which I then added header and footer icons. The DynaText version required adding SGML tags and manually adding codes for links.

In adapting the printed texts for all four kinds of hypertext systems, I found I had to make decisions about the appropriate length of lexias. In each case, I took chapters already divided into sections and created additional subdivisions. Whereas print technology emphasizes the capacity of language to form a linear stream of text that moves unrelentingly forward, hypermedia encourages branching and creating multiple routes to the same point. Hypertextualizing a document therefore involves producing a text composed of individual segments joined to others in multiple ways and by multiple routes. Hypermedia encourages the conception of documents in terms of separate brief reading units. Hypermedia permits linear linking but encourages parallel, rather than linear, arguments. Such structures necessarily require a more active reader. When creating hypermedia documents, one must bear in mind these characteristics of the medium, which derive from linked reading units. Therefore, when constructing webs, conceive the text units as brief passages, in order to take maximal advantage of the linking capacities of hypermedia.

Whatever its ultimate effect on new scholarly and creative writing, hypermedia today frequently contains text transferred from printed books. Such materials combine the two technologies of writing, and anyone preparing hypermedia documents confronts the problem of how best to preserve the integrity of the printed text, which may be a literary, philosophical, or other work whose overall structure plays an important role in its effect. The basic question that must be answered by someone placing a text created for print technology into hypermedia is Can one divide the original into reading units shorter than those in which it appeared in a book, or does such presentation violate its integrity? Some literary works, such as sonnet sequences or Pascal's *Pensées,* seem easily adapted to hypermedia, since they originally have the form of brief sections, but other works do not seem adaptable without violence to the original. Therefore, when adapting documents created for book technology, do not violate the original organization. When the text naturally divides into sections, though, these can provide the basis of text blocks, and one should take advantage of the presence of discrete subsections and other elements that are amenable to hypertextualization. However, the hy-

permedia version must contain linkages between previous and following sections to retain a sense of the original organization.

Converting Foot- and Endnotes. The treatment of notes in these four hypertext
versions of this book provides an object lesson in the complexities of working
in a new kind of writing environment. It reminds us, in particular, how specific
writing strategies depend upon a combination of equipment and often apparently trivial features of individual systems, some of which militate against
what seem to be intrinsic qualities of hypertext. For example, as we have
already observed in "Reconfiguring Text," hypertextualization tends to destroy the rigid opposition between main and subsidiary text, thereby potentially either removing notes as a form of text or else demanding that we
create multiple forms of them. Certainly, in hypertextualizing some of my
own works, longer foot- and endnotes containing substantive discussions became lexias in their own right.

Briefer notes that contain bibliographical citations embody a more complex problem. If one wishes the hypertext version of a printed original to
remain as close as possible to it, then simply converting notes into linked
lexias makes sense in certain kinds of hypertext systems but not in others.
This approach, which produces an axially structured hypertext, works well in
systems like Storyspace that follow such note-links in a split second, permit
opening several windows at once, and permit authors to save the location of
such windows. Even here one must be careful not to produce an absurd result: Storyspace automatically converts notes in Word into linked lexias, and
retains the then-irrelevant superscript number. Not only does it prove difficult
to select a single tiny character with a mouse, but, more important, numbered
notes only make sense when readers will consult them in sequence, and hypertextualizing them destroys that sequence. (When I convert notes this way
in Storyspace, I paste a more suitable text anchor in place of the superscript
number, removing it.)

However retrograde such direct translation of notes into hypertext might
seem, it can work perfectly well in systems like Storyspace, DynaText, and
Microcosm that both open note windows with extreme rapidity and permit
multiple windows to be open simultaneously. Direct translation of notes
makes no sense, however, in WWW translations of print documents, since
following links on the Web takes considerably longer. Furthermore, because
most HTML viewers replace a single text window with another, when readers
follow a link and discover a simple bibliographical citation, they have to wait
to reload the main document, whereas users of these other systems either

encounter the note to the side of the main text window or only have to click it shut to keep reading. Several obvious solutions to the problem of translating notation in WWW present themselves. First, convert all bibliographical notes to the current MLA in-text citation, linking all such citations to a list of references. Second, one might use a particular icon for bibliographical citations, thus creating a form of typed link (something we did in the first DynaText version of this book). Third, using Netscape frames, one can dedicate a portion of the page to such information.

In addition to dividing a print text into sections, adapting notes and bibliography, and adding header and footer icons, hypertextualizing a document involves adding features and materials that would be impractical or impossible in a printed version. Thus, as I have suggested above, the Storyspace, Microcosm, and WWW versions of both my Pre-Raphaelite materials and *Hypertext* contain a great many links that serve as cross-references and which provide additional paths through the text, and they have additional images, too. These webs also have elements such as multiple overviews that permit traversing them in ways difficult, or impossible, in a print version. The Intermedia, Storyspace, and DynaText translations of *Hypertext* all contain overviews for both critical theory and hypertext, and the Storyspace and Intermedia versions also have added ones for information technology, scribal culture, individual theorists, and so on.

Perhaps the most obvious difference—in addition to links—between the hypertext and print versions is size: the way links produce an open-ended, changing, multiply authored Velcro-text appears nowhere more clearly than in the fact that so much more material appears in *Hypertext in Hypertext* than in the print version. Once I created Intermedia and Storyspace versions for my course on hypertext and literary theory, my students interacted with them as active, even aggressive readers who could and did add links, comments, and their own subwebs to the larger web into which the print has version has transformed itself. Within a few years the classroom version contained five hundred of their interventions, criticizing, expanding, and commenting upon the text, often in ways that take it in very different directions than I had intended. I added some fifty of these new lexias to *Hypertext in Hypertext;* it also contains entries on individual theories and theorists from *The Johns Hopkins Guide to Literary Theory and Criticism,* edited by Michael Groden and Martin Kreiswirth, as well materials by Gregory Ulmer and Jacques Derrida. To these materials, we added, with permission, some of Malcom Bradbury's parodies of critical theory and all the reviews the book had received by the time the hypertext version went into production. These new lexias, which constitute a subweb of their own, serve to insert other voices, not always in agreement with mine, into the expanded text.

Because the planned electronic version of this second edition will appear on a CD-ROM rather than a pair of floppy disks, as did the first, it will have approximately one hundred times as much room. Therefore, I plan to include not only many color images but also webs in a number of environments and examples of sound, animated text, and motion, including dozens of student projects. Throughout, the principle of selection will be a cardinal rule of hypertext adaptation—use materials only when they serve a purpose and not just because you have them. Hypertext writing, in other words, should be driven by needs and not by technology.

Rules for Dynamic Data in Hypermedia. The preceding pages have focused upon writing hypertext with essentially static forms of data—words, images, diagrams, and their combinations—as opposed to kinetic or dynamic information, which includes animation and sound (animal cries, human speech, music). The essential difference between dynamic and static data is the former's time-boundedness. Speech or visual movement potentially immerses readers in a linear process or progression over which they have relatively less control than they do over static data, such as a passage of writing. One can stop and start one's reading at any point—when the phone rings, a child cries, or a thought strikes one. Turning one's attention away from time-bound linear media, in contrast, throws one out of one's position within a linear stream, and this place cannot be recovered, as it can with writing, simply by turning attention back to the text, since one's point, or location, or place within the text has moved on. Therefore, when one follows a link from a text discussing, say, mitosis to digitized animation of a cell dividing or from a work of criticism to a scene from Shakespeare, one cues a process. Such dynamic data places the reader in a relatively passive role and turns hypermedia into a broadcast, rather than an interactive, medium.

System designers and hypermedia authors therefore have to empower readers in at least two ways. First, they must permit readers to stop the reading process and exit the environment easily. Second, they must indicate that particular links lead to dynamic data. One may use labels or icons for this purpose, and one may also connect the link indicator to an additional document, such as a menu or command box, that shows users precisely the kind of process information they can activate. A control panel that permits the reader to manipulate the process to the extent of replaying all or part of a sequence makes the reader more active.

Many CD-ROMs employ sound and motion to present material that could have been conveyed more efficiently and more enjoyably as text. Using the talking heads approach, in which someone filmed from the chest or neck upward faces outward from the margin of the screen and talks to the "reader," can occasionally prove an effective strategy. However, this device expends two kinds of valuable resources: memory storage capacity and, because it occupies time, the reader's patience, or at least forbearance. One must allow readers to stop talking heads in midsequence. (Voyager's *Freak Show* CD-ROM makes a witty play on this capability by having its Master of Ceremonies or Ringmaster respond with different expressions of annoyance each time we cut him off in midsentence.) Too many creators of HTML and CD-ROM materials seem grossly unaware that one of the key advantages of written language lies precisely in the abstractness and indirection that permit communication of important information with great economy.

Nonetheless, there are applications for which sound and moving images convey information far more efficiently than verbal text. In *Prints and Visual Communication,* William Ivins demonstrated decades ago how certain key sciences and technologies could not develop until exact repeatability of fixed visual information became available, since without the appropriate technology, the equivalent of scribal drift crippled the transfer of information. Think how difficult following Euclid's reasoning was before printed diagrams, how impossible describing the color and shape of plants and animals! One wonders what the effects will be of similarly making sound and motion available in individually read documents.

Microsoft's *Art Gallery* (created by Ben Rubinstein of Cognitive Applications in Brighton, England) shows the fundamental value of such resources when properly employed to answer to specific needs. Opening the first screen of a series discussing an individual artist, one encounters an icon in the form of a loudspeaker next to the artist's name; clicking upon it produces a recorded voice that pronounces that name. This feature represents an effective, convenient use of resources on several counts: it requires little time, is easy to carry out, and is easily repeated.

Similarly, the *Art Gallery*'s animations show how effective even simple animated forms can be when well conceived. One use, exemplified in its discussion of Rubens' *Peace and War,* guides the viewer through the picture's iconography by reducing portions of the work to monochrome and then selectively restoring color to specific regions while also adding captions to them. Other animation screens use moving lines and geometrical shapes to explain optics and composition. The screen explaining the camera obscura

Adoration of the Kings (Tondo)

Analysing the Composition

The architecture leads our eye from foreground to background and back again. This compositional device derives from his training with Filippo Lippi, himself a great narrative painter.

The architecture has been constructed on the panel with a system of incised lines. There are also lines ruled in the sky on the right. This implies that Botticelli originally thought of placing extra architectural elements on the right hand side.

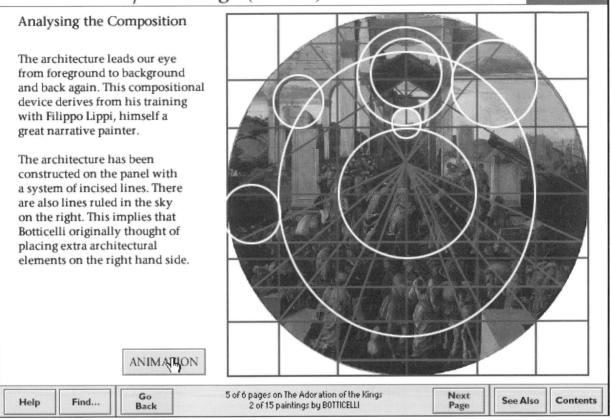

ANIMATION

| Help | Find... | Go Back | 5 of 6 pages on The Adoration of the Kings
2 of 15 paintings by BOTTICELLI | Next Page | See Also | Contents |

Figure 22. An Exemplary Use of Animation. The *Microsoft Art Gallery* makes an especially effective use of color and animation in its compositional analysis of Botticelli's *Adoration of the Kings*. This screen shot shows a monochrome version of the screen at the end of the animation. (Copyright National Gallery, London. Used by permission.)

linked to the Vermeer section uses moving lines to show inversion of the optical image.

A far more elaborate use of animation, involving colored lines, appears in the screen entitled "Analysing the Composition" in a study of Botticelli's *Adoration of the Kings* (Figure 22). Text to the left of the image explains:

The architecture leads our eye from foreground to background and back again. This compositional device derives from his training with Filippo Lippi, himself a great narrative painter.

The architecture has been constructed on the panel with a system of incised lines.

There are also lines ruled in the sky on the right. This implies that Botticelli originally thought of placing extra architectural elements on the right hand side.

Selecting an icon labeled "animation" (in the CD-ROM version one uses a mouse to do so, in the National Gallery installation a touch screen) prompts two red lines, one from the upper right of the circular image, another from the upper left, to move toward picture center, meet there, and continue until they reach the outer diameter of the painting. Five similar pairs of red lines move from the bottom of the picture upward, meeting at the same central point, describing narrow slices of the picture; two of these pairs of lines continue until they strike the tondo's upper edge, at which point they change direction and move toward each other. Then, one blue line bisects the picture vertically and another horizontally. Immediately afterward, additional blue lines move across and down the screen, creating a 6-by-6 rectangular grid. Finally, a series of white circles appears—first two concentric ones around the work's center and then six additional smaller ones elsewhere. The time and effort required to follow my description demonstrates the obvious superiority of animation for conveying this kind of information.

In explaining Nicholas Poussin's borrowing in *The Adoration of the Golden Calf* from one of his own earlier works, *A Bacchanalian Revel,* the *Art Gallery* exemplifies another effective use of moving images. Again, an accompanying text prepares readers for the animation, in this case informing them that the artist "took the design for the dancers from another of his paintings of this period, but turned them 180 degrees." This brilliantly conceived animation begins by making changes simultaneously in the juxtaposed representations of both *The Adoration of the Golden Calf* and *A Bacchanalian Revel.* As a group of four revelers detaches itself from the latter, which appears at the left, the group of figures in the other painting becomes rendered in monochrome. As the revelers move from one picture to the other, the group rotates 180 degrees, then fits in place in the scene from Exodus.

Yet other *Art Gallery* animations make especially effective use of the linear sequence intrinsic to animation and video. For example, in discussing *The Portrait of the Duke of Wellington,* the *Art Gallery* animates, as the accompanying text explains, "the sequences of changes Goya made" to his work. In another example, to explain the use of anamorphosis ("elongated perspectival distortion") in Hans Holbein's *The Ambassadors, Art Gallery* takes a different tack and moves the vantage point of the viewer. The animation screen first shows us an image of the painting hung alongside a staircase, explaining that "the bizarre subject at the sitters' feet is a skull. Its form has been stretched sideways. . . . The corrected shape of the skull can be seen from a particular point. If the painting were hung on a staircase, viewers would see the skull go through its cycle of distortion as they walked by." Appropriately, in a series of three jumps the animation moves us to the foot of the stairs and then up until the image of a skull—a memento mori—appears. As this example suggests, one does not need full-motion video, much less completely immersive virtual reality, to introduce simulation environments to hypermedia documents. Although an exquisite, richly textured graphic presentation of the proposed setting for Holbein's painting that had many historically verifiable details might prove elegant, it would not make its point more effectively.

Another instance of such efficient use of very rudimentary simulated environment appears in the *Art Gallery*'s discussion of Titian's *Bacchus and Ariadne*. Its reconstruction of the Camerino d'Albastro in Ferrara Castle takes the form of a bird's-eye view of the room with ceiling removed. The animation appears in the upper part of the screen above snapshots of *Bacchus and Ariadne* and four other works, by Bellini, Dosso Dossi, and Titian himself. The simple animation, really a very basic slide show, drops one down into the room, first showing the view from right to left and then from the opposite side. Again, using text effectively and knowing what one wants to accomplish prove more important than elaborate graphics.

Art Gallery's intertwining of static with dynamic media demonstrates how effectively the two can work together if basic principles of organization and design are followed. Nonetheless, since it presents the holdings of a traditional museum, most of its information is static, taking the form of words and images, and it does not offer examples of more time-bound forms of hyperwriting. Now let us look at a project that tries to make accessible the holdings of a museum containing chiefly, not unique static objects, but sound and film records. Gunnar Liestøl's *Kon-Tiki* CD-ROM extends the range of hypermedia rhetoric and stylistics by incorporating devices of orientation, navigation, arrival, and departure suitable to a video collection. It does not abandon title screens, overviews, essays, and link labels but builds upon them, creating methods appropriate to sound and motion.

Viewing the *Kon-Tiki* CD-ROM, after a title screen that changes, identifying in different combinations the work's publisher, title, editor, and production company, we encounter the multimedia equivalent of a book's preface— a screen on which appears an image of the Kon-Tiki in midocean. Then, against the sky, appears the first paragraph of Heyerdahl's two-paragraph summary of his life's work, which in the context seems especially appropriate, especially hypertextual: "The ocean currents run like salt rivers from coast to coast," his voice intones, "and tie the continents together instead of isolating them from each other." The second brief paragraph appears while he is still reading or reciting the first. We hear him read the second paragraph and then an animation of his signature appears along with the scratchy sound of pen on paper. After a screen containing a brief conceptual overview of his projects appears and then fades away, the first of several overviews presents itself (see Figure 18). Beneath the words "Kon-Tiki Interactive," against an image of the sea in soft focus, we find a globe representing the earth surrounded by seven small circles, each containing a photograph, the labels reading "Tigris," "Ra I & II," "Tucume," "Galapagos," "Easter Island," "Kon-Tiki," and "Heyerdahl." A deep musical tone sounds, and the globe turns. Then it stops, a line of white dots moves across the globe showing the route of the Tigris expedition, the still photograph in the "Tigris" icon transforms into a video clip, and a voice-over sums up the purpose and accomplishments of the expedition. At this point, readers may choose to learn more about the Tigris expedition, or wait until all the overviews have been previewed. Clicking upon any one of the circular items, which elegantly combine the functions of icon, preview, and conceptual overview, halts sound and animation and produces an overview for that topic.

Selecting the Tigris overview, for example, presents a large rectangular photograph from the expedition against the background of a map charting its route. This image animates, providing an introduction to the expedition. Three circular icons of the size and kind we have seen in the previous screen appear to the right and below the large rectangular one. Clicking upon any one produces multiple text screens, each bearing both detailed information and links indicated by blocks of contrasting color surrounding the anchors.

Readers can navigate this elegant project in a number ways, one of the most interesting of which for our purposes involves using the unlabeled icon, a mask or a gray shield (see Figures 18 and 23), that appears in the lower right-hand corner of every screen. Moving the mouse to the region of this icon halts all sound and video while simultaneously causing the face to flip over, revealing six choices: "Back," "Navigate," "Overview," "Start," "Help," and "Quit." Choosing navigate produces a menu of four choices; "Intro," "Start," "Overview," and "Retrace." Choosing "Overview" opens, not the original animated circular overview, but one shaped more like a flow chart. Selecting any of the items produces a menu of additional choices, each a segment of a narrative or exposition necessary for it (as shown in Figure 20).

Figure 23. The Help Function in the Kon-Tiki CD-ROM. Moving the mouse near the gray stone shield halts all sound and video while simultaneously revealing a menu of choices. (Used by permission of Gyldendal Publishers.)

Art Gallery and *Kon-Tiki Interactive* exemplify particularly effective, even exemplary, hypermedia replacements for the book—but at first glance, only for a single specific kind of book, the museum catalogue, a form whose characteristic combination of illustration, cross-references, and clear hierarchical organization seems especially well suited to electronic presentation. Like the dictionary and encyclopedia, the museum catalogue has a clear, easily perceived organization that militates against reader disorientation. Furthermore, the museum catalogue obviously benefits from the kinds of electronic enhancements offered by digital word, sound, and image: cross-references—

those simple pre-electronic links—work well as electronic links, which simultaneously enforce the catalogue's organization while also enhancing it by providing readers with additional ways through the information. Digital images permit an especially effective and efficient use of visual resources, since they allow the nearly instantaneous reuse of the same image in multiple sizes and scales, a feature of which *Art Gallery* takes fine advantage. When well used, as they are in these two products, sound valuably extends the catalogue's text, and animation its static illustrations.

The Voyager version of *Who Built America?* exemplifies an amplified textbook, one that adds a great deal of primary material in the form of text, image, sound, and film. Taking advantage of the storage capacities of the CD-ROM (which can hold more than 500 times the information found in the usual book), the author-designers have transformed the by-now venerable—and often scorned—textbook. In particular, they have redressed the way textbooks necessarily reductively present complex issues, by adding large amounts of additional interpretative commentary and, more important, many more primary materials. In so doing they have managed to extend students' notions of the materials involved in historical research while transforming a solid textbook into something like a miniature electronic library.

Like *Art Gallery, Who Built America?* extends the capacities of the codex book by adding to it additional forms or modes of information. A further extension of hypermedia writing occurs in two works that add yet another form of dynamic information technology essentially unavailable in books. The first, the courseware for a multidimensional mathematics course created by Thomas Banchoff, professor of mathematics at Brown University, combines simulation with the main text. While reading about certain kinds of equations, the student reader can examine the graphic presentation of them, much as one can in an ordinary printed textbook. Here, however, the student can add different values or otherwise reconfigure the variables, thus making immediately clear the effect of such action by visualizing data.

Electronic texts that similarly intend to develop nonverbal skills have been created for the arts. Kristin Hooper Woolsey, Scott Kim, and Gayle Curtis's *VizAbility,* which MetaDesign West created for PWS Publishing, takes the form of a CD-ROM version of a textbook originally created to develop visual thinking skills. Divided into subjects such as imagining, seeing, drawing, diagramming, and environment, this electronic textbook is designed with the expectation that its users, in addition to working on screen, will work off screen with a pencil and sketching pad. The on-screen materials consist of

introductions to a subject, such as contour drawing and perspective, demon-
strations in the form of QuickTime movies that contain sound and motion,
and examples that the user can consult. In addition, this amplified textbook
uses animation and simulation to do things a printed text cannot. For instance, after an introduction to creating multiple-point perspective and off-
screen exercises, the user can develop both seeing and drawing skills by trying to move a cube to a particular location on three perspective guide lines.
If the reader places the cube incorrectly, it simply moves back to its starting
point on the screen; if he or she places it correctly, it clicks into place and a
tone sounds indicating success. Many of these exercises, like those for visualizing the hidden surfaces of various three-dimensional objects, show the major value of such technology in developing skills or conveying information
that the printed book cannot.

Hypertext as Collage

Most current examples of hypertext take the form of texts
originally produced by the hypertext author in and for another
medium, generally print. In contrast, this section describes a
type of writing born of hypertext, though it also incorporates materials
ultimately derived from printed books.

On Tuesday, June 7, 1994, at 17:01:54 Eastern Standard Time, Pierre
Joris, a faculty member at the State University of New York, posted some
materials about collage on a electronic discussion group called Technoculture.[1] Joris wished to share with readers in this e-conference a gathering of
texts, "Collage between Writing and Painting," that he had delivered as a
combination of an academic paper and performance art while in graduate
school. His materials seemed to cry out for a hypertext presentation, and so,
after moving them from my mailbox to a file on the Brown University IBM
mainframe, I transferred them—in the jargon, "downloaded" them—into a
single document via a phone line to a Macintosh whirring away in my study
at home. Next, I opened them in Microsoft Word, and, passage by passage,
quickly copied the individual elements, pasting each into a separate writing
space or lexia in a new Storyspace web, and then linked them together. Along
the way, I created the following opening screen (or analogue to a book's
title page):

COLLAGE BETWEEN WRITING AND PAINTING

Pierre Joris

George P. Landow

being an assemblage starring

Kurt Schwitters & Tristan Tzara
with special guest appearances by
Georges Braque &
Pablo Picasso

and also featuring
dedicated to . . .

This opening screen, which also serves as a combination overview, information map, contents page, and index, contains links from the obvious places—such as all the proper names it lists. Clicking upon "Collage" takes one either to one possible terminal point of the web or to a definition of the term from *Le Petit Robert*. Since this dictionary definition, which mentions Picasso and Braque, serves as another ready-made overview or crossroads document, I linked various words to it, permitting readers to traverse Joris's materials in multiple ways. "Collage," for example, leads to a dozen-and-a-half mentions of the term, and the names of the artists link to illustrations of their work. Because I created this web largely as an experiment and not for publication, I did not have to worry at the moment about copyright issues, and I therefore scanned monochrome images of Braque's *Le Courrier* and Picasso's *Still Life with Chair Caning* and linked them to the names of the artists. At the same time, I added H. W. Janson's discussions of collage, linking them as well. Finally, I created a list of thirty authors whose statements Joris had included in "Collage between Writing and Painting," linking this list to the phrase "and also featuring" on the title screen.

At this point, some of the similarities between hypertext and collage will have become obvious. Having first appropriated Joris's materials by placing them in a web and then adding to them materials that they seemed to demand, I found that, like all hypertexts, it had become open-ended, a kind of Velcro-text to which various kinds of materials began attaching themselves. First, I included the discussion of Derrida and appropriation that appears on pages 34–35, after which I added definitions of hypertext and a list of qualities that it shares with collage. Next, I added several dozen screenshots, or pictures of how the screen appears while reading, of various hypertext webs;

these came from a since-published web that served as an introduction to a hypertext anthology that I edited, *Writing at the Edge.* Then, I added a dozen photographs, each involving issues of representation, illusion, simulation, or subject and ground. Finally, I added a new title page: *Hypertext and Collage: being in part, an appropriation of "Collage between Writing and Painting."*

After using this web to deliver my contribution to the August 1995 Digital Dialectic Conference at the Art Center College of Design, in Pasadena, California, I discovered I would have to transform it into a more or less traditional essay if it were to be part of the planned conference proceedings volume. Those pages thus represented a translation of *Hypertext and Collage.* When I write "translation," I cannot help thinking of the Italian maxim "traddutore traditore" or "translator equals traitor." Converting the essay from one information technology to another, I continually encountered the kind of reduction that one encounters when translating—or representing—something in three (or more) dimensions within a two-dimensional medium. An examination of the differences between the two versions will take us a way into understanding the reasons for describing hypertext as collage writing.

The on-line version of the *Oxford English Dictionary* defines collage, which it traces to the French words for pasting and gluing, as an "abstract form of art in which photographs, pieces of paper, newspaper cuttings, string, etc., are placed in juxtaposition and glued to the pictorial surface; such a work of art." The *Britannica Online* more amply describes it as the

artistic technique of applying manufactured, printed, or "found" materials, such as bits of newspaper, fabric, wallpaper, etc., to a panel or canvas, frequently in combination with painting. In the 19th century, *papiers collés* were created from papers cut out and put together to form decorative compositions. In about 1912–13 Pablo Picasso and Georges Braque extended this technique, combining fragments of paper, wood, linoleum, and newspapers with oil paint on canvas to form subtle and interesting abstract or semiabstract compositions. The development of the collage by Picasso and Braque contributed largely to the transition from Analytical to Synthetic Cubism.

This reference work, which adds that the term was first used to refer to Dada and Surrealist works, lists Max Ernst, Kurt Schwitters, Henri Matisse, Joseph Cornell, and Robert Rauschenberg as artists who have employed the medium.

In *The History of Art,* H. W. Janson, who explains the importance of collage by locating it within the history of Cubism, begins by describing Picasso's *Still Life* of 1911–12: "Beneath the still life emerges a piece of imitation chair caning, which has been pasted onto the canvas, and the picture is 'framed' by a piece of rope. This intrusion of alien materials has a most re-markable effect: the abstract still life appears to rest on a real surface (the chair caning) as on a tray, and the substantiality of this tray is further empha sized by the rope." According to Janson, Picasso and Braque turned from brush and paint to "contents of the wastepaper basket" because collage per-mitted them to explore representation and signification by contrasting what we in the digital age would call the real and the virtual. They did so because they discovered that the items that make up a collage, "'outsiders' in the world of art," work in two manners, or produce two contrary effects. First, "they have been shaped and combined, then drawn or painted upon to give them a representational meaning, but they do not lose their original iden-tity as scraps of material, 'outsiders' in the world of art. Thus their function is both to represent (to be part of an image) and to present (to be them-selves)" (522–23).

Hypertext writing shares many key characteristics with these works of Picasso, Braque, and other Cubists, particularly their qualities of juxtaposition and appropriation. Some of these qualities appear when one compares the hypertext and print versions of my discussion. First of all, despite my division of the print essay into several sections and the use of plates that a reader might inspect in different sequences, the essay really only allows one efficient way of proceeding through it. In contrast, the original hypertext version per-mits different readers to traverse it according to their needs and interests. Thus, someone well versed in twentieth-century art history might wish to glance only briefly at the materials on collage before concentrating on the materials about hypertext. Someone more acquainted with hypertext could concentrate upon the materials about collage. Others might wish to begin with one portion of the discussion, and then, using available links, return repeatedly to the same examples, which often gather meaning according to the contexts in which they appear.

Another difference between the two forms of "my" discussion of this sub-ject involves the length of quoted material and the way the surrounding texts relate it to the argument as a whole. Take, for example, the passage I quoted above from Janson's *History of Art*. In the Storyspace version the passage is several times longer than in the print one, and it appears without any intro-duction. The object here is to let the quoted, appropriated author speak for himself, or, rather, to permit his text to speak for itself without being summa-rized, translated, distorted by an intermediary voice. To write in this man-ner—that is to say, to copy, to appropriate—seems suited to an electronic environment, an environment in which text can be reproduced, reconfigured, and moved with very little expenditure of effort. In this environment, further-more, such a manner of proceeding also seems more honest: the text of the Other may butt up against that by someone else; it may even crash against it. But it does seem to retain more of its own voice. In print, on the other hand, one feels constrained to summarize large portions of another's text, if only to demonstrate one's command (understanding) of it and to avoid giving the appearance of that one has infringed copyright.

These two differences suggest some of the ways in which even a rudi-mentary form of hypertext reveals the qualities of collage. By permitting one so easily to make connections between texts and between text and images, the electronic link encourages one to think in terms of connections. To state the obvious: one cannot make connections without having things to connect. Those linkable items must not only have some qualities that make the writer want to connect them, they must also exist in separation, apart, divided. As Terence Harpold has pointed out in "Threnody," most writers on hypertext concentrate on the link, but all links simultaneously both bridge and maintain separation (174). This double effect of linking appears in the way it inevitably produces juxtaposition, concatenation, and assemblage. If part of the plea-sure of linking arises in the act of joining two different things, then this aes-thetic of juxtaposition inevitably tends towards catachresis and difference for their own ends and for the effect of surprise, sometimes surprised pleasure, that they produce.

On this level, then, all hypertext webs, no matter how simple, how lim-ited, inevitably take the form of textual collage, for they inevitably work by juxtaposing different texts, often appropriating them as well. Such effects ap-pear frequently in hypertext fiction. Joshua Rappaport's "The Hero's Face" (one of the webs included in *Writing at the Edge*) uses links, for example, to replace what in earlier literary writing would have been an element internal to the text; that is, the link establishes a symbolic as well as a literal relation-ship between two elements in a document. In reading "The Hero's Face," after making one's way through a series of lexias about the members of a rock band, their experiences on tour, and their musical rivalry—all of which might seem little more than matters of contemporary banality—one follows a link from a discussion of the narrator's seizing the lead during one perfor-mance and finds oneself in what at first appears to be a different literary world, that of the Finnish epic, the Kalelava.

Following Rappaport's link has several effects. First, readers find them-selves in a different, more heroic age of gods and myth, and then, as they realize that the gods are engaged in a musical contest that parallels the rock group's, they also see that the contemporary action resonates with the ancient one, thereby acquiring greater significance as it appears epic and archetypal. This single link in "Hero's Face," in other words, functions as a new form of both allusion and recontextualization. Juxtaposing two apparently unconnected and unconnectable texts produces the pleasure of recognition.

The combination of paying literary homage to a predecessor text while claiming to rival it has been a part of literature in the West at least since the ancient Greeks. But the physical separation between texts characteristic of earlier, nonelectronic information technologies required that their forms of linking—allusion and contextualization—employ indicators within the text, such as verbal echoing or the elaborate use of parallel structural patterns (such as invocations or catalogues). Hypertext, which permits authors to use traditional methods, also permits them to create these effects simply by connecting texts with links.

Hypertext here appears as textual collage—"textual" referring to alphanumeric information—but more sophisticated forms of this medium can produce visual collage as well. Any hypertext system (or, for that matter, any computer program or environment) that displays multiple windows produces such collage effects. Multiwindow systems, such as Microcosm, Storyspace, Intermedia, Sepia, and the like, have the capacity to save the size and position of individual windows. This capacity leads to the discovery of what seems a universal rule at this early stage of e-writing: authors will employ any feature or capacity that can be varied and controlled to convey meaning. All elements in a hypertext system that can be manipulated are potentially signifying elements. Controlled variation inevitably becomes semiosis. Hypertext authors like Stuart Moulthrop have thus far written poems in the interstices of their writing environments, creating sonnets in link menus and sentences in the arrangements of titles of lexias in the Storyspace view.

Inevitably, therefore, authors make use of screen layout, tiled windows, and other features to . . . write. For example, in an informational hypertext, such as *The "In Memoriam" Web,* tiling of documents constructs a kinetic collage whose juxtaposition and assembling of different elements permits easy reference to large amounts of information without the information's becoming intrusive. In addition to reading windows in their set positions, users can also move windows to compare two, three, or more poems that refer to one another in this proto-hypertextual poem.

Turning to another work of hypertext fiction, one sees that in Nathan Marsh's "Breath of Sighs and Falling Forever" lexias place themselves across and around the surface of the desktop, making the screen layout support the

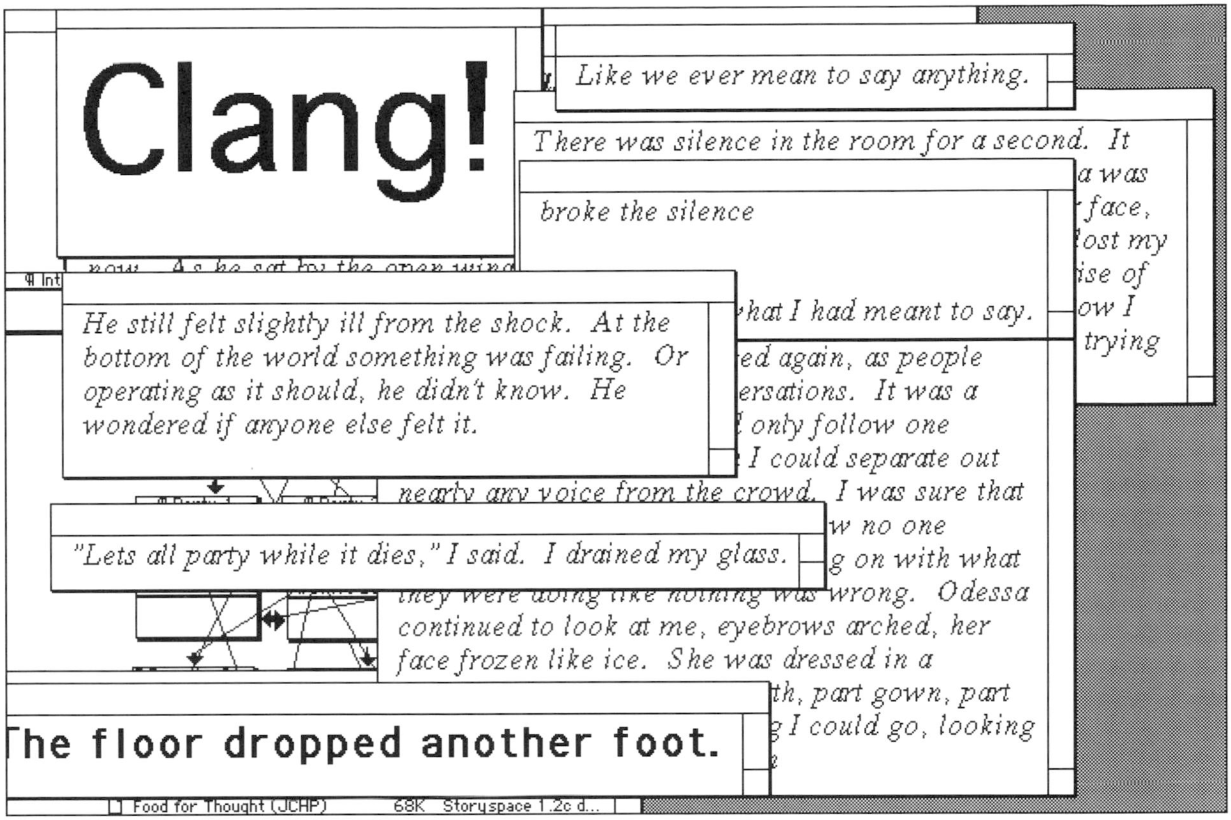

Figure 24. Digital Collage in Hypertext Narrative: Nathan Marsh's *Breath of Sighs and Falling Forever*. Marsh has arrayed the texts that make up his web so that some lexias show in their entirety, others only in part. In making their way through this fiction, readers encounter multiple narrative lines. The web continually changes the juxtaposition of texts as the reader navigates in the text. In the course of reading, one is repeatedly returned to the lexia "Clang!," which opens with the sound of an explosion, but the meaning of the word changes according to the lexia that one has read immediately before encountering it.

narrative as one crosses and recrosses the tale at several points (Figure 24). In *The "In Memoriam" Web* hypertext technology—the collage effect of tiling, separate windows, and juxtaposed text—was used to shed light on a work created for the world of print (see Figure 9). In "Breath of Sighs," the story arises from the medium itself. In making their way through this fiction, readers encounter multiple narrative lines and corollary narrative worlds both joined and separated by ambiguous events or phenomena. At certain points, readers cannot tell, for example, if one of the characters has experienced an earthquake tremor, a drug reaction, or a powerful illumination. Has the floor actually fallen, or are we supposed to take a character's experience as figurative? Certainly, one of the first lexias readers encounter could suggest any and all of these possibilities: "Andy paused for a second and let his senses adjust to the shock. The floor had been dropping all week now. As he sat by the open window and the frozen night air embraced the room, he realized that it was all part of the long slide down." Clicking upon this brief lexia leads one to the window "Clang!," which opens with a loud sound and displays its single word in eighty-point type. As one reads through "Breath of Sighs" one repeatedly returns to "Clang!" but finds that it changes its meaning according to the lexia that one has read immediately before encountering it.

As Marsh has arranged the texts that make up his web, some lexias show in their entirety, others only in part. As one reads through this web, one encounters a continually changing collage of juxtaposed texts. Two points about hypertext writing are illustrated by Marsh's web. First, such collage writing produces a new kind of reading, in which we must take into account not only the main text but also those that surround it. Second, because of this increasing importance of the spatial arrangement of individual lexias, writing has become visual as well as alphanumeric; or rather, since visual layout has always had a major impact on the way we read printed texts, perhaps it would be more accurate to say that hypertext authors, who have more control over layout than print authors, must write visually as well as alphanumerically. Marsh's web exemplifies a form of hypertext fiction that draws upon the collage qualities of a multiwindow system to generate much of its effect.

Despite interesting, even compelling, similarities, hypertext collage obviously differs crucially from that created by Picasso and Braque. Hypertext and hypermedia always exist as virtual, rather than physical, texts. Until digital computing, all writing consisted of making physical marks on physical surfaces. Digital words and images, in contrast, take the form of semiotic codes, and this fundamental fact about them leads to the defining qualities of digital infotechnology: virtuality, fluidity, adaptability, openness (or borderlessness), processabilty, infinite duplicablity, rapid portability, and finally, networkability. Digital text is virtual because we always encounter a virtual image, the simulacrum, of something stored in memory rather than any so-called text "itself" or physical instantiation of it. Digital text is fluid because, taking the form of codes, it can always be reconfigured, reformatted, rewritten. Digital text is hence infinitely adaptable to different needs and uses, and since it consists of codes that other codes can search, rearrange, and otherwise manipulate, digital text is also always open, borderless, unfinished and unfinishable, capable of infinite extension. Furthermore, since it takes the form of digital coding, it can easily be replicated without in any way disturbing the original coding or otherwise affecting it. Such replicability in turn permits digital text to be moved rapidly across great spaces, and this capacity has generated both new versions of old communication formats, such as the bulletin board, and entirely new forms of communication. Finally—at least for now—all the other qualities of digital textuality enable different texts (or lexias) to join together by means of electronic linking. Digitality, in other words, permits hypertextuality.

The connection of the fundamental virtuality of hypertext to the issue of collage becomes immediately clear when one recalls the history of collage and the reasons for its importance to Picasso, Braque, Schwitters, and other painters. As Janson explains, collage arose within the context of Cubism and had powerful effects because it offered a new approach to picture space. Facet Cubism, its first form, still retained "a certain kind of depth," and hence continued Renaissance perspectival picture space. "In collage Cubism, on the contrary, the picture space lies in front of the plane of the 'tray'; space is not created by illusionistic devices, such as modeling and foreshortening, but by the actual overlapping of layers of pasted materials" (522–23). The effect of Collage Cubism comes from the way it denies much of the recent history of Western painting, particularly that concerned with creating the effect of three-dimensional space on a two-dimensional surface. It does so by inserting some physically existing object, such as Picasso's chair caning and newspaper cuttings, onto and into a painted surface. Although that act of inclusion certainly redefines the function and effect of the three-dimensional object, the object nonetheless resists becoming a purely semiotic code and abrasively insists upon its own physicality.

The collage of Collage Cubism therefore depends for its effect upon a kind of juxtapositions not possible (or relevant) in the digital world—that between the physical and the semiotic. Both hypertext and painterly collage make use of appropriation and juxtaposition, but for better or worse the physical cannot be directly invoked within the digital information regime, for everything is mediated, represented, coded.

In a final example, "Sunset Montage" from my *Hypertext and Collage Web,* we move from this more traditional form of virtuality to that found in the world of digital information technology. In this lexia sections of all the images one may have seen in it (in whatever order) are repeated and blended with multiply repeated portions of a photograph of a sunset in Donegal, Ireland; yet the lexia also insists on the absence of any solid, physical ground: not only do different-sized versions of the same image appear to overlay one another, but in the upper center a square panel has moved aside, thus revealing what the eye reads as colored background or empty space. In this photographic collage or montage, appropriation and juxtaposition rule, but since all the elements and images are virtual, this lexia, like the entire web to which it contributes, does not permit us to distinguish (in the manner of Cubist collage) between virtual and real, illusion and reality.

"Sunset Montage" draws upon the secondary meaning of *montage* as photographic assemblage, pastiche, or, as the *OED* puts it, "the act or process of producing a composite picture by combining several different pictures or pictorial elements so that they blend with or into one another; a picture so produced." I titled this lexia "Sunset Montage" to distinguish the effect of photographic juxtaposition and assemblage from the painterly one, for in photography, as in computing, the contrast of physical surface and overlaying image does not appear. Upon hearing my assertion that hypertext should be thought of as collage-writing, Lars Hubrich, a student in my hypertext and literary theory course, remarked that he thought *montage* might be a better term than *collage*. He had in mind something like the first *OED* definition of *montage*, the "selection and arrangement of separate cinematographic shots as a consecutive whole; the blending (by superimposition) of separate shots to form a single picture; the sequence or picture resulting from such a process." Hubrich is correct in that, whereas *collage* emphasizes the stage effect of a multiwindowed hypertext system on a computer screen at any particular moment, *montage*, at least in its original cinematic meaning, places important emphasis upon sequence, and in hypertext one has to take into account the fact that one reads—one constructs—one's reading of a hypertext in time. Even though one can backtrack, take different routes through a web, and come upon the same lexia multiple times and in different orders, one nonetheless always experiences a hypertext as a changeable montage.

Hypertext writing, of course, does not coincide fully with either montage or collage. I do not chiefly employ these concepts to extend their history to digital realms, and, similarly, I am not much concerned to allay potential fears of this new form of writing by deriving it from earlier avant-garde work (though in another time and place either goal might provide the axis for a potentially interesting essay). Here I am more interested in helping us understand this new kind of hypertext writing as a mode that both

RECONFIGURING emphasizes and bridges gaps and that thereby inevitably becomes an art of
WRITING assemblage in which appropriation and catachresis rule. This is a new writing that brings with it implications for our conceptions of text as well as
of reader and author. It is a text in which new kinds of connections have
become possible.

Reconfiguring

Narrative

Approaches to Hypertext Fiction:

Some Opening Remarks

Not every digital narrative, we must remind ourselves, necessarily takes the form of hypertext. A case in point appears in Christy Sheffield Sanford's visually elegant World Wide Web fiction, *Safara in the Beginning* (1996), which the author describes as "a web-novel" written in the spirit of classical tragedy about "a young African princess taken as a slave from Senegal to Martinique." The opening screen, the first of twenty-one successive lexias, describes Sanford's design of each screen, explaining that to the left of the "main textual body, Bible quotations and natural history descriptions echo Old Testament Christianity and Animistic traditions at their point of contact: mythopoetization of nature." Essentially, Sanford works with the powers of digital information technology to add colors, images, and some motion to narrative, but the HTML links function solely to provide sequence. Among her twenty-one lexias, she includes what she describes as "five filmic scenes using the close-up, time-lapse and other cinematic effects. These techniques enable the conflict-crisis-resolution model to have conciseness and scope." These cinematic effects appear, not as full-motion video but as a kind of a film script, though Sanford's romantic tragedy does use occasional animations above and to the left of the main text spaces. I cite this elegant project not to criticize its lack of hypertextuality but to remind us that using the digital word and image, even on the World Wide Web, does not inevitably produce hypertextual narrative.

The examples of hypertext fiction at which we shall look in the following pages and have already examined in the earlier discussion of writing hypermedia suggest that, even in this early stage, hypertext has taken many forms, few of which grant readers the kind of power one expects in informational hypertext. As Michael Joyce, the first major author of hypertext fiction, has explained, the desire to create multiple stories out of a relatively small amount of alphanumeric text provided a major force in driving him to write *Afternoon:*

> I wanted, quite simply, to write a novel that would change in successive readings and to make those changing versions according to the connections that I had for some time naturally discovered in the process of writing and that I wanted my readers to share. In my eyes, paragraphs on many different pages could just as well go with paragraphs on many other pages, although with different effects and for different purposes. All that kept me from doing so was the fact that, in print at least, one paragraph inevitably follows another. It seemed to me that if I, as author, could use a computer to move paragraphs about, it wouldn't take much to let readers do so according to some scheme I had predetermined. (*Of Two Minds,* 31)

From one point of view, then, such an approach merely intensifies the agenda of high modernism, using linking to grant the author even more power.

Other authors take a self-consciously postmodern approach, using the multiplicity offered by branching links to create a combinatorial fiction that in some ways seems the electronic fulfillment of the French group, Oulipo. For example, in its forty-nine fictional lexias Tom McHarg's *The Late-Nite Maneuvers of the Ultramundane* attempts to "veer toward a narrative . . . not entirely dependent upon linearity, causality, and probable characterization" ("On Ultramundane" in Landow, *Writing at the Edge*). McHarg creates seven lexias for each day of the week, each a variation or transformation of the other. Choosing the first Monday, for example, the reader encounters the following narrative (which represents the first half of the lexia):

> Dwight awoke at 3:15 a.m. to find his girlfriend, Johnette, attempting to conceal a bomb under his pillow. "You've woken me up," he said. "And I've discovered your treachery."
>
> "The only treachery is yours," said Johnette.
>
> "I'm only sleeping," said Dwight. "You're the one planting bombs."
>
> "Perhaps you deserve it," said Johnette.
>
> "But I love you," said Dwight.
>
> "Then why do you accuse me of treachery?" said Johnette.
>
> "It's obvious," said Dwight. "You planned to murder me as I lay here dreaming of our sex."
>
> "You weren't dreaming," said Johnette. "I was watching your eyes."
>
> "Perhaps not, but at least I wasn't trying to murder you," said Dwight.
>
> "I only meant to scare you into loving me more," said Johnette.

"With a bomb?" said Dwight.

"You need to love me a lot more," said Johnette.

Each variation introduces a different weapon, a different betrayal, as *Ultramundane* explores how "a fictional text must be stretched, skewered, and sliced if it is to exploit the freedoms and accept the responsibilities offered by hypertext technology and its new writing spaces." Thus, on the first Tuesday a friend stands at the foot of their bed with a gun, on the first Wednesday the hero's hair has all fallen out, and on Sunday Dwight returns to find their home on fire. Like *Afternoon, The Late-Nite Maneuvers of the Ultramundane* combines into different narratives, many about sex and violence, producing different effects according to the route one follows through it. Otherwise, this web, whose tone and content suggest the influence of Coover's print fiction, contrasts entirely with Joyce's work. My point here is not that one should prefer the crystalline richness and emotional intensity of *Afternoon* to McHarg's playful postmodern removed sense of literature as its own laboratory, or that *Ultramundane* is in some way more hypertextual. Rather, I wish to emphasize that, like fiction in print, that produced as linked lexias can take many forms.

In some, the author compounds his power; in others, such as that exemplified by Carolyn Guyer's *Quibbling,* the author willingly shares it with readers. Similarly, in some fictional webs, such as *Afternoon,* readers construct or discover essentially one main narrative; in others, like *Semio-Surf, Freak Show,* or *Ultramundane,* one comes upon either a cluster of entirely separate stories or one finds narrative segments out of which one weaves one or more stories. A third opposition appears between those stories that, however allusive, consist largely of fictional lexias, and those like *Patchwork Girl* and *Semio-Surf,* that weave together theory and nonfiction materials with the narrative. A fourth such opposition separates fictional hypertext entirely derived from the author's "own" writing and those, like *Patchwork Girl* and Stuart Moulthrop's *Forking Paths,* that their authors wrote to varying degrees in the interstices of other works.

Hypertext narrative clearly takes a wide range of forms best understood in terms of a number of axes, including those formed by degrees or ratios of (1) reader choice, intervention, and empowerment; (2) inclusion of extralinguistic texts (images, motion, sound); (3) complexity of network structure; and (4) degrees of multiplicity and variation in literary elements, such as plot, characterization, setting, and so forth. Following the lead of Deleuze and Guattari, I prefer to think of the organizing structures in terms of ranges, spectra, or axes along which one can array phenomena, rather than in terms of diametric oppositions, such as male-female or alphanumeric versus multimedia text. I avoid such polarities because, particularly in the case of hypertext fiction and poetry, they hinder analysis by exaggerating difference, overrating uniformity, and suppressing our abilities to perceive complex mixtures of qualities or tendencies. Another reason for emphasizing a spectrum of possibilities when discussing hypertext is that neither end of any particular spectrum is necessarily superior to the other. For example, hyperfiction that demands intervention by readers, or otherwise empowers them, will not on those grounds alone turn out to surpass hyperfiction that employs links to solidify—indeed amplify—the power of the author.

Hypertext and the Aristotelian Conception of Plot

Hypertext, which challenges narrative and all literary form based on linearity, calls into question ideas of plot and story current since Aristotle. Looking at the *Poetics* in the context of a discussion of hypertext suggests one of two things: either one simply cannot write hypertext fiction (and the *Poetics* show why that could be the case) or else Aristotelian definitions and descriptions of plot do not apply to stories read and written within a hypertext environment. At the beginning of this study, I proposed that hypertext permits a particularly effective means of testing literary and cultural theory. Here is a case in point. Although hypertext fiction is quite new, the examples of it that I have seen already call into question some of Aristotle's most basic points about plot and story. In the seventh chapter of the *Poetics*, Aristotle offers a definition of plot in which fixed sequence plays a central role:

Now a whole is that which has beginning, middle, and end. A beginning is that which is not itself necessarily after anything else, and which has naturally something else after it; an end is that which is naturally after something itself, . . . as its necessary or usual consequent, and with nothing else after it; and a middle, that which is by nature after one thing and also has another after it. (1462)

Furthermore, Aristotle concludes, "a well-constructed Plot, therefore, cannot either begin or end at any point one likes; beginning and end in it must be of the forms just described. Again: to be beautiful, a living creature, and every whole made up of parts, must not only present a certain order in its arrangement of parts, but also be of a certain definite magnitude" (1462). Hypertext therefore calls into question (1) fixed sequence, (2) definite beginning and ending, (3) a story's "certain definite magnitude," and (4) the conception of unity or wholeness associated with all these other concepts. In hypertext fiction, therefore, one can expect individual forms, such as plot, characterization, and setting, to change, as will genres or literary kinds produced by congeries of these techniques.

When I first discussed hyperfiction in the earlier edition of this book, the novelty, the radical newness, of the subject appeared in the fact that almost all the sources cited were unpublished, in the process of being published, or published in nontraditional electronic forms: these sources included unpublished notes on the subject of hypertext and fiction by a leading American novelist, chapters in forthcoming books, and pre-release versions of hypertext fictions. Now, a few years later, substantial numbers of examples of both hypertext fiction and critical discussions of the subject have appeared. Following the strategy used in previous chapters, I shall therefore take almost all of my examples from widely available work, using whenever possible material published on floppy disks, CD-ROMs, and the World Wide Web.

Quasi Hypertextuality in Print Texts

Previous discussions of the effects of hypertext upon literary form either have sought to identify quasi hypertextuality in print text and then suggest what hypertext fiction might be like or have deduced the rules of hypertextual narrative from first principles, particularly that involving the removal of linearity as a dominant principle of form. This early approach to predicting the way hypertext would affect literary form pointed to *Tristram Shandy, In Memoriam, Ulysses,* and *Finnegan's Wake* and recent French, American, and Latin American fiction, particularly that by Michel Butor, Marc Saporta, Robert Coover, and Jorge Luis Borges (Bolter, *Writing Space,* 132–39). Such texts might not require hypertext to be fully understood, but to readers who have experienced hypertext they reveal new principles of organization or new ways of reading. Hypertext, the argument goes, makes certain elements in these works stand out for the first time. The example of these very different texts suggests that those poems and novels that most resist one or more of the characteristics of literature associated with print form, particularly linear narrative, will be likely to have something in common with new fiction in a new medium.

This approach therefore uses hypertext as a lens, or new agent of perception, to reveal something previously unnoticed or unnoticeable, and it then extrapolates the results of this inquiry to predict future developments. Because such an approach suggests that this new information technology has roots in prestigious canonical texts, it obviously has the political advantage of making the medium seem less threatening to students of literature and literary theory. At the same time, placing hypertext fiction within a legitimating narrative of descent from "great works," which offers the opportunity for new critical readings of significant print texts, makes those canonical texts appear especially forward looking, since they can be seen to provide the gateway to a different and unexpected literary future. I find all these genealogical analyses attractive and even convincing, but I realize that if hypertext has the kind and degree of power that previous chapters have indicated, it does threaten literature and its institutions as we know them. One *should* feel threatened by hypertext, just as writers of romances and epics should have felt threatened by the novel and Venetian writers of Latin tragedy should have felt threatened by the *Divine Comedy* and its Italian text. Descendants, after all, offer continuity with the past but only at the cost of replacing it.

One interesting approach to discussing hypertextual narrative involves deducing its qualities from the defining characteristics of hypertext—its non- or multilinearity, its multivocality, and its inevitable blending of media and modes, particularly its tendency to marry the visual and the verbal. Most who have speculated on the relation between hypertextuality and fiction concentrate, however, upon the effects it will have upon linear narrative. In order to comprehend the combined promise and peril with which hypertextuality confronts narrative, we should first recall that narratology generally urges that narration is intrinsically linear and also that such linearity plays a central role in all thought. As Barbara Herrnstein Smith argues, "there are very few instances in which we can sustain the notion of a set and sequence of events altogether prior to and independent of the discourse through which they are narrated" ("Narrative Versions," 225).[1]

Hayden White states only a particularly emphatic version of a common assumption when he asserts that "to raise the question of the nature of narrative is to invite reflection on the very nature of culture and, possibly, even on the nature of humanity itself. . . . Far from being one code among many that a culture may utilize for endowing experience with meaning, narrative is a metacode, a human universal on the basis of which transcultural messages about the nature of a shared reality can be transmitted" (1–2). What kind of a culture would have or could have hypertextual narration, which so emphasizes non- or multilinearity, and what happens to a culture that chooses such narration, when, as Jean-François Lyotard claims, in agreement with many other writers on the subject, "narration is the quintessential form of customary knowledge" (*Postmodern Condition,* 18)? Lyotard's own definition of postmodernism as "incredulity toward metanarratives" (xxiv) suggests one answer: any author and any culture that chooses hypertextual fiction will either already have rejected the solace and reassurance of linear narrative or will soon find their attachment to it loosening. Lyotard claims that "lamenting the 'loss of meaning' in postmodernity boils down to mourning the fact that knowledge is no longer principally narrative" (26), and for this loss of faith in narrative he offers several possible technological and political explanations, the most important of which is that science, which "has always been in conflict with narratives," uses other means "to legitimate the rules of its own game" (xiii).[2]

Even without raising such broader or more fundamental issues about the relation of narrative to culture, one realizes that hypertext opens major questions about story and plot by apparently doing away with linear organization. Conventional definitions and descriptions of plot suggest some of these questions. Aristotle long ago pointed out that successful plots require a "probable or necessary sequence of events" (1465). This observation occurs in the midst of his discussion of *peripeteia* (or in Bywater's translation, *peripety*); and in the immediately preceding discussion of episodic plots, which Aristotle considers "the worst," he explains that he calls "a Plot episodic when there is neither probability nor necessity in the sequence of its episodes" (1464).

Answering Aristotle: Hypertext and the Nonlinear Plot

One answer to Aristotle lies in the fact that removing a single "probable or necessary sequence of events" does not do away with all linearity. Linearity, however, then becomes a quality of the individual reader's experience within a single text and his or her experience following a reading path, even if that path curves back upon itself or heads in strange directions. Robert Coover claims that with hypertext "the linearity of the reading experience" does not disappear entirely, "but narrative bytes no longer follow one another in an ineluctable page-turning chain. Hypertextual story space is now multidimensional and theoretically infinite, with an equally infinite set of possible network linkages, either programmed, fixed or variable, or random, or both" ("Endings").

Coover, inspired by the notion of the active hypertext reader, envisions some of the ways the reader might contribute to the story. At the most basic level of the hypertext encounter, "the reader may now choose the route in the labyrinth she or he wishes to take, following some particular character, for example, or an image, an action, and so on." Coover adds that readers can become reader-authors not only by choosing their paths through the text but also by reading more actively, by which he means they "may even interfere with the story, introduce new elements, new narrative strategies, open new paths, interact with characters, even with the author. Or authors." Although some authors and audiences might find themselves chilled by such destabilizing, potentially chaotic-seeming narrative worlds, Coover, a freer spirit, mentions "the allure of the blank spaces of these fabulous networks, these green-limned gardens of multiply forking paths, to narrative artists" who have the opportunity to "replace logic with character or metaphor, say, scholarship with collage and verbal wit, and turn the story loose in a space where whatever is possible is necessary" ("Endings").

Coover offers a vision of possibilities, and now that many instances of hyperfiction have seen publication, one can make some first guesses about which of his suggestions seem most likely to be realized and which least so. Although it is true that readers in certain hypertext systems—those with search tools or something like Microcosm's compute links functions—can follow "some particular character, for example, or an image, an action, and so on," the software used for writing most hyperfiction thus far does not make such reading easy or, in some cases, even possible. Intermedia permitted reader-authors to enter the text freely, and students at Brown created works, such as *Hotel,* one version of which has since appeared on the Web and been recreated as a multi-user domain (MUD) (see Meyer, Blair, Hader). Group-authored productions seem, however, to represent a particular form or mode of hypertext fiction and not its dominant stream.

The way readers follow links presents an even more fundamental issue in hyperfiction. In contrast to informational hypertext, which must employ rhetorics of orientation, navigation, and departure to orient the reader, successful fictional hypertext and poetry do not always do so, with the result that their readers cannot make particularly informed or empowered choices. Webs created in systems like Storyspace that permit one-to-many links, link menus, and path names all provide authors the means to empower the reader; that is, authors can write in such a way as to provide the reader with informed choices. Taro Ikai's *Electronic Zen* exemplifies a web whose creator chose to do so: Using Storyspace's link menus (rather than its richer ability to name links and create paths), Ikai named the first destinations "water" and "chef." After reading even a few of his brief lexias, readers realize that he has created two paths, one characterized by Zen meditations and the other by details of the speaker's mundane existence. With that information, readers can now choose which path they wish to follow.

Similarly, in *Quibbling,* which employs the Storyspace View, Carolyn Guyer permits readers at any point to leave individual lexias and pursue the characters and narratives suggested by the names of individual folders and folders within folders. In *Victory Garden* Stuart Moulthrop uses path names, overviews, and other devices to encourage readers to make wise choices. A good many hypertext fictions published thus far show, in contrast, that authors prefer authorial power, reader disorientation, or both. Rather than concluding too quickly that Coover's vision has motes or blurs, we should recognize two things: First, that there will be—indeed, there already are—as many kinds of hyperfiction as occur in print fiction; there is probably no one ideal. And, second, that fictional hypertext has different purposes, modes, and effects than informational and educational hypertext.

Print Anticipations of Multilinear Narratives in E-Space

Doing away with a fixed linear text therefore neither necessarily does away with all linearity nor removes formal coherence, though coherence may appear in new and unexpected forms. Bolter points out that

in this shifting electronic space, writers will need a new concept of structure. In place of a closed and unitary structure, they must learn to conceive of their text as a structure of possible structures. The writer must practice a kind of second-order writing, creating coherent lines for the reader to discover without closing off the possibilities prematurely or arbitrarily. This writing of the second order will be the special contribution of the electronic medium to the history of literature (*Writing Space,* 144).

In "Poem Descending a Staircase," William Dickey, a poet who works with hypertext, proposes that authors can pattern their hypertexts by creating links that offer several sets of distinct reading paths: "The poem may be designed in a pattern of nested squares, as a group of chained circles, as a braid of different visual and graphic themes, as a double helix. The poem may present a single main sequence from which word or image associations lead into sub-sequences and then return" (147). Hypertext systems that employ single directional as opposed to bidirectional linking make this kind of organization easier, of course, but fuller and freer forms of the medium also make such quasi-musical organization possible and even inevitable. The main requirement, as Paul Ricoeur suggests, becomes "this 'followability' of a story," and followability provides a principle that permits many options, many permutations (1:67).

Another possible form of hypertextual literary organization involves parataxis, which is produced by repetition rather than sequence. Barbara Herrnstein Smith explains that in literary works that employ logical or temporal organization, "the dislocation or omission of any element will tend to make the sequence as a whole incomprehensible, or will radically change its effect. In paratactic structure, however (where the principle of generation does not cause any one element to 'follow' from another), thematic units can be added, omitted, or exchanged without destroying the coherence or effect of the poem's thematic structure." According to Smith, "'variations on a theme' is one of the two most obvious forms that paratactic structure may take. The other one is the 'list.'" The main problem with which parataxis, like hypertext, confronts narrative is that any "generating principle that produces a paratactic structure cannot in itself determine a concluding point" (*Poetic Closure,* 99–100).

Since some narratologists claim that morality ultimately depends upon the unity and coherence of a fixed linear text, one wonders if hypertext can convey morality in any significant form or if it is condemned to an essential triviality. White believes the unity of successful narrative to be a matter of ideology: "Narrativity, certainly in factual storytelling and probably in fictional storytelling as well, is intimately related to, if not a function of, the impulse to moralize reality, that is, to identify it with the social system that is the source of any morality that we can imagine" (14). Writing as a historian and historiographer, White argues that such ideological pressure appears with particular clarity in the "value attached to narrativity in the representation of real events," since that value discloses a desire to endow "real events" with a necessarily imaginary "coherence, integrity, fullness, and closure" possible only in fiction. The very "notion that sequences of real events possess the formal attributes of stories we tell about imaginary events," insists White, "could only have its origin in wishes, daydreams, reveries" (20, 23). Does this signify or imply that contemporary culture, at least its avant-garde technological phalanx, rejects such wishes, daydreams, and reveries? White's connection of plot and morality suggests several lines of inquiry. One could inquire if it is good or bad that linear narratives inevitably embody some morality or ideology, but first one should determine if rejecting linearity necessarily involves rejecting morality. After all, anyone taking seriously the fictional possibilities of hypertext wants to know if it will produce yet another form of postmodernist fiction that critics like John Gardener, Gerald Graff, and Charles Newman will attack as morally corrupt and corrupting (McHale, 219). If one wanted liberation from ideology, were such a goal possible, nonideological storytelling might be fine. But before concluding that hypertext produces either ideology-free miracles or ideology-free horrors, one should look at the available evidence. In particular, one should examine prehypertext attempts to create nonlinear or multilinear literary forms and evaluate the results.

A glance at previous experiments in avoiding the linearity of the printed text suggests that in the past authors have rejected linearity because it falsified their experience of things. Tennyson, for example, as we have already observed, created his poetry of fragments in an attempt to write with greater honesty and with greater truth about his own experience. Moreover, as several critics have pointed out, novelists at least since Laurence Sterne have sought to escape the potential confinements and falsifications of linear narrative.

One does not have to look back at the past for examples. In his review of *Dictionary of the Khazars,* a work by the Yugoslavian Milorad Pavič that Robert Coover describes as a hypertext novel, he asserts that "there is a tension in narrative, as in life, between the sensation of time as a linear experience, one thing following sequentiality (causally or not) upon another, and time as a patterning of interrelated experiences reflected upon as though it had a geography and could be mapped" ("He Thinks," 15) Nonlinear form, whether pleasing to readers or even practically possible, derives from attempts to be more truthful rather than from any amorality. Many contemporary works of fiction explore this tension between the linear and more spatial sensations of time that Coover describes. Graham Swift's *Waterland* (1983), for instance, questions all narrative based on sequence, and in this it agrees with other novels of its decade. Like Penelope Lively's *Moon Tiger* (1987), another novel in the form of the autobiography of a historian, *Waterland* relates the events of a single life to the major currents of contemporary history.

Using much the same method for autobiography as for history, Swift's protagonist, Tom Crick, would agree with Lively's Claudia Hampton, whose deep suspicion of chronology and sequence explicitly derive from her experience of simultaneity. Ricoeur suggests that "the major tendency of modern theory of narrative—in historiography and the philosophy of history as well as narratology—is to 'dechronologize' narrative," and these two novelists exemplify a successful "struggle against the linear representation of time" (1:30). Thinking over the possibility of writing a history of the world, Lively's heroine rejects sequence and linear history as inauthentic and false to her experience:

The question is, shall it or shall it not be linear history? I've always thought a kaleidoscopic view might be an interesting heresy. Shake the tube and see what comes out. Chronology irritates me. There is no chronology inside my head. I am composed of a myriad Claudias who spin and mix and part like sparks of sunlight on water. The pack of cards I carry around is forever shuffled and re-shuffled; there is no sequence, everything happens at once. (2)

Like Proust's Marcel, she finds that a simple sensation brings the past back flush upon the present, making a mockery of separation and sequence. Returning to Cairo in her late sixties, Claudia finds it both changed and unchanged. "The place didn't look the same but it felt the same; sensations clutched and transformed me." Standing near a modern concrete and plateglass building, she picked a "handful of eucalyptus leaves from a branch, crushed them in my hand, smelt, and tears came to my eyes. Sixty-seven-year-old Claudia . . . crying not in grief but in wonder that nothing is ever lost, that everything can be retrieved, that a lifetime is not linear but instant." Her lesson for narratology is that "inside the head, everything happens at once" (68). Like Claudia, Tom Crick takes historical, autobiographical narratives whose essence is sequence and spreads them out or weaves them in a nonsequential way.

The difference between quasi-hypertextual fictions and those in electronic form chiefly involves the greater freedom and power of the hypertext reader. Swift decided when Tom Crick's narrative branches and Lively decided when Claudia Hampton's does, but in Stuart Moulthrop's hypertext version of Borges's "Forking Paths" and in Leni Zumas's *Semio-Surf* or Carolyn Guyer's *Quibbling,* the reader makes this decision. Important prehypertextual narrative has, however, also required such reader decision. One of the most famous examples of an author's ceding power to the reader is found in "The Babysitter," in which Robert Coover, like an author of electronic hypertext, presents the reader with multiple possibilities, really multiple endings, with two effects. First, the reader, who takes over some of the writer's role and function, must choose which possibility, if any, to accept; and second, by encountering that need to decide, readers realize both that no true single narrative exists as the main or "right" one and that reading traditional narrative has brainwashed them into expecting and demanding a single right answer and a single correct story line. Coover's story not only makes a fundamentally moral point about the nature of fiction but also places more responsibility upon the reader. One may say of Coover's text, in other words, what Bolter says of Michael Joyce's interactive hypertext—that "there is no single story of which each reading is a version, because each reading determines the story as it goes. We could say that there is no story at all; there are only readings" (*Writing Space,* 124).

Narrative Beginnings

and Endings

As we have already observed in Chapter 3, the problems that hypertext branching creates for narrativity appear with particular clarity in the matter of beginning and ending stories. If, as Edward Said claims, "a 'beginning' is designated in order to indicate, clarify, or define a *later* time, place, or action," how can hypertext fiction begin or be said to begin? Furthermore, if, as Said also convincingly argues, "when we point to the beginning of a novel . . . we mean that from that beginning in principle follows *this* novel" (5), how can we determine what novel follows from the beginnings each reader chooses?

Thus far, most of the hypertext fictions I have read or heard described, like many hypertext collections of educational materials, take an essentially cautious approach to the problems of beginnings, by offering the reader a lexia labeled something like "start here" that combines functions of title page, introduction, and opening paragraph. They do so for several technological, rhetorical, and other reasons. Most authors writing with HyperCard, Guide, and Storyspace do not use these environments on networks that can distribute one's texts to other reading sites. To disseminate one's writings, the author must therefore copy it from one's own machine to a floppy disk and then give that disk to someone with another computer. This use of non-networked (or stand-alone) machines encourages writers to produce stories or poems that are both self-contained and small enough to fit on a single disk. In addition, since some of these early hypertextual environments do not give the reader the power to add links, authors working in them necessarily tend to consider their works to be self-contained, in a traditional manner. Another reason for using the "start here" approach appears in some writers' obvious reluctance to disorient readers upon their initial contact with a narrative, and some writers also believe that hypertextual fiction should necessarily change our experience of the middle but not the beginnings of narrative fiction.

In contrast, William Dickey, who has written hypertext poetry using Apple's HyperCard, finds it a good or useful quality of hypertext poetry that it "may begin with any one of its parts, stanzas, images, to which any other part of the poem may succeed. This system of organization requires that that part of the poem represented on any one card must be a sufficiently independent statement to be able to generate a sense of poetic meaning as it follows or is followed by any other statement the poem contains" (147), Dickey, who is writing about poetic rather than fictional structure, nonetheless offers organizational principles that apply to both.

Narrative Endings and Hypertext

Beginnings imply endings, and endings require some sort of formal and thematic closure. Using the image of "following" that is conventionally applied to narratives and that writers about hypertext also use to describe activation of links, Ricoeur explains that "to follow a story is to move forward in the midst of contingencies and peripeteia under the guidance of an expectation that finds its fulfillment in the 'conclusion' of the story." This conclusion "gives the story an 'end point,' which, in turn, furnishes the point of view from which the story can be perceived as forming a whole." In other words, to understand a story requires first comprehending "how and why the successive episodes led to this conclusion, which, far from being foreseeable, must finally be acceptable, as congruent with the episodes brought together by the story" (1:66–67).

In her classic study of how poems produce satisfying endings, Smith provides evidence that might prompt students of hypertext to conclude either that it creates fundamental problems in narrative and other kinds of literary texts or else that it opens them to entirely new forms of textuality. She explains that since "a poem cannot continue indefinitely" (*Poetic Closure,* 33), it must employ devices that prepare the reader for ending rather than continuing. These devices produce in the reader "the sense of stable conclusiveness, finality, or 'clinch' . . . referred to here as closure. . . . Whether spatially or temporally perceived, a structure appears 'closed' when it is experienced as integral: coherent, complete, and stable" (2)—qualities that produce a "sense of ultimate composure we apparently value in our experience of a work of art" and that we label "stability, resolution, or equilibrium" (34). Unlike texts in manuscript or print, those in hypertext apparently can continue indefinitely, perhaps infinitely, so one wonders if they can provide satisfying closure.[3] Or to direct this inquiry in ways suggested by Smith's analysis of closure, one should ask what techniques might provide something analogous to that desirable "sense of stable conclusiveness, finality, or 'clinch.'"

Taking another clue from fiction created for print publication, one perceives that many prehypertext narratives provide instances of multiple closure and also a combination of closure with new beginnings. Both Charles Dickens' novels written specifically for publication in periodicals at monthly intervals and those by other nineteenth-century novelists intended for first publication in the conventional triple-decker form make use of partial closure followed by continuation. Furthermore, Trollope's Palliser series, Lawrence Durrell's *Alexandria Quartet,* Faulkner's works, and countless trilogies and tetralogies in both fantastic and realistic modes suggest that writers of fiction have long encountered problems very similar to those faced by writers of hypertext fiction and have developed an array of formal and thematic solutions to them. In fact, the tendency of many a twentieth-century work to leave its readers with little sense of closure—either because they do not learn of the "final" outcome of a particular narrative or because they leave the story before any outcome occurs—shows us that as readers and writers we have long learned to live (and read) with more open-endedness than discussions of narrative form might lead us to expect.

Coover proclaims that endings will and must occur even in infinitely expandable, changeable, combinable docuverses:

> There is still movement, but in hyperspace it is that of endless expansion. "A" is, or may be, an infinite multiplicity of starting points, "B" a parenthetical "B" somewhere beyond the beyond, or within the within, yet clearly mapped, clearly routed, just somewhat less definite than, oh, say, dying. Which for all the networking maneuvers and funhouse mirrors cannot be entirely ignored. Sooner or later, whatever the game, the whistle is blown. Even in hyperspace, there is disconnection. One last windowless trajectory. ("Endings")

Hypertext fictions always end, because readings always end, but they can end in fatigue or in a sense of satisfying closure. Barbara Herrnstein Smith, writing of the printed text, reminds us that "the end of the play or novel will not appear as an arbitrary cut-off if it leaves us at a point where, with respect to the themes of the work, we feel that we know all there is or all there is to know" (*Poetic Closure,* 120). If individual lexias provide readers with experiences of formal and thematic closure, they can be expected to provide the satisfactions that Smith describes as requisite to the sense of an ending.

Michael Joyce's *Afternoon:*

The Reader's Experience

as Author

Michael Joyce, a hypertext author, is suspicious of closure. In Joyce's *Afternoon,* a hypertext fiction in 538 lexias, the section appropriately entitled "work in progress" advises readers: "Closure is, as in any fiction, a suspect quality, although here it is made manifest. When the story no longer progresses, or when it cycles, or when you tire of the paths, the experience of reading it ends." In other words, Joyce makes the responsibility for closure, for stopping, entirely the reader's. When the reader decides he or she has had enough, when he or she wishes to stop reading, why then the story is over. Joyce continues, however: "Even so, there are likely to be more opportunities than you think there are at first. A word which doesn't yield the first time you read a section may take you elsewhere if you choose it when you encounter the section again; and what sometimes seems a loop, like memory, heads off in another direction." Reading the highly allusive *Afternoon,* which has so many points of departure within each lexia as well as continually changing points of linkage, one sees what Joyce means (Figure 25).[4]

The successive lexias one encounters in *Afternoon* seem to take form as chains of narrative, and despite the fact that one shifts setting and narrator, one's choices produce satisfying narrative sets. Moving from section to sec-

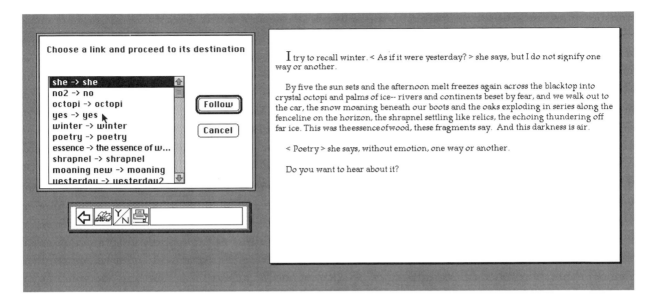

Figure 25. The Storyspace Page Reader: Michael Joyce's *Afternoon*. The Page Reader, one of several ways of distributing this system's webs to readers without the authoring environment, has a movable palette providing access to five functions: the arrow at left provides a backtracking function, and clicking upon the book icon provides a menu of all links from the current lexia, such as appears at the left. In addition, readers can respond positively or negatively to questions in the text, such as we encounter here, by choosing the appropriate button, or they can search for links relating to a specific word by typing it in the space at right. Finally, readers can print individual pages by using the icon at far right. (Courtesy of Eastgate Systems.)

tion, one every so often encounters puzzling changes of setting, narrator, subject, or chronology, but two things occur. After reading awhile one begins to construct narrative placements, so that one assigns particular sections to a provisionally suitable place—some lexias obviously have several alternate or rival forms of relation. Then, having assigned particular sections to particular sequences or reading paths—many, though not all, of which one can retrace at will—one reaches points at which one's initial cognitive dissonance or puzzlement disappears, and one seems satisfied. One has reached—or created—closure!

One might describe Joyce's hypertext fiction in the way Gérard Genette describes "what one calls Stendhal's *oeuvre*":

a fragmented, elliptical, repetitive, yet infinite, or at least indefinite, text, no part of which, however, may be separated from the whole. Whoever pulls a single thread must take the whole cloth, with its holes and lack of edges. To read Stendhal is to read the whole of Stendhal, but to read all of Stendhal is impossible, for the very good reason, among others, that the whole of Stendhal has not yet been published or deciphered, or discovered, or even written! I repeat, all the Stendhalian text, because the gaps, the interruptions are not mere absences, a pure non-text: they are a lack, active and perceptible as lack, as non-writing, as non-written text. (*Figures,* 165)

Genette, I suggest, describes the way a reader encounters the web of Joyce's hypertextual narrative. Even entering at a single point determined by the author, the reader chooses one path or another and calls up another lexia by a variety of means, and then repeats this process until she finds a hole or a gap. Perhaps at this point the reader turns back and takes another direction. One might just as well write something oneself or make present a remembered passage by another author in the manner that a book reader might begin a poem by Stevens, think of some parallel verses by Swinburne or a passage in a book by Helen Vendler or Harold Bloom, pull that volume off its shelf, find the passage, and then return to the poem by Stevens.

Whereas Genette's characterization of the Stendhalian *oeuvre* captures the reader's experience of the interconnectedness of *Afternoon* and other hypertext fictions, his description of temporality in Proust conveys the experience of encountering the disjunctions and jumps of hypertextual narrative. Citing George Poulet's observation that in *À la Recherche du temps perdu* time does not appear as Bergsonian duration but as a "succession of isolated moments," he points out that similarly "characters (and groups) do not evolve: one fine day, they find that they have changed, as if time confined itself to bringing forth a plurality that they have contained in potentia from all eternity. Indeed, many of the characters assume the most contradictory roles *simultaneously*" (216). In other words, in *À la Recherche du temps perdu* readers find themselves taking leaps and jumping into a different time and a different character. In a hypertext narrative it is the author who provides multiple possibilities by means of which the readers themselves construct temporal succession and choose characterization—though, to be sure, readers will take leaps, as we do in life, on the basis of inadequate or even completely inaccurate information.

So many different contexts cross and interweave that one must work at placing the characters one encounters in them. Joyce's world, which also inevitably includes the *other* Joyce, has many moving centers of interest, including marriage and erotic relationships, sexual politics, psychotherapy, advertising, film making and the history of cinema, computing, and myth, and literature of all kinds. Reading habits one has learned from print play a role in organizing these materials. If one encounters a speaker's mention of his marriage and, in a later lexia, finds him at the scene of an automobile accident from which the bodies of injured people have already been removed, one might take the accident as an event in the recent past; the emotional charge it carries serves to organize other reported thoughts and events, inevitably turning some of them into flashbacks, others into exposition. Conversely, one could take that event as something in the past, a particularly significant moment, and then use it as a point of origin either that leads to other events or whose importance endows events it has not caused with a significance created by explanation or contrast or analogy. Our assistance in the storytelling or storymaking is not entirely or even particularly random, since Joyce provides many hooks that can catch at our thoughts, but we do become reader-authors and help tell the tale we read.

Nonetheless, as J. Hillis Miller points out, we cannot help ourselves: we must create meaning as we read. "A story is readable because it can be organized into a causal chain. . . . A causal sequence is always an implicit narrative organized around the assumption that what comes later is caused by what comes before, 'post hoc, propter hoc.' If any series of random and disconnected events is presented to me, I tend to see it as a causal chain. Or rather, if Kant and Kleist are right, I must see it as a causal chain" (*Versions of Pygmalion,* 127, 130). Miller, who silently exchanges a linear model of explanation for one more appropriate to hypertextual narrative, later adds: "We cannot avoid imposing some set of connections, like a phantasmal spiderweb, over events that just happen as they happen" (139).

Miller's idea of reading printed text, which seems to owe a great deal to gestalt psychology's theories of constructionist perception, well describes the reader-author demanded by Joyce's *Afternoon* and other works of hypertext fiction. According to Miller, reading is always "a kind of writing or rewriting that is an act of prosopopoeia, like Pygmalion giving life to the statue" (186).[5] This construction of an evanescent entity or wholeness always occurs in reading, but in reading hypertext it takes the additional form of constructing, however provisionally, one's own text out of fragments, out of separate lexias. It is a case, in other words, of Lévi-Strauss's *bricolage,* for every hypertext reader-author is inevitably a *bricoleur.*

Such *bricolage,* I suggest, provides a new kind of unity, one appropriate to hypertextuality. As long as one grants that plot is a phenomenon created by the reader-author with materials the lexias offer, rather than a phenomenon belonging solely to the text, then one can accept that reading *Afternoon* and other hypertext fictions produces an experience very similar to that provided by reading the unified plot described by narratologists from Aristotle to White and Ricoeur. White, for example, defines plot as "a structure of relationships by which the events contained in the account are endowed with a meaning by being identified as parts of an integrated whole" (9). Ricoeur similarly defines plot, "on the most *formal* level, as an integrating dynamism that draws a unified and complete story from a variety of incidents, in other words, that transforms this variety into a unified and complete story. This formal definition opens a field of rule-governed transformations worthy of being called plots so long as we can discern temporal wholes bringing about a synthesis of the heterogeneous between circumstances, goals, means, interactions, and intended and unintended results" (2:8). According to Ricoeur, the metaphorical imagination produces narrative by a process of what he terms "predicative assimilation," which "'grasps together' and integrates into one whole and complete story multiple and scattered events, thereby schematizing the illegible signification attached to the narrative taken as a whole" (1:x). To this observation I would add, with Miller, that as readers we find ourselves *forced* to fabricate a whole story out of separate parts.

In his chapter on Heinrich von Kleist in *Versions of Pygmalion,* Miller provides us with an unexpectedly related model for this kind of extemporized construction of meaning-on-the-run. He quotes Kleist's claim that Mirabeau was "unsure of what he was about to say" (104) when he began his famous speech that ended "by creating the new French nation and a new parliamentary assembly." The speaker posits a "syntactically incomplete fragment, says Kleist, without any idea . . . of where the sentence is going to end, [and] the thought is gradually 'fabricated'"; and Kleist claims that the speaker's feelings and general situation in some way produce his proposals. Disagreeing with him, Miller argues in the manner of Barthes that Mirabeau's revolutionary "thought is gradually fabricated not so much by the situation or by the speaker's feelings" as Kleist suggests, "but by his need to complete the grammar and syntax of the sentence he has blindly begun" (104–5). Structuralists and poststructuralists have long described thinking and writing in terms of this extemporized, in-process generation of meaning, the belief in which does so much to weaken traditional conceptions of self and author. Hypertext fiction forces us to extend this description of meaning-generation to the reader's construction of narrative. It forces us to recognize that the active author-reader fabricates text and meaning from "another's" text in the same way that each speaker constructs individual sentences and entire discourses from "another's" grammar, vocabulary, and syntax.

Vladimir Propp, following Veselovsky, long ago founded the "structuralist study of plot" and with it modern narratology by applying notions of linguistic combination to the study of folk tales.[6] Miller, who draws upon this tradition, reminds us that folk tales, spoken discourses, and interpretative readings of print narratives follow an essentially similar process that entails the immediate, in-process construction of meaning and text. Miller's observations allow us to understand that one must apply the same notions to the activities of the reader of hypertext fiction. In brief, hypertext demands that one apply this structuralist understanding of speaker and writer to the reader as well, since in hypertext the reader is a reader-author. From this theory of the reader and from the experience of reading hypertext narratives, I draw the following, perhaps obvious but nonetheless important, conclusions: in a hypertext environment a lack of linearity does not destroy narrative. In fact, since readers always, but particularly in this environment, fabricate their own structures, sequences, and meanings, they have surprisingly little trouble reading a story or reading for a story. Obviously, some parts of the reading experience seem very different from reading a printed novel or a short story, and reading hypertext fiction provides some of that experience of a new orality that both McLuhan and Ong predicted. Although the reader of hypertext fiction shares some experiences, one supposes, with the audience of listeners who heard oral poetry, this active reader-author inevitably has more in common with the bard who constructed meaning and narrative from fragments provided by someone else, by another author or by many other authors.

Like Coover, who emphasizes the inevitable connection of death and narrative, Joyce seems to intertwine the two. In part it is a matter, as Brian McHale points out, of avant-garde authors using highly charged subjects (sexuality, death) to retain readers' interest, which might stray within puzzling and unfamiliar narrative modes. In part it is also a matter of endings: when the reader decides to stop reading *Afternoon,* he or she ends, kills, the story, because when the active reader, the reader-author, stops reading, the story stops, it dies, it has reached an ending. As part of that cessation, that willingness to stop creating and interpreting the story, certain acts or events in the story become deaths, because they make most sense that way; and by stopping reading, the reader prevents other alternatives from coming into being.

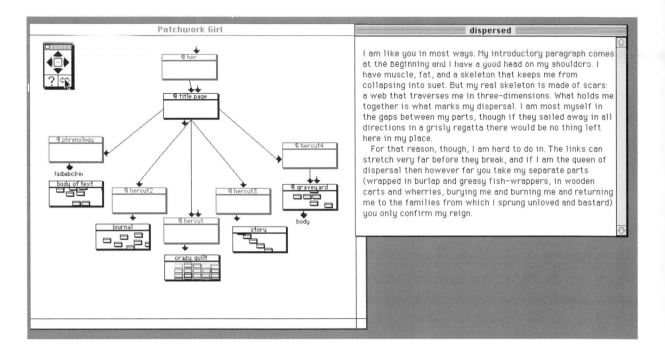

Figure 26. The Storyspace Reader: Shelley Jackson's *Patchwork Girl*. Readers can navigate the web (1) by simultaneously pressing option and keys to discover linked text and then double clicking upon it, (2) by mousing down upon the double-headed arrow on the movable palette (for default links), or (3) by exploring the Storyspace View, which consists of a folderlike arrangement of the web that authors can arrange as they wish. Unlike the Page Reader, which derives from the tiny size of original Macintosh screens, this form of Storyspace does not restrict documents to a card-like format and permits scrollable text that readers can reconfigure. (Courtesy of Eastgate Systems.)

Stitching together Narrative, Sexuality, and Self: Shelley Jackson's *Patchwork Girl*

Patchwork Girl, Shelley Jackson's brilliant hypertext parable of writing and identity, generates both its themes and its techniques from the kinds of collage writing intrinsic to hypertext (Figure 26). Jackson, a book illustrator as well as author, creates a digital collage out of her own words and images (and those of others, including Mary Shelley, Frank L. Baum, and Jacques Derrida) as she tells us about the female companion to Frankenstein's monster whose "birth takes place more than once. In the plea of a bygone monster; from a muddy hole by corpse-light; under the needle, and under the pen" ("birth").

One form of collage in *Patchwork Girl* appears in the thirty-lexia section entitled "Crazy Quilt." Karyn Raz explains in her section of "*Patchwork Girl*

Comments," a student-created portion of the *Cyberspace, Hypertext, and Critical Theory Web:* "Each patch in Jackson's quilt is composed of various other patches, various other texts, from theoretical to fictional, from pop cultural to hearsay, sewn together to form either a sentence or paragraph" ("Patches"). The lexia by Jackson entitled "seam'd" thus combines sentences from *Getting Started with Storyspace,* Frank L. Baum's *Patchwork Girl of Oz,* and Barbara Maria Stafford's *Body Criticism: Imagining the Unseen in Enlightenment Art and Medicine:* "You may emphasize the presence of text links by using a special style, color or typeface. Or, if you prefer, you can leave needles sticking in the wounds—in the manner of tailors—with thread wrapped around them. Being seam'd with scars was both a fact of eighteenth century life and a metaphor for dissonant interferences ruining any finely adjusted composition. 'The charm you need is a needle and thread,' said the Shaggy Man." As Raz points out, "Stitches, or links, connect one patch to another, one text to another. Jackson seems particularly interested in examining the points of union between texts, such that 'being seam'd with scars' becomes a fact not only of eighteenth-century life but of hypertext writing, and indeed of any sort of creative process" ("Patches").

Fittingly, my discussion of Jackson's web has already taken on much of the appearance of collage itself. I first wrote a good portion of what follows for the *Electronic Book Review,* one of an increasing number of critical and scholarly World Wide Web periodical publications, but after students in my course on cyberspace and critical theory supplemented it with an HTML web in the form of some two dozen commentaries, I decided to find some way to draw upon their work in a manner appropriate to print. In the *Cyberspace, Hypertext, and Critical Theory Web,* our lexias appear woven together, and I could *add to* my single lexia simply by using links. Here, following the conventions of print, I shall sum up and introduce these additional comments (which are now, of course, part of the "main" text, and hence no longer "additional"), citing some longer passages in the endnotes. Back to *Patchwork Girl* and hypertext collage.

Most of *Patchwork Girl's* collage effects occur, not within individual patches or lexias, but across them as we readers patch together a character and a narrative. Opening Jackson's web, we first encounter a black-and-white image of the stitched-together protagonist that she cuts and recombines into the images we come upon at various points throughout our reading. The first link takes us to her title page, a rich crossroads document to which we return repeatedly, that offers six paths out: "a graveyard," "a journal," "a quilt," "a story," "broken accents," and a list of sources. The graveyard, for example, takes us first to a patchwork image created by cutting and rearranging the title screen, after which we receive some directions and then reach the headstone, another overview or crossroads lexia that provides multiple paths; these paths take us to the lives of each of the beings, largely women, whose parts contributed to the Patchwork Girl.

According to Jason Williams, the graveyard section functions as a collage of "mini-narratives and fragmented character sketches" that serves as a "matrix for the meta-character and her story." Its removal from the narrative of the Patchwork Girl's own life avoids "interrupting the story's flow, and its compartmentalization encourages the application of its contents to the smaller narrative subsections. The graveyard itself focuses on the headstone and the list of the urns' contents, giving it a double-focus radial structure that unifies the parts without imposing a hierarchical order upon them. The introductory and concluding lexias temporally frame this structure and facilitate passage to the more linear sections of the text" ("Texture, Topology, Collage, and Biology in *Patchwork Girl*").

Jackson endows each tale, each life, encountered in the graveyard with a distinctive voice, thereby creating a narrative of Bakhtinian multivocality while simultaneously presenting a composite image of women's lives at the turn of the nineteenth century. The Everywoman Monster's left leg, we read,

belonged to Jane, a nanny who harbored under her durable grey dresses and sensible undergarments a remembrance of a less sensible time: a tattoo of a ship and the legend, Come Back To Me. Nanny knew some stories that astonished her charges, and though the ship on her thigh blurred and grew faint and blue with distance, until it seemed that the currents must have long ago finished their work, undoing its planks one by one with unfailing patience, she always took the children to the wharf when word came that a ship was docking, and many a sailor greeted her by name.

My leg is always twitching, jumping, joggling. It wants to go places. It has had enough of waiting. ("left leg")

Patchwork Girl makes us all into Frankenstein-readers stitching together narrative, gender, and identity, for as it reminds us, "you could say all bodies are written bodies, all lives pieces of writing" ("all written"). This digital collage-narrative assembles Shelley Jackson's (and Mary Shelley's and Victor Frankenstein's) female monster, forming a hypertext Everywoman who embodies assemblage, concatenation, juxtaposition, and blurred, recreated identities—one of many digital fulfillments of twentieth-century literary and pictorial collages. As the monster slyly informs us in a lexia one encounters early on, "I am buried here. You can resurrect me, but only piecemeal. If you want to see the whole, you will have to sew me together yourself. (In time you may find appended a pattern and instructions—for now, you will have to put it together any which way, as the scientist Frankenstein was forced to do.) Like him, you will make use of a machine of mysterious complexity to animate these parts" ("graveyard"). In emphasizing the way her readers have to start out without a map or plan and then do a lot of the assembling ourselves, Jackson playfully prepares us for the gaps and jumps we shall have to make.

In putting all readers into the mode of Dr. Frankenstein, she also strikes a Baudrillardian note. As David Goldberg argues in his HTML "Comments on *Patchwork Girl,*" "hypertext represents the fulfillment of the fantasy that Shelley proposes and Jackson revitalizes. A prevailing theme throughout the history of modern science and technology has been the simulation of life by artificial means. Frankenstein and his real-life predecessors . . . sought . . . to create new life, a copy without an original—Baudrillard's simulacrum." Reading *Patchwork Girl* offers "the opportunity to create a unique conformation of the text, of creating a copy without an original," something, one may add, characteristic of the collage form.[7]

Another source of such collage patchwork appears in the different link structures—what Jason Williams terms the link topologies—that characterize each section of the web. As Williams points out, that portion which tells the story of the Patchwork Girl herself relies upon unified setting and chronological change. "Because this section emphasizes temporal dynamics, its link structure correspondingly parallels our normal linear perception of time, regularly progressing from past lexias forward. Mary Shelley's encounter outdoors with the monster and the more ambiguous bedroom scene behave similarly but take the peculiar cast of ancillary narratives, like apocryphal stories or appended myths—complete units that draw upon and support material from other units" ("Texture, Topology").

In contrast, that portion of the web containing the nonfictional components takes a more characteristically hypertext form of what Williams terms "paths that intersect at lexias containing similar subject matter. This arrangement permits a digressive textual interrogation in which the reader pursues attractive ideas down branching paths. This mode feels appropriate to nonfiction because it mirrors the normal scholarly process of following references between texts." Although the "Crazy Quilt" section follows a stricter, more limited sequence, "its clear grid layout [in the Storyspace view], the arrow keys, and the chunked arrangement of its content allow a grazing approach to reading."

According to Williams, each of these linking topologies patterns the sequence in which a reader experiences, constructs, or reconstructs the text: "Each corresponds to a temporal texture" created by the reader's perception of transitions between lexias "as smooth and determined, chaotic, or ornately interlocking." *Patchwork Girl* then combines these "linking textures and their composition into a meta-collage with a meta-texture":

> Thematic, word-based links act as singular jumps between sections, but, ironically, a woven mass of them forms a canvas on which the author mounts scraps of structure. Links destabilize—or, more positively—stretch the text to flexibility, by pointing away from themselves, by suggesting the reader might read better elsewhere. But again ironically, this pulling apart lends the text its unity, because it permits meanings from separate subsections to bleed into one another through the cracks between them, permitting the text's colorings to mix throughout it.[8]

Finally, Williams concludes, he finds it less surprising that such qualities "appear so fundamental to hypertext and to *Patchwork Girl* than that earlier literary forms subdued them."

Having glanced at *Patchwork Girl*'s linking topologies and its collage-like features, let us next examine some of the ways they and its themes and techniques appear in its use of seams, sutures, links, and scars. As Tim McConville points out, cinema "theoreticians use the word suture to describe a film's ability to cover up cuts and fragments," thereby creating the appearance of "a fluid text that reads 'naturally.'" But because *Patchwork Girl,* "like all hypertext fiction, scoffs at the notion of a neat and tidy text," Jackson's patched-together protagonist defines herself by her scars. Thus, although, "like film, *Patchwork Girl* and all hypertext implement suture," unlike film, they do not do so "as a means of holding narrative together in one cohesive unit. Jackson uses sutures to tie various pieces together so that narrative may merely exist. After sutures have been set in place, the end result is a scar" ("Sutures and Scars").

And scars define the Patchwork Girl, *Patchwork Girl,* and, Jackson implies, all hypertext. In fact, according to Erica Seidel,

> scars are analogous to hypertextual links. The monster's scars are intimate, integral, the essence of her identity. Similarly, the essence of hypertext is the linking, the private ways that the author chooses to arrange her piece, and the reader uses to meander through it. Just as the monster finds pleasure and identity in her scars, good hypertext works are defined and distinguished by their unique linking structures. When Shelley and the monster become intimate, she first understands the significance of the monster's scars: "I see that your scars not only mark a cut, they also commemorate a joining." During this sexual en-

counter, Shelley genuinely identifies with the scars. "Her scars lay like living things be-tween us, inscribing themselves in my skin. What divided her, divided me." Just as the stitchings of skin unite Shelley and the monster, hypertext links unite author and reader. ("The Hypertextuality of Scars")[9]

Jeffrey Pack's mini-web discussing *Patchwork Girl* takes this analogy even farther, first looking at Webster's definitions of a scar as, "among other things, a 'mark left on the skin or other tissue after a wound, burn, ulcer, pustule, lesion, etc. has healed,' a 'marring or disfiguring mark on anything,' and 'the lasting mental or emotional effects of suffering or anguish.'" The first mean-ing, Pack explains, defines the scar "as a joining, that is, a visual signal that two pieces of skin that were not contiguous at one time now are. In this sense, a scar is the biological version of the seam, where Mother Nature (or, in the case of *Frankenstein* and *Patchwork Girl,* a human creator) sews flesh together in the same way a seamstress stitches together a quilt or the creator of a hypertext links texts together."

According to Pack, the next definition "presents the scar as a mark of disfigurement. Scars are ugly (in modern Western society, at least). They're jarring breaks in the otherwise even epidermis," and links similarly "disrupt, scar, an otherwise linear text." (Pack wrote his critique in HTML to be read with a WWW viewer, and he thus added that the appearance of the link "is even similar; most graphical browsers will display a 'scar' beneath the links on this page, though a user can play the role of cosmetic surgeon and opt to conceal this disfigurement of the text if they so choose.")

The last definition

gives the scar a more abstract meaning; it is now a sign of trauma. In order for a scar to exist, the flesh must have been torn. The formation of a scar is a kludge: its appearance is the result of haphazard regeneration rather than orderly growth. The link is similarly a textual trauma; the transitions between sentences and paragraphs give way to (presum-ably) intuitive leaps between texts and ideas. The replacement (as opposed to the ap-pending) of text caused by following an HTML link is disorienting to say the least; even the sudden appearance of another window (in an environment such as Storyspace) interferes with the reader's practiced down-and-to-the-right movement across a "page" of text.

Pack entitled his subweb "Frankenfiction," and his examination of scars, links, and seams in *Patchwork Girl* emphasizes the way Jackson uses them to create a textual "monster."

Like Donna J. Haraway, Jackson rejoices in the cultural value of monsters. Traveling within Jackson's multisequential narrative, we first wander along many paths, finding ourselves in the graveyard, then in Mary Shelley's journal, in scholarly texts, and in the life histories of the beings—largely women but also an occasional man and a cow—who provided the monster's parts. As we read, we increasingly come to realize an assemblage of points, one of the most insistent of which appears in the way we use our information technologies, our prosthetic memories, to conceive ourselves. Jackson's 175-year-old protagonist embodies the effects of the written, printed, and digital word. "I am like you in most ways," she tells us.

> My introductory paragraph comes at the beginning and I have a good head on my shoulders. I have muscle, fat, and a skeleton that keeps me from collapsing into suet. But my real skeleton is made of scars: a web that traverses me in three dimensions. What holds me together is what marks my dispersal. I am most myself in the gaps between my parts, though if they sailed away in all directions in a grisly regatta there would be no thing left here in my place.
>
> For that reason, though, I am hard to do in. The links can stretch very far before they break, and if I am the queen of dispersal then however far you take my separate parts (wrapped in burlap and greasy fish-wrappers, in wooden carts and wherries, burying and burning me and returning me to the families from which I sprung unloved and bastard) you only confirm my reign. ("dispersed")

Hypertext, Jackson permits us to see, enables us to recognize the degree to which the qualities of collage—particularly those of appropriation, assemblage, concatenation, and the blurring of limits, edges, and borders—characterize a good deal of the way we conceive of gender and identity.

Michael DiBianco points out, for example, that *Patchwork Girl* "addresses the issue of identity as it is inextricably linked to the author/subject relationship," particularly in relation to the narrator, who appears "as much a jumbled collection of disparate parts as her monster," something apparent in the way "Jackson continually incorporates different personas, different voices, at all levels of the text. There is a sense of unceasingly assuming new identities, trying them on briefly, then letting the hypertextual structure of the fiction erase them, only to be subsequently replaced by new identities" ("Commentary"). As the narrator puts it, "I hop from stone to stone and an electronic river washes out my scent in the intervals. I am a discontinuous trace, a dotted line." And: "I am a mixed metaphor. Metaphor, meaning something like 'bearing across,' is itself a fine metaphor for my condition. Every part of me is linked to other territories alien to it but equally mine."

Sooner or later all information technologies, we recall, have always convinced those who use them both that these technologies are natural and that they provide ways to describe the human mind and self. At the early stage of a digital information regime, *Patchword Girl* permits us to use hypertext as a powerful speculative tool that reveals new things about ourselves while at the same time retaining the sense of strangeness, of novelty.[10]

Quibbling,

a Feminist Rhizome Narrative

Quibbling, explains its author, Carolyn Guyer, "is about how women and men are together, it tends slightly toward the salacious, it is broadly feminist (so to speak), or, one could say it is the story of someone's life just before the beginning or a little after the end" ("Something about *Quibbling*"). I begin my discussion of *Quibbling* by directing attention to Guyer's words "how women and men *are* together." Her emphasis is upon a state of being rather than upon narrative drive, for in fact the tale accumulates, eddies, and takes the form, as Guyer puts it, of a "lake with many coves." *Quibbling*'s dispersed set of narratives includes those of four couples—Agnes and Will, Angela and Jacob, Hilda and Cy, and Heta and Priam—as well as a range of other characters, including several in a novel one of the characters is writing.

Quibbling sharply contrasts with Joyce's *Afternoon,* which seems the electronic translation of high modernist fiction—difficult, hieratic, earnest, allusive, and enigmatic. In essence, the opposition comes down to attitudes towards sharing authorial power with readers, and Coover therefore well describes *Quibbling* as a "conventional, but unconventionally designed, romance by one of the most radical proponents of readerly intervention in hyperfictions" ("And Now," 11). In contrast to *Afternoon,* which uses the resources of hypertext to assign even more authorial power to the reader, *Quibbling* tantalizes readers into wandering through its spaces in unexpected ways.

The contrast between the attitudes toward reader intervention taken by *Quibbling* and *Afternoon* clearly appears in the versions of Storyspace they employ. Like *Patchwork Girl,* Guyer's hypertext fiction uses the Storyspace reader, which presents a single scrollable page, similar to that which one encounters in WWW, along with the folderlike Storyspace view that permits readers to search the innards of the text. Although Joyce originally used the Storyspace reader for some of the prepublication versions of *Afternoon* (including one I illustrated in the first edition of this book), in the published version, he employed the simple Page Reader, which offers the reader far less power. In explaining her own choice, Guyer points out: "I want people to see the topographic structure itself, be able to go inside it and muck about directly. I want access left to the reader as much as possible." This choice means, as Coover correctly points out, that *Quibbling* "can be read by way of its multiple links, but it can also be read more 'geographically' simply by

exploring these nested boxes as though they constituted a kind of topographi-
cal map" ("And Now," 11)

Similarly, Guyer's approach to linking reveals her to be far more willing
to share power with the reader, as her changing attitude towards links suggests: "I've always felt dense linkage meant more options for the reader, and
so greater likelihood of her taking the thing for her own. But this idea now
seems wrong to me. Excessive linkage can actually be seen as something of
an insult, and certainly more directive. . . . In the end, I find I cannot bring
myself to make the physical links that are inherent in the writing, that is,
the 'obvious' ones (the motifs of glass, water, hands, color, walking, etc.)"
(journal).

Guyer's emphasis upon an active reader, as opposed to simply a respon-
sive, attentive one, relates directly to her conception of hypertext as a form
of feminist writing. In fact, like *Patchwork Girl, Quibbling* makes us wonder
whether hypertext fiction and, indeed, all hypertext is in some way a feminist
sort of writing, the electronic embodiment of that *l'écriture feminine* for which
Hélène Cixous called several decades ago. Certainly, like Ede and Lunsford,
whose alignment of collaborative authorship with feminist theory, we have
already observed, Guyer believes that hypertext—an intrinsically collaborative form as she employs it—speaks to the needs and experience of women:
"We know that being denied personal authority inclines us to prefer . . . decentered contexts, and we have learned, especially from our mothers, that
the woven practice of women's intuitive attention and reasoned care is a fuller, more balanced process than simple rational linearity" (quoted in Joyce,
Of Two Minds, 89).

According to Diane Greco, Guyer sees hypertext as the embodiment of
"ostensibly female (or perhaps, feminine) characteristics of intuition, atten-
tiveness, and care, all of which are transmitted from one woman to another
via the universal experience of having a (certain kind of) mother. The opportunities for non-linear expression which hypertext affords coalesce, in this
view, to form a writing that is 'female' in a very particular way: hypertext
writing embraces an ethic of care that is essentially intuitive, complicated,
detailed, but also 'fuller' and 'balanced.'" Reminding us that "some notable
hypertexts by women, such as Kathryn Cramer's *In Small and Large Pieces*
and Jane Yellowlees Douglas's *I Have Said Nothing,* feature violence, rupture,
and breakage as organizing imagery," Greco remains doubtful of any claims
that hypertext, or any other mode of writing, could be essentially female or
feminine (88).[11]

Whether we agree with Guyer that hypertext fiction necessarily embodies some essential form of women's writing, we have to recognize that she has written *Quibbling* as a non-Aristotelian networked cluster of stories, moods, and narrative fragments that gather and rearrange themselves in ways that embody her beliefs about female writing. In her essay about *Quibbling* published in *Leonardo,* she emphasizes how her fiction web lacks both conventional narrative and conventional aspirations to be literary: "It is hardly about anything itself, being more like the gossip, family discussions, letters, passing fancies and daydreams that we tell ourselves every day in order to make sense of things. These are not exactly like myths, or fairy tales, or literary fiction. They are instead the quotidian stream. In this sense, then, *Quibbling* is a work that tries not to be literary." Wending our ways through it, we encounter lexias that take the form of messages received via electronic mail, brief notes, and poetry, as well as more usual narrative, description, and exposition. The links that join these lexias do not produce straight-ahead, or even eddying, narratives but instead generate an open montage-textuality, like that of *In Memoriam,* in which lexias echo one another, gathering meaning to themselves and sharing it with other, apparently unrelated patches of writing.

Guyer's basic approach appears in the way individual lexias follow one another and hence come to associate with one another. If, after reading the lexia entitled "walking w/Will," which recounts an episode in the relationship of Agnes and Will, one double clicks on it to follow a link out, that action brings one to "following her," which relates how after their first date Priam secretly followed Hetta home to make sure she was safe; activating a link from this lexia brings one to an event or state in the relationship of Angela and Jacob. Reading along this link path, one perceives somewhat analogous situations, thus finding similarity, though not identity, in the lives of different couples. In some cases, only by looking at the lexia's location in the web's structure (presented by the Storyspace View) can readers discern which couple's story they are reading. These stories take form by gentle accretion, as one lexia rubs up against another. In contrast to *Afternoon,* in which our ignorance of a crucial event drives our reading, here no single core quickly comes to prominence as the necessary axis or center of all lexias. No single event endows the others with meaning. *Quibbling* seems far more a networked narrative in which similar situations bleed back and forth across the boundaries of individual lexias, gradually amassing meanings. It is, as Guyer explains,

in that rhythmic sense of ebb and flow, of multi-directional change, of events that disappear before they are quite intelligible but somehow come to mean something, that *Quib-*

bling was made. In hindsight, I can see why water and its properties became one of the pervasive, propelling metaphors in the work. A lake with many coves is how I saw it. The coves being where we focus, where individuals exist, where things are at least partly comprehensible; the lake being none of that, but, naturally, more than the sum of the coves, or more than what connects them. As a metaphor, the lake and coves stand not just for the form of this hyperfiction, but hyperfictions generally, and yes, for life itself. ("Something")

Guyer has stated that when she encountered *A Thousand Plateaus,* she recognized Deleuze and Guattari's ideas as something which she had long sought, and not surprisingly her conceptions of event and resolution in narrative are illuminated far more by their conceptions of nomadic thought than Aristotelian notions of plot. In *Quibbling,* she explains, "closure, resolution, achievement, the objects of our lives are inventions that operate somewhat like navigational devices, placemarkers if you will." Guyer's exposition of the ideas and attitudes that inform her fiction provide a valuable guide to her world of fluid narrative, a world of change and flux that has strong resemblances to that created by *In Memoriam,* a world in which "we go on like waves unsure of the shore, sometimes leaping backwards into the oncoming, but always moving in space-time, always finding someplace between the poles that we invent, shifting, transforming, making ourselves as we go" ("Buzz-Daze").

In discussing *Quibbling,* Guyer turns to Deleuze and Guattari's ideas of the smooth and the striated as a conceptual and fictional way of resolving problems created by the "nonexistent" sets of polarized abstractions in terms of which we lead our lives: "Female/Male, Night/Day, Death/Life, Earth/Sky, Intuitive/Rational, Individual/Communal.... We make these things up!" Deleuze and Guattari shift attention from polar oppositions to "the constant transformations of one pole into the other. What's important to recognize is not the impossible duality of the poles, but what happens between them. You might say it's What We Learn, what we actually experience in space-time as we conceive ourselves, as we conceive space-time" ("Buzz-Daze").

Storyworlds and Other Forms of Hypertext Narratives

Many hypertexts, like *Quibbling* and *Ultramundane,* exemplify what Michael Innis, head of Inscape, Inc., has termed a storyworld. Storyworlds, which contain multiple narratives, demand active readers because they only disclose their stories in response to the reader's actions. Obviously derived from computer-based adventure gaming, these storyworlds, however, generally play down elements of danger or fighting monsters as a means of approaching some goal. *Uncle Buddy's Phantom Funhouse,* which John McDaid created in HyperCard, seems the first of this electronic genre, whose more recent examples on CD-ROM include Laurie Anderson and Hsien-Chien Huang's *Puppet Motel* (1996), the Residents' *Freak Show* (1993) and *Bad Day at the Midway* (1995).

Like the extremely popular CD-ROM adventure game *Myst* (1993), these storyworlds reconfigure conflict and the role it plays in narrative and the reader's experience. All stories take the form of the conflict or the journey, and if one considers that distance serves as the antagonist in the journey narrative, then all stories turn out to involve various forms of conflict. The antagonist can be a personal opponent, a force, fate, or ignorance (or cognitive dissonance), which appear either as an internal state or as a relation between the self and environment. Whereas in both adventure narratives and adventure games the conflict requires some form of physical opposition, in the storyworld the role of antagonist is taken by mystery and enigma. The detective story becomes the paradigm for this electronic form—something already present in modernist and postmodern fictions such as *Absalom, Absalom!* and *Waterland.*

Like the detective working on a case, readers who find themselves within storyworlds must take an aggressive approach, even performing actions supposedly forbidden. In most narratives, as in real life, one learns that it is considered bad form or even criminal behavior to interrogate, trespass, or investigate behind the scenes. In hypertext storyworlds, one must do so or one will encounter very little in the way of story or world. In both *Myst* and *Freak Show* one receives very little in the way of clues or instructions and must gradually piece together a strategy. This process involves recognizing clues and determining what attitude one must take towards the environment in which one comes upon them. When *Freak Show* begins, we find ourselves outside a side show tent, and using a computer mouse we move inside it and encounter a ringmaster who introduces us to what he terms "the world's most disturbing collection of human oddities"—Herman the Human Mole, Harry the Head, Jelly Jack, Wanda the Worm Woman, and so on. He pauses before the doorway or curtain that leads to each, providing a brief introduction in the manner of the carnival barker. Finding ourselves within this carefully rendered three-dimensional overview, we can pause before each of several possible choices, which also include a sampling of the Residents' music and a historical archive of freaks and deformities, listening to the barker's description. After each introduction, we can approach the relevant exhibit, thus prompting its display, or we can cut off the barker in mid-sentence, causing him to cry out, "Forget it!" "Okay! Okay!" or a number of other expressions of irritation

More important, this storyworld rewards readers who repeatedly disobey his irritated pronouncements that they cannot go behind the scenes. On the third attempt, readers discover that they can in fact enter a passage that takes them to the trailers inhabited by members of the sideshow. Entering each environment similarly rewards the active, intrusive, curious reader. Finding ourselves projected into the cursor (or reduced to it), we probe objects until they yield stories. Entering Herman the Human Mole's area, we find his wagon and can get a brief glimpse of him through the porthole-like window of his circus wagon. At this point, we can turn around, returning to the main tent, or nosily wander around until we find a way into his wagon. Probing this environment successfully, we eventually find Herman in hiding and he tells us his sad tale in the form of a set of primitive cartoons in what appears to be his personal style. The narratives of Herman and the other characters, each of which takes a very different form, themselves have little of hypertextuality. They are simply the rewards of the reader's aggressive curiosity.

Readers or viewers of *Freak Show* find themselves in a situation quite different from that of the reluctant wedding guest whom Coleridge's Ancient Mariner forces to hear his tale. Here the reader-listener acts as the obsessive one, forcing the story out of a reluctant narrator, one who must be convinced by intrusive actions that the reader's obsessive curiosity matches his need to tell an explanatory narrative. Storyworlds, in other words, take the active, aggressive, intrusive critic as the paradigm of the ideal reader.

In the storyworld and noncombative adventure game, reader-viewers assume the position of protagonist and their reward comes in the form of experience, not as a reward one might attain. Both of these qualities involve repetitive narrative structure as in the picaresque novel of old or much Japanese fiction, neither of which builds toward a single unique climactic movement. But this form of hypertext narrative does not so much do away with climaxes as emphasize multiple ones. We have already observed something akin to this tendency in Joyce's *Afternoon* or Tennyson's *In Memoriam,* both of which achieve some sort of wholeness by formal terms. In Tennyson's case this derives from virtuoso formal closures, many of which pointedly do not coincide with intellectual or thematic ones, thereby making an individual lexia simultaneously self-sufficient and yet part of a larger whole; the formal closure makes them end satisfactorily, the lack of intellectual closure joins each into a larger whole. Joyce's similar effects arise not so much from any formal closure—something harder to achieve in prose since one doesn't have what

Figure 27. *HyperCafe*'s Overview Screen. This project employs an overview suited to its interactive materials, effectively mediating between the linear drive of video and the reader's desire for control. Although viewers cannot halt the videos, as they can in *Kon-Tiki Interactive,* they can choose among them. (Used by permission of the authors.)

J. V. Cunningam used to called "the exclusions of a rhyme"—but from ornate, rich prose, each example of which in some sense satisfies. Thus, in hypertext fiction, one needs a certain modicum of lexias that not only make sense when entered from multiple places but also satisfy, in some way seeming (partially) complete when they end or when one departs from them.

Another variant on the storyworld appears in the *HyperCafe* interactive video project created by Nitin Sawhney, David Balcom, and Ian Smith at the Georgia Institute of Technology (Figure 27). Their combination of digital video and hypertext, the authors explain, "places the user in a virtual cafe, composed primarily of digital video clips of actors involved in fictional conversations. . . . You enter the Cafe, and the voices surround you. Pick a table, make a choice, follow the voices. You're over their shoulders looking in, listening to what they say—you have to choose, or the story will go on without you" (1). This experiment in multiple narrative was created in part to explore and extend the rhetoric of hypermedia. In particular, Sawhney, Balcom, and Smith successfully devised a means of permitting choice—and hence branching—in so fundamentally linear an information technology as video.

Some work in interactive video concentrates upon creating branching within (or from) a narrative line, often by having the user able to switch from the position of one character to another. In *The Wrong Side of Town,* for example, a woman on a business trip—the exposition is provided by a telephone call to her husband at home—goes to a diner for supper, encounters a beggar, orders her meal, and leaves. The viewer can experience the encounter with the beggar from the vantage point of either person, and once the protagonist enters the diner, one can experience her interaction with a waiter and waitress from each of their positions as well as from hers. The creators of *The Wrong Side of Town* use this opportunity in a clever, if heavy-handed, way to produce a *Rashomon*-like divergence of events coded according to class and gender positions.

Bad Day at the Midway, an interactive CD-ROM created by some members of the team that produced *Freak Show,* takes the ability to exchange roles even further by employing it as a means of switching not just vantage points but entire lines of narrative. In this storyworld the areas one can explore, the facts one discovers, and the dangers that threaten one all depend upon which character one assumes. Thus, although the little boy "Bobby" cannot gain access to certain dangerous heights, he also seems safe from the predations of a homicidal maniac who inhabits the midway. In contrast, each of the adults has the capacity to make more discoveries than does Bobby, but each also exists in greater danger as well.

"The time-based, scenario-oriented hypermedia" of *HyperCafe* (2) takes a different approach, for rather than finding oneself within a narrative where one discovers choices, one begins by encountering a field of competing narratives—essentially a video version of the situation one has in certain static hyperfictions, such as *Adam's Bookstore,* in which one begins by choosing any lexia as one's starting point (Figure 28). As Sawhney, Balcom, and Smith explain: "In *HyperCafe,* the video sequences play out continuously, and at no point can they be stopped by actions of the user. The user simply navigates

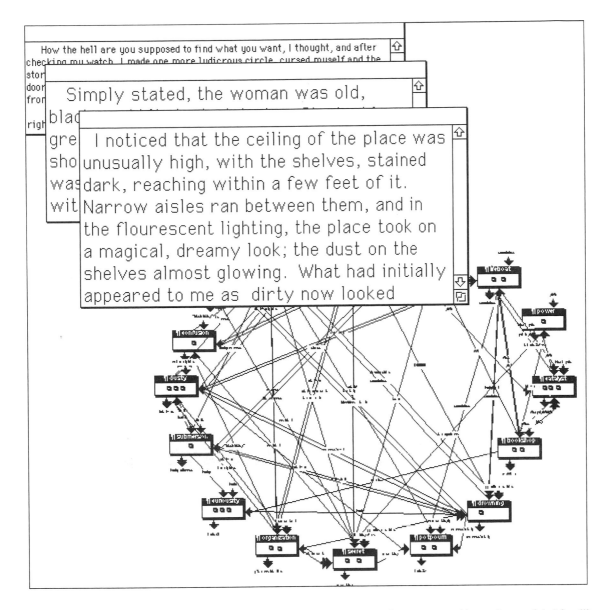

Figure 28. The Structure of Networked Hypertext. In creating a narrative that the reader can enter and leave at any point, Adam Wenger took advantage of the graphic capacities of Storyspace to arrange the individual lexias of *Adam's Bookstore* in the form of a circle or large polygon. (For the sake of legibility, I have increased the font size in two of the lexias in relation to the Storyspace view; in the original, one can easily read the titles of all the lexia icons.) (Used by permission of the author.)

Figure 29. Text and Image from *HyperCafe*. In this interactive video project viewers become aware of possible choices from text containing bits of dialogue that move across the screen and from overhearing conversations. (Used by permission of the authors.)

through the flow of the video and links presented. . . . The camera moves to reveal each table (3 in all), allowing the user 5–10 seconds to select any conversation. The video of the cafe overview scene plays continuously, forwards and then backwards, until the user selects a table" (2). Once viewers make a choice, they enter a particular scene, which then offers particular narrative lines.

The designers of the HyperVideo environment in which *HyperCafe* exists created three forms of linking—the temporal form we have already observed, one they term "spatial link opportunities," and a third kind, interpretive textual links. Viewers learn about the presence of spatial links by means of three "potential interface modes: flashing rectangular frames within the video, changes in the cursor, and/or possible playback of an audio-only preview of the destination video" (4). Finally, viewers learn about the choices they can make from text that scrolls across the screen, and these texts can take the form of random bits of dialogue or scripts for particular scenes (Figure 29). "Text intrudes on the video sequences, to offer commentary, to replace or even displace the videotext. Words, spoken by the participants are subverted and rewritten by words on the screen, giving way to tensions between word and image" (4). Building upon the research of workers at MIT, the University of Amsterdam, and the University of Oslo, *HyperCafe* demands active, intrusive reader-viewers who build narratives by following links.

The result, as the authors make clear, is that individual lexias participate in various story lines, or, as they put it, "narrative sequences may 'share' scenes" (5), and for this reason they specifically compare the kind of narrative found in *HyperCafe* to that of Joyce's *Afternoon*.

From Narration to Poetry?

By now many of the similarities of postmodernism, post-structuralism, and electronic media should have become obvious. Which raises the question, Whether or not there is a message in the medium, is there a genre and a style there? After all, each age of information technology, each information regime, has had its characteristic literary genres. The age of orality had the epic, heroic elegy, and tragedy, the age of manuscript had the romance, and that of print the novel. In his *Theory of the Novel* (1923), Georg Lukacs, who argued that every era had its own characteristic literary form, pointed for evidence to the classical epic, medieval romance, and modern novel, and considering each era's dominant information technology provides even more support for his proposition.

Writers on hypertext increasingly take it to be an intrinsically postmodern literary and artistic medium, but does it come with particular genres and modes, or does it at least favor particular ones? Coover has expressed the idea that hypertext might turn out to be more a poetic than a narrative form, and many of the webs at which we have already looked, particularly those by Guyer and Joyce, suggest that such might be the case. They reveal, as Jean Clement has argued, "a shift from narration to poetry in fiction hypertexts." According to Clement, "hypertexts produce—at the level of narrative syntax—the same 'upheaval' as poems produce at the level of phrastic syntax." In other words, the way links reconfigure narrative leads to a defamiliarization that parallels the effects of characteristically poetic departures from word order, common usage, and the like. Clement continues: "Hypertexts free narrative sequences from their subjection to the syntax of conventional narration to insert them into the multidimension[al] space of a totally new and open structure, as poems free words from their linkage to the straightness of the syntagmatic axis to put them in a network of thematic, phonetic, metaphoric (and so on) connections which create a multi-isotopic configuration" (71). The explanation may be even simpler: the link, the element that hypertext adds to writing, bridges gaps between text—bits of text—and thereby produces effects similar to analogy, metaphor, and others forms of thought, other figures, that we take to define poetry and poetic thought.

Yet another ground for believing that hypertext might privilege poetry, particularly its lyric forms, appears in Jerome J. McGann's argument that "the object of poetry is to display the textual condition. Poetry is language that calls attention to itself, that takes its own textual activities as its ground subject." He emphasizes that such a claim does not assume "poetic texts lack polemical, moral, or ideological materials and functions. The practice of language takes place within those domains. But poetical texts operate to display their own practices, to put them forward as the subject of attention" (*Textual Condition,* 10–11), or, as McGann explains later, "the object of the poetical text is to thicken the medium as much as possible—literally, to put the resources of the medium on full display, to exhibit the processes of self-reflection and self-generation which texts set in motion, which they *are*" (14). McGann refers to the bibliographical and linguistic resources of written and printed language, but hypertext adds a new element—the link—to the mix. Since the link and various associated functions, such as lists of destination lexias, serve as the defining resources of hypertext, one expects to find them foregrounded in literary webs, and such is in fact the case. Of course, at this point in the development of this new medium, one cannot tell whether the sheer novelty of the medium motivates one to make such emphases in these writing resources, and whether later hyperwriters will do so, though I must admit that I find it difficult imagining literary hypertext that does not in this poetic manner make the most of its unique features.

Certainly, as we have already seen, poetry appears throughout the docuverse, often in unexpected places. That is, we encounter poetry not only in the form of scholarly hypertext editions, such as Peter Robinson's Chaucer project, or in translations into the hypertextual, such as Espen Aarseth's HyperCard version of Raymond Queneau's *Cent Mille Milliards de Poèmes* or Jon Lanestedt's and my *"In Memoriam" Web*. It also appears brushing up against other forms and modes, sometimes merely as a defining allusion within the midst of a prose fiction (Joshua Rappaport's *Hero's Face*) and other times as part of a prose mystory (Taro Ikai, *Electronic Zen*). Karen Lee's *Lexical Lattice* demonstrates that poetry comes braided together with theory and literary history. Poetry also shows up in the most unexpected places within hypertext webs, nowhere more so than in Stuart Moulthrop's *Victory Garden,* where at least one of his Storyspace link menus forms a sonnet!

Hypertext poetry uses the link in a wide variety of ways. Following links in Aarseth's HyperCard version of Queneau's combinatorial poem, for example, produces the effect of replacing individual lines while leaving the remaining ones unchanged. In *Lexical Lattice,* on the other hand, links attach to individual words rather than to entire lines, and following any one of them produces a choice of between two and four destination poems. Much of the hypertext poetry I have seen employs one aspect of what I think of as the *In*

Memoriam model, in which lexias function as more-or-less self-sufficient poems that nonetheless take on additional meaning from the various collages and montages in which they appear.

Hypertext poets have created their work in a wide variety of software environments. A large number of them have used Storyspace, but William Dickey, one of the first (possibly the very first) of hypertext poets, uses HyperCard, some poets in France have used the help system for Windows, and Robert Kendall seems unique in writing in Visual Basic for Windows. His visually elegant *A Life Set for Two* embodies his belief that hypertext is "a medium of multiplicity and contingency" in which readers perform poems, thus creating effects similar to those found in "semi-improvised oral poetry" (74). In attempting to "parallel the random-access nature of human memory" (75), Kendall's lyric reflection on lost love employs what he terms "floating links" that allow readers many ways through his collection of lyrics. Assembling a virtuoso combination of his own poetry and programming, Kendall seats us at the table in his hypertext restaurant and lets us order and reorder his salty sweet, sometimes peppery dishes. After a linear introduction, readers encounter juxtaposed male and female menus from "Café Passé," each of which lists topics on the order of "Fall Fruit," "A Heart Well Done," "Manna from the Stars," and "Wild Game (in Season)." Clicking upon any item in the menu produces a lyric that, like an animation in Macromedia Director, assembles itself line-by-line and then occasionally displays a single word or phrase in a kind of exchange mode, in which it alternates every few seconds with its variant twin.

The poet has explained his conceptions of hypertext with fine clarity in "Hypertextual Dynamics," and so I shall remark only that *A Life Set for Two* makes no attempt to attach links to individual words or phrases, producing instead a poetic form based on section-to-section or lexia-to-lexia linking. Readers follow links by using a menu at bottom right that permits them to reread a section, go to the next, or change their options, which include choosing one of three "moods, or emotional perspectives" (75) denoted by blue, red, or black backgrounds, against which individual lyrics take appropriately different forms. In addition, Kendall adds yet other elements of variation by permitting readers to choose what he terms "secondary state" or motifs that add seasoning to the mix. "Potential Parenthood" or "Touch of Another Man" vary and complicate the overall mix as throughout *A Life Set for Two* Kendall braids together reader choice and authorial power in ways impossible to create in print.

Reading *A Life Set for Two* with a friend whose Windows machine I had appropriated for the purpose, I found Kendall's combination of accessible, relatively traditional poetry with an enriching technology very compelling. As we made our way through the web, retracing our steps occasionally and then changing the moods and motifs to experience slightly different seasoning, my friend remarked, "You know, this is a new art form." And so it is. Whether lyric poetry or narrative will draw more inspiration from the electronic link remains an open question. Similarly, it is hardly clear at this point whether hypertextual amplifications of the imperial author, collaboration among multiple authors, or collaboration between author and wreaders will all produce important work. But whatever interesting questions we have to consider, we realize that the arrival of hypertext represents not the death of literature but merely its latest transformation.

Reconfiguring

Literary Education

Threats and Promises

Like many other observers of the relations between information technology and education, Jean-François Lyotard perceives that "the miniaturization and commercialization of machines is already changing the way in which learning is acquired, classified, made available, and exploited. It is reasonable to suppose that the proliferation of information-processing machines is having, and will continue to have, as much of an effect on the circulation of learning as did advances in human circulation (transportation systems) and later, in the circulation of sounds and visual images (the media)" (*Postmodern Condition,* 4). One chief effect of electronic hypertext has been the way it challenges now-conventional assumptions about teachers, learners, and the institutions they inhabit. It changes the roles of teacher and student in much the same way it changes those of writer and reader. Its emphasis upon the active, empowered reader, which fundamentally calls into question general assumptions about reading, writing, and texts, similarly calls into question our assumptions about the nature and institutions of literary education that so depend upon these texts. Gary Marchionini, who created evaluation procedures for Project Perseus, reminds us that "each time a new technology is applied to teaching and learning, questions about fundamental principles and methods arise." ("Evaluating Hypermedia-Based Learning," 369). Hypertext, by holding out the possibility of newly empowered, self-directed students, demands that we confront an entire range of questions about our conceptions of literary education.

Hypertext systems promise—or threaten—to have major effects on literary education, and the nature of hypertext's potential effect on human thought appears in descriptions of it from its earliest days. Writing of Bush,

Englebart, Nelson, and other pioneers of hypertext, John L. Leggett and members of his team at the Hypermedia Lab at the University of Texas point out that "the revolutionary content of their ideas was, and continues to be, the extent to which these systems engage the user as an active participant in interactions with information" ("Hypertext for Learning," 27). Students making use of hypertext systems participate actively in two related ways, acting as reader-authors both by choosing individual paths through linked primary and secondary texts and by adding texts and links to the docuverse.[1]

Now that a decade has passed since I began teaching with hypertext—half a decade since I completed the typescript of the first edition of this book—I can see that this medium has been used in four ways. One cannot accurately term them stages, since several coincided with each other, and all continue in use today. Starting with Intermedia, read-only hypermedia helped students acquire both information and habits of thinking critically in terms of multiple approaches or causes. These first two uses or results represent the effects of employing an information medium based on connections to help students develop the habit of making connections. Next, almost immediately we discovered that Intermedia, which provided a participatory reading-and-writing environment, empowered students by placing them within—rather than outside—the world of research and scholarly debate. Finally, writing hypermedia enabled students to explore and create new modes of discourse appropriate for the kind of reading and writing we shall do increasingly in e-space, the writing necessary for the twenty-first century. In the first version of this book, by necessity I cited materials chiefly available only on Intermedia at Brown. Now, since many of these webs have moved into other systems, I shall use examples easily accessible to readers, choosing, whenever possible, materials either published in Storyspace or other environments or available on the Web.

All these effects or applications encourage and even demand an active student. The ways in which hypertext does so leads writers on the medium, such as David H. Jonassen and R. Scott Grabinger, to urge that "hypermedia learning systems . . . place more responsibility on the learner for accessing, sequencing and deriving meaning from the information." Unlike users of "most information systems, hypermedia users must be mentally active while interacting with the information" (4).

From this emphasis upon the active reader follows a conception of an active, constructivist learner and an assumption that, in the words of Philippe C. Duchastel, "hypermedia systems should be viewed not principally as teaching tools, but rather as learning tools" (139). As Terry Mayes, Mike

Kibby, and Tony Anderson, from the Edinburgh Centre for the Study of Human-Computer Interaction, point out, systems of computer-assisted education that use hypertext are "rightly called *learning systems,* rather than *teaching
systems.* Nevertheless, they do embody a theory of, at least an approach to,
instruction. They provide an environment in which *exploratory* or *discovery*
learning may flourish. By requiring learners to move towards nonlineal thinking, they may also stimulate processes of integration and contextualization
in a way not achievable by linear presentation techniques" ("Learning," 229).
Mayes and his collaborators therefore claim:

At the heart of understanding interactive learning systems is the question of how deliber-
ate, explicit learning differs from implicit, incidental learning. Explicit learning involves
the conscious evaluation of hypotheses and the application of rules. Implicit learning is
more mysterious: it seems almost like a process of osmosis and becomes increasingly important as tasks or material to be mastered become more complex. Much of the learning
that occurs with computer systems seems implicit. (228)

Rand J. Spiro, working with different teams of collaborators, has developed one of the most convincing paradigms yet offered for educational hypertext and the kind of learning it attempts to support. Drawing upon Ludwig
Wittgenstein's *Philosophical Investigations,* Spiro and his collaborators propose that the best way to approach complex educational problems—what he
terms "ill-structured knowledge domains"—is to approach them as if they
were unknown landscapes: "The best way to [come to] understand a given
landscape is to explore it from many directions, to traverse it first this way
and then that (preferably with a guide to highlight significant features). Our
instructional system for presenting complexly ill-structured 'topical landscape' is analogous to physical landscape exploration, with different routes
of traversing study-sites (cases) that are each analyzed from a number of
thematic perspectives" ("Knowledge Acquisition," 187). Concerned with developing efficient methods of nurturing the diagnostic skills of medical students, Spiro's team of researchers involve themselves in knowledge domains
that present problems similar to those found in the humanistic disciplines.
Like individual literary texts, patients offer the physician ambiguous com-
plexes of signs whose interpretation demands the ability to handle diachronic
and synchronic approaches. Young medical doctors, who must learn how to
"take a history," confront symptoms that often point to multiple possibilities.
They must therefore learn how to relate particular symptoms to a variety of
different conditions and diseases. Since patients may suffer from a combination of several conditions at once, say, asthma, gall bladder trouble, and high

blood pressure, physicians have to learn how to connect a single symptom to more than one explanatory system.

Spiro's explanation of his exploration-of-landscape paradigm provides an excellent description of educational hypertext:

> The notion of "criss-crossing" from case to case in many directions, with many thematic dimensions serving as routes of traversal, is central to our theory. The treatment of an irregular and complex topic *cannot be forced in any single direction* without curtailing that potential for transfer. If the topic can be applied in many different ways, none of which follows in rule-bound manner from the others, then limiting oneself in acquisition to, say, a single point of view or a single system of classification, will produce a relatively *closed* system instead of one that is open to context-dependent variability. By criss-crossing the complex topical landscape, the twin goals of highlighting multifacetedness and establishing multiple connections are attained. Also, awareness of variability and irregularity is heightened, alternative routes of traversal of the topic's complexities are illustrated, multiple entry routes for later information retrieval are established, and the general skill of working around that particular landscape (domain-dependent skill) is developed. *Information that will need to be used in a lot of different ways needs to be taught in lots of different ways.* (187–88; emphasis in original)

In such complex domains, "single (or even small numbers of) connecting threads" do not run "continuously through large numbers of successive cases." Instead, they are joined by "'woven' interconnectedness. In this view, strength of connection derives from partial overlapping of many different strands of connectedness across cases rather than from any single strand running through large numbers of the cases" (193).

Reconfiguring the Instructor

Educational hypertext redefines the role of instructors by transferring some of their power and authority to students. This technology has the potential to make the teacher more a coach than a lecturer, and more an older, more experienced partner in a collaboration than an authenticated leader. Needless to say, not all my colleagues respond to such possibilities with cries of glee and hymns of joy.

Before some of my readers pack their bags for the trip to Utopia and others decide that educational computing is just as dangerous as they thought all along, I must point out that hypertext systems have a great deal to offer instructors in all kinds of institutions of higher education. To begin with, a hypermedia corpus of multidisciplinary materials provides a far more efficient means of developing, preserving, and obtaining access to course materials than has existed before. One of the greatest problems in course development has been that it takes such a long time and that the materials developed, however pioneering or brilliant, rarely transfer to another teacher's course, because they rarely match that other teacher's needs exactly. Similarly, teachers often expend time and energy developing materials potentially useful in more than one course that they teach but do not use the materials because the time necessary for adaptation is lacking. These two problems, which all teachers face, derive from the classic, fundamental problem with hierarchical data structures that was Vannevar Bush's point of departure when he proposed the memex. A hypertext corpus, which is a descendent of the memex, allows a more efficient means of preserving the products of past endeavors because it requires so much less effort to select and reorganize them. It also encourages integrating all one's teaching, so that one's efforts function synergistically. A hypermedia corpus also preserves and makes easily available the efforts of others, as well as one's own.

Hypertext obviously provides us with a far more convenient and efficient tool than has previously existed for teaching courses in a single discipline that need the support of other disciplines. As I discovered in my encounter with the nuclear-arms materials that I discussed in Chapter 4, this educational technology permits instructors to teach in the virtual presence of other instructors and other subsections of their own discipline or other closely related disciplines. Thus, someone teaching a plant-cell biology course can draw upon the materials created for courses in very closely related fields, such as animal-cell biology, as well as slightly more distant ones, such as chemistry and biochemistry. Similarly, someone teaching an English course that concentrates on literary technique of the nineteenth-century novel can nonetheless draw upon relevant materials in political, social, urban, technological, and religious history. All of us try to allude to such aspects of context, but the limitations of time and the need to cover the central concerns of the course often leave students with a decontextualized, distorted view.

Inevitably, hypertext gives us an easy, effective way of teaching interdisciplinary courses, of doing that which almost by definition "shouldn't be done." (Except when they are applying for funding from external agencies, most departmental and university administrators use the term *interdisciplinary* to mean little more than "that which should not be done" or "that for which there is no money." After all, putting together biology and chemistry to study the chemistry of organisms is not interdisciplinary; it is the subject of a separate discipline called biochemistry.) Interdisciplinary teaching no longer has its earlier glamor for several reasons. First, some have found that the need to deal with several disciplines has meant that some or all end up being treated superficially or only from the point of view of another discipline. Second, such teaching requires faculty and administration to make often extraordinarily heavy commitments, particularly when such courses involve teams of two or more instructors. Then, when members of the original team take a leave or cover an essential course for their department, the interdisciplinary course comes to a halt. In contrast to previous educational technology, hypertext offers instructors the continual virtual presence of teachers from other disciplines.

All the qualities of connectivity, preservation, and accessibility that make hypertext an enormously valuable teaching resource make it equally valuable as a scholarly tool. The medium's integrative quality, when combined with its ease of use, offers a means of efficiently integrating one's scholarly work and work-in-progress with one's teaching. In particular, one can link portions of data upon which one is working, whether they take the form of primary texts, statistics, chemical analyses, or visual materials, and integrate these into courses. Such capabilities, which we have already tested in undergraduate and graduate courses at Brown, allow faculty to explore their own primary interests while showing students how a particular discipline arrives at the materials, the "truths of the discipline," that it presents as worthy of their knowledge. Materials on anti-Catholicism and anti-Irish prejudice in Victorian Britain created by Anthony S. Wohl, like some of my recently published work on Graham Swift and sections of this book, represent such integration of the instructor's scholarship and teaching. Such use of one's scholarly projects for teaching, which can highlight the more problematic aspects of a field, accustoms students to the notion that for the researcher and theorist many key problems and ideas remain in flux.

Hypermedia linking, which integrates scholarship and teaching in one discipline with others, also permits the faculty member to introduce beginners in the field to the way advanced students think and work, while it gives beginners access to materials at a variety of levels of difficulty. Such materials, which the instructor can make easily available to all or only advanced students, again permit a more efficient means than do textbooks of introducing students to the actual work of a discipline, which is often characterized by competing schools of thought. Because hypertext interlinks and interweaves a variety of materials at differing levels of difficulty and expertise, it encourages both exploration and self-paced instruction. The presence of such materials permits faculty members to accommodate the slower and the faster or more committed learners in the same class.

Reconfiguring the Student

For students hypertext promises new, increasingly reader-centered encounters with text. In the first place, experiencing a text as part of a network of navigable relations provides a means of gaining quick and easy access to a far wider range of background and contextual materials than has ever been possible with conventional educational technology. Students in schools with adequate libraries have always had the materials available, but availability and accessibility are not the same thing. Until students know how to formulate questions, particularly about the relation of primary materials to other phenomena, they are unlikely to perceive a need to investigate context, much less know how to go about using library resources to do so.

Even more important than having a means of acquiring factual material is having a means of learning what to do with such material when one has it in hand. Critical thinking relies upon relating many things to one another. Since the essence of hypertext lies in its making connections, it provides an efficient means of accustoming students to making connections among materials they encounter. A major component of critical thinking consists in the habit of exploring how various causes impinge upon a single phenomenon or event and then evaluating their relative importance, and hypertext encourages this habit.

Hypertext also offers a means for a novice reader to learn the habit of multisequential reading necessary for the use of both educational anthologies and scholarly apparatuses. Hypertext, which has been defined as text designed to be read multisequentially or in a nonlinear mode, efficiently models the kind of text characteristic of scholarly and scientific writing. These forms of writing require readers to leave the main text and venture out to consider footnotes, evidence of statistics and other authorities, and the like. Our experience at Brown University suggests that using hypertext teaches students to read in this advanced manner. This effect upon reading, which first appears in students' better use of anthologies and standard textbooks, exemplifies the way that hypertext and appropriate materials together can quickly get students up to speed.

In addition, a corpus of hypertext documents intrinsically joins materials that students encounter in separate parts of a single course and in other courses and disciplines. Hypertext, in other words, provides a means of integrating the subject materials of a single course with other courses. Students, particularly novice students, continually encounter problems created by necessary academic specialization and separation of single disciplines into individual courses. Arguing for the historic contextualization of literary works, Brook Thomas describes this all too familiar problem.

> The notion of a piece of literature as an organic, autonomous whole that combats the fragmentation of the modern world can easily lead to teaching practices that contribute to the fragmentation our students experience in their lives; a fragmentation confirmed in their educational experience. At the same time sophomores take a general studies literature course, they might also take economics, biology, math, and accounting. There is nothing, not even the literature course, that connects the different knowledge they gain from these different courses. . . . Furthermore, because each work students read in a literature course is an organic whole that stands on its own, there is really no reason why they should relate one work to another in the same course. As they read one work, then another, then another, each separate and unique, each reading can too easily contribute to their sense of education as a set of fragmented, unrelated experiences in which wholeness and unity are to be found only in temporary, self-enclosed moments. (229)

Experience teaching with hypertext demonstrates that its intrinsic capacity to join varying materials creates a learning environment in which materials supporting separate courses exist in closer relationship to one another than is possible with conventional educational technology. As students read through materials for one English course, they encounter those supporting others and thereby perceive relationships among courses and disciplines.

Learning the Culture of a Discipline

Hypertext also offers a means of experiencing the way a subject expert makes connections and formulates inquiries. One of the great strengths of hypertext lies in its capacity to use linking to model the kinds of connections that experts in a particular field make. By exploring such links, students benefit from the experience of experts in a field without being confined by them, as students would be in a workbook or book approach.

Hypertext thus provides novices with means of quickly and easily learning the culture of a discipline. From the fact that hypertext materials provide the student with a means of experiencing the way an expert works in an individual discipline it follows that such a body of electronically linked material also provides the student with an efficient means of learning the vocabulary, strategies, and other aspects of a discipline that constitute its particular culture.

The capacity of hypertext to inculcate the novice with the culture of a specific discipline and subject suggests that this new information medium has an almost totalitarian capacity to model encounters with texts. The intrinsically antihierarchical nature of hypertext, however, undercuts such possibilities and makes it a means of efficiently adapting the materials to individual needs. A body of hypertext materials functions as a customized electronic library that makes available materials as they are needed and not, as lectures and other forms of scheduled presentation of necessity must often do, just when the schedule permits.

The infinitely adaptable nature of hypertext also provides students a way of working up to their abilities by providing access to sophisticated, advanced materials. Considered as an educational medium, hypertext also permits the student to encounter a range of materials that vary in terms of difficulty, because authors no longer have to pitch their materials to a single level of expertise and difficulty. Students, even novice students, who wish to explore individual topics in more depth therefore have the opportunity of following their curiosity and inclination as far as they wish. At the same time, more advanced students always have available more basic materials for easy review when necessary.

The reader-centered, reader-controlled characteristics of hypertext offer student-readers means of shaping and hence controlling major portions of what they read. Since readers shape what they read according to their own needs, they explore at their own rate and according to their own interests. In addition, the ease of using hypertext means that any student can contribute documents and links to the system. Students can thus experience the way contributions in various fields are made.

Finally, hypertext produces an additional form of discussion and a new means of contributing to class discussions that assists many students. Jolene Galegher and Robert Kraut, like most students of cooperative work, point out that "one of the failures of group discussion is the social influence that inhibits the quantity of original ideas that the members would have generated had they been working in isolation." In this context, hypermedia exemplifies those "permissive technologies" that "allow current practices to be extended into new realms in which they had previously been impracticable" ("Technology for Intellectual Teamwork," 9). This feature of hypertext doubly permits students to contribute to the activity of a class: they can contribute materials in writing if they find group discussions difficult, and other students can cite and discuss their hypertext contributions. By giving an additional means of expression to those people shy or hesitant about speaking up in a group, electronic conferencing, hypertext, and other similar media shift the balance of exchange from speaking to writing, thus addressing Derrida's calls to avoid phonocentricism in that eccentric, unexpected, very literal manner that, as we have seen before, characterizes such hypertext instantiations of theory.

Nontraditional Students:

Distant Learners and Readers

outside Educational Institutions

The combination of the reader's control and the virtual presence of a large number of authors makes for an efficient means of learning at a distance. The very qualities that make hypertext effective at supporting interdisciplinary learning also permit students to work without having to be in residence at a geographical or spatial site. In other words, the adaptable virtual presence of hypermedia contributors serves both the distant, unconventional learner and the student in a more conventional setting. To those interested in the efficient and just distribution of costly educational resources, hypertext offers a way for students at one institution to share in the resources of another. Hypermedia efficiently allows students anywhere potentially to benefit from materials created at any participating institution.

The very strengths of hypertext that make it work so well in conventional educational settings also make it the perfect means of informing, assisting, and inspiring the unconventional student. Because it encourages students to choose their own reading paths with far more freedom than do such quasi-hypertext systems as those based on HyperCard, hypertext provides the individualistic learner a superior vehicle for exploration and enrichment. By permitting readers to move from relatively familiar areas to less familiar ones, a hypertext corpus encourages the autodidact, the continuing education student, and the student with little access to instructors to get in the habit of making precisely those kinds of connections that constitute such an important part of the liberally educated mind that is so necessary in government and business. At the same time, the manner in which hypertext places the distant learner in the virtual presence of many instructors both disperses the resources in a particularly effective manner and allows the student access to some of the major benefits of an institutional affiliation without as much cost to either party in terms of time and money.

Two of the most exciting and objectively verifiable effects of using educational hypertext systems involves the way they change the limiting effects of time. The modularization that John G. Blair has described as characteristic of American (as opposed to European) higher education appears in the concepts of credit hours, implicitly equivalent courses, and transcripts.[2] Modularization also appears, one may add, in the precise and necessarily rigid scheduling of the syllabus for the individual course, which embodies what

Joseph E. McGrath describes as a naively atomistic Newtonian conception of time:

> Two of the assumptions of the Newtonian conception of time, which dominates our culture and organizations within it, are (a) an atomistic assumption that time is infinitely divisible, and (b) a homogeneity assumption that all the "atoms" of time are homogeneous, that any one moment is indistinguishable from and interchangeable with any other. But these assumptions do not hold in our experience. . . . Ten 1-minute work periods, scattered throughout the day, are not of equivalent productivity value to one 10-minute period of work from 9:15 to 9:25 a. m. Nor is the day before Christmas equivalent to February 17th for most retailers. A piece of time derives its epochal meaning, and its temporal value, partly in terms of what activities can (or must) be done in it. (38)

The division—segregation, really—of individual weeks into isolated units to which we have all become accustomed has the unfortunate effect of habituating students to consider in isolation the texts and topics encountered during these units. The unfortunate effects of precise scheduling, which coverage requires, became apparent to me only after teaching with hypertext. Here, as in other cases, one of the chief values of teaching with a hypertext system has proved to be the light it unexpectedly has cast on otherwise unexamined, conventional assumptions about education.

The Effects of Hypermedia in Teaching

An example of the effects of hypermedia in teaching comes from the experience at Brown University of Peter Heywood, associate professor of biology, who used an Intermedia component in his upper-class course in plant-cell biology.[3] The term paper for his course, which he intends to be a means of introducing students to both the literature of the field and the way it is written, requires that students include all materials on their particular topic that have seen publication up to the week before papers are handed in. This demanding assignment required that Heywood devote a great deal of time to assisting individual students with their papers and their bibliographies, and one of the chief attractions of the Intermedia component to him lay in its potential to make such information more accessible. Using hypermedia greatly surprised Heywood by producing a completely unexpected effect. In the previous seventeen years that he had taught this course, he had discovered that many term papers came in after the deadline, some long after, and that virtually all papers concerned topics covered in the first three weeks of the course. The first year that students used the Intermedia component, all thirty-four papers came in on time. Moreover, their topics were equally distributed throughout the fourteen weeks of the semester. Heywood explains this dramatic improvement in student performance as a result of the way hypertext linking permitted students to perceive connections among materials covered at different times during the semester. Although all other components of the course remained the same, the capabilities of hypermedia permitted students to follow links to topics covered later in the course and thereby encounter attractive problems for independent work. For example, while reading Intermedia materials about the cell membrane in the first weeks of the course, students could follow links that brought them to related materials not covered until week eight, when the course examined genetics, or until the last weeks of the course, when it addressed ecological questions or matters of bioengineering. Many who enrolled in this upper-division course had already taken other advanced courses in genetics, biochemistry, or similarly related subjects; linking also permitted these students to integrate materials encountered in plant-cell biology with those previously encountered in other courses.

Educational hypertext in this way serves as what McGrath describes as one of those "technological tools . . . designed in part to ease the constraints of the time/activity match in relation to communication in groups. For example, certain forms of computer conference arrangements permit so-called asynchronous communication among group members" (39). As the example from Heywood's course shows, hypertext systems also support asynchronous communication between students and between chronologically ordered modular components of the course.

Hypertext's trait of freeing learners from constraints of scheduling without destroying the structure and coherence of a course has been noted in the more impressionistic observations reported by members of both biology and English courses. One of Heywood's students described working with hypertext as providing something like the experience of studying for a final examination every week, by which he meant that each week, as students encountered a new topic, they discovered they were rearranging and reintegrating the materials they had previously learned, an experience that previously they had encountered only during preparations for major examinations. English students similarly contrasted their integrative experience of course readings with those of acquaintances in sections of the survey course that had not used Intermedia. The English students, for example, expressed surprise that whereas they placed each new poem or novel within the context of those read previously as a matter of course—considering, say, the relation of *Great Expectations* to "Tintern Abbey" and "The Vanity of Human Wishes" as well as to *Pride and Prejudice* and *Gulliver's Travels*—their friends in other sections assumed that, once a week was over, one should set aside the reading for that week until the final exam. In fact, students in other sections apparently expressed surprise that my students wanted to make all these connections.

A second form of asynchronous communication involves the creation by hypertext of a course memory that reaches beyond a single semester. Galegher and Kraut propose that "technologies that allow users to observe each others' contributions (such as computer conferences and hypermedia systems) may provide a system for sustaining group memory independent of the presence of specific individuals in an organization" (15). The contributions of individual student (and faculty) reader-authors, which automatically turned Intermedia into a fully collaborative learning environment, remain on the system for future students to read, quote, and argue against. Students in the survey course at the present time already encounter essays, comments, concept maps, and imitations in poetry and prose by at least nine groups of students from earlier years.[4] Coming upon materials created by other students, some of whom one may know or whose name one recognizes, serves to convince students that they are in a very different, more active kind of learning situation. As we shall also observe when we return to this subject in discussing the political implications of such educational media, this technology of memory produces effects quite unusual in a university setting.

**Reconfiguring Assignments
and Methods of Evaluation**

To take advantage of hypertext's potential educational effects, instructors must decide what role it will play and must consciously teach with it. Therefore, students unacquainted with this new information medium must use it from the beginning of the course. At the same time, teachers must make clear to students both the goals of the course and the role of the hypertext system in meeting them. Peter Whalley correctly points out that "the most successful uses of hypertext will involve learners and lead them to adopt the most appropriate learning strategy for their task. They must . . . allow the learner to develop higher-level skills, rather than simply become the passive recipients of a slick new technology" (68). Instructors therefore must create assignments that emphasize precisely those qualities and features of hypertext that furnish the greatest educational advantages. In another work, I have described in detail such an initial assignment; I will summarize it below before providing the example of a more complex exercise.

Whether it is true or not that readers retain less of the information they encounter while reading text on a screen than while reading a printed page, electronically linked text and printed text have different advantages. One should therefore prepare an initial assignment that provides the student with experience of hypertext's advantages—the advantages of connectivity. Obviously, instructors wishing to introduce students to the capacity hypertext gives them to choose their own reading paths and hence construct their own document must employ assignments that encourage students to do so.

The first hypertext assignment in all my courses derives from one first developed for Intermedia and then modified to fit the features of Storyspace and later Netscape. This assignment instructs students to follow links from the same location or link marker and then report what they encounter. Similarly, since I employ a corpus of linked documents to accustom students to discovering or constructing contexts for individual blocks of text or data, my assignments require multiple answers to the same question or multiple parts to the same answer. If one wishes to accustom students to the fact that complex phenomena involve complex causation, one must arrange assignments in such a way as to make students summon different kinds of information to explain the phenomena they encounter. Since my courses have increasingly taken advantage of hypertext's capacity to promote collaborative learning, my assignments, from the beginning of the course, require students to comment upon the materials and links they find, suggest new ones, and add materials. Instructors employing educational hypertext must also rethink examinations and other forms of evaluation. If hypertext's greatest educational strength as well as its most characteristic feature is its connectivity, then tests and other evaluative exercises must measure the results of using that connectivity to develop the ability to make connections.

Independent of educational use of hypertext, dissatisfaction with American secondary school students' ability to think critically has recently led to a new willingness to try evaluative methods that emphasize conceptual skills— chiefly making connections—rather than those that stress simple data acquisition. Taking advantage of the full potential of hypertext obviously forces instructors to rethink the goals and methods of education. If one wishes to develop student skills in critical thinking, then one might have to make one's goal elegance of approach rather than quantitative answers. Particularly when dealing with beginning students, instructors will have to recognize that several correct answers may exist for a single problem and that such multiplicity of answers does not indicate that the assigned problem is subjective or that any answer will do. If, for example, one asks students to provide a context in contemporary philosophy or religion for a literary technique or historical event, one can expect to receive a range of correct solutions.

A Hypertext Exercise. Several of the courses that I teach with hypertext employ the following exercise, which may take the form of either an in-class exercise or a take-home exam that students have a week or more to complete. The exercise consists of a series of passages from the assigned readings that students have to identify and then relate to a single work in brief essays; in the past, these exercises have used Wordsworth's "Tintern Abbey," *Great Expectations,* and Austen's *Pride and Prejudice* as the central texts; those for courses in Victorian literature have similarly employed Charlotte Brontë's *Jane Eyre,* Elizabeth Barrett Browning's *Aurora Leigh,* Thomas Carlyle's "Signs of the Times," and other works. The instructions for the exercise ask students to relate passages to a specific text thusly:

Begin each essay by identifying the full name, exact title, and date of the passage, after which you should explain at least three ways in which the passage relates (whatever you take that term to mean) to the poem. One of these connections should concern theme, a second should concern technique, and a third some aspect of the religious, philosophical, historical, or scientific context. . . . Not all the relations you discover or create will turn out to be obvious ones, such as matters of influence or analogous ideas and techniques. Some may take the form of contrasts or oppositions that tell us something interesting about the authors, literary forms, or times in which these works appeared.

To emphasize that demonstrating skill at formulating possible explanations and hypothesizing significant relations counts as much as factual knowledge alone, the directions explain that some subjects, "particularly matters of context, may require you to use materials" in whatever hypermedia corpus they use "to formulate an hypothesis," and the assignment goes on to warn that in many cases, the hypermedia materials, like the library, may provide "the materials to create an answer but not answers themselves."

Using this exercise in six iterations of the survey course as well as in two other courses has convinced me that it provides a useful and accurate means of evaluation that has several additional beneficial effects. Although the exercise does not directly ask for specific factual information other than titles, authors, and dates, students soon recognize that without such information they cannot effectively demonstrate connections between or among texts. In comparing a passage from Pope's "Essay on Man" with "Tintern Abbey," for example, they soon realize that only specific examples and specific comments on those examples produce effective discussion. Gary Marchionini points out that "hypermedia is an enabling technology rather than a directive one, offering high levels of user control. Learners can construct their own knowledge by browsing hyperdocuments according to the associations in their own *cognitive structures*. As with access, however, control requires re-sponsibility and decision making" ("Evaluating Hypermedia Based Learn-ing," 356). By making students choose which literary techniques, themes, or aspects of context they wish to relate, the exercise emphasizes the major role of student choice.

This assignment proves an effective educational tool because while at-tempting to carry it out many students realize that they have difficulty handling matters of context, which at the beginning they often confuse with the theme or main idea of a passage. Discussions of context require one to posit a connection between one phenomenon, say, the imagery in a poem, and some other, often more general, phenomenon, such as conceptions of the human mind, gender roles, or religious belief contemporaneous with that imagery. Perceiving possible connections and then arguing for their validity is a high-level intellectual skill. Since students are permitted and in fact en-couraged to perform the exercise as many times as they wish, it simultane-ously furnishes students the opportunity to make conceptual breakthroughs and teachers the opportunity to encourage and then measure them.

Two additional advantages of this exercise for the courses in which it appears involve writing. Since both the survey course and the more advanced courses are intended to be intensive writing courses, the chance to do a large amount of writing (and rewriting) supports one of the goals of these courses; in other kinds of courses, particularly those with large enrollments, the large output of written material might prove a hindrance. Second, the several short essays that the structure of the assignment requires seem to accomplish more than did a single long essay. At the same time that students find writing many short essays easier than constructing a single much longer one, they cover far more material than they could with a more conventional assign-ment and they cover different approaches, each demanding the kind of mate-rials generally available only in a hypermedia corpus.

Another advantage of this exercise, which I find well suited to courses with hypertext supplements, lies in the fact that, particularly in its take-home version, it demonstrates the usefulness of the hypertext system at the same time that it draws on skills encouraged by using it. The hypertext materials show students possible connections they might wish to make and furnish the information with which to make their own connections. Our hypermedia corpus also permits them to range back and forth throughout the course, thereby effecting their own syntheses of the materials.

A final utility of this exercise is that by encouraging the students to take a more active, collaborative approach to learning, it creates more materials for students to read. In one of the last years I used Intermedia (1991), approximately one third of the students in my survey wrote their answers to these exercises directly on the system, and the writers of the most successful ones later linked them to relevant documents. Other students almost all wrote their essays with Intermedia-compatible word-processing programs, such as Microsoft Word, producing documents that could be placed directly onto Intermedia; integrating these new student materials into the docuverse therefore proved easy and efficient and hence required little time or technical support. Moving to Storyspace, which imports text very easily, made such bootstrap course materials very convenient to manage; and the World Wide Web similarly makes adding lexias and simple linking very easy, though maintaining the web structure and overviews becomes vastly more difficult. (Although I do not add all student writing to the HTML versions of webs originally created in courses, as a matter of fairness, I require students to submit their assignments both in paper copies and in HTML versions on disks, which I have provided along with templates; otherwise those students who wrote the finest essays would end up having to do more work.) Increasingly, students who have used the World Wide Web versions of the Victorian and other webs themselves suggest that they write exercises directly for the web.

Examples
of Collaborative Learning

In the early days of developing and using Intermedia, the reader's shaping of the text and choice of link paths provided the only form of student collaborative work. Those of us who created the first version of the survey's hypertext component, four graduate or postdoctoral students and I, worked collaboratively, of course, but only in ways characteristic of traditional group projects. Each person wrote documents on a set of authors and topics and also gathered relevant graphic materials. Acting in the manner of the editor of an encyclopedia or anthology, I then coordinated the materials and made them conform to a uniform style. Once we reached the stage of adding documents to the course web, some of the contributors modified materials created by others and linked them to their own creations. At this point, the Intermedia materials were still the product of the five original contributors alone.

Ever since students in the survey course began using the hypertext component, however, they have become collaborators, and their collaboration has proved increasingly important. The first assignment acquaints the student with the nature of the hypertext system and the materials it contains. After instructing students to open an overview file and follow various links, the assignment asks them to record what they encounter and then asks for suggestions of additional links or materials. Another part of the assignment asks the students to choose a passage from the week's reading and append it to one of the maps or other graphic documents. From the first, somewhat to our surprise, these assignments had the happy effect of convincing a substantial portion of the class that they had control over the material and could contribute to it. Students therefore offered proofreading corrections, suggestions for links, and requests for additional materials throughout the semester. In fact, after students expressed the view that discussions of technical devices, such as imagery and narration, worked best with specific proof-texts, we created new materials for later readings. In addition to the clearly demonstrated general acceptance by students of participation and collaboration in shaping the hypermedia materials, several students took further initiative and, after receiving permission (and passwords), began to make their own links as well as obvious corrections (for example, moving links that had been labeled mistakenly or correcting typographical errors).

During Intermedia's first year, it supported an upper-class seminar in Victorian poetry. The fourteen students enrolled in this course used it to work in a more intensively collaborative manner than had the students in the more basic survey. They created documents, and some entered them on the system themselves and also made links. Observing students from an upper-class course reading and benefiting from materials created by those in another class convinced me that I should attempt an even more elaborate experiment in collaborative hypertext with graduate students, some of whom had begun to use Intermedia to prepare for their qualifying examinations. Therefore, the following term, when our hypertext materials again supported the teaching of the survey, I also used it for my graduate seminar in Victorian literature, whose six members contributed to the *In Memoriam* project.

Writing in hypertext, a student makes four kinds of contributions to the course materials, each of which, as we shall see, involves collaborative work: (1) reading, in which the reader plays a more important role in shaping the reading path than does the reader of a book, (2) creating links among documents present on the system, (3) creating text documents and linking them to others, and (4) creating graphic documents and linking them to others. Contributors to the system have produced graphics documents by adding digitized images, such as maps or reproductions of pictures, and by creating concept maps accompanied by varying degrees of text. Students have both created entirely new concept maps in the form of overview or literary relations documents and used earlier ones as templates, making minor modifications and changing the texts.

The way hypertext changes both our notions of collaborative work and our experience of it is apparent in student contributions. The most basic kind of contribution to a hypertext web, and the most fundamental, is the addition of a link, something students are encouraged to do by an assignment due a few days after each course begins. As I described above, introductory exercises require them to explore the materials by following links and then to suggest other possible links. Students have to link a text from the first week's reading in Graham Swift's *Waterland* to one of several maps intended to illuminate that novel. (In my hypertext and literary theory classes, students add links to the electronic version of this text.)

The next most complex form of student contributions to a hypermedia corpus involves creating a document, either textual or graphic, and then linking it to existing documents. Two things about this type of student contribution demand comment. First, presented by means of print technology, they seem separate, discrete documents created as student exercises that do not collaborate with anything else. But on a hypertext system, they are experienced differently because they link to other documents, which qualify and supplement them. Second, these student documents mingle with ones created by faculty members. They therefore represent a radical departure from current modes of learning and scholarship. Although college teachers encourage students to think independently, may even prompt them to challenge our pet theories and interpretations, and occasionally in our books and articles thank students for having helped us formulate theories in the pressure of discussion or for having uncovered some interesting bit of evidence, we do not usually publish their comments in our books. Hypertext, however, promotes student-faculty collaboration, by allowing easy inclusion of a large number of links and documents created by students. Whereas few students can contribute general essays or much in the way of original scholarly research, all can contribute links and many can produce valuable graphic and text documents that supplement faculty-created ones. These documents, as we shall observe, can add materials not included previously, qualify existing approaches, and even simply contradict existing presentations of individual topics.

In the Intermedia and Storyspace versions of this work used in my course on hypertext and critical theory, student interventions cause Barthes's *S/Z* to play a different, and more important, role in the work than it does in this print version. I incorporated a small selection of student-produced lexias into

Hypertext in Hypertext. They discuss issues including (1) the conflict of author and reader for status and power, (2) the degree to which hypertext describes *S/Z,* and *S/Z* defines hypertext, (3) *S/Z*'s veiling and unveiling enigma, (4) its dividing and reassembling of the female body, (5) the work's simulation of a critical act, (6) its exemplification of the male language that Luce Irigaray opposes, (7) its treatment of suspense, (8) its existence as an open or closed text, (9) its relation to chronology, and (10) Barthes's legal ability to use Balzac's tale at all.

In addition, students employed Barthes's work to create independent webs. Testing the proposition that hypertext might provide a laboratory for certain ideas characteristic of poststructuralism, Karen Kim analyzed Borges's "Grains of Sand" in terms of Barthes's five codes, Lisa Rose did the same with Guy de Maupassant's "Necklace," and Eliel Mamousette worked with X-Clan's rap, "Grand Verbalizer, What Time Is It?" Adam Wenger, skeptical of the value and relevance of these codes, applied them to his own *Adam's Bookstore,* an open-ended hypertext written in Storyspace that the reader begins and leaves at any point (for an illustration of his web, see Figure 28).

Turning back to the first Intermedia days, one can observe less elaborate forms of collaboration in the graphic concept maps that students in several courses created. Laura M. Henrickson, a member of my graduate seminar on Victorian poetry, produced, for example, a graphic image of *In Memoriam*'s intertextuality that takes the form of a modified wheel-diagram in which the poem's title appears in a rectangle at the center; this rectangle is surrounded by seven others, each of which indicates a work in some way related to Tennyson's poem. One box includes the text "Malory's *Morte d'Arthur:* compare Elaine, the Maid of Astolat, to the Lady of Shalott," and another suggests a far older source: "Sappho's fragment 102: especially for the weaving. Tennyson marked this fragment in his copy of *Poetae Lyrici Graeci.*" Other rectangles suggest a fourteenth-century Italian analogue, Spenser's *Faerie Queene,* poems by Shelley, and nineteenth-century collections of fairy stories. The center of the diagram also contains the words "for another view" and an accompanying link marker that permits access to other documents, which include a concept map, created earlier by a student in my undergraduate seminar, that offers a quite different approach to the poem.

In what ways does this wheel-diagram exemplify collaborative work? First, it adds something new to the Tennyson materials. Second, it links to various documents on one particular poem, "The Lady of Shalott," thereby working together with them. Third, one of those documents to which it links, another concept map, was created by a student in an undergraduate course, and Henrickson's document therefore exists in relation to one produced by an undergraduate student. It is worthwhile emphasizing this point, because just as teachers do not ordinarily produce work with our students, so, too, graduate and undergraduate students rarely collaborate. I have observed graduate students reading hypertext documents written by freshmen and freshmen reading ones created by advanced graduate students. I have also observed students at widely divergent places in their academic careers creating links to documents produced by those at different academic levels. Hypertext, in other words, allows collaboration not only among those of equivalent academic rank or status but also among those of widely different rank or status.

The In Memoriam *Project.* The early *In Memoriam* project, which ultimately provided the basis of the published *"In Memoriam" Web,* employed all the forms of collaborative work described thus far and took advantage of the capacities of hypermedia to do things virtually impossible with book technology. In particular, the dual capacity of hypertext to record relations between text blocks and to allow readers quickly to navigate these links offers enormous possibilities to the humanistic disciplines. As an experiment in collaboration to determine precisely how one goes about creating, maintaining, and using hypertext to study the internal and external connections implicit in a major literary work, the members of the graduate seminar and I placed a particularly complex poem on the hypertext system and then linked to it (1) variant readings from manuscripts, (2) published critical commentary, as well as (3) commentary by members of the seminar, and (4) passages from works by other authors. Tennyson's *In Memoriam,* a radically experimental mid-Victorian poem, perfectly suited this experiment, in part because Tennyson's attempt to create new versions of traditional major poetic forms produced 133 separate poems, each a work that can stand on its own and yet contributes to a greater whole. *In Memoriam* makes extensive use of echoing, allusion, and repetition, all of which are ideal for hypertext linking.

The *In Memoriam* project made use of documents created as an exercise for the undergraduate seminar in Victorian poetry. The assignment directed students to take a single section of the work and "show either by an essay of no more than two pages (typed) or by a one-page diagram its connections or relations to other sections of the poem." Kristen Langdon's "Relations of *In Memoriam* 60 to Other Sections," which relies on a wheel diagram in which blocks of text are connected by spokes to a center, reinvents the Intermedia concept map by making a more concrete use of it. Langdon demonstrates how Tennyson enriches his straightforward, simple diction by linking individual phrases, such as "dark house," "some poor girl," and "sphere," to other sections of the poem. This author's decision to link partial blocks of text to a complete one and avoid generalizing statements or summaries distinguished her approach from most previous material on the system. Her solution to the assignment, which was paralleled by those of several other students, manages to convey on one page or screen information that would take many more words in an essay format.

The six members of the graduate seminar added links and documents to the body of materials already on line. In addition to the 133 sections of the poem, these included several dozen files on the poet and his other poems and relevant materials on Victorian religion, science, history, and art. Students from the undergraduate seminar created approximately a dozen graphic or text documents and linked them to individual sections of *In Memoriam*. I had already created an overview file for the poem itself, basing it on the one for Tennyson; and to this, student consultants, room monitors, and I linked individual sections and a few of the relevant motifs.

Between January and April 1988 the members of the graduate seminar added more than a hundred documents, each student commenting specifically on one or more sections of the poem and on one another's work. The first assignment for the project required them to create five documents to append to individual sections of the poem. Each week members of the seminar read the contributions of others, added more documents, and then made links. The final assignment required each student to put on line the texts of poems by another poet, Christina Rossetti, that had obvious relevance to individual sections of Tennyson's work. Members of the class had earlier added texts from work by writers other than Tennyson, and this assignment was intended to explore hypertext presentation of interauthor relations in specific terms.

Working independently and yet together, the members of the seminars have created a presentation of a major nineteenth-century literary work that makes obvious many of its internal and external relations. Equally interesting, graduate students in English have worked collaboratively in a manner rare in their discipline, and since their work takes the form of contributions to a hypertext document, those who follow them will have access to what they have created.

One can argue, of course, that all writing inevitably follows this form of collaboration, however much book-bound technology hides or obscures it.

Such is precisely the argument made by structuralists, who continually emphasize that each speaker or writer manipulates a complex semiotic system containing layers of linguistic, semantic, rhetorical, and cultural codes with which one always collaborates. Unlike book technology, however, hypertext does not hide such collaborative relationship. Even if all texts (however defined) always exist in some relation to one another, before the advent of hypertext technology, such interrelations could exist only within the individual minds that perceived these relations or within other texts that asserted the existence of such relations. The texts themselves, whether art objects, laws, or books, existed in physical separation from one another.

Networked hypermedia systems, in contrast, record and reproduce the relations among texts, one effect of which is that they permit the novice to experience the reading and thinking patterns of the expert. Another result of such linking appears in the fact that all texts on a hypertext system potentially support, comment upon, and collaborate with one another. Once placed within a hypertext environment, a document no longer exists alone. It always exists in relation to other documents in a way that a book or printed document never does and never can. From this follow two corollaries. First, any document placed on a networked system that supports electronically linked materials potentially exists in collaboration with any and all other documents on that system. Second, any document electronically linked to any other document collaborates with it.

To create a document or a link in hypertext is to collaborate with all who have used the document previously and will use it in future. The essential connectivity of hypertext encourages and demands collaboration. By making each document in the docuverse exist as part of a larger structure, hypertext places each document in what one can term the "virtual presence" of all previously created documents and their creators. This electronically created virtual presence transforms individual documents created in an assembly-line mode into ones that could have been produced by several people working at the same time. In addition, by permitting individual documents to contribute to this electronically related overarching structure, hypertext also makes each contribution a matter of versioning. In so doing, it provides a model of scholarly work in the humanities that better records what actually takes place in such disciplines than does traditional book technology.

The twenty students in the survey course during the second semester of the 1989–90 academic year provided an indication of the way students work collaboratively with the documents already present on the system. On receiving one of the assignments, a student in the course asked how I wanted members of the class to indicate indebtedness, and I responded that they should avoid footnotes and simply use parenthetical, in-text citations. Since several students either missed class or later told me that they (correctly) believed citing one's sources was not required, the following figures represent a particularly conservative picture of the way students make use of lexias created by other students. Ten students, or 50 percent of the class, cited an average of 4.3 documents on Intermedia, and of these students, six, or 30 percent, cited work by students in earlier classes an average of 3.3 times each. In comparison eight, or 40 percent, cited the *Norton Anthology of English Literature* or *Oxford Companion to English Literature,* which is not on the reading list, an average of 5.4 times each. One student cited Intermedia documents 6 times, none of which had student authors, and she cited the introductions and other critical materials in the Norton anthology a dozen times. Another cited 4 documents by faculty and graduate student developers, InterLex (an electronic version of the Houghton Mifflin *American Heritage Dictionary*) once, students' documents twice, and the Norton anthology 8 times. In contrast, seven students, 35 percent, mentioned no outside specific sources, though in at least two of these cases the use of large numbers of Intermedia documents was clear. Since I observed most of the students working on the Intermedia system various times during the semester, these citations demonstrate to me not the use of the system per se but the fact that, in the role of authors, the students wished to connect their texts with those of other students. Whether or not they agreed with the student authors they cited, they inserted their own work into an existing network of textual relations.[5]

The Soyinka Web *and* Context34. Another, perhaps more interesting, example of collaborative writing involved the *Soyinka Web*—a set of more than seventy, mostly student-created, documents, and its various offspring: first, the Intermedia corpus *Context34,* which was six times larger than *Soyinka,* and then the far larger descendants in Storyspace and HTML. As an experiment, I had taught the second half of the 1989–90 survey course during the autumn semester in order to align it with Brown University's Curricular Advising Program, in which freshmen enroll in a course taught by their advisor. Students were apparently not notified about the existence of this course, and it ended up with the enrollment of a seminar—an even dozen. With a class this small, I decided to try an experiment in the collaborative production of a hypertext work on a single author, Wole Soyinka, a contemporary Nigerian poet, about whom Intermedia provided little material. After putting onto Intermedia several maps of Nigeria, the standard graphic overview for an author, a detailed list of works, and a chronology based upon James Gibbs's *Critical Perspectives on Wole Soyinka* (1980), I asked students to write at least two brief Intermedia essays, one on any poem from *The Shuttle in the Crypt,* Soyinka's prison poems, and a second on any aspect of the writer's context—political, historical, literary, religious, artistic, or whatever. It was late in the semester and the class had already done a great deal of writing in this intensive reading course, so I did not have high hopes for the quality of work they would produce on short notice while many were already preparing for term papers and final examinations in other courses.

To my surprise, the class produced twenty-one documents of high enough quality to remain on the system for use by later students. In addition to interpretations of individual poems, their documents included discussions of Nigeria under British colonial rule, a bibliography of materials on Yoruban religion, "Soyinka and the Biafran War," "The Yoruba Oba or King," "Negritude," and "Soyinka's Use of Jungian Archtypes." Students interested in the relation of Soyinka's poems to his other works added essays on a novel, *The Interpreters,* and an introduction to his drama; those who wanted to set him in the context of other writers produced "Wole Soyinka and Dylan Thomas: Time and Mystery" and a comparison of Soyinka's "Ulysses" to Joyce's novel. I realized this class had created the basis for a body of materials on the poet and his African context.

Adding a concept map for Soyinka's literary relations based on what students had already created, I gave the same assignment when I repeated the course the following semester, the only difference being that this time I asked the students not to write about something already covered unless they disagreed with the previous contribution. Those twenty students, who contributed an additional forty documents to the *Soyinka Web,* seem to have been inspired by the materials they encountered, for they wrote a wide range of essays that clearly integrate this Nigerian poet into the canon of English literature while providing a foundation for future work by other students.[6]

The success of this ongoing experiment led me to expand the *Soyinka Web* into *Context34,* a set of more than five hundred largely student-created documents that support the teaching of a new course on recent postcolonial fiction and autobiography in English. Work done by students in English 32 and other courses had provided, I realized, the basis for a rich hypertext corpus. After creating graphic overviews for the thirteen authors read in the course and for relevant topics, such as Nigeria (Figure 30) and women in India, Pakistan, and Bangladesh, I proceeded to edit and then link a range of

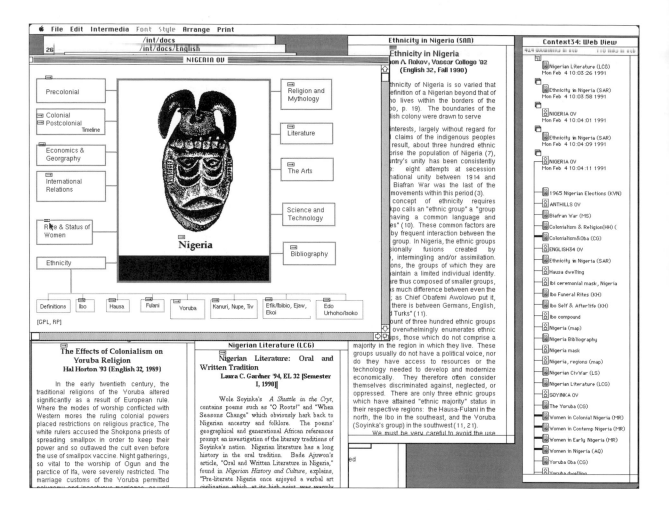

Figure 30. Student-Created Documents Linked to NIGERIA OV. The overview for materials relating to Nigeria, the home of two authors read in the course on postcolonial fiction, resembles those for individual literary works. Tribal and ethnic groupings, however, occupy the positions filled by literary techniques in the directory for novels. Beneath the overview appear "The Effects of Colonialism on Yoruba Religion," by Hal Horton '93, and "Nigerian Literature: Oral and Written Tradition," by Laura C. Gardner '94; and at the right appears "Ethnicity in Nigeria," by Simon A. Rakov '92, from Vassar College. The reader has activated the link marker for "Role and Status of Women," thereby darkening connecting lines to five of the icons in the Web View at right.

student documents to these overviews and to one another. The sheer practicality of a hypertext system like Intermedia for teachers is demonstrated by the fact that I managed to create *Context34* between the end of the first semester and beginning of the second. (*Context34* later migrated into Storyspace, gathering new student lexias as it went, and during the summer of

1996 these materials were reconfigured as *The Postcolonial and Postimperial Web*.)

Reconceiving

Canon and Curriculum

The same features of hypertext—connectivity, virtual presence, and shifting of the balance between writer and reader—that have prompted major, perhaps radical, shifts in teaching, learning, and the organization of both activities inevitably have the potential to affect the related notions of canon and curriculum. A work's entering the literary canon—or, more properly, being entered into the canon—gains it certain obvious privileges. That the passive grammatical construction more accurately describes the manner in which books, paintings, and other cultural texts receive that not-so-mysterious stamp of cultural approval reminds us that those in positions of power decide what enters this select inner circle. The gatekeepers of the fortress of high culture include influential critics, museum directors and their boards of trustees, and a far more lowly combine of scholars and teachers. One of the chief institutions of the literary canon is the middlebrow anthology, that hanger-on of high culture that in the Victorian period took the form of pop anthologies like *Golden Treasury* and today exists principally in the form of major college anthologies. In America, to be in the Norton or the Oxford anthology is to have achieved, not greatness, but what is more important, certainly—status. And that is why, of course, it matters that so few women have managed to gain entrance to such anthologies.

The notion of a literary canon descends from that of the biblical one, in which, as Gerald L. Bruns explains, canonization functions as "a category of power":

What is important is not only the formation, collection, and fixing of the sacred texts, but also their application to particular situations. A text, after all, is canonical, not in virtue of being final and correct and part of an official library, but because it becomes *binding* upon a group of people. The whole point of canonization is to underwrite the authority of a text, not merely with respect to its origin as against competitors in the field . . . but with respect to the present and future in which it will reign or govern as a binding text. . . . From a hermeneutic standpoint . . . the theme of canonization is *power*. (81, 67)

One sees the kind of privileges and power belonging to canonization in the conception that something is a work of art; the classification of some object or event as a work of art enters it into a form of the canon. Such categorization means that the work receives certain values, meanings, and modes of being perceived. A work of art, as some modern aestheticians have pointed out, is functionally what someone somewhere takes to be a work of art. Saying it's so makes it so. If one says the found object is a work of art, then it is; and having become such (however temporarily), it gains a certain status, the most important factor of which is simply that it is looked at in a certain way: taken as a work of art, it is contemplated aesthetically, regarded as the occasion for aesthetic pleasure or, possibly, for aesthetic outrage. It enters, one might say, the canon of art; and the contemporary existence in the Western world of galleries permits it to inhabit, for a time, a physical space that is taken by the acculturated to signify, "I am a work of art. I am not (simply) an object for holding open a door. Look at me carefully." If that object is sold, bartered, or given *as a work of art* to one who recognizes the game or accedes in the demand to play his role in it, then it brings with it the capacity to generate that special space around it that signals it to be an object of special notice and a special way of noticing.

In a precisely the same way, calling something a work of literature invokes a congeries of social, political, economic, and educational practices. If one states that a particular text is a work of literature, then for one it is, and one reads it and relates it to other texts in certain definite ways. As Terry Eagleton correctly observes, "anything can be literature, and anything which is regarded as unalterably and unquestionably literature—Shakespeare, for example—can cease to be literature. Any belief that the study of literature is the study of a stable, well-definable entity, as entomology is the study of insects, can be abandoned as a chimera. . . . Literature, in the sense of a set of works of assured and unalterable value, distinguished by certain shared inherent properties, does not exist" (*Literary Theory,* 10–11). The concept of literature (or literariness) therefore provides the fundamental and most extended form of canonization, and classifying a text as a work of literature is a matter of social and political practice.

I first became aware of the implications of this fact a bit more than several decades ago when I was reading the sermons of the Evangelical Anglican, Henry Melvill, in an attempt to understand Victorian hermeneutic practice. Upon encountering works by a man who was the favorite preacher of John Ruskin, Robert Browning, W. E. Gladstone, and many of their contemporaries, I realized that his sermons shared literary qualities found in writings by Ruskin, Carlyle, Arnold, and Newman. At first Melvill interested me solely as an influence upon Ruskin and as a means of charting the sage's changing religious beliefs. In several studies, I drew upon his extraordinarily popular sermons as extraliterary sources or as indications of standard Victorian interpretative practice. If I were to write my study of Ruskin now, two decades later, I would treat Melvill's sermons also as works of literature, in part because contemporaries did so and in part because classifying them as literature would foreground certain intertextual relations that might otherwise remain invisible. At the time, however, I never considered discussing Melvill's sermons as literary texts rather than as historical sources, and when I mentioned to colleagues that his works seemed in some ways superior to Newman's, none of us considered the implications of that remark for a concept of literature. Remarks by colleagues, even those who specialized in Victorian literature, made clear their perception that paying close attention to such texts was in some way eccentric and betokened a capacity to endure reading large amounts of necessarily boring "background material." When I taught a course in Anglo-American nonfiction some fifteen years after first discovering Melvill, I assigned one of his sermons, "The Death of Moses," for students to read in the company of works by Thomas Carlyle and Henry David Thoreau. Reading Melvill's sermon for an official course given under the auspices of the Department of English, the students assumed that it was a work of literature and treated it as such. Considering "The Death of Moses," which had probably never before appeared in an English course, as a work of "real" literature, my students, it became clear, assumed that Melvill's writing possessed a certain canonical status.

The varieties of status that belonging to the canon confers—social, political, economic, aesthetic—cannot easily be extricated one from the others. Belonging to the canon is a certification of quality, and that accreditation of high aesthetic quality serves as a promise, a contract, that announces to the viewer, "Here is something to be enjoyed as an aesthetic object. Complex, difficult, privileged, the object before you has been winnowed by the sensitive few and the not-so-sensitive many, and it will *repay* your attention. You will receive a frisson; at least you're supposed to, and if you don't, well, perhaps there's something wrong with your apparatus." Such an announcement of status by the poem, painting, building, sonata, or dance that has appeared ensconced within a canon serves, as I have indicated, a powerful separating purpose: the work immediately stands forth as different, better, to be valued, loved, enjoyed. It is the wheat winnowed from the chaff, the rare survivor, and has all the privileges of such survival.

Anyone who has studied literature in a secondary school or university in the Western world knows what that means. It means that the works in the canon get read, read by neophyte students and expert teachers. It also means that to read these privileged works is a privilege and a sign of privilege. It is also a sign that one has been canonized oneself—beautified by the experience of being introduced to beauty, admitted to the ranks of those of the inner circle, who are acquainted with the canon and can judge what belongs and does not. Becoming acquainted with the canon, with those works at the center, allows (indeed forces) one to move to the center or, if not absolutely to the center, at least much closer to it than one had been before.

This canon, it turns out, appears far more limited to the neophyte reader than to the instructor, for few of the former read beyond the reading list of the course, few know that one *may* read beyond; most believe that what lies beyond is by definition dull, darkened, dreary. One can look at this power, this territoriality of the canonized work in two ways. Gaining entrance clearly allows a work to be enjoyed; failing to do so thrusts it into the limbo of the unnoticed, unread, unenjoyed, unexisting. Canonization, in other words, permits the member of the canon to enter the gaze and to exist. Like the painting accepted as a painting and not, say, a mere decorative object or even paint spill, it receives a conceptual frame; and although one can remark upon the obvious fact that frames confine and separate, it is precisely such appearance within the frame that guarantees its aesthetic contemplation—its likelihood of making the viewer respect it.

The very narrowness of the frame and the very confinement within such a small gallery of framed objects produces yet another effect, for the framed object, the member of the canon, gains an intensification not only from its segregation but also because, residing in comparative isolation, it gains splendor. Canonization both permits a work to be seen and, since there are so relatively few objects thus privileged, intensifies the gaze; potentially distracting objects are removed from the spectator's view, and those that are left benefit from receiving exclusive attention.

Within academia, however, to come under the gaze, works must be teachable. They must conform to whichever currently fashionable pedagogy allows the teacher to discuss this painting or that poem. In narrating the formation of the modernist canon, Hugh Kenner explains that "when Pound was working in his normal way, by lapidary *statement,* New Critics could find nothing whatever to say about him. Since 'Being-able-to-say-about' is a pedagogic criterion, he was largely absent from a canon pedagogues were defining. So was Williams, and wholly. What can Wit, Tension, Irony enable you to say about 'The Red Wheelbarrow'?" (371). Very little, one answers, and the same is true for the poetry of Swinburne, which has many similarities to that of Stevens but which remains unteachable for many trained in the New Criticism.[7] In painting the situation is much the same: critics of purely formalist training and persuasion have nothing to say about the complex semiotics of Pre-Raphaelite painting. To them it does not really seem to be art.

Thematic as well as formal filters render individual texts teachable. As Sandra M. Gilbert and Susan Gubar, Ellen Moers, Elaine Showalter, and many others have repeatedly demonstrated, people who for one reason or another do not find interesting a particular topic—say, the works, fates, and subjectivities of women—do not see them and have little to say about them. They remove them from view. If belonging to the canon brings a text to notice, thrusts it into view, falling out of the circle of light or being absent or exiled from it keeps a text out of view. The work is in effect excommunicated. For, as in the Church's excommunication, one is not permitted to partake of the divine refreshing acts of communion with the divinity, one is divorced from sacramental life, from participation in the eternal, and one is also kept from communicating with others. One is exiled from community. Likewise, one of the most savage results of not belonging to the canon is that these works do not communicate with one another. A work outside the canon is forgotten, unnoticed, and if a canonical author is under discussion, any links between the uncanonical work and the canonical tend not to be noticed.

I write *tend* because under certain conditions, and with certain gazes, they can be at the other end of the connections. But within the currently dominant information technology, that of print, such connections and such linkages to the canonical require almost heroic and certainly specialized efforts. The average intelligent educated reader, in other words, is not expected to be able to make such connections with the noncanonical work. For him or her they do not exist. The connections are made among specialized works and by those readers—professionalized by the profession of scholarship— whose job it is to explore the reader's equivalent of that "darkest Africa" of the nineteenth- and early-twentieth-century imagination—the darkest stacks of the library where reside the unimportant, unnoticed books, those one is not expected to know, not even to have seen. The real situation, not so strangely, resembles that of the unknown dark continent—which certainly was not dark nor unknown to itself or to its inhabitants but only to Europeans, who labeled it so because to them, from their vantage point, it was out of view and perception. They did so for obviously political—indeed, obviously colonialist—reasons, and one may inquire if this segregation, this placement at a distance accurately figures the political economy of works canonized and uncanonized.

Like the colonial power, say, France, Germany, or England, the canonical work acts as a center—the center of the perceptual field, the center of values, the center of interest, the center, in short, of a web of meaningful interrelations. The noncanonical works act as colonies or as countries that are unknown and out of sight and mind. That is why feminists object to the omission or excision of works by women from the canon, for by not appearing within the canon those works do not . . . appear. One solution to this more or less systematic dis-appearance of women's works is to expand the canon.

A second approach to the noncanonization of works is the creation of an alternate tradition, an alternate canon. Toril Moi points to the major problems implicit in the idea of a feminist canon of great works (though she does not point to the possibility of reading without a canon) when she argues that all ideas of a canon derive from the humanist belief that literature is "an excellent instrument of education" and that the student becomes a better person by reading great works. "The great author is great because he (occasionally even she) has managed to convey an authentic vision of life." Furthermore, argues Moi—and thus incriminates all canons, and all bodies of special works with the same brush—"the literary canon of 'great literature' ensures that it is this 'representative experience' (one selected by male bourgeois critics) that is transmitted to future generations, rather than those deviant, unrepresentative experiences discoverable in much female, ethnic, and working-class writing. Anglo-American feminist criticism has waged war on this self-sufficient canonization of middle-class male values. But they have rarely challenged the very notion of such a canon." Arguing against the creation of a separate canon of women's writing, she points out that "a new canon would not be intrinsically less oppressive than the old" (78).

Unfortunately, one cannot proclaim the end of canons, or do away with them, since they cannot be ended by proclamation. "To teach, to prescribe a curriculum, to assign one book for a class as opposed to another," Reed Way Dasenbrock points out, "is ineluctably to call certain texts central, to create a canon, to create a hierarchy" ("What to Teach When the Canon Closes Down," 67). Rather, we must learn to live with them, appreciate them, benefit from them, but, above all, remain suspicious of them. Grandiose announcements that one is doing away with The Canon fall into two categories: announcements, doomed to failure, that one is no longer going to speak in prose, and censorship that in totalitarian fashion tells others what they cannot read. Doing away with the canon leaves one not with freedom but with hundreds of thousands of undiscriminated and hence unnoticeable works, works we cannot see or notice or read. Better to recognize a canon, or numerous versions of one, and argue against it, revise it, add to it.

Having thus far paraphrased—but I hope not parodied—now-popular notions of the positive and negative effects of a literary canon, I have to express some reservations. I have little doubt that a canon focuses attention, provides status, and screens noncanonical works from the attention of most people. That seems fairly clear. But I do not believe that the one canon about which I know very much, that for English and American literature, has ever been terribly rigid. The entire notion of world literature, great touchstones, and studying English academically has a comparatively brief history. Victorian literature, that area of literature to which I devote most of my attention, certainly shows astonishing changes of reputations. When I first encountered the Victorians in undergraduate courses some thirty years ago, Tennyson, Browning, and Arnold claimed positions as the only major poets of the age, and Hopkins, when he was considered, appeared as a proto-modernist. In the following decades, Swinburne and the Pre-Raphaelites, particularly Christina Rossetti and her brother Dante Gabriel Rossetti, have seemed more important, as has Elizabeth Barrett Browning, who had a major reputation during her own lifetime. Arnold, meanwhile, has faded rather badly. Looking at older anthologies, one realizes that some of the poets whose reputations have of late so taken a turn for the better had fairly strong reputations in the 1930s and '40s but had disappeared into a shade cast by modernism and the New Criticism.

Such evidence, which reminds us how ideological and critical fashions influence what we read as students and what we have our students read now, suggests, perhaps surprisingly, that the literary canon, such as it is, changes with astonishing speed. Viewing it over a scholarly or critical career, only the historically myopic could claim that the academic canon long resists the pressures of contemporary interests. No matter how rigid and restrictive it may be at any one moment, it has shown itself to be characterized by impermanence, even transience, and by openness to current academic fashion. Over a university "generation," a far shorter span of time, the lag seems intolerably long. What good does it do an individual student to know that students will be able to study, say, a particular Nigerian writer a few years after *they* graduate?

Nonetheless, the canon, particularly that most important part of it represented by what educational institutions offer students in secondary school and college, takes a certain amount of time to respond. One factor in such resistance to change derives from interest and conviction, though as we have seen, such conviction can change surprisingly quickly in the right circumstances—right for change, not necessarily right according to any other standard. Another factor, which every teacher encounters, derives from book technology, in particular from the need to capitalize a fixed number of copies of a particular work. Revising, making additions, taking into account new works require substantial expenditures of time and money; and the need to sell as many copies as possible to cover publication costs means that one must pitch any particular textbook, anthology, or edition towards the largest possible number of potential purchasers.

As Richard Ohmann has so chillingly demonstrated in "The Shaping of a Canon: U.S. Fiction, 1960–1975," the constraints of the marketplace have even more direct control of more recent fiction, both bestsellers and those few books that make their way into the college curriculum. The combination of monopoly capitalism and a centralized cultural establishment, entrenched in a very few New York–based periodicals, has meant that for a contemporary novel to "lodge itself in our culture as precanonical—as 'literature,'" however briefly, it has to be "selected, in turn, by an agent, an editor, a publicity department, a review editor (especially the one at the Sunday *New York Times*), the New York metropolitan book buyers whose patronage [is] necessary to commercial success, critics writing for gatekeeper intellectual journals, academic critics, and college teachers" (381). Once published, "the single most important boost" for a novel is a "prominent review in the Sunday *New York Times*," which, Ohmann's statistics suggest, heavily favors the largest advertisers, particularly Random House (380).[8]

Historians of print technology have long argued that the cost of book technology necessitates standardization, and although education benefits in many ways from such standardization, it is also inevitably harmed by it as well. Most of the great books courses, which had so much to offer within all their limitations, require some fixed text or set of texts.

Although hypertext can hardly provide a universal panacea for all the ills of American education, it does allow one to individualize any corpus of materials by allowing reader and writer to connect them to other contexts. In fact, the connectivity, virtual presence, and shifting of the balance between writer and reader that permit interdisciplinary team teaching do away with this kind of canonical time lag while simultaneously permitting one to preserve the best parts of book technology and its associated culture. Let me give an example of what I mean. Suppose, as is the case, that I am teaching a survey course in English literature, and I wish to include works by women. A few years ago, if one turned to the Oxford or Norton anthologies, one received the impression that someone had quite consciously excluded female authors from them—and therefore from most beginning undergraduates' sense of literature. One could of course complain, and in fact many did complain. After a number of years, say, seven or eight, a few suitable texts began to appear in these anthologies, though Norton also took the route of publishing an anthology of women's literature in English. This new presence of women is certainly better than the former nonpresence of women, but it takes and is taking a long time. What is worse, many of the texts that appear at last in these anthologies may well not be those one would have chosen.

Let us consider a second problem I have encountered in the attempt to introduce new materials into my teaching, one less likely to find redress anywhere as quickly as has the first. I refer to the difficulty of introducing authors of non-English ethnic backgrounds who write in English. This problem, which precisely typifies the difficulties of redefining the canon and the curriculum alike, arises because a good many of Britain's major authors during the past century have not been English.[9] In England, where the inhabitants distinguish quite carefully among English, Welsh, Scots, and Irish, the major figures since the rise of modernism have not necessarily been English: Conrad was Polish; James, American; Thomas, Welsh; and Joyce and Yeats, Irish. Generally, anthologies work in these figures without placing too much emphasis on their non-Englishness, which shows a nice capacity to accommodate oneself to the realities of literary production. Of course, such accommodation has taken a rather long time to materialize.

Today the situation has become far more complex, and in Great Britain's postcolonial era, if one wishes to suggest the nature of writing in English—which is how I define English literature—one must include writers of both Commonwealth and ex-Commonwealth countries and also those with a wide range of ethnic origins who live in the United Kingdom and write in English. Surveying leading novelists writing in English in Britain, one comes upon important English men and women, of course, like Graham Swift, A. S. Byatt, and Penelope Lively, but such a survey almost immediately brings up the matter of national origins. After all, among the novelists who have won prestigious prizes of late, one must include Salman Rushdie (India and Pakistan), Kazuo Ishiguro (Japan), and Timothy Mo (Hong Kong), and if one includes novels in English written by authors occasionally resident in Britain, one must include the works of the Chinua Achebe and Nobel Prize winner Wole Soyinka (both of Nigeria), and of Anita Desai (India). And then there are all the Canadian, Australian, not to mention American, novelists who play important roles on the contemporary scene. The contemporary English novel, in other words, is and is not particularly English. It is English in that it is written in English, published in England, and widely read in England and the rest of Britain; it is non-English insofar as its authors do not have English ethnic origins or even live in England.

The canon, such as it is, has rather easily accommodated itself to such facts, and while the academic world churns away attacking or defending the supposedly fearsome restrictions of the canon and the virtual impossibility of changing it, contemporary writers, their publishers, and readers have made much of the discussion moot, if not downright comical. The problem faced by the teacher of literature, then, is how, in the case of contemporary English literature, to accommodate the curriculum to a changing canon. Of course, one can include entire novels in a course on fiction, but that means that the new does not enter the curriculum very far. In practice, the academic version of the expanded canon of contemporary literature will almost certainly take the form of Afro-American literature, which now appears in separate courses and is experienced as essentially unconnected to the central, main, defining works.

Hypertext offers one solution to the problem of accommodating the curriculum to a changing canon. In my section of the standard survey course, which is a prerequisite for majoring in English at Brown University, I include works by Derek Walcott (St. Lucia) and Wole Soyinka and plan in future years to add fiction by Mo or Achebe. How can hypertext aid in conveying to students the ongoing redefinition, or rather self-redefinition, of English literature? First of all, since Soyinka writes poems alluding to *Ulysses* and *Gulliver's Travels,* one can easily create electronic links from materials on Joyce and Swift to Soyinka, thus effortlessly integrating the poems of this Nigerian author into the literary world of these Irish writers.

Since hypertext linking also encourages students to violate the rigid structure of the standard week-by-week curriculum, it allows them to encounter examples of Soyinka's work or questions about its relation to earlier writers in the course of reading those writers earlier in the curricular schedule. By allowing students to range throughout the semester, hypertext permits them to see various kinds of connections, not only historical ones of positive and negative influence but equally interesting ones involving analogy. In so doing, this kind of educational technology effortlessly inserts new work within the total context.

Such contextualization, which is a major strength of hypermedia, has an additional advantage for the educator. One of the great difficulties of introducing someone like Soyinka into an English literature course, particularly one that emphasizes contextualization, involves the time and energy—not to mention additional training required—to add the necessary contextual information. Our hypertext component, for example, already contains materials on British and continental history, religion, politics, technology, philosophy, and the like. Although Soyinka writes in English, received his undergraduate degree from Leeds, and wrote some of his work in England, he combines English and African contexts; and therefore, to create for him a context analogous to that which one has created for Jonathan Swift and Robert Browning, one has to provide materials on colonial and postcolonial African history, politics, economics, geography, and religion. Since Soyinka combines English literary forms with Yoruban myth, one must provide information about that body of thought and encourage students to link it to materials on Western and non-Western religions.

Such an enterprise, which encourages student participation, draws upon all the capacities of hypertext for team teaching, interdisciplinary approaches, and collaborative work and also inevitably redefines the educational process, particularly the process by which teaching materials, so called, develop. In particular, because hypertext corpora are inevitably open-ended, they are inevitably incomplete. They resist closure, which is one way of saying that they never die; and they also resist appearing to be authoritative: they can provide information beyond a student's or teacher's wildest expectations, yes, but they can never make that body of information appear to be the last and final word.

Inventing the New Writing

Since writing the first version of *Hypertext* my interest in the educational applications of this information technology has increasingly shifted from read-only informational hypertext to those forms created by one or more students. Although I continue to use hypertext in the ways described in the preceding sections for courses on both literature and critical theory, students in the theory-related courses have begun to invent the ways of writing hypermedia at which we looked in Chapter 5. Equally important, they have, in often brilliant and unexpected ways, tested my proposal that hypertext offers a rare laboratory in which to experiment with the ideas of poststructuralist theory.

As part of my courses in hypertext and critical theory, I developed the electronic versions of this volume in Intermedia and other systems described in Chapter 5 as an example of translating a print book into hypertext. As I explained, students radically reconfigured the original in several ways, since they read *Hypertext* as wreaders—as active, even aggressive readers who can and do add links, comments, and their own subwebs to the larger web into which the print version has been transformed.

Although students continued to make similar contributions while working with the Storyspace version of *Hypertext,* they also began to create their own independent, discrete webs. The move from Intermedia, a truly real-time, or synchronous, collaborative environment, to Storyspace saw many of the changes, advantages, and disadvantages that occurred when my institution switched most of its word-processing activities from centralized networked mainframe computing to stand-alone personal computers: the personal computer brought with it both greater convenience and resultant wider usage but also a marked loss in certain forms of computer literacy based upon networked computing. Many more people used computers, though often inefficiently as little more than typewriters; but comparatively few took advantage of electronic mail, bulletin boards, and discussion groups. Similarly, when students moved from the kind of networked textuality provided by Intermedia to a hypertext system that did not join individual machines, they found synchronous collaboration more difficult to carry out. Fortunately, in moving from Intermedia to Storyspace a great deal also has been gained.

The sophistication and intellectual accomplishments exemplified by the first student webs on Storyspace compensated in many ways for the loss of an immensely powerful, if occasionally unstable, networked environment. The very first webs demonstrated more clearly than could any theoretical argument that writing in this medium creates new genres and new expectations. As one looks at these webs, it is clear that new kinds of academic writing were taking form. A few of them, like David Stevenson's *Freud Web,* whose dozen and a half lexias offer an introduction to Freud's theories, represent attempts to create hypertext versions of the standard academic term paper. Intrigued by the possibilities of hypertext, which he had encountered in the survey course, Stevenson asked permission to create his term paper in Intermedia, and not surprisingly he followed the approaches used in developing the lexias he had seen in *Context32;* that is, like the developers of the course materials, he wrote each of his substantial discussions of free association, libido, and the like, and to these he added a chronology, bibliography, and various graphic presentations of Freud's model of the mind.

The Freud Web, like a number of others, moved first to Storyspace and thence to HTML, but in its Intermedia version Stevenson interlinked it with the text of Rudyard Kipling's "Mary Postgate," a narrative of psychosexual violence that he believed Freud's theories would illuminate. Looking in retrospect at this pioneering student web, one sees how it combines two kinds of writing. *The Freud Web* itself contains only materials written by Stevenson, but he then pushed the resulting web up against a literary text, thereby creating a hybrid form of writing in which the intellectual connections and interpretations consist only in links.

In contrast to Stevenson's approach of linking *from outside,* Steve Boyan's adaptation of Edgar Lee Master's *Spoon River Anthology,* like *The "In Memoriam" Web,* uses paths or trails of links through an existing text to permit reading the poem more easily in ways that the print version already encourages or even demands. Its added interpretative link paths serve as readings, or rather as records of readings that, if we wish, we can make into our own.

Most student academic webs, however, rely less on either central print texts or on ways of writing associated with them. Once students began to use Storyspace, a hypertext environment that easily imports text, I began to notice something that I have since realized characterizes hyperwriting—its tendency, already observed in the discussion of hypertext as collage, to take the form of appropriation and abrupt juxtaposition. For example, Tom Meyer's *Plateaus* appropriates and interlinks a broad variety of materials to explain the relation of Deleuze and Guattari's thought to hypertext. Along with its substantial discussion-lexias and material garnered from the Internet, Meyer's Storyspace web incorporates folders containing multiple documents from *A Thousand Plateaus,* the Cabbala, Calvino's *Invisible Cities,* Burrough's *Naked Lunch,* and *The Satyricon.*

In addition to this tendency to exploit electronic collage for purposes of interpretive juxtaposition and comparison, the student webs share other qualities, one of which involves joining what one might consider academic and so-called creative writing, that is, poetry and fiction. This tendency appeared again in some of the earliest Storyspace webs. *Adam's Bookstore* by Adam Wenger developed in two stages, the first as hyperfiction and the second as a laboratory for theory. As a midterm exercise Wenger created a Borgesian tale that readers can enter and leave at any point, something enforced by the fact that he provided no title screen and arranged his lexias as a circle in the Storyspace view. For his final project, Wenger, who was highly skeptical of Barthes's approach in *S/Z,* applied the theorist's five codes to his own work, producing a very heavily linked web. Of the 51 lexias and 354 links that constitute *Adam's Bookstore* approximately half consist of the original story, and if one clicks on the hot text in a specific lexia, one receives a list of six, eight, or even more links, the first several constructing the narrative, those that appear farther down in the list constructing Wenger's Barthesian reading (see Figure 28).

Although few webs thus self-consciously apply critical theory to the student author's own texts, a large number move effortlessly between theory and fiction or poetry. Karen Kim's *Lexical Lattice,* Shelley Jackson's *Patchwork Girl,* and Michael DiBianco's *Memory, Inc.* (created in HTML and now part of the *Cyberspace Web*) all interweave substantial lexias containing text similar to standard academic discourse with fiction or poetry.

Lars Hubrich's *In Search of the Author, or Standing Up Godot,* first created in Storyspace and then recreated for the Web, exemplifies the playful examination of central critical issues that often characterize this writing. An introductory title screen explains that readers can choose to begin with either of its two separate parts or subwebs, one of which, "Killing Me," wryly meditates on the ways hypertext reconfigures our conceptions of authorship. In the WWW version, "Killing Me" begins with a screen shot of the Storyspace original (Figure 31), showing six layered, overlapping lexias on this theme, three of which are entirely visible—those from Barthes's "The Death of the Author," Tristran Tzara's *Dada Manifesto,* and my *Hypertext.* Beneath the defining image provided by this screenshot, Hubrich places a brief introduction that explains several ways in which his web reveals the problematic nature of conventional understandings of authorship, after which the text directs readers to use an immediately following set of thirteen cryptic magenta-and-yellow icons that stretch across the screen. Clicking upon them brings the reader to individual statements about issues of authorship, intellectual property, and our assumptions about them. Thus, in addition to the three statements one can read in the screenshot, one comes upon additional passages from Barthes, Emile Benveniste's definition of the self, and Michel Foucault's "What Is an Author?" as well as questions to the reader about Hubrich's educational background and a humorous example of the way people use the author function in making aesthetic choice and evaluation: "I have a friend who hates U2. One day, I went to his house to find him very excited. He had just recorded a song from the radio and wanted to play it to me. He said that this was the best song he had heard for months and that he had to find out which band recorded it. What he finally played to me was U2's 'The Fly.' When I told him that, he frowned and shut off the music mumbling something like 'That can't be. . . . sounded much better last time I heard it.' He never again mentioned U2 to me" ("U2").

Other brief lexias challenge our habit of reading a coherent authorial self out of a text. In fact, the very first lexia readers are likely to select—that obtained by clicking on the icon at the extreme left—reads: "I paid someone to do this midterm assignment for me. I really had no time at all to get it done. Therefore, everything you are going to read and what you already read has been written by someone else." Another announces: "I don't know if you

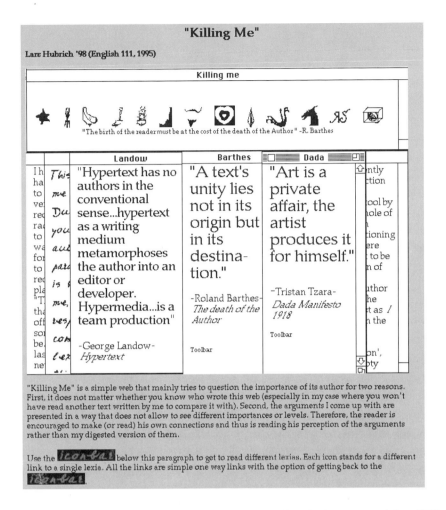

Figure 31. Lars Hubrich's *Killing Me*. This web, which represents another translation of a Storyspace web into HTML, playfully explores the notions of authorship in e-space, braiding together texts from Foucault, Barthes, and Landow with the student-author's own challenges to the reader.

care, but you are misinterpreting this web. I never meant what you think this web is about." And yet another entitled "Handwriting" takes the form of an image of what appears to be a handwritten three-paragraph statement, which begins: "This was written by me and Marcel Duchamp. Who do you think holds the authorship of this paragraph?" Duchamp, "for it is his handwriting," or Hubrich, who wrote the lexia? Using a computer font named "Duchamp" based upon the artist's handwriting, Hubrich created his lexia in Storyspace and then made an image of it for the HTML translation. With effective playfulness he uses it to question our assumptions about authorship on several levels. As he explains in his introductory lexia, he has arranged his materials nonhierarchically in a way that makes his text multivocal. "Therefore, the reader is encouraged to make (or read) his own connections and thus is reading his perception of the arguments rather than my digested version of them."

A great many of the several hundred other webs that Brown students have created in Storyspace take the form of similar experiments, for they use hypertext to test the theories of Barthes, Derrida, and others. Borges often appears as the Vergilian guide to these electronic explorations. Karen Kim created a hypertext version of Borges's "Grains of Sand" in which she linked the individual lexias containing text by Borges to analyses in the manner of Barthes's *S/Z*, and other students have taken similar approaches to works of Carroll, Lorca, Maupassant, and Proust. Derrida, Bakhtin, Baudrillard, Haraway, and other theorists also appear within such laboratory-for-theory webs.

Many student-created webs exemplify that new form of discourse proposed in Gregory Ulmer's *Teletheory* (where, however, he presents it in the context of video and film; he has since discovered hypertext and become a major innovator using it, particularly in the form of the WWW, to teach large classes at the University of Florida in writing and literature). This genre, which Ulmer terms *mystory*, combines autobiography, public history, and popular myth and culture. As Ulmer explains, his proposed new mode of writing "brings into relationship the three levels of sense—common, explanatory, and expert—operating in the circulation of culture from 'low' to 'high' and back again," and thereby offers a means of

researching the equivalencies among the discourses of science, popular culture, everyday life, and private experience. A mystory is always specific to its composer, constituting a kind of personal periodic table of cognitive elements, representing one individual's intensive reserve. The best response to reading a mystory would be a desire to compose another one, for myself. . . . mystory assumes that one's thinking begins not from the generalized classifications of subject formation, but from the specific experiences historically situated, and that one always thinks by means of and through these specifics, even if that thinking is directed against the institutions of one's own formation. (vii–viii)

Although Ulmer presented his Derridean notions of the new writing in *Teletheory*, a work subtitled *Grammatology in the Age of Video*, it turns out to describe not so much—or at least not only—the kind of textuality one finds in the analogue media of film and video but that emanating from (or instantiated by) digital word and digital image. As we have several times observed, hypertext, a border- and genre-crossing mode of writing, inevitably stitches together lexias written "in" different modes, tones, genres, and so on. Ulmerian mystory provides us with a first, possibly preliminary, model of how to write hypermedia.

Taking a quick glance at webs published in the collection *Writing at the Edge,* we see that Jane Park's *Food for Thought,* for example, combines personal history, literary discussions of cooking in Asian-American and Asian fiction, and discussions of eating disorders. Limarys Caraballo's *Guyabaya and Cream Cheese,* which attempts to come to terms with her Cuban-American heritage, relates her family's emigration from Cuba, discussions of Hispanic culture, her youth, family pictures, music, pro- and anti-Castro discussions of contemporary Cuba, and the like.

One of the most interesting of such mystories is Taro Ikai's *Electronic Zen,* which uses hypertext linking to allow the reader to travel among lexias relating his experiences as a security guard in Tokyo, work with a zen master, and Japanese poetry. Following directions and clicking upon the introduction, one encounters two possible routes—"water" or "chef"—and following the first, one encounters four lexias that, taken together, produce the following:

1. Water flows, unceasingly.

2. It never stops. Not for a second.

3. To hear it makes me think that I can hear the sound of time trickling down like water.

4. Look without your eyes, straight—at all that has life, and simply to obey them.

Following the link from this last lexia opens an image of the night sky, from which one can take a dozen different paths, some of which cycle back through the sky. At first, like the lexia entitled "chef," some on this path appear to contrast sharply with the tone and subject of the zen materials, but increasingly as one encounters and re-encounters them, these supposedly disparate subjects begin to penetrate and illuminate one another, drawing closer together, as it were: the hard-working short-order cook turns out to fulfill the Nun Aoyama's injunction "Don't think about yourself," while the words of a half-witted co-worker, obsessed with the weather, blend eerily with those of his zen master.

Some mystories, to be sure, may well be fictional through and through; that is, like *Jane Eyre* and *Great Expectations,* they imitate or simulate autobiographies, and however much autobiographical material may permeate them, they nonetheless take the form of autobiographies of fictional characters. Helene Zumas's *Semio-Surf,* at which we have already looked when discussing the rhetoric of writing hypermedia for WWW, exemplifies such a possibly fictional mystory, and so do several other works submitted as course projects.

In contrast, Jeffrey Pack's *Growing Up Digerate,* which now forms a part or subweb of the *Cyberspace, Hypertext, and Critical Theory Web,* combines theory, here chiefly relating to cyberspace, and autobiography of someone who grew up "'digitally literate'; that is, having a familiarity with computers." As Pack's Introduction points out,

most autobiographies start at birth, or with a short prelude describing how one's parents met. For this web, however, such things aren't very important. A birthdate (February 14, 1977) may prove useful if you're the sort of person who likes to do the math and figure out how old I was when various things happened, but isn't very necessary since I *am* that sort of person and will probably do it for you if I feel it's important. Where this story *really* begins is in 1983, when our family purchased its first computer.

At this point one can follow links within the text from the phrases "William Gibson's *Neuromancer*" or "its first computer," or one can use Pack's footer links to open an index that lists alphabetically approximately forty items ranging from America On-Line and Apple IIe through MS-DOS and MUD to World Wide Web and Zork. One can read this mystory more or less linearly, or one can go to the index or cycle through it by means of its many links— the lexia entitled "MS-DOS," for example, has seven links in addition to the four footer links—and as one proceeds one receives both a personal history of computer literacy and a personal history.

As these few examples show, hypertext is here, and undergraduate students are already mapping out the new forms of discourse that this combined information technology promises. After giving readings of these and similar webs at conferences and workshops, I am often asked how I go about evaluating them, and I respond that I combine the requirements of the old and the new; that is, accuracy, quality of research, writing at the level of the individual sentence and paragraph, and rhetorical effectiveness still count for a great deal; but webs also have to show visual literacy, skillful linking, clear and effective organization, and the like.

After Intermedia

As I pointed out in the first chapter, after changes in Apple Computers' hard- and software effectively ended the Intermedia project, my students and I used various other hypertext systems, each of which has its own distinctive strengths and disadvantages and its corresponding educational effects. Experiences with these different systems revealed several important points of interest to anyone working with educational hypermedia, the first of which is that the apparently most minute technological change, such as system speed or screen size, can have unexpected, broad effects on reading, writing, and learning with hypertext.

Storyspace, which works on both Macintosh and Windows machines, does not have Intermedia's UNIX-based system of varying permissions (which allow an instructor to fix or freeze a document while permitting students to link to it), and it also does not have either Intermedia's structured graphics editor or its ability to permit individual documents to participate in multiple webs. On the other hand, it has a range of valuable qualities, not the least of which is that it will work on any Macintosh or Windows machine; unfortunately, moving webs between environments is not entirely automatic. Importing text and images, making links between words and phrases, full-text searching, and organizing documents are all very easy in Storyspace, and although this system does not have Intermedia's Web View, the Storyspace Roadmap (see Figure 16), which one can call up by pressing a simple key combination, provides a partial analogue to this invaluable feature by furnishing a reading history and list of link destinations for each individual document.

Perhaps most important, the simple fact that Storyspace runs on any Macintosh created novel portability for all the webs originally created for Intermedia. Since students can copy any web from a server that is situated in the Computing and Information Technology building but electronically accessible from various parts of the university, including some residence halls, they can both read and write webs anywhere they have access to a Macintosh. (Since Storyspace permits one to copy linked sets of lexias easily, one can create comments at home and later paste them into the master or server version of any web to share with others.) The ease and convenience of working with this "poor man's Intermedia" led, particularly in my hypertext and literary theory courses, to students creating their own considerable hypertext webs, some of them quite massive.

Storyspace has proved itself extremely useful but in comparison to Intermedia has reduced the ability of students to read spontaneously as wreaders. Yes, students can add links but, without Intermedia's UNIX-based system of hierarchical privileges, they can add links only if they meet in lab with the person having the course password. In retrospect, one can see that the convenience of using a hypertext system based on the standard Macintosh operating system meant that we gained greater ease of use, particularly when importing materials, and far greater accessibility. In return, we lost a real-time—as opposed to asynchronous—collaborative work environment. None-theless, having had experience working with Intermedia, I could easily de-velop strategies to ensure that students created valuable collaborative webs and even added their own links. Collaborative authoring of text, however, proved, and remains, a much easier matter than does adding links. One of the first exercises using both Intermedia and Storyspace involved students' creating their own links in the course webs, but the absence of a convenient way of doing so in Storyspace meant that students did not tend to think of working in this manner unless an assignment called for them to do so.

Using Storyspace also affected the kinds of visual materials students cre-ated, paradoxically reducing the visual literacy of student work in the purely literary courses while radically increasing it in students of digital culture and critical theory. Whereas Intermedia had a simple graphics editor that permit-ted student wreaders to create diagrams, concept maps, and overviews within the system, Storyspace and WWW viewers do not, thus requiring wreaders to use Photoshop or similar graphics software. One immediate ef-fect of the switch from Intermedia to Storyspace, therefore, was that students in my survey and Victorian courses stopped producing the interesting simple graphic concept maps but that students experienced in using Photoshop, Il-lustrator, and image scanning programs found adding more sophisticated vis-ual materials to their webs very easy to do. (In Storyspace one simply elec-tronically copies images from a graphics program and pastes them directly into a lexia.) Consequently, they began to use complex images (and video and sound) much more often.

Another difference, which we had anticipated, appeared in the way stu-dents manipulated the Storyspace view to convey information. Although both Intermedia and Storyspace share what at first appear nearly identical folder structures, authors can arrange the individual items in the Storyspace View to create patterns and hence display a web's organization. Experiment-ing with this feature, students quickly began to use it as a visual element in their writing (for examples, see Figures 14 and 26).

Using the World Wide Web again confronts the teacher with a set of advantages and disadvantages. Most obviously, the availability of resources and potential for collaborations are truly worldwide rather than limited to a single class or campus, and students find creating basic HTML documents very easy to do, particularly if instructors provide simple templates. Although including images in a document consumes time and resources, they are easy to employ, and the sheer visual literacy has risen greatly with WWW. Assum-ing that students have access to a server on which they can place their own documents, WWW once again grants student collaborators the power to create both their own documents and sets of links.

On the other hand, as we have already seen, HTML viewers come with a heavy cost as well. HTML produces a relatively flat version of hypertext, and students accustomed to working with two features shared by Intermedia and Storyspace—one-to-many linking and various aspects of the multi-window feature—often complain bitterly about how confining and disorienting they find the Web to be. As I have already explained in Chapter 5, course templates, identifying headers, and sets of linked footer icons solve many of the potential problems of navigation and orientation in HTML-based systems. One-to-many linking, which I take to be one of the defining qualities of a true hypertext system and one of the most valuable to education, proves harder to replace or find an equivalent for. The laborious task of creating and then maintaining suboverviews for each item in an author and text overview solves the problem of using effective overview and crossroads documents on the web, but the common Intermedia, Storyspace, and Microcosm practice of attaching several links to a word or phrase in a text document—particularly useful because multiple links produce a valuable preview function in the form of automatically generated menus—simply disappears on the Web.

What Chance Has Hypertext in Education?

My experience of teaching with hypertext since 1987 convinces me that even the comparatively limited systems and bodies of literary materials thus far available demonstrate that hypertext and hypermedia have enormous potential to improve teaching and learning. Skeptical as I was when I first became involved with the Intermedia experiment, I had discovered two years later that the hypertext component of my courses allowed me to accomplish far more with them than had ever been possible. In the decade since I began to work with educational hypermedia, I have observed increasingly computer-literate students either demand hypertext materials or, now that the World Wide Web has arrived, go in search of them independently of their instructors' suggestions, wishes, or even knowledge. One of my favorite stories of this behavior involves a student in one of the earliest classes to use Intermedia who took a visiting year at another Ivy League institution. After the opening meeting of a course on James Joyce, he perplexed the lecturer by asking, "Where is your Intermedia web on *Ulysses*?" Students have begun increasingly to drive the use of hypertext—just as they did the use of silent reading in the late middle ages.

Nonetheless, even with the enormous impetus provided by the World

Wide Web, I do not expect to see dramatic changes in educational practice for some time to come, in large part because of the combination of technological conservatism and general lack of concern with pedagogy that characterizes the faculty at most institutions of higher learning, particularly at those that have pretensions to prestige. There is, however, occasion to hope, because as one of those attending a 1988 conference on educational hypermedia at Dartmouth commented: "It took only twenty-five years for the overhead projector to make it from the bowling alley to the classroom. I'm optimistic about academic computing; I've begun to see computers in bowling alleys."

The Politics

of Hypertext:

Who Controls

the Text?

Answered Prayers;

or, The Politics of Resistance

After a lecture I had delivered at an Ivy League campus on the role of hypertext in literary education, a distinguished historical scholar worried aloud in conversation with me that the medium might serve primarily to indoctrinate students into poststructuralism and Marxist theory. After another talk at a large state university in the Deep South, a younger academic, concerned with critical theory and the teaching of writing, argued (on the basis of my use of Intermedia in a historical survey) that hypertext would necessarily enforce historical approaches and prevent the theorizing of literature. Such responses have proved typical of a sizable minority of those to whom I and others who work with this new medium have introduced educational and other applications of hypertext. Many with whom I have spoken have shown interest and enthusiasm, of course, and some of those concerned with critical theory as a major professional interest have responded with valuable suggestions and advice, even while remaining guardedly skeptical. For that sizable minority, however, hypertext represents the unknown, and one is not surprised to find that they project their fears upon it, as people do on any unknown Other.

Not all observers find themselves troubled by the entrance of this latest educational technology into the portals of academe. Jean-François Lyotard, for example, argues that "it is only in the context of the grand narratives of legitimation—the life of the spirit and/or the emancipation of humanity— that the partial replacement of teachers by machines may seem inadequate or even intolerable" (*Postmodern Condition*, 51). Since he has abandoned these "grand narratives," he does not resist technology that might threaten them. The historical record reveals, however, that university teachers have

fiercely resisted all educational technology and associated educational practice at least since the late Middle Ages. Those who feel threatened by hypertext and associated technologies might do well to remember that, as Paul
Saenger points out, when the introduction of spacing between words made
reading to oneself possible, in "fourteenth-century universities, private silent
reading [was] forbidden in the classroom" (155). One can easily imagine the
objections to the new technology and its associated practice, because those
objections have not changed very much in the last seven centuries: "Students, if left to their own devices, will construe the texts incorrectly. Everyone
knows that permitting them such control over their own education before
they are ready for it is not good for them. They don't yet know enough to
make such decisions. And besides, what is to become of us if they use this
insidious technology by themselves? What are we to *do*?" Similarly, when
books appeared, many faculty members feared these dangerous new teaching machines, which clearly ceded much of the instructor's knowledge and
power to the student. The mass production and wide distribution made possible by printing, which threatened to swamp ancient authority in a flood
of modern mediocrity, also permitted people to teach themselves outside
institutional control. Therefore, well into the eighteenth century, undergraduates in European universities had access to the library only a few hours per
week.

Just as printed books did, hypertext systems are dramatically changing
the roles of student, teacher, assignment, evaluation, reading list, and relations among instructors, courses, departments, and disciplines. No wonder
so many faculty find so many "reasons" not to look at hypertext. Perhaps
scariest of all for the teacher, hypertext answers teachers' sincere prayers for
active, independent-minded students who take more responsibility for their
education and are not afraid to challenge and disagree. The problem with
answered prayers is that one may get that for which one asked, and then . . .
How terrifying for professors of English, who for decades have called for
creativity, independent mindedness, and *all those other good things,* to receive
them from their students! Complaining, hoping, even struggling heroically,
perhaps, to awaken their students, they have nonetheless accommodated
themselves to present-day education and its institutions, which include the
rituals of lecture, class discussions, examinations through which they themselves have passed and which (they are the evidence) have some good effects
on some students.

The Marginalization of Technology and the Mystification of Literature

Discussions of the politics of hypertext have to mention its power, at least at the present time, to make many critical theorists, particularly Marxists, very uncomfortable. Alvin Kernan wryly observes, "That the primary modes of production affect consciousness and shape the superstructure of culture is, not since Marx, exactly news, but . . . both Whiggish theories of progress and Marxist historical dialectic have failed to satisfy the need to understand the technologically generated changes or to provide much real help in deciding what might be useful and meaningful responses to such radical change" (3). Anyone who encounters the statements of Frederic Jameson and other critical theorists about the essential or basic lack of importance of technology, particularly information technology, to ideology and thought in general recognizes that these authors conspicuously marginalize technology. As Terry Eagleton's fine discussions of general and literary modes of production demonstrate, contemporary Marxist theory has drawn upon the kind of materials Kernan, McLuhan, and other students of information technology have made available (*Criticism and Ideology,* 44–63).[1] For this reason, when other Marxists, like Jameson, claim that examining the effects of technology on culture inevitably produces technological determinism, one should suspect that such a claim derives more from widespread humanist technophobia than from anything in Marxist thought itself. Jameson's statements about technological determinism bear directly upon the reception of ideas of hypertext within those portions of the academic world for which it has the most to offer but which, history suggests, seem most likely to resist its empowerment. This rejection of a powerful analytic tool lying ready to hand appears particularly odd given that, as Michael Ryan observes, "technology—form-giving labor—is, according to Marx, the 'nature' of human activity, thereby putting into question the distinction between nature and culture, at least as it pertains to human life" (60).[2]

In *Marxism and Form,* Jameson reveals both a pattern of and the reason for an apparently illogical resistance to work that could easily support his own. There he argues that

however materialistic such an approach to history may seem, nothing is farther from Marxism than the stress on invention and technique as the primary cause of historical change. Indeed, it seems to me that such theories (of the kind which regard the steam engine as the cause of the Industrial Revolution, and which have been rehearsed yet again, in streamlined modernistic form, in the works of Marshall McLuhan) function as a substitute for Marxist historiography in the way they offer a feeling of concreteness comparable to economic subject matter, at the same time that they dispense with any consideration of the human factors of classes and of the social organization of production. (74)

One must admire Jameson's forthrightness here in admitting that his parodied theories of McLuhan and other students of the relations of technology and human culture potentially "function as a substitute for Marxist historiography," but the evidence I have presented in previous pages makes it clear that Eisenstein, McArthur, Chartier, Kernan, and many other recent students of information technology often focus precisely on "the human factors of classes and of the social organization of production." In fact, these historians of information technology and associated reading practices offer abundant material that has potential to support Marxist analyses.

Jameson attacks McLuhan again a decade later in *The Political Unconscious*. There he holds that an old-fashioned naive conception of causality, which he "assumed to have been outmoded by the indeterminacy principle of modern physics," appears in what he calls "that technological determinism of which McLuhanism remains the most interesting contemporary expression, but of which certain more properly Marxist studies like Walter Benjamin's ambiguous *Baudelaire* are also variants." In response to the fact that Marxism itself includes "models which have so often been denounced as mechanical or mechanistic," Jameson gingerly accepts such models, though his phrasing suggests extraordinary reluctance: "I would want to argue that the category of mechanical effectivity retains a purely local validity in cultural analysis where it can be shown that billiard-ball causality remains one of the (nonsynchronous) laws of our particular fallen social reality. It does little good, in other words, to banish 'extrinsic' categories from our thinking, when they continue to have a hold on the objective realities about which we plan to think." He then offers as an example the "unquestioned causal relationship" between changes in "the 'inner form' of the novel itself" and the late nineteenth-century shift from triple-decker to single-volume format (25). I find this entire passage very confusing, in part because in it Jameson seems to end by accepting what he had begun by denying—or at least he accepts what those like McLuhan have stated rather than what he apparently assumes them to have argued. His willingness to accept that "mechanical effectivity retains a purely local validity in cultural analysis" seems to do no more than describe what Eisenstein, Chartier, and others do. The tentativeness of his acceptance also creates problems. I do not understand why Jameson writes, "I would want to argue," as if the matter were as yet only a distant possibility, when the end of this sentence and those that follow show that he definitely makes that argument. Finally, I find troubling the conspicuous muddle of his apparently generous admission that "it does little good . . . to banish 'extrinsic' categories from our thinking, when they continue to have a hold on the objective realities about which we plan to think." Such extrinsic categories might turn out to match "the objective realities about which we plan to think," or again, these objective realities might turn out to support the hypothesis contained in extrinsic categories, but it only mystifies things to describe categories as having "a hold on . . . objective realities."

Such prose from Jameson, who often writes with clarity about particularly difficult matters, suggests that this mystification and muddle derives from his need to exclude technology and its history from Marxist analyses. We have seen how hard he works at it, and we have also observed that technological factors not only offer no threat to Jamesonian Marxism but even have potential to support it.[3] Jameson's exclusions, I suggest, therefore have little to do with Marxism. Instead, they exemplify the humanist's common technophobia, which derives from that "venerable tradition of proud ignorance of matters material, mechanical, or commercial" that Eisenstein observes in students of literature and history (706).

Such resistance to the history of technology does not appear only in Marxists, though in them, as I have suggested, the exclusion strikes one as particularly odd. While reading Annette Lavers's biography of Roland Barthes, I encountered another typical instance of the humanist's curious, if characteristic, reticence to grant any importance to technology, however defined, as if so doing would grant status and power to it: "The contemporary expansion of linguistics into cybernetics, computers, and machine translation," she tells us, "probably played its part in Barthes's evolution on this subject; but the true reason is no doubt to be found in the metaphysical change in outlook which resulted in his new literary doctrine" (138). After pointing to Barthes's obvious intellectual participation in some of the leading currents of his own culture (or strands that weave his own cultural context), she next takes back what she has granted. Although her first clause announces that computing and associated technologies "probably" played a part in "Barthes's evolution on this subject," she immediately takes back that "probably" by stating unequivocally that "the true reason"—the other factors were apparently false reasons, now properly marginalized—"no doubt" lies in Barthes's "metaphysical change." One might have expected to encounter a phrase like "the most important reason," but Lavers instead suddenly changes direction and brings up matters of truth and falsity and of doubt and certainty.

Two things about Lavers's discomfort deserve mention: First, when confronted with the possibility that technology may play a contributing role in some aspect of culture, Lavers, like Jameson and so many other humanists, resorts to devices of mystification, thereby suggesting that such matters intrude in some crucial way upon matters of power and status. Second, her mystification consists of reducing complexity to simplicity, multivocality to univocality. Her original statement proposes that several possible contributing factors shaped Barthes's "evolution," but once we traverse the semicolon, the possibilities, or rather probabilities, that she herself has just proposed instantly vanish into error, and a "metaphysical change in outlook" in all its vagueness becomes the sole causation.

One wonders why critical theorists thus marginalize technology, which, like poetry and political action, is a production of society and individual imagination. Since marginalization results from one group's placement of itself at a center, one must next ask which group places itself at the center of power and understanding, and the answer must be one that feels itself threatened by the importance of technology. Ryan asks, "What is the operation of exclusion in a philosophy that permits one group, or value, or idea to be kept out so that another can be safeguarded internally and turned into a norm?" (3). One such operation that I have frequently encountered after talks on educational hypertext takes the form of a statement something like "I am a Luddite" or "What you say is very interesting, but I can't use (or teach with) computers, because I'm a Luddite." (Can you imagine the following? "I can't use lead pencils—ballpoint pens—typewriters—printed books—photocopies—library catalogues because I'm a Luddite.") All the self-proclaimed Luddites in academe turn out to oppose only the newest machines, not machines in general and certainly not machines that obviate human drudgery. Such proclamations of Luddism come permeated by irony, since literary scholars as a group entirely depend on the technologies of writing and printing. The first of these technologies, writing, began as the hieratic possession of the politically powerful, and the second provides one of the first instances of production-line interchangeable parts used in heavily capitalized production. Scholars and theorists today can hardly be Luddites, though they can be suspicious of the latest form of information technology, one whose advent threatens, or which they believe threatens, their power and position. In fact, the self-presentation of knowledge workers as machine-breakers defending their chance to survive in conditions of soul-destroying labor in bare, subsistence conditions tells us a lot about the resistance. Such mystification simultaneously romanticizes the humanists' resistance while presenting their anxieties in a grotesquely inappropriate way. In other words, the self-presentation of the modern literary scholar or critical theorist as Luddite romanticizes an unwillingness to perceive actual conditions of their own production.

Perhaps my favorite anecdote and one that may make a particularly significant contribution to our understanding of resistance is this: after giving a lecture on hypertext and critical theory at one institution, a young European-trained faculty member who identified his specialty as critical theory candidly admitted to me, "I've never felt old-fashioned before." As the latest of the newfound, new-fangled developments, hypertext and computing in general have the (apparent) power to make those who position themselves as the advocates of the new appear to themselves and others as old-fashioned.

The Politics of

Particular Technologies

Discussions of hypertext all raise political questions—questions of power, status, and institutional change. All these changes have political contexts and political implications. Considerations of hypertext, like all considerations of critical theory and literature, have to take into account what Jameson terms the basic "recognition that there is nothing that is not social and historical—indeed, that everything is 'in the last analysis' political" (*Political Unconscious,* 20). A fully implemented embodiment of a networked hypertext system such as I have described obviously creates empowered readers, ones who have more power relative both to the texts they read and to the authors of these texts than readers of print materials have. The reader-author as student similarly has more power relative to the teacher and the institution. This pattern of relative empowerment, which we must examine with more care and some skepticism, appears to support the notion that the logic of information technologies, which tends toward increasing dissemination of knowledge, implies increasing democratization and decentralization of power.

Technology always empowers someone. It empowers those who possess it, those who make use of it, and those who have access to it. From the very beginnings of hypertext (which I locate in Vannevar Bush's proposals for the memex), its advocates have stressed that it grants new power to people. Writers on hypertext almost always continue to associate it with individual freedom and empowerment. "After all," claim the authors of a study concerning what one can learn about learning from the medium, "the essence of hypertext is that users are entirely free to follow links wherever they please" (Mayes, Kibby, and Anderson, 228). Although Bush chiefly considered the memex's ability to assist the researcher or knowledge worker in coping with large amounts of information, he still conceived the issue in terms of ways to empower individual thinkers in relation to systems of information and decision. The inventors of computer hypertext have explicitly discussed it in terms of empowerment of a more general class of reader-authors. Douglas Englebart, for example, who invented the first actual working hypertext environment, called his system Augment; and Ted Nelson, who sees Xanadu as the embodiment of the Sixties' New Left thought, calls on us to "imagine a new accessibility and excitement that can unseat the video narcosis that now sits on our land like a fog. Imagine a new libertarian literature with alternative explanations so that anyone can choose the pathway or approach that best suits him or her; with ideas accessible and interesting to everyone, so that a new richness and freedom can come to the human experience; imagine a rebirth of literacy" (*Literary Machines,* 1/4).[4]

Like other technologies, those centering on information serve as artificial, human-made means of amplifying some physical or mental capacity. Jean-François Lyotard describes computing and other forms of information technology in terms usually assigned to wooden legs and artificial arms: "Technical devices originated as prosthetic aids for the human organs or as physiological systems whose function it is to receive data or condition the context. They follow a principle, and it is the principle of optimal performance: maximizing output (the information or modifications obtained) and minimizing input (the energy expended in the process)" (*Postmodern Condition,* 44). According to the *American Heritage Dictionary,* the term *prosthesis* has the two closely related meanings of an "artificial replacement of a limb, tooth, or other part of the body" and "an artificial device used in such replacement." Interestingly, *prosthesis* has an early association with language and information, since it derives from the late Latin word meaning "addition of a letter or syllable," which in turn comes from the Greek for "attachment" or "addition, from *prostithenai,* to put, add: *pros-,* in addition + *tithenai,* to place, to put." Whereas its late Latin form implies little more than an addition following the rules of linguistic combination, its modern application suggests a supplement required by some catastrophic occurrence that reduced the individual requiring the prosthesis to a condition of severe need, as in the case of a person who has lost a limb in war, in an automobile accident, or from bone cancer or, conversely, of a person suffering as a result of a "birth defect." In each case the individual using the prosthesis requires an artificial supplement to restore some capacity or power.

Lyotard's not uncommon use of this term to describe all technology suggests a powerful complex of emotional and political justifications for technology and its promises of empowerment. Transferring the term *prosthesis* from the field of rehabilitation (itself an intriguing term) gathers a fascinating, appalling congeries of emotion and need that accurately conveys the attitudes contemporary academics and intellectuals in the humanities hold towards technology. Resentment of the device one needs, resentment at one's own need and guilt, and a Romantic dislike of the artificiality of the device that answers one's needs mark most humanists' attitudes toward technology, and these same factors appear in the traditional view of the single most important technology we possess—writing. These attitudes result, as Derrida has shown, in a millennia-long elevation of speech above writing, its supposedly unnatural supplement.

Walter J. Ong, who reminds us that writing is technology, exemplifies the comparatively rare scholar who considers its artificiality as something in its favor: "To say that writing is artificial is not to condemn it but to praise it. Like other artificial creations and indeed more than any other, it is utterly invaluable and indeed essential for the realization of fuller, interior, human potentials. . . . Alienation from a natural milieu can be good for us and indeed is in many ways essential for full human life. To live and to understand fully, we need not only proximity but also distance" (*Orality and Literacy,* 82). Like McLuhan, Ong claims that "technologies are not mere exterior aids but also interior transformations of consciousness" (82), and he therefore holds that writing created human nature, thought, and culture as we know them. Writing empowers people by enabling them to do things otherwise impossible—permitting them not just to send letters to distant places or to create records that preserve some information from the ravages of time but to think in ways otherwise impossible.

Abstractly sequential, classificatory, explanatory examination of phenomena or of stated truths is impossible without writing and reading. . . . In the total absence of any writing, there is nothing outside the thinker, no text, to enable him or her to reproduce the same line of thought again or even to verify whether he or she has done so. . . . In an oral culture, to think through something in non-formulaic, non-patterned, non-mnemonic terms, even if it were possible, would be a waste of time, for such thought, once worked through, could never be recovered with any effectiveness, as it could be with the aid of writing. It would not be abiding knowledge but simply a passing thought. (8–9, 34–35)

Technology always empowers someone, some group in society, and it does so at a certain cost. The question must always be, therefore, What group or groups does it empower? Lynn White showed in *Medieval Technology and Social Change* that the introduction from Asia of three inventions provided the technological basis of feudalism: the horse collar and the metal plow produced far higher yields than had scratch plowing on small patches of land, and these two new devices produced food surpluses that encouraged landowners to amass large tracts of land. The stirrup, which seems to have come from India, permitted a heavily armored warrior to fight from horseback; specifically it permitted him to swing a heavy sword or battle axe, or to attack with a lance, without falling off his mount. The economic power created by people employing the horse collar and the metal plow provided wealth to pay for the expensive weaponry, which in turn defended the farmers. According to White, these forms of farming and military technology provided crucial, though not necessarily defining, components of feudalism. Whom did this technology empower? Those who ultimately became knights and landowners in an increasingly hierarchical society obviously obtained more power, as did the Church, which benefited from increasing surplus wealth. Those who made and sold the technology also obtained a degree of status, power, and wealth. What about the farm worker? Those freemen in a tribal society who lost their land and became serfs obviously lost power. But were any serfs better off, either safer or better fed, than before feudalism, as apologists for the Middle Ages used to argue? I do not know how one could answer such questions, though one component of an answer is certain: even if one had far more detailed evidence about living conditions of the poor than we do, no answer will come forth garbed in neutrality, because one cannot even begin to consider one's answer without first deciding what kind of weight to assign to matters such as the relative value of nutrition, safety, health, power, and status both in our own and in an alien culture. Another thing is clear as well: the introduction of new technology into a culture cuts at least two ways.

Like other forms of technology, those involving information have shown a double-edged effect, though in the long run—sometimes the run has been very long indeed—the result has always been to democratize information and power. Writing and reading, which first belonged to a tiny elite, appears in the ancient Middle East as an arcane skill that supports the power of the state by recording taxes, property, and similar information. Writing, which can thus conserve or preserve, has other political effects, Ong tells us, and "shortly after it first appeared, it served to freeze legal codes in early Sumeria" (*Orality and Literacy,* 41). Only careful examinations of the historical evidence can suggest which groups within society gained and which lost from such recording. In one society within a particular battle of forces, only nobility or nobility and priesthood could have gained, whereas in other situations the common person could have benefited from stability and clear laws.

Another political implication inheres in the fact that a "chirographic (writing) culture and even more a typographic (print) culture can distance and in a way denature even the human, itemizing such things as the names of leaders and political divisions in an abstract, neutral list entirely devoid of a human action context. An oral culture has no vehicle so neutral as a list" (42). The introduction of writing into a culture effects many changes, and all of them involve questions of power and status. When it first appeared in the ancient world, writing made its possessors unique. Furthermore, if writing changes the way people think as radically as McLuhan, Ong, and others have claimed, then writing drove a sharp wedge between the literate and the illiterate, encouraged a sharp division between these two groups that would rapidly become classes or castes, and greatly increased the power and prestige of the lettered. In the millennia that it took for writing to diffuse through large proportions of entire societies, however, writing shifted the balance from the state to the individual, from the nobility to the polis.

Writing, like other technologies, possesses a logic, but it can produce different, even contrary, effects in different social, political, and economic contexts. Marshall McLuhan pointed to its multiple, often opposing effects when he remarked, "If rigorous centralism is a main feature of literacy and print, no less so is the eager assertion of individual rights" (220). Historians have long recognized the contradictory roles played by print in the Reformation and in the savage religious wars that followed. "In view of the carnage which ensued," Eisenstein observes, "it is difficult to imagine how anyone could regard the more efficient duplication of religious texts as an unmixed blessing. Heralded on all sides as a 'peaceful art,' Gutenberg's invention probably contributed more to destroying Christian concord and inflaming religious warfare than any of the so-called arts of war ever did" (319).[5] One reason for these conflicts, Eisenstein suggests, derives from the fact that when fixed in print—that is, put down in black and white—"positions once taken were more difficult to reverse. Battles of books prolonged polarization, and pamphlet wars quickened the process" (326).

I contend that the history of information technology from writing to hypertext reveals an increasing democratization or dissemination of power. Writing begins this process, for by exteriorizing memory it converts knowledge from the possession of one to the possession of more than one. As Ryan correctly argues, "writing can belong to anyone; it puts an end to the ownership or self-identical property that speech signaled" (29). The democratic thrust of information technologies derives from their diffusing information and from the power that such diffusion can produce.[6]

Such empowerment has always marked applications of new information technology to education. As Eisenstein points out, for example, Renaissance treatises, such as those for music, radically reconfigured the cultural construction of learning by freeing the reader from a subordinate relation to a particular person: "The chance to master new skills without undergoing a formal apprenticeship or schooling also encouraged a new sense of independence on the part of many who became self-taught. Even though the new so-called 'silent instructors' did no more than duplicate lessons already being taught in classrooms and shops, they did cut the bonds of subordination which kept pupils and apprentices under the tutelage of a given master" (244). Eisenstein cites Newton as an example of someone who used books obtained at "local book fairs and libraries" to teach himself mathematics with little or no outside help (245). First with writing, then with print, and now with hypertext one observes that an increasing synergy is produced when readers widely separated in space and time build upon one another's ideas.

Tom McArthur's history of reference materials provides another reminder that all developments and inflections of such technology serve the interests of particular classes or groups. The early-seventeenth-century "compilers of the hard-word dictionaries" did not, in the manner of modern lexicographers, set out to record usage. Instead, they achieved great commercial success by "transferring the word-store of Latin wholesale into their own language. . . . They sought (in the spirit of both Renaissance and Reformation) to broaden the base of the educated Elect. Their works were for the nonscholarly, for the wives of the gentry and the bourgeoisie, for merchants and artisans and other aspirants to elegance, education, and power" (87). These dictionaries served, in other words, to diffuse status and power, and the members of the middle classes who created them for other members of their classes self-consciously followed identifiable political aims.

The dictionary created by the French Academy, McArthur reminds us, also embodies a lexicographical program that had clear and immediate political implications. Claude Favre de Vaugelas, the amateur grammarian who directed the work of the Academy, sought "to regulate the French language in terms of aristocratic good taste" as a means of making French the "social, political and scientific successor to Latin" (93). This dictionary is one of the most obvious instances of the way print technology sponsors nationalism, the vernacular, and relative democratization. It standardizes the language in ways that empower particular classes and geographical areas, inevitably at the expense of others. Nonetheless, it also permits the eventual homogenization of language and a corollary, if long-in-coming, possibility of democratization.

By the end of the eighteenth century, Kernan argues, print technology had produced many social and political changes that altered the face of the literary world. "An older system of polite or courtly letters—primarily oral, aristocratic, amateur, authoritarian, court-centered—was swept away at this time and gradually replaced by a new print-based, market-centered, democratic literary system" (4). Furthermore, by changing the standard literary roles of scholar, teacher, and writer, print "noticeably increased the importance and the number of critics, editors, bibliographers, and literary historians" at the same time that it increasingly freed writers from patronage and state censorship. Print simultaneously transformed the audience from a few readers of manuscripts to a larger number "who bought books to read in the privacy of their homes." Copyright law, which dates from this period, also redefined the role of the author by making "the author the owner of his own writing" (4–5).

Like earlier technologies of information and cultural memory, electronic computing has obvious political implications. As Gregory Ulmer argued during a recent conference on electronic literacy, artificial intelligence projects, which use computers either to model the human mind or to make decisions that people would make, necessarily embody a particular ideology and a particular conception of humanity.[7]

What, then, are the political implications of hypertext and hypertext systems? I propose to begin examining that question by looking at the political implications of events described in a scenario that opened an article on hypertext in literary education that I published several years ago: It is 8:00 p.m. After having helped put the children to bed, Professor Jones settles into her favorite chair and reaches for her copy of Milton's *Paradise Lost* to prepare for tomorrow's class. A scholar who specializes in the poetry of Milton's time, she returns to the poem as one turns to meet an old friend. Reading the poem's opening pages, she once again encounters allusions to the Old Testament, and because she knows how seventeenth-century Christians commonly read these passages, she perceives connections both to a passage in Genesis and to its radical Christian transformations. Furthermore, her previous acquaintance with Milton allows her to recall other passages later in *Paradise Lost* that refer to this and related parts of the Bible. At the same time, she recognizes that the poem's opening lines pay homage to Homer, Vergil, Dante, and Spenser and simultaneously issue them a challenge.

Meanwhile John H. Smith, one of the most conscientious students in Professor Jones's survey of English literature, begins to prepare for class. What kind of a poem, what kind of text, does he encounter? Whereas Professor

Jones experiences the great seventeenth-century epic situated within a field of relations and connections, her student encounters a far barer, less connected, reduced poem, most of whose allusions go unrecognized and almost all of whose challenges pass by unperceived. An unusually mature student, he pauses in his reading to check the footnotes for the meaning of unfamiliar words and allusions, a few of which he finds explained. Suppose one could find a way to allow Smith to experience some of the connections obvious to Professor Jones. Suppose he could touch the opening lines of *Paradise Lost,* for instance, and the relevant passages from Homer, Vergil, and the Bible would appear, or that he could touch another line and immediately encounter a list of other mentions of the same idea or image later in the poem or elsewhere in Milton's writing—or, for that matter, interpretations and critical judgments made since the poem's first publication—and that he could then call up any or all of them.

This scenario originally ended with my remark that hypertext allows students to do "all these things." Now I would like to ask what such a scenario implies about the political relations that obtain between teachers and students, readers and authors. These issues, which writers on hypertext have long discussed, also arose in questions I encountered when delivering invited talks on my experiences in teaching with hypertext. One of the administrators at my own university, for example, asked a question I at first thought rather curious but have since encountered frequently enough to realize is quite typical for those first encountering the medium. After I had shown some of the ways that Intermedia enabled students to follow far more connections than ever before possible between texts and context, she asked if I was not worried because hypertext limited the students too much, because it restricted them only to what was available on the system. My first response then as now was to remark that as long as I used print technology and the limited resources of a very poor university library, no administrator or member of the faculty ever worried that I found myself unable to suggest more than a very limited number of connections, say, five or six, in a normal class discussion; now that I can suggest six or ten times that number, thus permitting students a far richer, less controlled experience of text, helpful educators suddenly begin to worry that I am "limiting" students by allowing them access to some potentially totalitarian system.

One part of the reason for this reaction to educational hypertext lies in a healthy skepticism. Another appears in the way we often judge new approaches to pedagogy as simultaneously ineffective, even educationally useless, and yet overpoweringly and dangerously influential. Nonetheless, the skeptical administrator raised important questions, for she is correct that the information available limits the freedom of students and general readers alike. At this early, still experimental stage in the development of hypertext, one must pay great attention to ensuring a multiplicity of viewpoints and kinds of information. For this reason I emphasize creating multiple overviews and sets of links for various document sets, and I also believe that one must produce educational materials collaboratively whenever possible; as I have suggested, such collaboration is very easy to carry out between individual instructors in the same department as well as between those in different disciplines and different institutions.

Several key features of hypertext systems intrinsically promote a new kind of academic freedom and empowerment. Reader-controlled texts permit students to choose their own way. The political and educational necessity for this feature provides one reason why hypertext systems must always contain both bidirectional links and efficient navigational devices; otherwise, developers can destroy the educational value of hypertext with instructional systems that alienate and disorient readers by forcing them down a predetermined path as if they were rats in a maze. A second feature of hypertext that has crucial political implications is the sheer quantity of information the reader encounters, because that quantity simultaneously protects readers against constraint and requires them to read actively, to make choices. A third liberating and empowering quality of hypertext is that the reader also writes and links; this power, which removes much of the gap in conventional status relations between reader and author, permits readers to read actively in an even more powerful way—by annotating documents, arguing with them, leaving their own traces. As long as any reader has the power to enter the system and leave his or her mark, neither the tyranny of the center nor that of the majority can impose itself. The very open-endedness of the text also promotes empowerment of the reader.

The Political Vision of Hypertext; or, The Message in the Medium

Does hypertext as medium have a political message? Does it have a particular bias? As the capacity of hypertext systems to be infinitely recenterable suggests, they have the corollary characteristic of being antihierarchical and democratic in several different ways. To start, as the authors of "Reading and Writing the Electronic Book" point out, in such systems, "ideally, authors and readers should have the same set of integrated tools that allow them to browse through other material during the document preparation process and to add annotations and original links as they progress through an information web.

In effect, the boundary between author and reader should largely disappear" (Yankelovich, Meyrowitz, and van Dam, 21). One sign of the disappearance of boundaries between author and reader consists in its being the reader, not the author, who largely determines how a reading proceeds through the system, for the reader can determine the order and principle of investigation. Hypertext has the potential, thus far only partially realized, to be a democratic or multicentered system in yet another way: as readers contribute their comments and individual documents, the sharp division between author and reader that characterizes page-bound text begins to blur and threatens to vanish, with several interesting implications: first, by contributing to the system, users accept some responsibility for materials anyone can read; and second, students thus establish a community of learning, demonstrating to themselves that a large part of any investigation rests on the work of others.

Writing about electronic information technology in general rather than about hypertext in particular, McLuhan proposed: "The 'simultaneous field' of electronic information structures, today reconstitutes the conditions and need for dialogue and participations, rather than specialism and private initiative in all levels of social experience" (141). McLuhan's point that electronic media privilege collaborative, cooperative practice, which receives particular embodiment in hypertext, suggests that such media also embody and possibly support a particular political system or construction of relations of power and status. J. Hillis Miller similarly argues that "one important aspect of these new technologies of expression and research is political. These technologies are inherently democratic and transnational. They will help create new and hitherto unimagined forms of democracy, political involvement, obligation, and power." Writing in the spring of 1989, Miller commented: "Far from being necessarily the instruments of thought control, as Orwell in *1984* foresaw, the new regime of telecommunications seems to be inherently democratic. It has helped bring down dictator after dictator in the past few months" ("Literary Theory," 18).

Michael Ryan, who is also not writing about hypertext, nonetheless offers more specific clues to its political implications and effects. Beginning from the assumption that "there is a necessary relationship between conceptual apparatuses and political institutions" (8), he argues that Derridean deconstruction implies

that absolute truth, defined as the adequacy of language to conscious intention, without any unconscious remains or side effects, is not a justifiable norm of political theory and practice [and should] . . . be abandoned in favor of multiple, situationally defined, complexly mediated, differentiated strategies. In other words, the "decentering" of the metaphysical assumption implies a decentering of the political project. . . . What is at stake, then, is a politics of multiple centers and plural strategies, less geared toward the restoration of a supposedly ideal situation held to be intact and good than to the micrological fine-tuning of questions of institutional power, work and reward distribution, sexual political dynamics, resource allocation, domination, and a broad range of problems whose solutions would be situationally and participationally defined. . . . Deconstruction comes closest to theorizing (and discursively practicing) this decentered plurality, but the nature of the object described defuses any potential centering privilege this theoretical insight might bestow. (114–16)

The political vision Ryan offers, which he terms "critical marxism," resembles that implied by hypertextuality, Bakhtinian multivocality, and the dialogic mode of collaborative endeavor proposed by Lisa Ede and Andrea Lunsford. Like Bakhtin, whose emphasis upon multivocality and critical practice responded to Stalinism, Ryan's amalgam of Marxism and Derridean deconstruction responds to the threat of a totalitarian Marxist-Leninism by dissolving the latter's conceptual foundations, which include a rigid linearity.[8]

Ryan defines his critical Marxism specifically in contrast to Russian communism. The economic theory of critical Marxism, for example, which rejects "the model of authoritarian central state communism," instead advances "models of socialism which are dehierarchized, egalitarian, and democratic. Whereas the Soviet model privileges productive forces (technology, heavy industry, and the like) over productive relations, thus permitting the preservation of capitalist work relations, critical marxists demand a complete transformation of the form of work and of all social relations, in 'private' as much as in the 'public' sphere. They see capital and patriarchy as equally important adversaries" (xiii–xiv).

Ryan defines critical Marxist politics and political organization by means of an equally sharp contrast to the Soviet model:

Critical marxists depart from the leninist tradition in that they call for political organizational forms that are not exclusive, elitist, hierarchical, or disciplinarian. The postrevolutional "arrangement of things," to use Marx's phrase, should include the political advances made by the bourgeoisie (such as democracy and civil rights), just as a socialist economy must necessarily presuppose the technological and economic advances that capitalism produces. . . . Rather than to anarchism, as some might contend, this critique leads, I shall argue, to a radical socialism that is more akin to the participatory and egalitarian models of self-government and self-management proposed by democratic socialists, socialist feminists, and autonomists than to the hierarchical and party-elitist, central state, leninist variety that exists in the East. (xv, 7)

Ryan draws upon major points of deconstruction, particularly upon Derrida's meditations on textuality that theorize hypertextuality, to construct a defense against communist totalitarianism. Like decenteredness and plurality, the theorized "inconclusivity," "indeterminacy," and "undecidability" of deconstruction keep the iron doors of the Leninist tradition from slamming shut on Ryan's appealing political vision. Critical Marxism, according to Ryan, is a politics of continuing process that will never lead to either utopian stasis or dystopian tyranny. The openness of deconstruction offers the caution that removing the metaphysical roots of ideology "can never be completed, either *at one go* or *once and for all.* The work involved is constant and repetitive, like, as Gayatri Spivak put it, keeping a house clean" (117). Ryan uses the word *caution,* but in doing so he simultaneously reassures himself and us that critical Marxism will not—cannot—repeat the horrors of Stalinism.

I have my doubts, I admit, that Ryan offers an authentically Marxist political vision. Attractive as I find the goals his critical Marxism embraces, I suspect that he tries to eat his cake and still have it. He clearly wages a war on two fronts, trying to attack both Marxist-Leninism and capitalism. He tries to convince the leftist audience, from which he clearly assumes most of his readers will come, and works hard to win converts from orthodox Marxism to his decentralized quasi-Marxism. To achieve this end, he relies primarily on two strategies. He tries to establish his credentials as an authentic radical by relating his personal history of political belief, and he attacks Western capitalist democracies, and only them, when both they and Marxist countries provide abundant targets for his criticism. For example, his mentioning "the poisoning of the world by transnationals" (43) appears rather unnecessarily biased, particularly now that countries formerly in the Eastern bloc freely admit they have created some of the world's most toxically polluted environments and are asking for assistance. I emphasize Ryan's one-sidedness not to create a balance by claiming, "See, the Commies do it, too!" Rather, if one attempts to construct a politico-economic system that combines the best of East and West, of Marxism and capitalism, as Ryan proposes to do, one must clearly locate the sources of major problems, such as ravaging the environment. Attacking only "transnationals," however justly, for destroying the environment while classical Marxist regimes bear equal responsibility will not help one perceive that the problems derive from a certain kind of industrial technology rather than from economic systems.

Whatever rhetorical and other difficulties Ryan stumbles over in his advocacy of critical Marxism, he manages to offer the vision of a truly decentered, or multiply centered, politics that seems the political equivalent of Richard

Rorty's edifying philosophy whose purpose is "to keep the conversation going rather than to find objective truth. . . . The danger which edifying discourse tries to avert is that some given vocabulary, some way in which people might come to think of themselves, will deceive them into thinking that from now on all discourse could be, or should be, normal discourse. The resulting freezing-over of culture would be, in the eyes of edifying philosophers, the dehumanization of human beings" (377).[9] Like Bakhtin, Derrida, and Rorty, Ryan presents his views as an explicit reaction against totalitarian centrism. He and Bakhtin have the example of Marxist-Leninism, particularly during the Stalin years, whereas Derrida and Rorty react against Plato and his heirs in a manner reminiscent of Karl Popper in *The Open Society and Its Enemies*.[10] Hypertext is the technological embodiment of such a reaction and such a politics.

Gregory Ulmer comments that "the use of communications technology is a concretization of certain metaphysical assumptions, consequently that it is by changing these assumptions (for example, our notion of identity) that we will transform our communicational activities" (*Applied Grammatology*, 147). We may add that the use of communications technology is also a concretization of certain political assumptions. In particular, hypertext embodies Ryan's assumptions of the necessity for nonhierarchical, multicentered, open-ended forms of politics and government.

The Politics of Access: Who Can Make Links, Who Decides What Is Linked?

Mixed with the generally democratic, even anarchic tendencies of hypertext is another strain that might threaten to control the most basic characteristics of this information medium. Readers in hypertext obviously have far more control over the order in which they read individual passages than do readers of books, and to a large extent the reader's experience also defines the boundaries of the text and even the identity of the author, if one can conveniently speak of such a unitary figure in this kind of dispersed medium.

The use of hypertext systems involves four kinds of access to text and control over it: reading, linking, writing, and networking. Access to hypertext begins with the technology to read and produce hypertext, and this technology has only recently begun to become available. Once it becomes widespread enough to serve as a dominant, or at least major, form of publication, issues of the right and power to use such technology will be multiplied.

One can easily envision reading a text for which one has only partial permission, so that portions of it remain forbidden, out of sight, and perhaps entirely unknown. An analogy from print technology would be having access to a published book but not to the full reports by referees, the author's contract, the manuscript before it has undergone copyediting, and so on. Conventionally, we do not consider such materials to be *part* of the book. Electronic linking has the potential, however, radically to redefine the nature of the text, and since this redefinition includes connection of the so-called main text to a host of ancillary ones (that then lose the status of ancillary-ness), issues of power immediately arise. Who controls access to such materials—the author, the publisher, or the reader?

Linking involves the essence of hypertext technology. One can expect that in the future all hypertext systems will offer the capacity to create links to texts over which others have editorial control. This ability to make links to lexias for which one does not possess the right to make verbal or other changes has no analogy in the world of print technology. One effect of this kind of linking is to create an intermediate realm between the writer and the reader, thus further blurring the distinction between these roles.

When discussing the educational uses of hypertext, one immediately encounters the various ways that reshaping the roles of reader and author quickly reshape those of student and teacher, for this information medium enforces several kinds of collaborative learning. Granting students far more control over their reading paths than does book technology obviously empowers students in a range of ways, one of which is to encourage active explorations by readers and another of which is to enable students to contextualize what they read. Pointing to such empowerment, however, leads directly to questions about the politics of hypertext.

Hypertext demands the presence of many blocks of text that can be linked to one another. Decisions about relevance obviously bear heavy ideological freight, and hypertext's very emphasis upon connectivity means that excluding any particular bit of text from the metatext places it comparatively much further from sight than would be the case in print technology. When every connection requires a particular level of effort, particularly when physical effort is required to procure a copy of an individual work, availability and accessibility become essentially equal, as they are for the skilled reader in a modern library. When, however, some connections require no more effort than does continuing to read the same text, *un*connected texts are experienced as lying much further off, and availability and accessibility become very different matters.

Complete hypertextuality requires gigantic information networks of the kind now being planned and created. This vision of hypertext as a means of democratic empowerment depends ultimately upon the individual reader-author's access to enormous networks of information. As Norman Meyrowitz admits, "Down deep, we all think and believe that hypertext is a vision that sometime soon there will be an infrastructure, national and international, that supports a network and community of knowledge linking together myriad types of information for an enormous variety of audiences" (2). The person occupying the roles of reader and author must have access to information, which in practice means access to a network. For the writer this access to a network becomes essential, for in the hypertext world access to a network is publication.

Considered as an information and publication medium, hypertext presents in starkest outline the contrast between availability and accessibility. Texts can be available somewhere in an archive, but without cataloguing, support personnel, and opportunities to visit that archive, they remain unseen and unread. Since hypertext promises to make materials living within a hypertext environment much easier to obtain, it simultaneously threatens to make any materials not present seem even more distant and more invisible than absent documents are in the world of print. The political implications of this contrast seem clear enough: gaining access to a network permits a text to exist as a text in this new information world. Lyotard, who argues that knowledge "can fit into the new channels, and become operational, only if learning is translated into quantities of information," predicts that "anything in the constituted body of knowledge that is not translatable in this way will be abandoned and that the direction of new research will be dictated by the possibility of its eventual results being translatable into computer language" (*Postmodern Condition,* 4). Antonio Zampolli, the Italian computational linguist and recent president of the Association of Literary and Linguistic Computing, warns about this problem when he suggests an analogy between the Gutenberg revolution and what he terms the *informatization* of languages: "Languages which have not been involved with printing, have become dialects or have disappeared. The same could happen to languages that have not been 'informatized'" (47), transferred to the world of electronic text storage, manipulation, and retrieval. As Lyotard and Zampolli suggest, individual texts and entire languages that do not transfer to a new information medium when it becomes culturally dominant will become marginalized, unimportant, virtually invisible.

Although a treatise on poetry, horticulture, or warfare that existed in half a dozen manuscripts may have continued to exist in the same number of copies several centuries after the introduction of printing, the manuscripts lost power and status, except as collector's items, and became far harder to use than before printed copies were available. Few readers cared to locate a manuscript copy, much less make an inconvenient, costly, and possibly dangerous trip to peruse it when far cheaper printed books existed close at hand. As habits and expectations of reading changed during the transition from manuscript to print, the experience of reading texts in manuscript changed in several ways. Although they retained the aura of unique objects, texts in manuscript became scarcer, harder to locate, and more difficult to read in comparison with books. Moreover, as readers quickly accustomed themselves to the clarity and uniformity of printed fonts, they tended to lose the skill for or find annoying certain reading tasks and certain characteristics associated with manuscripts, including the copious use of abbreviations that made the copyist's work easier and faster. Similarly, book readers who had begun to take for granted tables of contents, pagination, and indices found locating information in manuscripts particularly difficult. Finally, readers in a culture of print, who enjoyed the convenience of abundant maps, charts, and pictures, soon realized that they could not find certain kinds of information in manuscripts at all.

In the past, transitions from one dominant information medium to another have taken so long—millennia with writing and centuries with printing—that the surrounding cultures adapted gradually. Those languages and dialects that did not make the transition remained much the same for a long time but gradually weakened, attenuated, or even died out because they could not do many of the things printed languages and dialects could do. Because during the early stages of both chirographic and typographic cultures so many resources were devoted to transferring texts from the earlier to the current medium, these transitions were somewhat masked. The first centuries of printing, as McLuhan points out, saw the world flooded with versions of medieval manuscripts in part because the voracious, efficient printing press could reproduce texts faster than authors could write them. This flood of older work had the effect of thus using radically new means to disseminate old-fashioned, conservative, and even reactionary texts.

We can expect that many of the same phenomena of transition will repeat themselves during this transition, though often in forms presently unexpected and unpredictable. We can count on hypertext and print to exist side by side for some time to come, particularly in elite and scholarly culture, and when the shift to hypertext makes it culturally dominant, it will appear so natural to the general reader-author that only specialists will notice the change or react with much nostalgia for the way things used to be. Whereas certain inventions, such as vacuum cleaners and dishwashers, took almost a century between their initial development and commercial success, recent discoveries and inventions, such as the laser, have required less than a tenth the time to complete the same process. This acceleration of the dispersal of technological change suggests, therefore, that the transition from print to electronic hypertext, if it comes, will therefore take far less time than did earlier transitions.

The history of the print technology and culture also suggests that if hypertext becomes culturally dominant, it will do so by enabling large numbers of people either to do new things or to do old things more easily. Furthermore, one suspects that such a shift in information paradigms will see another version of what took place in the transition to print culture: an overwhelming percentage of the new texts created, like Renaissance and later how-to-do-it books, will answer the needs of an audience outside the academy and hence will long remain culturally invisible and objects of scorn, particularly among those segments of the cultural elite who claim to know the true needs of "the people." The active readers that hypertext creates can meet their needs only if they can find the information they want, and to find that information they must have access to networks such as the Internet. Similarly, authors cannot fully assume the authorial function if they cannot place their texts on a network. The following section provides a scenario that embodies some of the darker implications of a future hypertext author's attempt to gain access to the Net. Appropriately, an earlier electronic version of "Ms. Austen's Submission" appeared (was "published"?) in *IF,* an electronic periodical edited by Gordon Howell in Edinburgh, and from there was disseminated internationally on computer networks.

Ms. Austen's Submission

She knew that some like to make their Submissions in the privacy of their own living quarters. Other fragile souls, who had to work themselves up to such an important act, made theirs on the spur of the moment by making use of a foneport they encountered while away from home. Austen, however, had decided to do it the traditional way, the right way, as she thought of it, or perhaps, she had admitted to herself, it was just that she found such older forms comforting. At any rate, she had risen early, bathed, put on her best outfit, treated herself to an elegant breakfast at Rive Gauche, the restaurant frequented by would-be's, and then made her way to the Agency of Culture, outside of whose main portal she now stood.

Taking several deep, careful breaths to remain calm, she entered the forbidding building and sought the elevator that would take her to the eighty-ninth floor of the west tower. She found herself alone in the elevator for the last half of her ascent, and superstitiously taking anything she encountered as an omen, she wondered if that meant that she was to be one of the lucky ones who would rise fast and alone, one of those few who would make it. As the elevator eased to a halt and its bronze-colored doors slid back, she automatically stepped out of the elevator; but before proceeding down the long corridor, she carefully checked the number of the floor, though, like any other Apprentice Author, she had recognized it immediately. Smiling wryly at the way her nervous hesitation masked itself as a traveler's caution, Austen began an inner harangue that she sometimes carried on for hours at a time. "Come on, you know this is the right floor, and you recognized it immediately. Jane, you can recite the names of the worthies whose portraits line the halls, since they haven't changed in a hundred years. They certainly haven't since your disastrous last visit. There's Shakespeare, Homer, Dante, the first three on the left, and Woolf, Dickinson, Johnnes, and all the rest on the right."

Arriving at the end of the corridor, Austen paused, took a deep breath, and opened the door marked "Submissions." Now that she was here, she began to worry that perhaps she had been too hasty. Perhaps her story was not quite ready. Maybe she had better go home and let it sit for a few days or maybe a week. Her mouth was dry, so dry she licked her lips several times without much effect. "Relax," she told herself. "There's no sense in waiting any longer. You know it's the best thing you've ever done; you can feel it in your bones, and you knew this was the one as soon as it began to take shape last week. Besides," she added, "it's only your second Submission. If something crazy happens and it is not accepted, you still have one more."

Deciding that this was no time to hesitate, the young woman stepped firmly up to the central console, pressed her palm against the recognition pad, plugged in her Authorpad, and said in a voice that was slightly deeper and more hoarse than usual, "I, Jane Austen, Apprentice Author, would like to make a Submission."

"Submission. Are you fully aware that if this one is not accepted, you have only a single opportunity remaining?"

"I am."

"Please press the white button to make your Submission." She had promised herself that, win or lose, she would make her Submission like a true Author. She would not close her eyes, take a deep breath, or mumble any prayers. She would just press the white button that had been pressed by so many thousands of fingers before her and would be pressed by so many thousands after.

Austen tried to summon courage by recalling how full of confidence and how eager to complete her submission draft she had been yesterday. In fact, when the clerk at the writing bureau, a man in his sixties who always wore an old-fashioned ill-fitting suit, had looked in her direction, she had left her chair in the waiting room and headed directly toward the door even before he called her name. "Fourteen, Ms. Austen," he said in his sad, thin voice, when she looked back at him before opening the door to the workrooms. Silently counting the rooms on her right—"one, two, three, four"—she made her way to number fourteen, which she recognized immediately as one of the newly reconditioned units. Pressing her hand against the recognition pad that would charge her time in the workroom to her personal account at CenterBank, Austen waited until the door opened and then, full of barely repressed excitement, entered the little chamber that would be her working place for the next four hours, unslung a battered light blue case, and proceeded to open her Authorpad. Glancing at the portable writer that had been hers since the Agency of Culture had assigned it to her six years ago when she declared for authorship as a career, Austen plugged it into the narrow shelf before her and seated herself in the authorship chair, which immediately shaped itself to her back and sides.

"Welcome, Ms. Austen," she heard slightly behind her and to her left—that's where the sound always seemed to emanate from in this unit, she recalled. "Today we can offer you a fine selection of environments suitable for inspiration or editorial activities. First, we have Off Puerto Rico, 25 June, a calm seascape whose quiet waves many have found most suitable, and which Andros van Hulen, the recent winner of the Prix de Rome, used while composing the crucial third chapter of his brilliant prose epic. Second, you might like to work within Far Himalayas, 1 August, a bare, chilling setting far from human and other distractions. The third environment, which is new since your last session, is entitled Jungle Vista, Amazon Basin, 3 February, which, in contrast to the other new offerings, seethes with energy and strange life forms and is well worth the supplementary fee. Several of our young authors," the huckstering machine continued, "have already worked with it and claim that the resultant work produced within this surround is simply wonderful."

"Thank you, Surround, but today I think I need something better known, more familiar. Please let me have Browning's study, personalized version no. 32–345B." Immediately, the narrow confines of her cramped workunit appeared to shift until she found herself seated at a large oak work table covered with manuscript and leather-covered rectangular solids in a walnut-paneled room the likes of which had not existed for several hundred years. She had no idea who this Robert Browning had been or even what kind of work he had created—whether it was, say, adventure tales or erotic epics—but she had felt at home in his work room since she first came upon it while idly browsing through infrequently used scenarios. Austen felt the temperature of the air around her drop slightly as Surround changed it to match the qualified realism that marked her own personalized version of this ancient writer's workplace.

When she turned it on, her Authorpad model 73.2 automatically called up the last wordfile she had entered before going to sleep a very few hours before. Austen had caught fire late yesterday afternoon, and unwilling to spare attention or energy for anything else, she had composed until her latest tale—her best, she knew—arrived at the conclusion for which she had been searching. Anxious lest the passages, which had seemed so perfect before she had returned home and thrown herself down on her rumpled sheets and slept at last, would now appear awkward and imprecise, she nervously rubbed her left hand over her mouth and cheek. She had waited long for this one, so long that she was terrified lest she had deluded herself into thinking, as all beginners must, that she had a winner. No, she was certain. This time her submission would move the Agency to promote her from Apprentice Author Class 1C to Author.

Like all those many thousands of student and apprentice authors, she had wasted far too much creative energy, she knew, dreaming of making it. She wanted the enormously greater convenience of having her own work unit at home, of course, and like everyone else, she naturally wanted the stipend that came with promotion as well. And the status of being a real Author and not one of the hangers-on, the would-be's, so many of whom eventually dropped out of the struggle and ended their days as clerks or worse, well, that was wonderful, to be sure. But it was publication, gaining access to the literary network, that made it all worthwhile.

Sure, it wasn't much, not like achieving the status of Mass Author or even Serious Author, but it was a first step, the one that allowed and encouraged her to take others. Some legendary Apprentice Authors had made it real big. Why, not more than two or three years ago, she remembered, a young man had shot out of obscurity, scored big with a Mass Novel about the last war that had made the international network, where it had been picked up and used for videos throughout the world. There was even one of those weird pop fairy-tale versions in New Delhi, and the French had taken it, dividing the main character into six states of consciousness or moods, and creating a phantasmagoria that made the art channels.

Today she felt hopeful, energetic, sure that she would make it to the network. Moods are funny, she thought, for not more than a week ago she felt crushed beneath the base of this massive pyramid that stretched from students, authors-in-training, and would-be authors to fully accredited practitioners and from them upward to the minor and major Mass Authors, and above them, in turn, to the Serious Ones, whose works would be allowed to exist for one hundred years after their death. And, then, way off in the distance, at the peak of this pyramid, there were the Canonical Authors, those whose works had lasted and would be allowed to last, those whose works could be read and were even taught in schools to those who didn't want to be writers.

She knew how difficult creating something new had proved. And she certainly had learned the hard way that there were no shortcuts to success. In particular, she remembered with embarrassment how she had tried to crash through the gates of success with a little piece on a young author struggling to succeed, and she still squirmed when she remembered how Evaluator, the Agency of Culture's gateway computer, had responded to her first Submission with an extreme boredom and superior knowledge born of long experience, "Ah, yes, Ms. Austen, a story on a young author, another one. Let's see, that's the eighth today—one from North America, one from Europe, two from Asia, and the rest from Africa, where that seems a popular discovery of this month. Your ending, like your concentration on classroom action and late night discussions among would-be authors, makes this a clear example of Kunstlerroman type 4A.31. Record this number and check the library, which at the last network census had 4,245 examples, three of which are canonical, 103 Serious Fiction, and the remainder ephemera.

"Your submission has been erased, and the portions of your Authorpad memory containing it have been cleared, thus allowing you to get on with more promising work. Thank you for your submission. Good day, Apprentice Author Austen."

That, she thought, must be her most painful memory, but another concerning her attempt at truly original creativity rivaled it. A year before the first incident, which took place this last November, she had decided that she had been relying too much on the Authorpad's tie-ins to the Agency's plot, character, and image generators. No, she promised, she would be her own woman, and though she had found it difficult working without the assistance of that friendly voice that made suggestions and allowed her to link instantly to source texts and abundant examples, she had forced herself to slog on, hour after hour, confident that she would return the craft of authorship to its past glories, the glories of the Back-Time, when computers had not offered their friendly assistance and authors, so it was rumored, actually created heavy things called books (though how one was supposed to store or even read them she wasn't quite certain). She remembered her chagrin when the Practice Evaluator at school, which was programmed to emulate the Agency's official one, pointed out how sadly derivative her contribution had turned out to be. When she emphasized how she had composed it entirely "on her own"—that was the phrase she used—the knowing voice commanded, "Look, Austen," and then before she realized what the Evaluator was doing, the scene vanished from her Surround, replaced by sets of flow charts, concept maps, and menus, some of which bore labels like "Parallels to Plots of Submitted Work" or "Forty-One Types of Novels about Young Authors." She found herself particularly embarrassed to discover that even the title of which she was so proud, "A Portrait of the Artist as a Young Man," had already been used by an obscure twentieth-century author who resided in the distant reaches of the canon.

Worst, she had to listen, this time forced to pay close attention, to another lecture on the foolish egotism of would-be authors. She had taken all the requisite courses in literary theory, naturally, and now Evaluator was accusing her of theoretical naiveté and ideological illiteracy. Her main problem, she had to admit, was that she had such a firm sense of herself, such a firm conviction that she existed apart, different, that she found the Culture Agency's emphasis on inevitable creation uncongenial, and well, yes, threatening. It all went back, the machine was reminding her, to language, the condition of all intelligence, whether human, artificial, or a combination of the two. "All of us, Apprentice Austen, use it to communicate our thoughts and to shape our reality, but although you speak ComEnglish, you do not create it, even though no one may ever have combined those words that you use at this instant in precisely that way before. In fact, as your teachers have reminded you so many times, the thoughtful Author confronts the fact that language speaks her as much as she speaks language. And since literature is but another level of language and linguistically organized codes, you cannot assume that you are in sole control of the stories you produce. Your job as an author, Ms. Austen, involves recombinations and possible discoveries, not origins, not originations. An author is a weaver of tapestries and not a sheep producing wool fibre."

Austen had learned her lesson, she felt sure, and this story would be the one to realize all that potential her teachers had seen so many years earlier.

Austen pressed the white button, transmitting her story from the Authorpad to Evaluator in the legally required act of Submission. She thereupon stepped back and waited. Slightly more than seven seconds later, Evaluator's melodious womanly voice, now warmer and more enthusiastic than before, announced, "Congratulations, Author Austen, your story has been accepted. It will appear this Thursday on the regional network and we predict solid interest. Please check the official reviews and abstracts that will be circulated on this date in order to provide author's confirmation of the abstract. Additional congratulations are in order, Ms. Austen: Requests have just been received for translation rights from Greater Germany, Nepal, and Japan."

Austen lifted her finger to press the white button that would transmit her story from the Authorpad to Evaluator in the legally required act of Submission. She placed her finger near the white button, paused a second, and then another. Slowly unplugging her Authorpad, she left the cell, and holding herself rigid by sheer force of will, walked briskly back toward the elevator.

Austen pressed the white button, transmitting her story from the Authorpad to Evaluator in the legally required act of Submission. She was still seated, eyes shut and holding her breath, when less than ten seconds later, Evaluator announced, "Congratulations, Author Austen, your story has been accepted for a collaborative fiction! Your text will mingle with those of eleven other authors, only two of them brand new like yourself. That is quite an honor, I must say. Would you like to learn the identities of your collaborators?

Austen pressed the white button, transmitting her story from the Authorpad to Evaluator in the legally required act of Submission. She had not time to remove her index finger from the button, when the firm motherly voice of Evaluator gently announced, "I am sorry, Ms. Austen. Your Submission is not accepted. Please try not to be upset. At another time, your work might have been admitted to the Net, but this past week has seen an unusual number of texts submitted. If you find yourself in need of a tranquilizing agent now or something to help you sleep later, I am authorized to prescribe one at your local pharmacia."

Several years after writing "Ms. Austen's Submission," I encountered Gordon Wu's review of Paula Milne's *Earwig*. According to Wu's description, in Milne's play a "feminist novelist in need of money" works on "soap operas plotted by a committee of tired hacks working for a television network. Their success is judged by a computer, EARWIG, which projects audience ratings for their scripts" (777). When I first wrote my description of a future author's experience of trying to publish her work, I thought Ms. Austen's new world of publishing as a dystopia, though one, of course, that extrapolated strands found in contemporary England and America. However, after reading Richard Ohmann's account of the relations that obtain among authors, publishers, advertisers, reviewers, and leading periodicals in contemporary America ("Shaping of a Canon"), I wonder if machines could do worse. Then, of course, I recalled Ulmer's observation that machine intelligence necessarily reproduces *someone's* ideology. . . .

Pornography, Gambling, and Law on the Internet: Vulnerability and Invulnerability in E-Space

The Associated Press reported on December 5, 1994, that Robert and Carleen Thomas, who operated a computer bulletin board in California, were convicted in Memphis, Tennessee, of eleven counts of transmitting obscene materials to a members-only computer bulletin board via a telephone line. "The prosecution of the Thomases marked the first time that operators of a computer bulletin board were charged with obscenity in the city where the material was received, rather than where it originated." The Thomases, who lived in Milpitas, California, near San Francisco, claimed that the prosecutors shopped around until they found a Bible Belt jurisdiction to increase chances of conviction. "If the 1973 Supreme Court standard is applied to cyberspace," the AP story continued, "juries in the most conservative parts of the country could decide what images and words get onto computer networks, said Stephen Bates, a senior fellow with the Annenberg Washington Program, a communications think-tank." To be sure, this case involves digital networked culture and not hypertext itself, since the crime with which the Thomases were charged involved a commercial bulletin board rather than the WWW. Nonetheless, the same issues pertain to the World Wide Web.

According to the presiding judge in the Thomas case, the virtual space that permits disseminating information at great speed turned out to have extended—grotesquely, many have argued—the legal and hence physical space in which one is legally vulnerable. The Internet, in effect, was understood to have dissolved one kind of legal boundary—that of the more liberal municipal authorities and of the state of California—while simultaneously extending that of Tennessee to override wishes of voters and judiciary in another state.

One does not know if the Thomases' conviction will be upheld, finally, and its legal implications certainly have more importance to the United States, with its conflicting legal jurisdictions, than to many other countries. Their case also presents some odd features, one of the most obvious being that local Tennessee Internet providers offering the same kind of sexually explicit materials were supposedly not prosecuted either before or after the prosecutor went after the California couple. But the issue of jurisdiction in virtual space reminds us that in cyberspace the basic definitions of rights and responsibilities, law and its limits, are currently up for grabs—and, as James Boyle suggests, since law works by analogy to often outmoded conditions, one can expect that crucial precedents will be made by those unaware of differences between physical and virtual space.

Granted that many people find such erotica offensive, the recent hysteria about pornography and exploitation of children on the Internet seems more than a little fishy, particularly given that an astonishing amount of similar, equally degrading material is available via telephone chat-lines. Unless I have missed that article in my local newspaper, I don't recall reading that politicians and local law enforcement officers have proposed to imprison the CEOs of AT&T, the Baby Bells, and local phone companies, much less seize phone lines and equipment. One common interpretation of the high moral dudgeon about possibilities of seduction and corruption on the Internet is that it involves asserting control of the vast, great financial potential of its resources. In an article in *PC Magazine* (which I encountered in its WWW form), John C. Dvorak convincingly argues that the entire Thomas case has little to do with the ostensible issues of moral standards: "The purpose of this interstate arrest was to set a legal precedent for all interstate activity done over a computer network. Authorities hope the result of this case (along with that of a parallel case against the Thomases pending in the Utah courts) will be effective control of interstate banking, interstate sales tax collection for on-line mall activity, and interstate gambling for the purpose of collecting taxes (which authorities would like to ban outright)."

In this and other ways authorities might hope to control financial resources, in essence using virtual space to reshape physical and legal space within the boundaries of the United States of America. What can they do, however, when illegal activities originate outside the country? Dvorak sees the entire Thomas matter as related essentially to the desire by individual states to control—that is, tax—gambling and other financial transactions by Americans on the Internet, but offshore servers have already shown how difficult this might be in an open society.

The easy, convenient access to Internet resources provided by WWW has, as one might expect, quickly produced distant gambling casinos that, however virtual themselves, require real money—as if money were itself not always virtual! In addition to providing advertising for legal gambling in Las Vegas (Vegas.Com!) and books on the subject, the WWW also hosts both discussion groups and several virtual gambling casinos whose servers are located outside the United States. WagerNet, based in Belize, and Sports International, based in Antigua, permit one to place sports wagers—$50 minimum bet for Sports International—and the Caribbean Casino, which is based in Turks and Caicos Islands, offers blackjack and lotteries as well as wagering on sports. These establishments escape local American laws against gambling both because the activity takes place in virtual space and because the server lies outside a boundary that would permit law enforcement. According to William M. Bulkley, "the Justice Department says cyberspace casinos are illegal. But the companies' offshore venues may protect them. And authorities will have a tough time detecting who's actually betting because many people will be playing the same games for free" (B1). The effect of cyberspace here is the opposite of that observed in the Thomas case: whereas in the pornography case, local authorities in one jurisdiction (with the assistance of U.S. postal authorities) asserted their control over another jurisdiction, in this case the limits of U.S. sovereignty mean that no control is possible. Perhaps the Thomases should move offshore.

"What becomes of government in an electronic revolution?" asks James K. Glassman, who asserts that "government's regulatory functions could weaken, or vanish. It's already a cinch on the Internet to get around the rules; censorship, telecommunications restrictions and patent laws are easily evaded. Even tax collection could become nearly impossible when all funds are transferred by electronic impulses that can be disguised." Glassman describes the cyberpunk science fiction worlds of William Gibson, Bruce Sterling, and Neal Stephenson in which the new information technologies prevent national governments from controlling the flow of money and information, thereby inevitably destroying them and transferring their power to other entities, such as multinational corporations and organized crime.

To forestall such a future, China and Singapore are trying to impose their own cyberspace dystopias. As an article in the *Wall Street Journal* explains, China "is determined to do what conventional wisdom suggests is impossible: Join the information age while restricting access to information" (Kahn, Chen, and Brauchli, A1), and its authorities hope to do so by creating an electronic Wall of China, a heavily filtered and censored "'intranet' or Internet-lite" (A4) with a "monolithic Internet backbone, centrally administered, that minimizes the threat of the Internet's amoeba-like structure" and thereby controls the "two things China's authoritarian government most dreads, political dissent and pornography" (A4).

The government of Singapore, "one of the world's most enthusiastic users of the Internet," also wishes to take advantage of the new technology while simultaneously silencing any liberatory message that might be in the medium. As Dan McDermott wrote on March 6, 1996,

Chill winds blew through Singapore cyberspace yesterday, as the government announced sweeping plans to filter what the average Singaporean can see and say on the Internet. Joining several other governments in seeking to filter the rivers of words and pictures pouring onto the Internet, Singapore said it will hold both content providers and access providers responsible for keeping pornographic and politically objectionable material out of the country's 100,000 Internet accounts. (A1)

Singapore has already blocked computer sites objectionable to the government, shutting down access both to Playboy Enterprises' homepage and to that of the Socratic Circle, "an informal discussion group that . . . briefly held some animated political discussions last year" (A1).

The apparently odd collocation of politics and pornography that appears so explicitly in China and Singapore turns out to be a common theme in the intertwined histories of information technology, democratization, and modernity. In fact, as Lynn Hunt has shown, "pornography as a regulatory category was invented as a response to the perceived menace of the democratization of culture. . . . It was only when print culture opened the possibility of the masses gaining access to writing and pictures that pornography began to emerge as a separate genre of representation" (12–13). If one defines pornography as "explicit depiction of sexual organs and sexual practices with the aim of arousing sexual feelings," then it almost always appears in the context of other genres and modes, "until the middle or end of the eighteenth century. In early modern Europe, that is, between 1500 and 1800, pornography was most often a vehicle for using the shock of sex to criticize religious and political authorities" (10), and it was therefore linked "to freethinking and heresy, to science and natural philosophy, and to attacks on absolutist political authority" (11).

As these examples suggest, the WWW and Internet bring with them the threat and promise of democratized access to information—all sorts of information, not all of it savory or sane—but the degree to which information technology will change culture, government, and society very much remains an open question. If, as we have observed, the very slightest changes in technology (the size of a screen, the presence or absence of color, forms of linking) often have surprisingly major effects on the way we read, write, and think in e-space, then one cannot predict if governments will finally control the forms of hypertext we shall encounter, or if hypertext will appear in forms that will prove too powerful to fit into our present conceptions of space and power or to be controlled by the laws that shape them.

Access to the Text and the Author's Right (Copyright)

Conceptions of authorship are a matter of convention, and they relate importantly to whatever information technology currently prevails. When that technology changes or shares its power with another, the cultural construction of authorship changes, too, for good or for ill. In hypertext, which reconceives both reader and author, rights of authorship comingle with rights of readership. Readers' access to a network implies access to the texts "on" that network, and not just in order to read those texts but potentially to link to them as well. Who, then, has the right to have access to a text?

The issue of readers' rights relates directly to the fate of authorial rights. Michael Heim has pointed out that "as the model of the integrated private self of the author fades, the rights of the author as a persistent self-identity also become more evanescent, more difficult to define. If the work of an author no longer carries with it definite physical properties as a unique original, as a book in definite form, then the author's rights too grow more tenuous, more indistinct" (*Electric Language,* 221). If the author, like the text, becomes dispersed or multivocal, how does society fairly assign legal, commercial, and moral rights?

Before we can begin to answer such a question, we have to recognize that our print-based conceptions of authorial property and copyright even now do harm as well as good. They produce economically irrational effects, hindering as well as stimulating invention. Indeed, as James Boyle reminds us in his splendid book about law and the construction of an information society,

Copyright is a fence to keep the public out as well as a scaffolding for the billboards displayed in the marketplace of ideas; it can be used to deny biographers the ability to quote from or to paraphrase letters; to silence parody; to control the packaging, context, and presentation of information. To say that copyright promotes the production and circulation of ideas is to state a conclusion and not an argument. At the very least we might wonder if, *in our particular copyright regime,* the gains outweigh the losses. (18–19, emphasis in original)

Boyle forcefully argues that the author paradigm that provides the center of copyright law and our current visions of intellectual property "produces effects that are not only unjust, but unprofitable in the long term" (xiv), in part because it rewards only certain kinds of creation, to the detriment of others.

Posing a hypothetical example based on the way Western scientists and corporations copyright materials that are based on information derived from communities in the Third World, he demonstrates how laws supposedly intended to promote innovation by rewarding creators recognize only creativity and originality based on a romantic conception of authorship:

Centuries of cultivation by Third World farmers produces wheat and rice strains with valuable qualities—in the resistance of disease, say, or in the ability to give good yields at high altitudes. The biologists, agronomists, and genetic engineers of a Western chemical company take samples of these strains and engineer them a little to add a greater resistance to fungus or a thinner husk. . . . The chemical company's scientists fit the paradigm of authorship. The farmers are everything authors should not be—their contribution comes from a community rather than an individual, from tradition rather than innovation, from evolution rather than transformation. Guess who gets the copyright? Next year the farmers may need a license to resow the grain from their crops. (126)

In a situation marked by diametrically opposed conceptions of intellectual property, each side believes the other has stolen something: whereas countries like the United States and Japan that base their conceptions of intellectual property on the author paradigm accuse Third World nations of pirating their ideas, the latter countries in turn accuse the United States and Japan of stealing something that belongs to an entire community.

An even more crucial problem with copyright is that notions of intellectual property based on the author paradigm, which supposedly reward and hence stimulate originality, "can actually *restrict* debate and slow down innovation—by limiting the availability of the public domain to future users and speakers" (155). Those who write about intellectual property often point out that many corporations elect to rely on secrecy rather than copyright law to protect their inventions, and, anyway, as Boyle urges, "innovators can recover their investment by methods other than intellectual property—packaging, reputation, being first to market, trading on knowledge of the more likely economic effects of the innovation, and so on" (140). If electronic information technology threatens to reconfigure our conceptions of intellectual property, we can take reassurance from several things, among them not only that our fundamentally problematic ideas of copyright often do not achieve what they are supposed to do but also that other means of rewarding innovation already exist.

As we have observed, one problem challenging print-based conceptions of intellectual property in an age of the digital word and image involves our changing understanding of authorship. A second problem concerning intellectual property derives from the nature of virtual textuality, any example of which by definition exists only as an easily copiable and modifiable version—as a derivative of something else or as what Baudrillard would call a simulacrum. Traditional conceptions of literary property derive importantly from ideas of original creation, and these derive in turn from the existence of multiple copies of a printed text that is both fixed and unique. Electronic text processing changes, to varying degrees, all aspects of the text that had made conceptions of authorial property practicable and even possible. Heim correctly warns that an outmoded conception of "proprietary rights based on the possession of an original creation no longer permits us to adapt ourselves to a world where the technological basis of creative work makes copying easy and inevitable," and that to protect creativity we "must envision a wholly new order of creative ownership" (*Electric Language*, 170). But the problem we face, Boyle warns, is that our "author-vision" of copyright and intellectual property "downplays the importance of fair use and thus encourages an absolutist rather than a functional idea of intellectual property" (139).

As Steven W. Gilbert testified before a congressional committee, technology already both extends conventional conceptions of intellectual property and makes its protection difficult or even inconceivable:

It may soon be technically possible for any student, teacher, or researcher to have immediate electronic access from any location to retrieve and manipulate the full text (including pictures) of any book, sound recording, or computer program ever published—and more. When almost any kind of "information" in almost any medium can now be represented and processed with digital electronics, the range of things that can be considered "intellectual property" is mind-boggling. Perhaps the briefest statement of the need to redefine terms was made by Harlan Cleveland in the May/June 1989 issue of *Change* magazine: "How can 'intellectual property' be 'protected'? The question contains the seed of its own confusion: it's the wrong verb about the wrong noun." (16)

Attitudes toward the correct and incorrect use of a text written by someone else depend importantly upon the medium in which that text appears. "To copy and circulate another man's book," H. J. Chaytor reminds us, "might be regarded as a meritorious action in the age of manuscript; in the age of print, such action results in law suits and damages."[11] From the point of view of the author of a print text, copying, virtual textuality, and hypertext linking must appear wrong. They infringe upon one person's property rights by appropriating and manipulating something over which another person has no proper rights. In contrast, from the point of view of the author of hypertext, for whom collaboration and sharing are of the essence of "writing," restrictions on the availability of text, like prohibitions against copying or linking, appear absurd, indeed immoral, constraints. In fact, without far more access to originally printed text than is now possible, true networked hypertextuality cannot come into being.

Difficult as it may be to recognize from our position in the midst of the transition from print to electronic writing, "it is an asset of the new technology, not a defect," Gilbert reminds us, "that permits users to make and modify copies of information of all kinds—easily, cheaply, and accurately. This is one of the fundamental powers of this technology and it cannot be repressed" (18). Therefore, one of the prime requisites for developing a fully empowering hypertextuality is to improve, not the technology, but the laws concerning copyright and authorial property. Otherwise, as Meyrowitz warns, copyrights will "replace ambulances as the things that lawyers chase" (24). We do need copyright laws protecting intellectual property, and we shall need them for the foreseeable future. Without copyright, society as a whole suffers, for without such protection authors receive little encouragement to publish their work. Without copyright protection they cannot profit from their work, or they can profit from it only by returning to an aristocratic patronage system. Too rigid copyright and patent law, on the other hand, also harms society by permitting individuals to restrict the flow of information that can benefit large numbers of people.

Hypertext demands new classes or conceptions of copyright that will protect the rights of the author while permitting others to link to that author's text. Hypertext, in other words, requires a new balancing of rights belonging to those entities whom we can describe variously as primary versus secondary authors, authors versus reader-authors, or authors versus linkers. Although no one should have the right to modify or appropriate another's text any more than one does now, hypertext reader-authors should be able to link their own texts or those by a third author to a text created by someone else, and they should also be able to copyright their own link sets should they wish to do so. A crucial component in the coming financial and legal reconception of authorship involves developing schemes for equitable royalties or some other form of payment to authors. We need, first of all, to develop some sort of usage fee, perhaps of the kind that ASCAP levies when radio stations transmit recorded music; each time a composition is broadcast, the copyright owner earns a minute sum that adds up as many "users" employ the same information—an apposite model, it would seem, for using electronic information technology on electronic networks.

Gilbert warns us that we must work to formulate new conceptions of copyright and fair use, since "under the present legal and economic conventions, easy use of the widest range of information and related services may become available only to individuals affiliated with a few large universities or corporations" (14). Thus dividing the world into the informationally rich and informationally impoverished, one may add, would produce a kind of techno-feudalism in which those with access to information and information technology would rule the world from electronic fiefdoms. William Gibson, John Shirley, and other practitioners of cyberpunk science fiction have convincingly painted pictures of a grim future, much like that in the movie *Blade Runner,* in which giant multinational corporations have real power and governments play with the scraps left over. Now is the time to protect ourselves from such a future. Like many others concerned with the future of education and electronic information technology, Gilbert therefore urges that we must develop "*new economic mechanisms to democratize the use of information, and economic mechanisms beyond copyright and patent.* It would be a tragedy if the technology that offers the greatest hope for democratizing information became the mechanism for withholding it. We must make information accessible to those who need it. . . . Any pattern that resembles information disenfranchisement of the masses will become more obviously socially and politically unacceptable" (17–18; emphasis in original).

Most of the discussions of copyright in the electronic age that I have encountered recently fall into two sharply opposing camps. Those people, like Gilbert, who consider issues of authorial property from the vantage point of the hypertext reader or user of electronic text and data emphasize the need for access to them and want to work out some kind of equitable means of assigning rights, payment, and protection to all parties. Their main concern, nonetheless, falls upon rights of access. Others, mostly representatives of publishers, often representatives of university presses, fiercely resist any questioning of conventional notions of authorship, intellectual property, and copyright as if their livelihoods depended upon such resistance, as indeed they well might. They argue that they only wish to protect authors and that without the system of refereed works that controls almost all access to publication by university presses, standards would plummet, scholarship would grind to a halt, and authors would not benefit financially as they do now. These arguments have great power, but it must be noted that commercial presses, which do not always use referees, have published particularly important scholarly contributions and that even the most prestigious presses invite thesis advisors to read the work of their own students or have scholars evaluate the manuscripts of their close friends. Nonetheless, publishers do make an important point when they claim that they fulfill a crucial role by vetting and then distributing books, and one would expect them to retain such roles even when their authors begin to publish their texts on networks.

Although almost all defenses of present versions of copyright I have encountered clearly use the rights of the author or society in large part as a screen to defend commercial interests, one issue, that of the author's moral rights, is rarely discussed, certainly not by publishers. As John Sutherland explains in "Author's Rights and Transatlantic Differences," Anglo-American law treats copyright solely in terms of property. "Continental Europe by contrast enshrines moral right by statute. In France and West Germany the author has the right to withdraw his or her work after it has been (legally) published—something that would be impossible in Britain or the United States without the consent of the publisher. . . . In [France and West Germany], publishers who acquire rights to the literary work do not 'own it,' as do their Anglo-American counterparts. They merely acquire the right to 'exploit' it" (554).[12]

The occasion for Sutherland's article raises important questions about rights of the hypertext author as well as the print author. In 1985 an American historian, Francis R. Nicosia, published *The Third Reich and the Palestine Question* with the University of Texas Press, which subsequently sold translation rights to Duffel-Verlag, a Neo-Nazi publisher whose director "is (according to Nicosia) identified by the West German Interior Ministry as the publisher of the *Deutscher Monatschefte,* a publication that, among other matters, has talked about 'a coming Fourth Reich in which there will be no place for anti-Fascists. The path to self-discovery for the German people will be over the ruins of the concentration camp memorials'" (554). Believing that an association with Duffel-Verlag would damage his personal and professional reputation, the author has complained vigorously about his American publisher's treatment of his book. Traditional Anglo-American law permits the author no recourse in such situations, but Sutherland points out that "on October 31, 1988, Ronald Reagan signed into law America's ratification of the Berne Convention," which grants the author moral rights including protection from a publisher's acting in ways "prejudicial to his honour and reputation" (554).

The question arises, Would an author whose text appears on a hypertext system find that text protected more or less than the work of a comparable print author? At first glance, one might think that Nicosia would find himself with even fewer rights if his work appeared as a hypertext, since anyone, including advocates of a Fourth Reich, could link comments and longer texts to *The Third Reich and the Palestine Question*. Such an answer is, I believe, incorrect for two reasons. First, in its hypertext version Nicosia's monograph would not appear isolated from its context in the way its print version does. Second (and this is really a restatement of my previous point), a hypertext version would permit the author to append his objections and any other materials he wished to include. Linking, in other words, has the capacity to protect the author and his work in a way impossible with printed volumes. Allowing others to link to one's text therefore does not sacrifice the author's moral rights.

An Open-Ended Conclusion; or, The Dispatch Comes to an End

As my readers will no doubt have observed, this book is simultaneously an enthusiastic hard sell, a prophecy, a grim warning, and a report from the front. Above all, it is an invitation to make connections. Take it, then, as a plea to link up very different areas of endeavor—contemporary critical and literary theory and late-twentieth-century state-of-the-art computing—that supposedly have little in common. Contemporary theory can illuminate the design and implementation of hypertext, and hypertext in turn offers theory an empirical laboratory, a means of practice, refinement, and extension, a space, in other words, in which to test imaginings.

One of the most interesting, exciting things about hypertext appears in the way it offers us a means of looking a short way into one or more possible futures, an electronic Pisgah Sight, as it were, a vision of a future that we ourselves will probably not reach. Equally important, it permits another glance, a re-vision of aspects of our past and present, because even a brief experience of reading and writing in a hypertext environment denaturalizes and demystifies the culture of the printed book. The strangeness, the newness, the difference of hypertext permits us, however transiently and however ineffectively, to decenter many of our culture's assumptions about reading, writing, authorship, and creativity.

Electronic hypertext, the latest extension of writing, raises many questions and problems about culture, power, and the individual, but it is no more (or less) natural than any other form of writing, which is the greatest as well as the most destructive of all technologies.

Notes

1. An important caveat: Here, right at the beginning, let me assure my readers that although I urge that the theories of Barthes and Derrida relate in interesting and important ways to computer hypertext, I do not claim that these theories, or those of semiotics, and poststructuralism—or, for that matter, structuralism—are essentially the same as hypertext.

2. Although the following pages examine some aspects of the history of hypertext theory, they do not provide a history of earlier pioneering systems, such as NLS, Augment, HES, FRESS, Guide, and Hyperties, or of later developments, since valuable basic surveys can be found in Jakob Nielsen, *Multimedia and Hypertext: The Internet and Beyond,* and Wendy Hall, Hugh Davis, and Gerard Hutchings, *Rethinking Hypermedia: The Microcosm Approach.*

3. A second important caveat: By hypertext I mean only one of at least five possible forms of the digital word. In addition to hypertext, there are four other important kinds of electronic textuality, each of which can exist within hypertext environments but is not itself hypertextual:

   1. Graphic representations of text: Using computer graphics to represent text produces images of it that cannot be searched, parsed, or otherwise manipulated linguistically. The resulting images can be animated, made to change in size, accompanied by sound, and so on. This kind of e-text, which is familiar from television advertising, is often created using Macromedia Director.

   2. Simple alphanumeric digital text: this form of electronic text, which functions linguistically, appears in electronic mail, bulletin boards, and word-processing environments.

   3. Nonlinear text: This form does not, like hypertext, enable multisequential reading. According to Espen Aarseth (whose "Nonlinearity and Literary Theory" [in *Hyper/Text/Theory,* ed. Landow] provides the essential discussion of its subject), the various forms of nonlinear textuality include (a) computer games, (b) text-based collaborative environments, such as multi-user domains (MUDs) and MUDs that employ object-oriented programming methods (MOOs), and (c) cybertext, or text generated on the fly. See essays by Carreño, Donguy, Lenoble, Vuillemin, and Balpe in *A:\Littérature ⌐: Colloque Nord Poésie et Ordinateur.* See Meyer, Blair, and Hader for a MOO for WWW.

   4. Simulation: Text in simulation environments can range from computationally produced alphanumeric text (and hence have much in common with the nonlinear form) to instances of fully immersive virtual (or artificial) reality. For discussions of the educational use of such simulation environments within electronic books, see my "Twenty Minutes into the Future, or How Are We Moving beyond the Book?" For general discussions of virtual reality, see *Cyberspace: First Steps,* ed. Michael Benedikt; Michael Heim, *The Metaphysics of Virtual Reality;* and *Virtual*

Reality Systems, ed. R. A. Earnshaw, M. A. Gigante, and H. Jones, and Alex Wexelblat, *Virtual Reality: Applications and Explorations.*

4. A third (and last) caveat: As I pointed out in the introduction to *Hyper/Text/Theory,* some hypertext environments, though not chiefly text- or image-based, employ logical and conceptual links as a means of assisting organization, collaborative work, and decision making. Systems like Xerox PARC's Acquanet and IDE thus far have appealed to workers in computer and cognitive science who are investigating the business applications of information technology. For Acquanet see the articles by Catherine C. Marshall listed in the bibliography; for IDE see those by Daniel Russell.

5. The developers of Microcosm, currently the richest and the most advanced hypertext system available, similarly argue: "*There should be no artificial distinction between author and reader.* Many systems have an authoring mode and a reading mode; such a system is not open from the reader's point of view. We believe that all users should have access to all parts of the system; this does not imply that one user will be able to access or change another's data, but implies that this aspect should be controlled by the granted rights of access to the operating system. Users should be able to create their own links and nodes within their private workspace, then change the access rights so that other users may view or edit them as required" (Hall, Davis, and Hutchings, *Rethinking Hypermedia,* 30; emphasis in original).

6. When I wrote the first edition, Intermedia was the hypertext system with which my students at Brown University and I worked; but shortly after the print publication of *Hypertext,* we found ourselves forced to use several other systems, after Apple Computers, which had funded a portion of the Intermedia development project, fundamentally changed its version of UNIX, thus halting development—and eventually even the use—of Intermedia. Two fully illustrated articles describe IRIS Intermedia in detail: Nicole Yankelovich, Norman Meyrowitz, and Stephen Drucker, "Intermedia: The Concept and the Construction of a Seamless Information Environment," and Bernard J. Haan, Paul Kahn, Victor A. Riley, James H. Coombs, and Norman K. Meyrowitz, "IRIS Hypermedia Services." The Intermedia section of my *Hypertext at Brown* web site, which contains a detailed introduction to the system with many screenshots, can be found at "http://www.stg.brown.edu/projects/hypertext/landow/HTatBrown/Intermedia.html." This URL (uniform resource locator) also provides information about obtaining Paul Kahn's archival video, *Intermedia: A Retrospective,* from the Association for Computing Machinery.

7. In *Writing Space,* Bolter explains some of these costs: "Electronic text is the first text in which the elements of meaning, of structure, and of visual display are fundamentally unstable. Unlike the printing press, or the medieval codex, the computer does not require that any aspect of writing be determined in advance for the whole life of a text. This restlessness is inherent in a technology that records information by collecting for fractions of a second evanescent electrons at tiny junctions of silicon and metal. All information, all data, in the computer world is a kind of controlled movement, and so the natural inclination of computer writing is to change" (31).

8. Terry Eagleton's explanation of the way ideology relates the individual to his or her society bears an uncanny resemblance to the conception of the virtual machine in computing: "It is as though society were not just an impersonal structure to me, but a 'subject' which 'addresses' me personally—which recognizes me, tells me that I am valued, and so makes me by that very act into a free, autonomous subject. I come to feel, not exactly as though the world exists for me alone, but as though it is significantly 'centred' on me, and I in turn am significantly 'centred' on it. Ideology, for Althusser, is the set of beliefs and practices which does this centring" (*Literary Theory*, 172).

9. Chartier bases his remarks in part on Marie-Elizabeth Ducreux's "Reading unto Death: Books and Readers in Eighteenth-Century Bohemia," also in *The Culture of Print*, 191–230.

**Chapter 2
Hypertext and
Critical Theory**

1. I am thinking of Richard Rorty's description in *Philosophy and the Mirror of Nature* (378) of edifying philosophy as a conversation: "To see keeping a conversation going as a sufficient aim of philosophy, to see wisdom as consisting in the ability to sustain a conversation, is to see human beings as generators of new descriptions rather than beings one hopes to be able to describe accurately. To see the aim of philosophy as truth—namely, the truth about the terms which provide ultimate commensuration for all human inquiries and activities—is to see human beings as objects rather than subjects, as existing en-soi rather than as both pour-soi and en-soi, as both described objects and describing subjects." To a large extent, Rorty can be thought of as the philosopher of hypertextuality.

2. Examples include GodSpeed Instant Bible Search Program, from Kingdom Age Software in San Diego, California, and the Dallas Seminary CD-Word Project, which builds upon Guide, a hypertext system developed by OWL International (Office Workstations Limited). See Steven J. DeRose, "Biblical Studies and Hypertext," in *Hypermedia and Literary Studies*, ed. Delany and Landow, 185–204.

3. Jorge Luis Borges, "The Aleph," in *The Aleph and Other Stories*, 13: "In that single gigantic instant I saw millions of acts both delightful and awful; not one of them amazed me more than the fact that all of them occupied the same point in space, without overlapping or transparency. What my eyes beheld was simultaneous, but what I shall now write down will be successive, because language is successive. . . . The Aleph's diameter was probably little more than an inch, but all space was there, actual and undiminished. Each thing (a mirror's face, let us say) was infinite things, since I saw it from every angle of the universe."

4. For a description of existing networks, see Tracy LaQuey, "Networks for Academics." For a description of the proposed National Research and Education Network, see Albert Gore, "Remarks on the NREN," and Susan M. Rogers, "Educational Applications of the NREN."

5. Gregory L. Ulmer pointed out this fact to me during our conversations at the October 1989 Literacy Online conference at the University of Alabama in Tuscaloosa.

**Chapter 3
Reconfiguring
the Text**

1. In fact, a primitive form of hypertext appears whenever one places an electronic text on a system that has capacities for full-text retrieval or a built-in reference device, such as a dictionary or thesaurus. For example, I wrote the manuscript of the first version of the book you are reading on an Apple Macintosh II, using a word-processing program called Microsoft Word; my machine also ran (and still runs) On Location, a program that quickly locates all occurrences of an individual word or phrase, provides a list of them, and, when requested, opens documents containing them. Although somewhat clumsier than an advanced hypertext system, this software provides the functional analogue to some aspects of hypertext.

2. When I first used *intratextuality* in an article some years ago to refer to such referential and reverberatory relations within a text, or within a metatext conceived as a "work," I mistakenly believed I had coined the term. So did my editor, who was not enthusiastic about the coinage. But we were both wrong: Tzvetan Todorov used it in "How to Read" (1969), which appears in *The Poetics of Prose,* 242.

3. IBM Mainframe computers running the CMS operating system call each user's electronic mailbox or message center the "reader."

4. J. David Bolter, in *Writing Space* (63–81), provides an excellent survey of visual elements in writing technologies from hieroglyphics to hypertext. The periodical *Visible Language,* which has appeared since 1966, contains discussions of this subject from a wide variety of disciplines ranging from the history of calligraphy and educational psychology to book design and human-computer interaction.

5. In discussing Barthes's *Elements of Semiology,* Annette Lavers exemplifies the usual attitude toward nonalphanumeric information when she writes that Barthes's notion of narrative "acknowledges the fact that literature is not only 'made of words' but also of representational elements, although the latter can of course only be conveyed in words" (134). That pregnant "of course" exposes conventional assumptions about textuality.

**Chapter 4
Reconfiguring
the Author**

1. Lévi-Strauss's observation, in a note on the same page of *The Raw and the Cooked* (12), that "the Ojibiwa Indians consider myths as 'conscious beings, with powers of thought and action'" has some interesting parallels to remarks by Pagels on the subject of quasi-animate portions of neural nets: "Networks don't quite so much compute a solution as they settle into it, much as we subjectively experience our own problem solving. . . . There could be subsystems within supersystems—a hierarchy of information and command, resembling nothing so much as human society itself. In this image the neuron in the brain is like an individual in society. What we experience as consciousness is the 'social consciousness' of our neuronal network" (126, 224).

2. Lévi-Strauss also employs this model for societies as a whole: "Our society, a particular instance in a much vaster family of societies, depends, like all others, for its coherence and its very existence on a network—grown infinitely unstable and complicated among us—of ties between consanguineal families" (*The Scope of Anthropology,* 33).

3. Said in fact prefaces this remark by the evasive phrase, "it is quite possible to argue,"

and since he nowhere qualifies the statement that follows, I take it as a claim, no matter how nervous or half-hearted.

4. According to the scientists that Galegher, Egido, and Kraut studied, people in these fields work collaboratively not only to share material and intellectual resources: "Working with another person was simply more fun than working alone. They also believed that working together increased the quality of the research product, because of the synthesis of ideas it afforded, the feedback they received from each other, and the new skills they learned. In addition to these two major motives, a number of our respondents collaborate primarily to maintain a preestablished relationship. In a relationship threatened by physical separation, the collaboration provided a reason for keeping in touch. Finally some researchers collaborated for self-presentational or political reasons, because they believed that working with a particular person or being in a collaborative relationship per se was valuable for their careers. Of course, these motives are not mutually exclusive" (*Intellectual Teamwork,* 152).

5. For a classical statement of the historicizing elements in humanistic study, see "The History of Art as a Humanistic Discipline" in Erwin Panofsky's *Meaning in the Visual Arts* (1–25).

6. The large number of individuals credited with authorship of scientific papers— sometimes more than one hundred—produces problems, too, as does the practice of so-called honorary authorship, according to which the head of a laboratory or other person of prestige receives credit for research whose course he or she may not have followed and about which he or she may know very little. In this latter case problems arise when the names of such scientists of reputation serve to authenticate poor quality or even falsified research. See Walter W. Stewart and Ned Feder, "The Integrity of Scientific Literature," *Nature* 15 (1987): 207–214; cited by Ede and Lunsford.

**Chapter 5
Reconfiguring
Writing**

1. I have discussed the first year of Technoculture's existence in "Electronic Conferences and Samiszdat Textuality: The Example of Technoculture," in the 1993 MIT volume, *The Digital Word,* which I edited with Paul Delany.

**Chapter 6
Reconfiguring
Narrative**

1. Dorothy Lee finds an exception to linearity in the language of Trobriand Islanders, which reveals that they "do not describe their activity lineally; they do no dynamic relating of acts; they do not use even so innocuous a connective as *and*" (157). According to Lee, they do not use causal connections in their descriptions of reality, and "where valued activity is concerned, the Trobrianders do not act on an assumption of lineality at any level. There is organization or rather coherence in their acts because Trobriand activity is patterned activity. One act within this pattern gives rise to a preordained cluster of acts"—much as, Lee explains, when knitting a sweater the "ribbing at the bottom does not cause the making of the neckline" (158). Similarly, "a Trobriander does not speak of roads either as connecting two points, or as running from point to point. His paths are self-contained, named as independent units; they are not to and from, they are at. And hc himself is at; he has no equivalent for our *to* or *from*" (159). Appropriately, therefore, when an inhabitant of the Trobriand Islands

"relates happenings, there is no developmental arrangement, no building up of emotional tone. His stories have no plot, no lineal development, no climax" (160), and this absence of what we mean by narrativity relates directly to the fact that "to the Trobriander, climax in history is abominable, a denial of all good, since it would imply not only the presence of change, but also that change increases the good; but to him value lies in sameness, in repeated pattern, in the incorporation of all time within the same point" (161).

Lee, incidentally, does not claim that the people of the Trobriand Islands cannot perceive linearity, just that it possesses solely a negative value in their culture and it is made difficult to use by their customs and language. If one accepts the accuracy of her translations of Trobriand language and her interpretations of Trobriand culture, one can see that what Lee calls nonlineal thought based on the idea of clustering differs significantly from both linear and multilinear thought. If placed upon a spectrum from Trobriand culture at one extreme to Western print culture at the other, hypertextuality would appear only a moderate distance from other Western cultural patterns. Lee's description of Trobriand structuration by cluster, however, does possibly offer means of creating forms of hypertextual order.

2. Lyotard also proposes that "the decline of narrative can be seen as an effect of the blossoming of techniques and technologies since the Second World War, which shifted emphasis from the ends of action to its means; it can also be seen as an effect of the redeployment of advanced liberal capitalism after its retreat under the protection of Keynesianism during the period 1930–60, a renewal that has eliminated the communist alternative and valorized the individual enjoyment of good and services" (*Postmodern Condition,* 37–38). His use of "can be seen as" suggests that Lyotard makes less than a full commitment to these explanations.

3. Hypertext is not the first information technology to make closure difficult. In *Writing Space,* Bolter reminds us that "the papyrus scroll was poor at suggesting a sense of closure" (85).

4. The following discussion of Joyce's pioneering hyperfiction, substantially unchanged from the first edition, has been the subject of numerous detailed discussions since I first wrote about it. See, in particular, the chapters by J. Yellowlees Douglas and Terence Harpold in Landow, *Hyper/Text/Theory,* as well as Jean Clement, "Afternoon, a Story: From Narration to Poetry in Hypertextual Books" and Robert Coover, "And Now, Boot Up the Reviews" (10).

5. The term *prosopopoeia,* Miller explains, describes "the ascription to entities that are not really alive first of a name, then of a face, and finally, in a return to language, of a voice. The entity I have personified is given the power to respond to the name I invoke, to speak in answer to my speech. Another way to put this would be to say that though my prosopopoeia is a fact of language, a member of the family of tropes, this tends to be hidden because the trope is posited a priori" (5).

6. The quoted phrase is from Jonathan Culler, *Structuralist Poetics,* 207. For Propp, see Vladimir Propp, "Fairy Tale Transformations" (1928), *Morphology of the Folktale* (1958);

and sections relating to Propp in Groden and Kreisworth, *Guide to Literary Theory.* See also Robert Scholes, *Structuralism in Literature,* 59–141.

7. Goldberg continues: "In *Simulacra and Simulation,* Baudrillard who claims that 'of all the prostheses that mark the history of the body, the double is doubtless the oldest,' discusses science's desire to create life artificially:

> Cloning radically abolishes the Mother, but also the Father, the intertwining of their genes, the imbrication of their differences, but above all, the joint act that is procreation. The cloner does not beget himself: he sprouts from each of his segments. One can speculate on the wealth of each of these vegetal branchings that in effect resolve all oedipal sexuality in the service of "nonhuman" sex, of sex through immediate contiguity and reduction—it is still the case that it is no longer a question of the fantasy of auto-genesis. The Father and the Mother have disappeared, not in the service of an aleatory liberty of the subject, but in the service of a matrix called code. No more mother, no more father: a matrix. And it is the matrix, that of the genetic code, that now infinitely "gives birth" based on a functional mode purged of all aleatory sexuality.

"This statement," Goldberg points out, "has many implications for both hypertext and critical theory, particularly about the relationship between the author and her work. The author does not beget herself: she sprouts from each of her segments" ("Comments on *Patchwork Girl*").

8. Perhaps one may see this tension between order and disorder most clearly in life. *Patchwork Girl*'s functioning mirrors a cell's life. The "cytoplasm" of links serves as a permeable medium through which disparate parts pass signs. Its global disorder accommodates the local structure of organelles, which may have been conceived autonomously, but together rely on one another's differentiated function to achieve their fullest existence. Cells that incorporated subunits with diverse textures—wrinkled mitochondria, knotted DNA, smooth and rough endoplasmic reticulum—had sufficient complexity as biological collages to form entities such as readers of texts.

9. In the lexia Lars Hubrich added to the work, he argues that in *Patchwork Girl* scars become more than emblems of disfigurement, since we encounter

> the story of a long struggle, of an emancipation that ends not in a mourning about the lost battles but in new strength, as the monster explains: "Scar tissue does more than flaunt its strength by chronicling the assaults it has withstood. Scar tissue is new growth. And it is tougher than skin innocent of the blade." In fact, the scars become a new, living organ, opening up a new sensorium that goes straight into the chest of the monster. The scars are hot, responding to other people's input. And they have the ability to share their experience, to inscribe themselves one someone else's skin.
>
> The scars hold together the individual parts, each one having its own history, and gain their strength from the parts' experiences. But they do not point back, they rather are signs of an active, progressive look into a future that has learned from history.

I have a navel like any other person. Does Shelley's monster have one? Of course, it has to. Not that it gets mentioned, though, as far as I have read Patchwork Girl. It would be rather odd for a monster like the one in the story to have a navel. Its origins lie somewhere else, not at one single point.

And then we realize what those scars really are: birthmarks. Birthmarks of a new history, arisen from endless struggles. Donna Haraway would smile. ("Stitched Identity")

10. In his lexia entitled "A Spotlight on the Haze: Notions of Origin in *Patchwork Girl*," Brian Perkins claims, however, that "hypertext is not so much a harbinger of the new possibilities, but a spotlight on the old machinations. It makes manifest the problems involved in defining the author as producer and the reader as consumer, problems which are not specific to hypertext, but which encompass all of language and signification. The transmission of meaning has forever been a blurry and complicated phenomenon. Hypertexts like *Patchwork Girl* are not novel because the reader is decisive in determining their meaning, they are novel because they more clearly demonstrate the process which has always been at work."

11. Greco continues:

Any claim that hypertext is a privileged preserve of female or even feminist writing is suspicious for other reasons as well. Who is to say how and why hypertext might in some essential way fulfill a dream of an equal or even superior voice and representation for a group whose voices, interests, and hopes are themselves diverse and difficult to define? Those who make this claim commit themselves to a patronizing ideology of dominance masquerading as support and concern; for it is the privilege of the powerful to appropriate domains of discourse on behalf of others. Moreover, discovering alternatives to "rational linearity" is not the same as resisting and transforming the structures whose power and authority give rise to the need for alternatives in the first place. (Joyce, *Of Two Minds,* 88)

**Chapter 7
Reconfiguring
Literary Education**

1. We have been observing ways that hypertext embodies literary theory, and we should also notice that it also instantiates related pedagogical theory. The hypertextual reader-author, for instance, matches R. A. Shoaf's claim in "Literary Theory, Medieval Studies, and the Crisis of Difference" that "every reader, in fact, from the beginning student to the seasoned professional, is also a writer, or more accurately a rewriter—and must be aware of that" (80).

2. John G. Blair, *Modular America,* 11, 20: "The modularity in question emerges when the Americans take something the Europeans considered as a whole, namely undergraduate education, and break it up into small, self-contained and implicitly recombinable units commonly called course credits or credit hours. . . . The implications of the new system show up most clearly in the new artifact to which they give rise: the student transcript. . . . The transcript, by tracing one person's passage through the curriculum, is an additive record bounded by the number of credits required for graduation. Equivalence of parts dictates that a course is a course is a course, though locally defined restraints on combinability (majors, distribution requirements, and the like)

may sometimes lead a student to accumulate more credits than the minimum required for graduation." A full hypertext version of the present book would, at this point, link to the entire text of Blair's book (most likely through a section or chapter that, in turn, would link to the entire text) and also to the enormous body of internal reports produced in recent decades by individual American colleges and universities discussing the results of such modular approaches.

3. That part of the Intermedia development plan funded by the Annenberg/CPB Project included an intensive three-year evaluation carried out by a team of ethnographers, who taped, attended, and analyzed all class meetings and who frequently surveyed and interviewed students for the two years before the introduction of the hypertext component and for the year following. Many of my observations on conventional education and the educational effects of hypertext upon it derive from their data and from conversations with Professor Heywood. See William O. Beeman and others, *Intermedia*.

4. *Context32* and other Intermedia webs contains materials created by my students in six iterations of English 32 (the survey course), two of English 61 (Victorian poetry), one each of English 137 (Anglo-American nonfiction) and English 263 (graduate seminar in Victorian poetry), plus a handful of undergraduate and graduate independent research projects that include Graham Swift's fiction (Barry J. Fishman); World War I, technology, and literature (Thomas G. Bowie); the semiotics of emblem literature (Gary Weissman); Italian Renaissance cultural history and an anthropological approach to women's fashion, 1700 to the present (Shoshana M. Landow); postcolonial fiction (Melissa Culross); and selected authors from the Women Writers Project (Elizabeth Soucar).

5. Six students, or 30 percent of the class, composed their documents directly on Intermedia, rather than on typewriters or personal computers located in clusters or in their own rooms.

6. The authors and essays from the second semester include Melinda Barton, "Soyinka as a Romantic"; Jonathan Clough, "Jonathan Swift's Influences on Soyinka with Reference to 'Gulliver'"; Andrew Colcord Curtis, "Notions of Progress in Swift's *Waterland* and Soyinka's 'When Seasons Change'"; Mary Jane Ebert, "Soyinka's Drama"; Andrew Frumovitz, "Religion, the Earth, and the City in the Drama and Poetry of Wole Soyinka," "The Swamp Dwellers," "The Trials of Brother Jero," and "Soyinka's 'Ujamaa'"; Jonathan Protass, "Soyinka's Battle against Insanity in 'The Man Died'"; Abra Reid, "Christianity and Yoruba: The Fusing of Influences in Wole Soyinka's Work"; Rob Rosenthal, "Swift and Soyinka as Satirists"; Anujeet Sareen, "Wole Soyinka and A. D. Hope"; Valerie Steinberg, "Wole Soyinka's 'Gulliver' and the Perils of Vision"; Emily Steiner, "Changes in African Poetry" and "Soyinka's Roots and the Oral Tradition"; Leslie Stern, "Soyinka's Use of the Yoruba Conception of Man"; Karen van Ness, "The Nigerian Elections of 1965"; Amelia Warren, "Soyinka's 'Gulliver' and Gulliver's Travels," "Wole Soyinka: 'The Critic and Society: Barthes, Leftocracy, and Other Mythologies'"; and Kelley Wilson, "The Test of Idealism in 'The Man Died.'" In general, these documents created by beginning students who had used Intermedia for a semes-

ter match or surpass in usefulness (and often in quality) those produced by graduate developers who had not yet used hypertext. Of course, the present *Soyinka Web* cannot rival what specialists in African literature, history, and culture might create were they given a year or so, but until the WWW how many institutions had available such a flexible, growing resource?

7. Writing in terms of the broadest canon, that constituted by the concept of literature and the literary, Eagleton observers: "What you have defined as a 'literary' work will always be closely bound up with what you consider 'appropriate' critical techniques: a 'literary' work will mean, more or less, one which can be usefully illuminated by such means of enquiry" (*Literary Theory*, 80).

8. In 1968, for example, Random House, which that year purchased seventy-four pages of advertisements in the *New York Times* to Harper's twenty-nine, "had nearly three times as many books mentioned in the feature 'New and Recommended' as Doubleday or Harper, both of which published as many books as the Random House group" (381). Ohmann also points out that "it may be more than coincidental" that in the same year in the *New York Review of Books,* founded by a Random House vice president, "almost one-fourth of the books granted full reviews . . . were published by Random House (. . . including Knopf and Pantheon)—more than the combined total of books from Viking, Grove, Holt, Harper, Houghton Mifflin, Oxford, Doubleday, Mac-Millan, and Harvard so honored; or that in the same year one-fourth of the reviewers had books in print with Random House and that a third of those were reviewing other Random House books, mainly favorably; or that over a five-year period more than half the regular reviewers (ten or more appearances) were Random House authors" (383).

9. According to Hugh Kenner, "since Chaucer, the domain of English literature had been a country, England. Early in the 20th century its domain commenced to be a language, English" (366).

**Chapter 8
The Politics
of Hypertext**

1. Although Eagleton never cites McLuhan or other students of the history of information technology, he several times compares manuscript and print cultures within the context of Marxist theory; see 47–48, 51–52.

2. Ryan also offers an oddly limited description of technology when he writes: "Technology is the human mind working up the natural world into machines. And, as I have argued, it is motivated by the desire of a class of subjects—capitalists—to maintain power over another class of subjects—workers" (92). The problems with this statement include, first, the fact that Ryan confuses "capitalists" with "owners of production," even though he makes clear elsewhere that what he calls the Leninist tradition also relies upon heavy technology; and second, such a bizarrely narrow definition apparently restricts technology to heavy machinery, thereby omitting both everything before the Industrial Revolution and everything in the electronic and atomic age other than old-fashioned rust-belt manufacturing. The context makes difficult determining whether Ryan's dislike of technology or capitalism leads him to such an obsolete definition.

3. Elizabeth L. Eisenstein makes a particularly astute point when discussing arguments about the role of print technology in radical social change during the Reformation: "Given the convergence of interests among printers and Protestants, given the way that the new media implemented older evangelical goals, it seems pointless to argue whether material or spiritual, socio-economic or religious 'factors' were important in transforming Western Christianity. Not only do these dichotomies seem to be based on spurious categories, but they also make it difficult to perceive the distinctive amalgam which resulted from collaboration between diverse pressure groups" (406). One does not have to espouse pluralism to recognize that Marxist analyses could easily incorporate evidence provided by Eisenstein.

4. Nelson also points out: "Tomorrow's hypertext networks have immense political ramifications, and there are many struggles to come. Many vested interests may turn out to be opposed to freedom. . . . For rolled into such designs and prospects is the whole future of humanity and, indeed, the future of the past and the future of the future—meaning the kinds of future that become forbidden, or possible" (3/19).

5. In *The Gutenberg Galaxy* (216), McLuhan quotes Harold Innis, *The Bias of Communication* (Toronto: University of Toronto Press), 29: "The effect of the discovery of printing was evident in the savage religious wars of the sixteenth and seventeenth centuries. Application of power to communication industries hastened the consolidation of vernaculars, the rise of nationalism, revolution, and new outbreaks of savagery in the twentieth century."

6. In print this thrust appears with particular clarity in the radically new discovery that the best way to preserve information lies in disseminating large numbers of copies of a text containing it rather than keeping it secret; see Eisenstein, 116.

7. Professor Ulmer made these comments in the course of the 1988 University of Alabama conference *Literacy Online*.

8. Ryan, whose prose clots and stutters at this point, explains: "The deconstructive rewriting of the classical dialectic removes the justification for the conservative marxist model a linearly evolutionary and finalistically resolutive progress to socialism, while implicitly furthering a politics predicated upon a more realistic assessment of the antagonistic forces and irreducible differences that characterize capitalist social and productive relations" (43).

9. He continues on the same page: "The edifying philosophers are thus agreeing with Lessing's choice of the infinite striving for truth over 'all of Truth.' For the edifying philosopher the very idea of being presented with 'all of Truth' is absurd, because the Platonic notion of Truth itself is absurd."

10. Karl Popper, *The Open Society and Its Enemies,* argues that Plato developed his conceptions of humanity, society, and philosophy in reaction to the political disorder of his time. Plato's "theory of Forms or Ideas," according to Popper, has three main functions within his thought: (a) as a methodological device that "makes possible pure scientific knowledge"; (b) as a "clue" to a theory of change, decay, and history; and (c)

as the basis of an historicist "social engineering" that can arrest social change (1:30–31). Popper argues that Plato bases his ideal state on Sparta, "a slave state, and accordingly Plato's best state is based on the most rigid class distinctions. It is a caste state. The problem of avoiding class war is solved, not by abolishing classes, but by giving the ruling class a superiority which cannot be challenged" (1:46). Popper, who attacks him for providing the ultimate ideological basis of fascism, claims that in *The Republic* Plato "used the term 'just' as a synonym for 'that which is in the interest of the best state.' And what is in the interest of this best state? To arrest all change, by the maintenance of a rigid class division and class rule. If I am right in this interpretation, then we should have to say that Plato's demand for justice leaves his political programme at the level of totalitarianism" (1:89).

11. H. J. Chaytor, *From Script to Print* (Cambridge: Heffer and Sons, 1945), 1, cited by McLuhan (87) and credited on the previous page as "a book to which the present one owes a good deal of its reason for being written."

12. Sutherland quotes E. Plowman and L. C. Hamilton's explanation in *Copyright* (1980) that in France and Germany moral rights include "the rights to determine the manner of dissemination, to ensure recognition of authorship, to prohibit distortion of the work, to ensure access to the original or copies of the work, and to revoke a license by reason of changed convictions against payment of damages" (554).

Bibliography

Printed Materials

A:\ Littérature ⌐: Colloque nord poésie et ordinateur. Lille: Université de Lille3, and Villeneuve D'Ascq: MOTS-VOIR, 1994.

Aarseth, Espen. *Texts of Change: Towards a Poetics of Nonlinearity.* Bergen: University of Bergen, 1991.

Accame, Lorenzo. *La decostruzione e il testo.* Florence: G. C. Sansoni, 1976.

Akscyn, Robert M., Donald L. McCracken, and Elise Yoder. "KMS: A Distributed Hypermedia System for Managing Knowledge Organizations." *Communications of the ACM* 31 (1988): 820–35.

Althusser, Louis. *For Marx.* Trans. Ben Brewster. London: Verso, 1979.

Amerika, Mark. *The Kafka Chronicles.* Boulder: Black Ice, 1993.

———. "Notes from the Digital Overground." *American Book Review* (December–January 1995–96): 1, 12.

Amerika, Mark, and Lance Olsen. "Smells Like Avant Pop: An Introduction, Of Sorts." *In Memoriam to Postmodernism.* Ed. Mark Amerika and Lance Olsen. San Diego: San Diego State University Press, 1995. 1–31.

Anderson, Jean. "STELLA: Software for Teaching English Language and Literature." *Hypermedia at Work: Practice and Theory in Higher Education.* Ed. W. Strang, V. B. Simpson, and D. Slater. Canterbury: University of Kent, 1995. 89–98.

Aristotle. *Poetics.* Trans. Ingram Bywater. *Basic Works.* Ed. Richard McKeon. New York: Random House, 1941.

Bakhtin, Mikhail. *Problems of Dostoevsky's Poetics.* Ed. and trans. Caryl Emerson. Minneapolis: University of Minnesota Press, 1984.

Barrett, Edward, ed. *Sociomedia: Multimedia, Hypermedia, and the Social Construction of Knowledge.* Cambridge: MIT Press, 1992.

———. *Text, ConText, and Hypertext: Writing with and for the Computer.* Cambridge: MIT Press, 1988.

Barth, John. "The State of the Art." *Wilson Quarterly* 36 (1996): 37–45.

Barthes, Roland. "Authors and Writers." *A Barthes Reader.* Ed. Susan Sontag. New York: Hill and Wang, 1982. 185–93.

———. *The Eiffel Tower and Other Mythologies.* Trans. Richard Howard. New York: Hill and Wang, 1979.

———. *Elements of Semiology.* Trans. Annette Lavers and Colin Smith. London: Jonathan Cape, 1967.

BIBLIOGRAPHY ———. *Mythologies.* Trans. Annette Lavers. New York: Hill and Wang, 1972.

———. *Sade, Fourier, Loyola.* Trans. Richard Miller. New York: Hill and Wang, 1976.

———. *S/Z.* Paris: Éditions du Seuil, 1970.

———. *S/Z.* Trans. Richard Miller. New York: Hill and Wang, 1974.

———. *Writing Degree Zero.* Trans. Annette Lavers and Colin Smith. London: Jonathan Cape, 1967.

Bass, Randall. "The Syllabus Builder: A Hypertext Resource for Teachers of Literature." *Journal of Computing in Higher Education* 4 (1993): 3–26.

Bates, Stephen. "The First Amendment in Cyberspace." *Wall Street Journal* June 1, 1994: A15.

Baudrillard, Jean. *The Ecstasy of Communication.* Trans. Bernard and Caroline Schutze. Ed. Sylvère Lotringer. New York: Semiotext(e), 1988.

———. *Fatal Strategies.* Trans. Philip Beitchman and W. G. J. Niesluchowski. New York: Semiotext(e)/Pluto, 1990.

———. *Simulations.* New York: Semiotext(e), 1983.

Beeman, William O., Kenneth T. Anderson, Gail Bader, James Larkin, Anne P. McClard, Patrick McQuillian, and Mark Shields. *Intermedia: A Case Study of Innovation in Higher Education.* Providence, R.I.: Office of Program Analysis / Institute for Research in Information and Scholarship, 1988.

Benedikt, Michael, ed. *Cyberspace: First Steps.* Cambridge: MIT Press, 1991.

Benjamin, Walter. *Illuminations.* Ed. Hannah Arendt. Trans. Harry Zohn. New York: Schocken, 1969.

Benstock, Shari. *Textualizing the Feminine: On the Limits of Genre.* Norman: University of Oklahoma Press, 1991.

Berger, Peter L., and Thomas Luckmann. *The Social Construction of Reality: A Treatise in the Sociology of Knowledge.* Garden City, N.Y.: Doubleday, 1966.

Berners-Lee, Tim, Robert Calliau, Ari Luotonen, Henrik Frystyk Nielksen, and Arthur Secret. "The World-Wide Web." *Communications of the ACM* 37 (August 1994): 76–82.

Bikson, Tora K., and J. D. Eveland. "The Interplay of Work Group Structures and Computer Support." *Intellectual Teamwork.* Ed. Jolene Galegher, Carmen Egido, and Robert Kraut. Hillsdale, N.J.: Lawrence Erlbaum, 1990.

Blackwell, Lewis, and David Carson. *The End of Print: The Graphic Design of David Carson.* San Francisco: Chronicle, 1996.

Blair, John G. *Modular America: Cross-Cultural Perspectives on the Emergence of an American Way of Life.* New York: Greenwood, 1988.

BIBLIOGRAPHY Bloom, Harold, et al. *Deconstruction and Criticism*. London: Routledge and Kegan Paul, 1979.

Bolter, J. David. "Beyond Word Processing: The Computer as a New Writing Space." *Language and Communication* 9 (1989): 129–42.

———. *Turing's Man: Western Culture in the Computer Age*. Chapel Hill: University of North Carolina Press, 1984.

———. *Writing Space: The Computer in the History of Literacy*. Hillsdale, N.J.: Lawrence Erlbaum, 1990.

Borges, Jorge Luis. *The Aleph and Other Stories, 1933–1969*. Trans. Norman Thomas di Giovanni. New York: Bantam, 1971.

———. *Other Inquisitions, 1937–1952*. Trans. Ruth L. C. Simms. New York: Washington Square Press, 1966.

Bornstein, George, and Ralph G. Williams, eds. *Palimpsest: Editorial Theory in the Humanities*. Ann Arbor: University of Michigan Press, 1993.

Boyle, James. *Shamans, Software, and Spleens: Law and the Construction of the Information Society*. Cambridge: Harvard University Press, 1996.

Brown, Peter J. "Creating Educational Hyperdocuments: Can It Be Economic?" *Hypermedia at Work: Practice and Theory in Higher Education*. Ed. W. Strang, V. B. Simpson, and D. Slater. Canterbury: University of Kent, 1995. 9–20.

Bruns, Gerald L. "Canon and Power in the Hebrew Scriptures." *Canons*. Ed. Robert von Halberg. Chicago: University of Chicago Press, 1984.

Bulkley, William M. "New On-Line Casinos May Thwart U.S. Laws." *Wall Street Journal* May 10, 1995: B1, 8.

Bush, Vannevar. "As We May Think." *Atlantic Monthly* 176 (July 1945): 101–8.

———. *Endless Horizons*. Washington, D.C.: Public Affairs Press, 1946.

———. "Memex Revisited." *Science Is Not Enough*. New York: William Morrow, 1967. 75–101.

Calvino, Italo. *If on a Winter's Night a Traveler*. Trans. William Weaver. San Diego: Harcourt Brace Jovanovitch, 1981.

Carlyle, Thomas. "Signs of the Times." *Collected Works*. London: Chapman and Hall, 1858. 98–118.

Catano, James. "Poetry and Computers: Experimenting with Communal Text." *Computers and the Humanities* 13 (1979): 269–75.

Chartier, Roger. *The Cultural Uses of Print in Early Modern France*. Trans. Lydia G. Cochrane. Princeton: Princeton University Press, 1987.

BIBLIOGRAPHY ———. *The Culture of Print: Power and the Uses of Print in Early Modern Europe*. Trans. Lydia G. Cochrane. Princeton: Princeton University Press, 1987.

———. "Meaningful Forms." Trans. Patrick Curry. *Liber* 1 (1989): 8–9.

Chatman, Seymour. *Story and Discourse: Narrative Structure in Fiction and Film*. Ithaca, N.Y.: Cornell University Press, 1978.

Cixous, Hélène. *Readings: The Poetics of Blanchot, Joyce, Kafka, Kleist, Lispector, and Tsvetayeva*. Minneapolis: University of Minnesota Press, 1981.

Cixous, Hélène, and Catherine Clement. *The Newly Born Woman*. Trans. Betsy Wing. Minneapolis: University of Minnesota Press, 1986.

Clement, Jean. "Afternoon, a Story: From Narration to Poetry in Hypertextual Books." *A:\ Littérature ⅃: Colloque nord poésie et ordinateur*. Lille: Université de Lille3, and Villeneuve D'Ascq: MOTS-VOIR, 1994.

Collaud, G., J. Monnard, and J. Pasquier-Boltuck. *Untangling Webs: A User's Guide to the Woven Electronic Book System*. Fribourg, Switzerland: University of Fribourg (IAUF), 1989.

Conklin, E. Jeffrey. "Hypertext: An Introduction and Survey." *IEEE Computer* 20 (1987): 17–41.

Coombs, James H. "Hypertext, Full Text, and Automatic Linking," SIGIR 90 (technical report). Providence, R.I.: Institute for Research in Information and Scholarship, 1990.

Coover, Robert. "And Hypertext Is Only the Beginning. Watch Out!" *New York Times Book Review* August 29, 1993: 8–9.

———. "And Now, Boot Up the Reviews." *New York Times Book Review* August 29, 1993: 10–12.

———. "Endings: Work Notes." Manuscript, 1990.

———. "The End of Books." *New York Times Book Review* June 21, 1992: 1, 11, 24–25.

———. "He Thinks the Way We Dream." *New York Times Book Review* November 20, 1988: 15.

———. "Hyperfiction: Novels for the Computer." *New York Times Book Review* August 29, 1993: 1, 8–10.

———. *Pricksongs and Descants*. New York: New American Library, 1969.

Cortázar, Julio. *Hopscotch*. Trans. Gregory Rabassa. New York: Random House, 1966.

Cotton, Bob, and Richard Oliver. *Understanding Hypermedia: From Multimedia to Virtual Reality*. London: Phaidon, 1993.

Crane, Gregory. "Redefining the Book: Some Preliminary Problems." *Academic Computing* 2 (February 1988): 6–11, 36–41.

BIBLIOGRAPHY   Culler, Jonathan. *Framing the Sign: Criticism and Its Institutions.* Norman: University of Oklahoma Press, 1988.

———. *On Deconstruction: Theory and Criticism after Structuralism.* Ithaca, N.Y.: Cornell University Press, 1982.

———. *The Pursuit of Signs: Semiotics, Literature, Deconstruction.* Ithaca, N.Y.: Cornell University Press, 1981.

———. *Structuralist Poetics: Structuralism, Linguistics and the Study of Literature.* Ithaca, N.Y.: Cornell University Press, 1975.

Daniele, Daniela. "Travelogues in a Broken Landscape: Robert Smithson's Mixed-Media Tribute to William Carlos Williams." *Rivista di Studi Anglo-Americani* 8 (1994): 95–104.

Dasenbrock, Reed Way. "What to Teach When the Canon Closes Down: Toward a New Essentialism." *Reorientations: Critical Theories and Pedagogies.* Ed. Bruce Henricksen and Thaïs Morgan. Urbana: University of Illinois Press, 1990. 63–76.

deCerteau, Michel. *The Practice of Everyday Life.* Trans. Steven Rendall. Berkeley: University of California Press, 1984.

Deegan, Marilyn, Nicola Timbrell, and Lorraine Warren. *Hypermedia in the Humanities.* Oxford: Universities of Oxford and Hull, 1993.

Delany, Paul, and George P. Landow, eds. *Hypermedia and Literary Studies.* Cambridge: MIT Press, 1991.

Deleuze, Gilles, and Félix Guattari. *A Thousand Plateaus: Capitalism and Schizophrenia.* Trans. Brian Massumi. Minneapolis: University of Minnesota Press, 1987.

Del Monaco, Emanuella, and Alessandro Pamini. *Ernest Lubitsch: L'Arte della variazone nel cinema.* Rome: Ente dello Spectacola, 1995.

DeRose, Steven J. *CD Word Tutorial: Learning CD Word for Bible Study.* Dallas: CD Word Library, 1990.

———. "Expanding the Notion of Links." *Hypertext '89 Proceedings.* New York: Association for Computing Machinery, 1989. 249–57.

DeRose, Steven J., David F. Durand, Elli Mylonas, and Allen H. Renear. "What Is Text, Really?" *Journal of Computing in Higher Education* 1 (1990): 3–26.

Derrida, Jacques. *De la grammatologie.* Paris: Les Éditions de Minuit, 1967.

———. *La dissémination.* Paris: Éditions du Seuil, 1972.

———. *Dissemination.* Trans. Barbara Johnson. Chicago: University of Chicago Press, 1981.

———. "Living On." *Deconstruction and Criticism.* Harold Bloom et al. London: Routledge and Kegan Paul, 1979. 75–176.

BIBLIOGRAPHY

———. *Of Grammatology.* Trans. Gayatri Chakravorty Spivak. Baltimore: Johns Hopkins University Press, 1976.

———. "Signature Event Context." *Glyph 1.* Johns Hopkins Textual Studies. Baltimore: Johns Hopkins University Press, 1977.

———. "Structure, Sign, and Play in the Discourse of the Human Sciences." *The Structuralist Controversy: The Languages of Criticism and the Sciences of Man.* Ed. Richard Macksey and Eugenio Donato. Baltimore: Johns Hopkins Press, 1972.

———. *Writing and Difference.* Trans. Alan Bass. Chicago: University of Chicago Press, 1978.

Designing Hypermedia Applications. Issue of *Communications of the ACM* 38 (August 1995).

Dickey, William. "Poem Descending a Staircase: Hypertext and the Simultaneity of Experience." *Hypermedia and Literary Studies.* Ed. Paul Delany and George P. Landow. Cambridge: MIT Press, 1991. 143–52.

Digital Libraries. Issue of *Communications of the ACM* 38 (April 1995).

Duchastel, Philippe C. "Discussion: Formal and Informal Learning with Hypermedia." *Designing Hypertext / Hypermedia for Learning.* Ed. David H. Jonassen and Heinz Mandl. Heidelberg: Springer-Verlag, 1990. 135–46.

Dyson, Esther. "If You Don't Love It, Leave It." *New York Times Sunday Magazine* July 16, 1995: 26–27.

Eagleton, Terry. *Criticism and Ideology: A Study in Marxist Theory.* London: NLB, 1976.

———. *Literary Theory: An Introduction.* Minneapolis: University of Minnesota Press, 1983.

Earnshaw, R. A., M. A. Gigante, and H. Jones, eds. *Virtual Reality Systems.* London: Academic Press, 1993.

Eco, Umberto. *The Open Work.* Trans. Anna Cancogni. Cambridge: Harvard University Press, 1989.

———. *A Theory of Semiotics.* Bloomington: Indiana University Press, 1979.

Ede, Lisa, and Andrea Lunsford. *Singular Texts / Plural Authors: Perspectives on Collaborative Writing.* Carbondale: Southern Illinois University Press, 1990.

Eisenstein, Elizabeth L. *The Printing Press as an Agent of Change: Communications and Cultural Transformations in Early-Modern Europe.* Cambridge: Cambridge University Press, 1980.

Flaxman, Rhoda L. *Victorian Word Painting and Narrative: Toward the Blending of Genres.* Ann Arbor, Mich.: UMI Research Press, 1987.

BIBLIOGRAPHY

Foster, Hal, ed. *The Anti-Aesthetic: Essays on Postmodern Culture.* Port Townsend, Wash.: Bay Press, 1983.

Foucault, Michel. *The Archeology of Knowledge and the Discourse on Language.* Trans. A. M. Sheridan Smith. New York: Harper and Row, 1976.

———. *The Order of Things: An Archeology of the Human Sciences.* New York: Vintage, 1973.

———. "What Is an Author?" *Language, Counter-Memory, Practice: Selected Essays and Interviews.* Trans. Donald F. Bouchard and Sherry Simon. Ithaca, N.Y.: Cornell University Press, 1977. 113–38.

Frow, John. *Marxism and Literary History.* Cambridge: Harvard University Press, 1986.

Galegher, Jolene, Carmen Egido, and Robert Kraut, eds. *Intellectual Teamwork.* Hillsdale, N.J.: Lawrence Erlbaum, 1990.

Galegher, Jolene, and Robert Kraut. "Technology for Intellectual Teamwork: Perspectives on Research and Design." *Intellectual Teamwork.* Hillsdale, N.J.: Lawrence Erlbaum, 1990. 1–20.

Geertz, Clifford. *Works and Lives: The Anthropologist as Author.* Stanford, Calif.: Stanford University Press, 1988.

Genette, Gérard. *Figures of Literary Discourse.* Trans. Alan Sheridan. New York: Columbia University Press, 1982.

———. *Narrative Discourse: An Essay in Method.* Trans. Jane E. Lewin. Ithaca, N.Y.: Cornell University Press, 1980.

Gibson, William. *Burning Chrome.* New York: Ace, 1987.

———. *Mona Lisa Overdrive.* New York: Bantam, 1988.

———. *Neuromancer.* New York: Ace, 1984.

Giedion, Sigfried. *Mechanization Takes Command: A Contribution to Anonymous History.* New York: Norton, 1969.

Gilbert, Steven W. "Information Technology, Intellectual Property, and Education." *EDUCOM Review* 25 (spring 1990): 14–20.

Glassman, James K. "What Becomes of Government in an Electronic Revolution?" *Providence Journal-Bulletin,* September 3, 1995: D13.

Gore, Albert. "Remarks on the NREN." *EDUCOM Review* 25 (summer 1990): 12–16.

Gray, Chris Hables, Heidi J. Figueroa-Sarriera, and Steven Mentor. *The Cyborg Handbook.* London: Routledge, 1995.

Greco, Diane. "Hypertext with Consequences: Recovering a Politics of Hypertext." *Hypertext '96.* New York: Association for Computing Machinery, 1996. 85–92.

BIBLIOGRAPHY   Grigely, Joseph. *Textualterity: Art, Theory, and Textual Criticism*. Ann Arbor: University of Michigan Press, 1995.

Groden, Michael, and Martin Kreiswirth, eds. *The Johns Hopkins Guide to Literary Theory and Criticism*. Baltimore: Johns Hopkins University Press, 1994.

Grudin, Robert. *Book: A Novel*. New York: Random House, 1992.

Guyer, Carolyn. "Buzz-Daze Jazz and the Quotidian Stream." Paper delivered at MLA panel "Hypertext, Hypermedia: Defining a Fictional Form." December, 1992

———. Journal kept during writing of *Quibbling*. Unpublished manuscript.

———. "Something about *Quibbling*." *Leonardo* (October 1992): 258.

Haan, Bernard J., Paul Kahn, Victor A. Riley, James H. Coombs, and Norman K. Meyrowitz. "IRIS Hypermedia Services." *Communications of the ACM* 35 (1992): 36–51.

Hall, Wendy. "Making Hypermedia Work in Education." *Hypermedia at Work: Practice and Theory in Higher Education*. Ed. W. Strang, V. B. Simpson, and D. Slater. Canterbury: University of Kent, 1995. 1–19.

Hall, Wendy, Hugh Davis, and Gerard Hutchings. *Rethinking Hypermedia: The Microcosm Approach*. Boston: Kluwer, 1996.

Hamilton, David P. "Japanese Embrace a Man Too Eccentric for Silicon Valley: After Years of Failure in the U.S., Ted Nelson Is Continuing His Quest for Xanadu." *Wall Street Journal* April 26, 1996: A1, 10.

Harpold, Terence. "Threnody: Psychoanalytic Digressions on the Subject of Hypertexts." *Hypermedia and Literary Studies*. Ed. Paul Delany and George P. Landow. Cambridge: MIT Press, 1991. 171–84.

Heim, Michael. *Electric Language: A Philosophical Study of Word Processing*. New Haven: Yale University Press, 1987.

———. *The Metaphysics of Virtual Reality*. New York: Oxford, 1993.

Hertz, J. H., ed. *The Pentateuch and Haftorahs*. 2nd ed. London: Soncino Press, 1962.

Howard, Alan. "Hypermedia and the Future of Ethnography." *Cultural Anthropology* 3 (1988): 304–15.

Hunt, Lynn, ed. *The Invention of Pornography: Obscenity and the Origins of Modernity, 1500–1800*. New York: Zone, 1993.

Huyssen, Andreas. *After the Great Divide: Modernism, Mass Culture, and Postmodernism*. Bloomington: Indiana University Press, 1987.

Institute for Research in Information and Scholarship. *The Dickens Web: User's and Installation Guide*. Providence, R.I.: Institute for Research in Information and Scholarship, 1990.

BIBLIOGRAPHY　　*IRIS Intermedia System Administrator's Guide: Release 3.0.* Providence, R.I.: Institute for Research in Information and Scholarship, 1989.

IRIS Intermedia User's Guide: Release 3.0. Providence, R.I.: Institute for Research in Information and Scholarship, 1989.

Ivins, William M. *Prints and Visual Communication.* New York: Da Capo, 1969.

Jameson, Fredric. *Marxism and Form: Twentieth-Century Dialectical Theories of Literature.* Princeton: Princeton University Press, 1971.

————. *The Political Unconscious: Narrative as a Socially Symbolic Act.* Ithaca, N.Y.: Cornell University Press, 1981.

Janson, H. W., with Dora Jane Janson. *History of Art: A Survey of Major Visual Arts from the Dawn of History to the Present Day.* New York: Harry N. Abrams, 1962.

Johnson, Barbara. *A World of Difference.* Baltimore: Johns Hopkins University Press, 1987.

Jonassen, David H. "Information Mapping: A Description, Rationale and Comparison with Programmed Instruction." *Visible Language* 15 (1981): 55–66.

————. "Hypertext Principles for Text and Courseware Design." *Educational Psychologist* 21 (1986): 269–92.

Jonassen, David H., and R. Scott Grabinger. "Problems and Issues in Designing Hypertext/Hypermedia for Learning." *Designing Hypertext/Hypermedia for Learning.* Ed. David H. Jonassen and Heinz Mandl. Heidelberg: Springer-Verlag, 1990. 3–26.

Jonassen, David H., and Heinz Mandl, eds. *Designing Hypertext/Hypermedia for Learning,* Heidelberg: Springer-Verlag, 1990.

Jones, Loretta L., Jennifer L. Karloski, and Stanley G. Smith. "A General Chemistry Learning Center: Using the Interactive Videodisc." *Academic Computing* 2 (September 1987): 36–37, 54.

Joyce, Michael. "My Body the Library." *American Book Review* (December–January 1995–96): 6, 31.

————. *Of Two Minds: Hypertext Pedagogy and Poetics.* Ann Arbor: University of Michigan Press, 1995.

————. "Storyspace as a Hypertext System for Writers of Varying Ability." *Hypertext '91.* New York: Association for Computing Machinery, 1991. 381–88.

Kahn, Joseph, Kathy Chen, and Marcus W. Brauchli. "Chinese Firewall: China Seeks to Build Version of the Internet that Can Be Censored." *Wall Street Journal* January 31, 1996: A1, A4.

Kahn, Paul D. "Isocrates: Greek Literature on CD ROM" *CD ROM: The New Papyrus: The Current and Future State of the Art.* Ed. Steve Lambert and Suzanne Ropiequet. Redmond, Wash.: Microsoft Press, 1986.

BIBLIOGRAPHY   ———. "Linking together Books: Experiments in Adapting Published Material into Intermedia Documents." *Hypermedia* 1 (1989): 111–45.

Kahn, Paul D., Julie Launhardt, Krzysztof Lenk, and Ronnie Peters. "Design Issues of Hypermedia Publications: Issues and Solutions." *EP 90: International Conference on Electronic Publishing, Document Manipulation, and Typography.* Ed. Richard Furuta. Cambridge: Cambridge University Press, 1990. 107–24.

Kahn, Paul D., and Krzysztof Lenk. "Typography for the Computer Screen: Applying the Lessons of Print to Electronic Documents." *Seybold Report on Desktop Publishing* 7 (July 5, 1993): 3–16.

Kahn, Paul D., and Norman Meyrowitz. "Guide, HyperCard, and Intermedia: A Comparison of Hypertext/Hypermedia Systems." Technical Report No. 88-7. Providence, R.I.: Institute for Research in Information and Scholarship, 1987.

Kapoor, Mitchell. "Democracy and New Information Highway." *Boston Review* (October–November 1993): 19–21.

Kendall, Robert. "Hypertextual Dynamics in *A Life Set for Two.*" *Hypertext '96.* New York: Association for Computing Machinery, 1996. 74–84.

Kenner, Hugh. "The Making of the Modernist Canon." *Canons.* Ed. Robert von Halberg. Chicago: Unviersity of Chicago Press, 1984. 363–76.

Kermode, Frank. *The Sense of an Ending: Studies in the Theory of Fiction.* New York: Oxford University Press, 1967.

Kernan, Alvin. *Printing Technology, Letters, and Samuel Johnson.* Princeton: Princeton University Press, 1987.

Kerr, Stephen T. "Instructional Text: The Transition from Page to Screen." *Visible Language* 20 (1986): 368–92.

King, Kenneth M. "Evolution of the Concept of Computer Literacy." *EDUCOM Bulletin* 20 (1986): 18–21.

Kittler, Friedrich A. *Discourse Networks 1800 / 1900.* Trans. Michael Metteer and Chris Cullins. Stanford: Stanford University Press, 1992.

Kosko, Bart. *Fuzzy Thinking: The New Science of Fuzzy Logic.* London: Flamingo, 1994.

Kuhn, Thomas S. *The Structure of Scientific Revolutions.* 2nd ed. Chicago: University of Chicago Press, 1970.

Lacan, Jacques. *The Language of the Self: The Function of Language in Psychoanalysis.* Trans. Anthony Wilden. Baltimore: Johns Hopkins Press, 1968.

Landow, George P., ed. *Hyper/Text/Theory.* Baltimore: Johns Hopkins University Press, 1994.

———. "Newman and the Idea of an Electronic University." *The Idea of a University.* Ed. Frank Turner. New Haven: Yale University Press, 1996. 339–61.

BIBLIOGRAPHY

———. "The Rhetoric of Hypermedia: Some Rules for Authors." *Journal of Computing in Higher Education* 1 (1989): 39–64.

———. "Twenty Minutes into the Future, or How Are We Moving beyond the Book?" *The Future of the Book.* Ed. Geoffrey Nunberg. Berkeley: University of California Press, 1996. 209–38.

———. *Victorian Types, Victorian Shadows: Biblical Typology and Victorian Literature, Art, and Thought.* Boston: Routledge and Kegan Paul, 1980.

Landow, George P., and Paul Delany, eds. *The Digital Word: Text-Based Computing in the Humanities.* Cambridge: MIT Press, 1993.

Landow, George P., and Paul Kahn. "The Pleasures of Possibility: What Is Disorientation in Hypertext." *Journal of Computing in Higher Education* 4 (1993): 57–78.

———. "Where's the Hypertext? The Dickens Web as a System-Independent Hypertext." *ECHT'92.* New York: ACM, 1992.

Lanham, Richard A. *The Electronic Word: Democracy, Technology, and the Arts.* Chicago: University of Chicago Press, 1993.

LaQuey, Tracy. "Networks for Academics." *Academic Computing* 4 (November 1989): 32–34, 39, 65.

Larson, James A. "A Visual Approach to Browsing in a Database Environment." *IEEE Computer* (1986): 62–71.

Lavers, Annette. *Roland Barthes: Structuralism and After.* Cambridge: Harvard University Press, 1982.

Lee, Dorothy. "Lineal and Nonlineal Codifications of Reality." *Symbolic Anthropology: A Reader in the Study of Symbols and Meanings.* Ed. Janet L. Dolgin, David S. Kemnitzer, and David M. Schneider. New York: Columbia University Press, 1977. 151–64.

Leggett, John J., John L. Schnase, and Charles J. Kacmar. "Hypertext for Learning." *Designing Hypertext/Hypermedia for Learning.* Ed. David H. Jonassen and Heinz Mandl. Heidelberg: Springer-Verlag, 1990. 27–38.

Leitch, Vincent B. *Deconstructive Criticism: An Advanced Introduction.* New York: Columbia University Press, 1983.

Lévi-Strauss, Claude. *The Raw and the Cooked: Introduction to a Science of Mythology: I.* Trans. John and Doreen Weightman. New York: Harper and Row, 1969.

———. *The Savage Mind.* Chicago: University of Chicago Press, 1966.

———. *The Scope of Anthropology.* Trans. Sherry Ortner Paul and Robert A. Paul. London: Jonathan Cape, 1967.

Liestøl, Gunnar. "Aesthetic and Rhetorical Aspects of Linking Video in Hypermedia." *ECHT'94.* New York: Association for Computing Machinery, 1994.

BIBLIOGRAPHY *Linking the Continents of Knowledge: A Hypermedia Corpus for Discovery and Collaborative Work in the Sciences, Arts, and Humanities.* Providence, R.I.: Institute for Research in Information and Scholarship, 1988.

Lively, Penelope. *Moon Tiger.* New York: Harper and Row, 1989.

Lukacs, Georg. *The Theory of the Novel: A Historico-Philosophical Essay on the Forms of Great Epic Literature.* Trans. Anna Bostock. Cambridge: M.I.T. Press, 1971.

Lyotard, Jean-François. *The Inhuman.* Trans. Geoffrey Bennington and Rachel Bowlby. Stanford: Stanford University Press, 1991.

———. *The Postmodern Condition: A Report on Knowledge.* Trans. Geoff Bennington and Brian Massumi. Minneapolis: University of Minnesota Press, 1984.

Machery, Pierre. *A Theory of Literary Production.* Trans. Geoffrey Wall. London: Routledge and Kegan Paul, 1978.

Marchionini, Gary. "Evaluating Hypermedia-Based Learning." *Designing Hypertext/ Hypermedia for Learning.* Ed. David H. Jonassen and Heinz Mandl. Heidelberg: Springer-Verlag, 1990. 355–73.

Marshall, Catherine C., Frank G. Halasz, Russell A. Rogers, and William A. Janssen, Jr. "Acquanet: A Hypertext Tool to Hold Your Knowledge in Place," *Hypertext '91.* New York: Association for Computing Machinery, 1991. 261–75.

Marshall, Catherine C., and Russell A. Rogers. "Two Years before the Mist: Experiences with Acquanet." *ECHT'92.* New York: Association for Computing Machinery, 1992. 53–62.

Massumi, Brian. *A User's Guide to Capitalism and Schizophrenia: Deviations from Deleuze and Guattari.* Cambridge: MIT Press, 1992.

Matejka, Ladislav, and Krystyna Pomorska, eds. *Readings in Russian Poetics: Formalist and Structuralist Views.* Cambridge: MIT Press, 1971.

Matejka, Ladislav, and Irwin R. Titunik. *Semiotics of Art: Prague School Contributions.* Cambridge: MIT Press, 1976.

Mayes, Terry, Mike Kibby, and Tony Anderson. "Learning about Learning for Hypertext." *Designing Hypertext/Hypermedia for Learning.* Ed. David H. Jonassen and Heinz Mandl. Heidelberg: Springer-Verlag, 1990. 227–50.

McArthur, Tom. *Worlds of Reference: Lexicography, Learning and Language from the Clay Tablet to the Computer.* Cambridge: Cambridge University Press, 1986.

McCaffrey, Larry. "13 Introductory Ways of Looking at a Post-Pop-Modernist Aesthetic Phenomenon Called 'Avant-Pop.'" *In Memoriam to Postmodernism.* Ed. Mark Amerika and Lance Olsen. San Diego: San Diego State University Press, 1995. 32–47.

McCartney, Scott. "For Teens, Chatting on Internet Offers Comfort of Anonymity." *Wall Street Journal* December 8, 1994: B1, 4.

BIBLIOGRAPHY McClintlock, Robert. "On Computing and the Curriculum." *SIGCUE Outlook* (spring–summer 1986): 25–41.

McCorduck, Pamela. *Machines Who Think: A Personal Inquiry into the History and Prospects of Artificial Intelligence.* New York: W. H. Freeman, 1979.

McDermott, Dan. "Singapore Unveils Sweeping Measures to Control Words, Images on Internet." *Wall Street Journal* March 6, 1996: A1.

McGann, Jerome J. "The Complete Writings and Pictures of Dante Gabriel Rossetti: A Hypermedia Research Archive." Unpublished manuscript.

———. *A Critique of Modern Textual Criticism.* Chicago: University of Chicago Press, 1983.

———. *The Textual Condition.* Princeton: Princeton University Press, 1991.

McGrath, Joseph E. "Time Matters in Groups." *Intellectual Teamwork.* Ed. Jolene Galegher, Carmen Egido, and Robert Kraut. Hillsdale, N.J.: Lawrence Erlbaum, 1990. 23–62.

McHale, Brian. *Postmodernist Fiction.* New York: Methuen, 1987.

McKnight, Cliff, John Richardson, and Andrew Dillon. "Journal Articles as a Learning Resource: What Can Hypertext Offer." *Designing Hypertext / Hypermedia for Learning.* Ed. David H. Jonassen and Heinz Mandl. Heidelberg: Springer-Verlag, 1990. 277–90.

McLuhan, Marshall. *The Gutenberg Galaxy: The Making of Typographic Man.* Toronto: University of Toronto Press, 1962.

McQuillan, Patrick. "Computers and Pedagogy: The Invisible Presence." *Journal of Curriculum Studies* 26 (1994): 631–53.

Meyer, Tom, David Blair, and Suzanne Hader. "*WAXweb:* A MOO-based Collaborative Hypermedia System for WWW." *Computer Networks and ISDN Systems* 28 (1995): 77–84.

Meyrowitz, Norman. "Hypertext—Does It Reduce Cholesterol, Too?" *Vannevar Bush and the Mind's Machine: From Memex to Hypertext.* Ed. James M. Nyce and Paul D. Kahn. San Diego: Academic Press, 1991.

Miller, J. Hillis. "The Critic as Host." *Deconstruction and Criticism.* Harold Bloom et al. London: Routledge and Kegan Paul, 1979. 217–53.

———. *Fiction and Repetition: Seven English Novels.* Cambridge: Harvard University Press, 1982.

———. *Illustration.* Cambridge: Harvard University Press, 1992.

———. "Literary Theory, Telecommunications, and the Making of History." *Scholarship and Technology in the Humanities.* Ed. May Katzen. London: British Library Research / Bowker Saur, 1991. 11–20.

———. *Versions of Pygmalion.* Cambridge: Harvard University Press, 1990.

Minsky, Marvin. *The Society of Mind.* New York: Simon and Schuster, 1986.

Mitchell, W. J. T., ed. *On Narrative.* Chicago: University of Chicago Press, 1980.

Mitchell, William J. *City of Bits: Space, Place, and the Infobahn.* Cambridge: MIT Press, 1995.

Moi, Toril. *Sexual/Textual Politics: Feminist Literary Theory.* London: Methuen, 1985.

Morgan, Thaïs E. "Is There an Intertext in This Text?: Literary and Interdisciplinary Approaches to Intertextuality." *American Journal of Semiotics* 3 (1985): 1–40.

Morrell, Kenneth. "Teaching with *HyperCard.* An Evaluation of the Computer-based Section in Literature and Arts C-14: The Concept of the Hero in Hellenic Civilization." Perseus Project Working Paper 3. Cambridge: Department of Classics, Harvard University, 1988.

Moulthrop, Stuart. "Beyond the Electronic Book: A Critique of Hypertext Rhetoric." *Hypertext '91.* New York: Association for Computing Machinery, 1991. 291–98.

———. "Containing the Multitudes: The Problem of Closure in Interactive Fiction." *Association for Computers in the Humanities Newsletter* 10 (summer 1988): 29–46.

———. "Hypertext and 'the Hyperreal.'" *Hypertext '89 Proceedings.* New York: Association for Computing Machinery, 1989. 259–68.

———. "Reading from the Map: Metonomy and Metaphor in the Fiction of 'Forking Paths.'" *Hypertext and Literary Studies.* Ed. Paul Delaney and George P. Landow. Cambridge: MIT Press, 1991. 119–33.

———. "Rhizome and Resistance: Hypertext and the Dreams of a New Culture." *Hyper/Text/Theory.* Ed. George P. Landow. Baltimore: Johns Hopkins University Press, 1994. 299–322.

———. "Toward a Paradigm for Reading Hypertext: Making Nothing Happen in Hypermedia Fiction." *Hypertext/Hypermedia Handbook.* Ed. Emily Berk and Joseph Devlin. New York: McGraw-Hill, 1991. 65–78.

Mowitt, John. *Text: The Genealogy of an Antidisciplinary Object.* Durham, N.C.: Duke University Press, 1992.

Murray, Oswyn. "The Word Is Mightier than the Sword." *Times Literary Supplement* June 16–22, 1989: 655.

Mylonas, Elli. "Design by Exploration: An Academic Hypertext." *Hypermedia at Work: Practice and Theory in Higher Education.* Ed. W. Strang, V. B. Simpson, and D. Slater. Canterbury: University of Kent, 1995. 39–54.

———. "The Perseus Project: Ancient Greece in Texts, Maps and Images." *Electronic Books—Multimedia Reference Works.* Bergen: Norwegian Computing Centre, 1991. 173–88.

BIBLIOGRAPHY   Negroponte, Nicholas. *Being Digital*. New York: Knopf, 1995.

Nelson, Theodor H. *Computer Lib/Dream Machines*. Seattle, Wash.: Microsoft Press, 1987.

———. "Hypermedia Unified by Transclusion." *Communications of the ACM* 38 (August 1995): 31–32.

———. *Literary Machines*. Swarthmore, Pa.: Self-published, 1981.

Newman, John Henry. *The Idea of a University*. Ed. Frank Turner. New Haven: Yale University Press, 1996.

Nielsen, Jakob. "The Art of Navigating through Hypertext." *Communications of the ACM* 33 (1990): 296–310.

———. *Multimedia and Hypertext: The Internet and Beyond*. Boston: Academic Press, 1995.

Novak, Joseph D., and D. Bob Gowin. *Learning How to Learn*. New York: Cambridge University Press, 1984.

Nyce, James M., and Paul Kahn. "Innovation, Pragmatism, and Technological Continuity: Vannevar Bush's Memex." *Journal of the American Society for Information Science* 40 (1989): 214–20.

———, eds. *From Memex to Hypertext: Vannevar Bush and the Mind's Machine*. Boston: Academic Press, 1991.

Ohmann, Richard. "The Shaping of a Canon: U.S. Fiction, 1960–1975." *Canons*. Ed. Robert von Halberg. Chicago: University of Chicago Press, 1984. 377–401.

Ong, Walter J. *Orality and Literacy: The Technologizing of the Word*. London: Methuen, 1982.

———. *Rhetoric, Romantic, and Technology: Studies in the Interaction of Expression and Culture*. Ithaca, N.Y.: Cornell University Press, 1971.

Pagels, Heinz R. *The Dreams of Reason: The Computer and the Rise of the Sciences of Complexity*. New York: Bantam, 1989.

Panofsky, Erwin. *Meaning in the Visual Arts*. Garden City, N.Y.: Doubleday Anchor, 1955.

Paul, Christiane. "Reading/Writing Hyperfictions: The Psychodrama of Interactivity." *Leonardo* 28, no. 4 (1995): 265–72.

Paulson, William R. *The Noise of Culture: Literary Texts in a World of Information*. Ithaca, N.Y.: Cornell University Press, 1988.

Pavic, Milorad. *Dictionary of the Khazars: A Lexicon Novel in 100,000 Words*. Trans. Christina Pribicevic-Zoric. New York: Knopf, 1988.

Peckham, Morse. *Man's Rage for Chaos: Biology, Behavior, and the Arts*. New York: Schocken, 1967.

BIBLIOGRAPHY   Perkins, D. N. "The Fingertip Effect: How Information-Processing Technology Shapes Thinking." *Educational Researcher* (August–September 1985): 11–17.

Perseus: An Interactive Curriculum on Ancient Greek Civilization. 3 vols. Cambridge: Harvard University, 1988.

"The Pleasures of the (Hyper)Text." *New Yorker* June 27 and July 4, 1994: 43–44.

Popper, Karl. *The Open Society and Its Enemies.* 2 vols. 5th ed. rev. Princeton: Princeton University Press, 1966.

Propp, Vladimir, "Fairy Tale Transformations." *Readings in Russian Poetics: Formalist and Structuralist Views.* Ed. Ladislav Matejka and Krystyna Pomorska. Cambridge: MIT Press, 1971. 94–116.

———. *Morphology of the Folktale.* Trans. Laurence Scott. 2nd ed., rev. Austin: University of Texas Press, 1968.

Provenzo, Eugene F. *Beyond the Gutenberg Galaxy: Microcomputers and the Emergence of Post-Typographic Culture.* New York: Teachers College Press, 1986.

Ricoeur, Paul. *Time and Narrative.* Trans. Kathleen McLaughlin and David Pellauer. 2 vols. Chicago: University of Chicago Press, 1984.

Rigden, Joan E. "Homebound and Lonely, Older People Use Computers to Get 'Out.'" *Wall Street Journal* December 8, 1994: B1, 14.

Rogers, Susan M. "Educational Applications of the NREN." *EDUCOM Review* 25 (summer 1990): 25–29.

Ronell, Avital. *The Telephone Book: Technology, Schizophrenia, Electric Speech.* Lincoln: University of Nebraska Press, 1989.

Rorty, Richard. *Philosophy and the Mirror of Nature.* Princeton: Princeton University Press, 1979.

Rosen, Jeffrey. "Cheap Speech: Will the Old First Amendment Battles Survive the New Technologies?" *New Yorker* August 7, 1995: 75–80.

Rosenau, Pauline Marie. *Post-Modernism and the Social Sciences: Insights, Inroads, and Intrusions.* Princeton: Princeton University Press, 1992.

Rosenheim, Andrew. "The Flow That's Becoming a Flood." *Times Literary Supplement* May 12, 1995: 10–11.

Russell, Daniel M. "Creating Instruction with IDE: Tools for Instructional Designers." *Intelligent Learning Media* 1 (1990): 1.

Russell, Daniel M., Daniel S. Jordan, Anne-Marie S. Jensen, and Russell A. Rogers. "Facilitating the Development of Representations in Hypertext with IDE." *Hypertext '89 Proceedings.* New York: Association for Computing Machinery, 1989. 93–104.

BIBLIOGRAPHY Russell, Daniel M., and Peter Piroli. "The Instructional Design Environment: Technology to Support Design Problem Solving." *Instructional Science* 19 (1990): 121–44.

Ryan, Michael. *Marxism and Deconstruction: A Critical Articulation.* Baltimore: Johns Hopkins University Press, 1982.

Saenger, Paul. "Books of Hours and the Reading Habits of the Later Middle Ages." *The Culture of Print: Power and the Uses of Print in Early Modern Europe.* Ed. Roger Chartier, trans. Lydia G. Cochrane. Princeton: Princeton University Press, 1987. 141–73.

Said, Edward W. *Beginnings: Intention and Method.* New York: Columbia University Press, 1985.

Sandberg, Jared. "Fringe Groups Can Say Almost Anything and Not Worry About Getting Punched." *Wall Street Journal* December 8, 1994: B1, 4.

———. "Regulators Try to Tame the Untameable On-Line World." *Wall Street Journal* July 5, 1995: B1, 3.

Sawhney, Nitin, David Balcom, and Ian Smith. "HyperCafe: Narrative and Aesthetic Properties of HyperVideo." *Hypertext '96.* New York: Association for Computing Machinery, 1996. 1–10.

Schmitz, Ulrich. "Automatic Generation of Texts without Using Cognitive Models: Television News." *The New Medium: ALLC-ACH 90 Book of Abstracts.* Siegen, Germany: University of Siegen, Association for Literary and Linguistic Computing, and the Association for Computers and the Humanities, 1990. 191–95.

———. *Postmoderne Concierge: Die "Tagesschau." Wortwelt und Weltbild der Fernsehnachrichten.* Opladen, Germany: Westdeutscher Verlag, 1990.

Schneiderman, Ben, and Greg Kearsley. *Hypertext Hands-On! An Introduction to a New Way of Organizing and Accessing Information.* Reading, Mass.: Addison-Wesley, 1989.

Scholes, Robert. *Structuralism in Literature: An Introduction.* New Haven: Yale University Press, 1974.

———. *Textual Power: Literary Theory and the Teaching of English.* New Haven: Yale University Press, 1985.

Scholes, Robert, and Robert Kellogg. *The Nature of Narrative.* New York: Oxford University Press, 1966.

Shoaf, R. A. "Literary Theory, Medieval Studies, and the Crisis of Difference. *Reorientations: Critical Theories and Pedagogies.* Ed. Bruce Henricksen and Thaïs Morgan. Urbana: University of Illinois Press, 1990. 77–94.

Smith, Barbara Herrnstein. "Narrative Versions, Narrative Theories." *On Narrative.* Ed. W. J. T. Mitchell. Chicago: University of Chicago Press, 1980. 209–32.

———. *Poetic Closure: A Study of How Poems End.* Chicago: University of Chicago Press, 1968.

BIBLIOGRAPHY Smith, Tony C., and Ian H. Witten. "A Planning Mechanism for Generating Story Text." *The New Medium: ALLC-ACH '90 Book of Abstracts.* Siegen, Germany: University of Siegen, Association for Literary and Linguistic Computing, and the Association for Computers and the Humanities, 1990. 201–4.

Spiro, Rand J., Richard L. Coulson, Paul J. Felktovich, and Daniel K. Anderson, "Cognitive Flexibility Theory: Advanced Knowledge Acquisition in Ill-structured Domains." *Program of the Tenth Annual Conference of the Cognitive Science Society.* Hillsdale, N.J.: Lawrence Erlbaum, 1988. 375–83.

Spiro, Rand J., Walter P. Vispoel, John G. Schmitz, Ala Samarapungavan, and A. E. Boerger. "Knowledge Acquisition for Application: Cognitive Flexibility and Transfer in Complex Content Domains." *Executive Control Processes in Reading.* Ed. B. K. Britton and S. McGlynn. Hillsdale, N.J.: Lawrence Erlbaum, 1987. 177–99.

Steigler, Marc. "Hypermedia and Singularity." *Analog Science Fiction* (1989): 52–71.

Steinberg, S. H. *Five Hundred Years of Printing.* 2nd ed. Baltimore: Penguin, 1961.

Suckale, Robert. *Studien zu Stilbildung und Stilwandel de Madonnenstatuen der Ile-de-France zwischen 1240 und 1300.* Munich: University of Munich, 1971.

Sutherland, John. "Author's Rights and Transatlantic Differences." *Times Literary Supplement* May 25–31, 1990: 554.

Taylor, Mark C., and Esa Saarinen. *Imagologies: Media Philosophy.* London: Routledge, 1994.

Thomas, Brook. "Bringing about Critical Awareness through History in General Education Literature Courses." *Reorientations: Critical Theories and Pedagogies.* Ed. Bruce Henricksen and Thaïs Morgan. Urbana: University of Illinois Press, 1990. 219–47.

Thorpe, James. *Principles of Textual Criticism.* San Marino, Calif.: Huntington Library, 1972.

Timpe, Eugene F. "Memory and Literary Structures." *Journal of Mind and Behavior* 2 (1981): 293–307.

Todorov, Tzvetan. *The Poetics of Prose.* Trans. Richard Howard. Ithaca, N.Y.: Cornell University Press, 1977.

Ulmer, Gregory L. *Applied Grammatology: Post(e)-Pedagogy from Jacques Derrida to Joseph Beuys.* Baltimore: Johns Hopkins University Press, 1985.

———. *Heuretics: The Logic of Invention.* Baltimore: Johns Hopkins University Press, 1994.

———. "The Object of Post-Criticism." *The Anti-Aesthetic: Essays on Postmodern Culture.* Ed. Hal Forster. Post Townsend, Wash.: Bay Press, 1983. 83–110.

———. *Teletheory: Grammatology in the Age of Video.* London: Routledge, 1989.

BIBLIOGRAPHY ———. "Textshop for an Experimental Humanities." *Reorientations: Critical Theories and Pedagogies.* Ed. Bruce Henricksen and Thaïs Morgan. Urbana: University of Illinois Press, 1990.

Utting, Kenneth, and Nicole Yankelovich, "Context and Orientation in Hypermedia Networks." *ACM Transactions on Information Systems* 7 (1989): 58–84.

von Hallberg, Robert, ed. *Canons.* Chicago: University of Chicago Press, 1984.

Waldrop, M. Mitchell. *Complexity: The Emerging Science at the Edge of Order and Chaos.* New York: Simon and Schuster, 1992.

Walsh, Peter. "Are Words Dead?: Designer David Carson's Revenge on the Stony Roman Alphabet Looks Softer in the Context of Calligraphy." *Providence Phoenix* March 1, 1996: 2.3–4.

Walter, John L. "On Phonography: How Recording Techniques Change Music and Musicians." *Times Literary Supplement* April 26, 1996: 10.

Weissman, Ronald F. E. "From the Personal Computer to the Scholar's Workstation." *Academic Computing* 3 (October 1988): 10–14, 30–34, 36, 38–41.

Wexelblat, Alex. *Virtual Reality: Applications and Explorations.* Boston: Academic Press Professional, 1993.

Whalley, Peter. "Models of Hypertext Structure and Models of Learning." *Designing Hypertext/Hypermedia for Learning.* Ed. David H. Jonassen and Heinz Mandl. Heidelberg: Springer-Verlag, 1990. 61–70.

White, Hayden. "The Value of Narrativity in the Representation of Reality." *On Narrative.* Ed. W. J. T. Mitchell. Chicago: University of Chicago Press, 1980. 1–24.

White, Lynn T. *Medieval Technology and Social Change.* Oxford: Clarendon Press, 1963.

Wilson, Kathleen S. "Palenque: An Interactive Multimedia Optical Disc Prototype for Children." Working paper no. 2. New York: Bank Street College of Education / Center for Children and Technology, 1986.

Wittgenstein, Ludwig. *Philosophical Investigations.* 3rd ed. Trans. G. E. M. Anscombe. New York: Macmillan, 1968.

Wittig, Rob. *Invisible Rendezvous: Connection and Collaboration in the New Landscape of Electronic Writing.* Hanover, N.H.: Wesleyan University Press / University Press of New England, 1995.

Wolf, Gary. "The Curse of Xanadu." *Wired* 3 (June 1995): 137–52, 194–202.

Wu, Gordon. "Soft Soap." *Times Literary Supplement* July 20–26, 1990: 777.

Yankelovich, Nicole. "From Electronic Books to Electronic Libraries: Revisiting 'Reading and Writing the Electronic Book.'" *Hypermedia and Literary Studies.* Ed. Paul Delany and George P. Landow. Cambridge: MIT Press, 1991. 133–41.

BIBLIOGRAPHY   Yankelovich, Nicole, Norman Meyrowitz, and Stephen Drucker. "Intermedia: The Concept and the Construction of a Seamless Information Environment." *IEEE Computer* 21 (1988): 81–96.

Yankelovich, Nicole, Norman Meyrowitz, and Andries van Dam. "Reading and Writing the Electronic Book." *IEEE Computer* 18 (October 1985): 15–30.

Zachary, G. Pasal. "Digital Age Spawns 'Neo-Luddite' Movement." *Wall Street Journal* April 12, 1996: B1, 3.

Zampolli, Antonio. "Technology and Linguistics Research." *Scholarship and Technology in the Humanities.* Ed. May Katzen. London: British Library Research / Bowker Saur, 1991. 21–51.

Zeleny, Jeff. "Poetic License on the Internet: Odes to Spam Renew / Literary Zest On-Line / Haiku Craze Is Back." *Wall Street Journal* July 22, 1996: B1–2.

Zimmer, Carl. "Floppy Fiction." *Discover* (November 1989): 34–36.

Electronic Materials and Videos   Aarseth, Espen. A hypertext version of Raymond Queneau's *Cent Mille Milliards de Poèmes* (1961). Environment: HyperCard, n.d.

Adelman, Ian, and Paul Jahn. *Memex Animation.* Environment: Director. Providence, R.I.: Dynamic Diagrams, 1995. Also available at http://dynamicdiagrams.com/services_ipp_memex.html.

Amerika, Mark. *Alt-X.* Available at http://www.altx.com/.

———. *Hypertextual Consciousness.* Available at http://www.altx.com/htc/title.html.

Anderson, David, Robert Cavalier, and Preston K. Covey. *A Right to Die? The Dax Cowart Case.* London: Routledge, 1996. CD-ROM.

Anderson, Laurie, with Huang Hsien-Chien. *Puppet Motel.* New York: Voyager, 1995. CD-ROM.

Bolter, J. David. *Writing Space: A Hypertext.* Environment: Storyspace. Hillsdale, N.J.: Lawrence Erlbaum, 1990.

Buchanan, Dorothy, and Stacie Hibino. *A Voice in the Silence.* Environment: Toolbook. Ann Arbor, Mich.: Project FLAME, 1996. An unpublished hypermedia project centering on the seventeenth-century Mexican poet Sor Juana Inese de la Cruz; demonstrated at Hypertext '96.

CD Word. The Interactive Bible Library. Environment: Specially amplified Guide. Dallas: CD Word Library, 1990.

Cecchi, Alberto. *Ipertesto tratto da "Il castello dei destini incrociati," di Italo Calvino.* Environment: Storyspace. Unpublished disk. ca. 1995.

Critical Mass: Graduate Projects. Environment: Projector. Pasadena, Calif.: Art Center College of Design, 1995.

BIBLIOGRAPHY   Daniele, Daniela. *Travelogues in a Broken Landscape: Robert Smithson's Visual/Textual Works.* Environment: Windows 3.1 Help System. Unpublished disks, 1993.

The Dickens Web. Developer: George P. Landow. Editors: Julie Launhardt and Paul D. Kahn. (1) Environment: Intermedia 3.5. Providence, R.I.: Institute for Research in Information and Scholarship, 1990. (2) Environment: Storyspace. Watertown, Mass.: Eastgate Systems, 1992. (3) Interleaf Worldview. Unpublished.

Dynamic Diagrams. "Introducing MAPA." Available at http://www.dynamicdiagrams.com/products/htm.

Exploring the Moon. Developers: Katie Livingston, Jayne Aubele, and James Head. Editors: Paul D. Kahn and Julie Launhardt. Environment: Intermedia 3.5. Providence, R.I.: Institute for Research in Information and Scholarship, 1988.

Fishman, Barry J. *The Works of Graham Swift: A Hypertext Honors Thesis.* Environment: Intermedia. Providence, R.I.: Brown University, 1989.

Greco, Diane. *Cyborg: Engineering the Body Electric.* Environment: Storyspace. Watertown, Mass.: Eastgate Systems, 1995.

Guyer, Carolyn. *Quibbling.* Environment: Storyspace. Watertown, Mass.: Eastgate Systems, 1993.

"In Memoriam" Web, The. Editors: Jon Lanestedt and George P. Landow. Environment: Storyspace. Watertown, Mass.: Eastgate Systems, 1992.

Intermedia: From Linking to Learning. Director: Deborah Dorsey. Cambridge, Mass.: Cambridge Studios, and the Annenberg / Corporation for Public Broadcasting Project, 1986. 27-minute video.

Jackson, Shelley. *Patchwork Girl.* Environment: Storyspace. Cambridge, Mass.: Eastgate Systems, 1995.

Joyce, Michael. *Afternoon.* (1) Environment: Storyspace Beta 3. 3. Jackson, Mich.: Riverrun Limited, 1987. (2) Environment: Storyspace. Cambridge, Mass.: Eastgate Systems, 1990.

Kahn, Paul D. *Intermedia: A Retrospective.* New York: Association for Computing Machinery, 1992. 53-minute video.

Kendall, Robert. *A Life Set for Two.* Environment: Visual Basic for Windows. Watertown, Mass.: Eastgate, 1996.

Kolb, David. *Socrates in the Labyrinth: Text, Argument, Philosophy.* Environment: Storyspace. Cambridge, Mass.: Eastgate Systems, 1994.

Lafaille, J. M. *Fragments d'une histoire.* Environment: Windows 3.1 Help System. Unpublished disk, 1994.

Landow, George P. *Hypertext at Brown.* Available at http://www.stg.brown.edu/projects/hypertext/landow/HTatBrown/BrownHT.html. Includes screen shots of

BIBLIOGRAPHY IRIS Intermedia, bibliography of IRIS publications, and materials on earlier systems, including FRESS.

————. *Hypertext in Hypertext.* Environment. DynaText. Baltimore: Johns Hopkins University Press, 1993.

————, ed. *Cyberspace, Hypertext, and Critical Theory Web.* Available at http://www.stg.brown.edu/projects/hypertext/landow/cpace/cspaceov.html.

————. *Postcolonial and Postimperial Literature in English.* Available at http://www.stg.brown.edu/projects/hypertext/landow/post/misc/postov.html.

————. *The Victorian Web.* Available at http://www.stg.brown.edu/projects/hypertext/landow/victorian/victov.html.

————. *Writing at the Edge.* Environment: Storyspace. Watertown, Mass.: Eastgate Systems, 1995.

Lanham, Richard A. *The Electronic Word: Democracy, Technology, and the Arts.* Environment: Voyager Expanded Book. Chicago: University of Chicago Press, 1993.

Larsen, Deena. *Marble Springs.* Environment: Storyspace. Watertown, Mass.: Eastgate Systems, 1994.

Liestøl, Gunnar. *Kon-Tiki Interactive.* Oslo: Gyldendal Norsk Forlag, 1996. CD-ROM.

Malloy, Judy, and Cathy Marshall. *Forward Anywhere.* Environment created specifically for project. Watertown, Mass.: Eastgate Systems, 1996.

McDermott, Anne, ed. Samuel Johnson, *A Dictionary of the English Language.* On CD-ROM. Environment: DynaText. Cambridge: Cambridge University Press, 1996.

McLaughlin, Tim. *Notes toward Absolute Zero.* Environment: Storyspace. Watertown, Mass.: Eastgate Systems, 1996.

Meyer, Tom. *Plateaus.* In *Writing at the Edge,* ed. George P. Landow. Environment: Storyspace. Watertown, Mass.: Eastgate Systems, 1995.

Microsoft Art Gallery. Environment by Cognitive Applications, Brighton, England. Redmond, Wash.: Microsoft, 1993.

Moulthrop, Stuart. *Forking Paths: An Interaction.* Environment: Storyspace Beta 3. 3. Jackson, Mich.: Riverrun Limited, 1987.

————. *Victory Garden.* Environment: Storyspace. Cambridge, Mass.: Eastgate Systems, 1991.

————. "You Say You Want a Revolution? Hypertext and the Laws of Media." *Postmodern Culture* 1 (May 1991).

Myst. Novato, Calif.: Broderbund, 1993. CD-ROM.

New Oxford Annotated Bible with the Apocrypha. New Revised Standard Version. Environment: CompLex. New York: Oxford, 1995.

BIBLIOGRAPHY Paul, Christiane. *Unreal City: A Hypertext Guide to T. S. Eliot's "The Waste Land."* Environment: Storyspace. Watertown, Mass.: Eastgate Systems, 1995.

Perseus 1.0b1: Interactive Sources and Studies on Ancient Greek Civilization (Beta pre-release version). Developers: Gregory Crane and Elli Mylonas. Environment: Hyper-Card. Washington, D.C.: Annenberg / Corporation for Public Broadcasting Project, 1990.

Residents, The. *Freak Show.* New York: Voyager, 1994. CD-ROM.

Robinson, Peter, ed. Chaucer, *The Wife of Bath's Prologue.* On CD-ROM. Environment: DynaText. Cambridge: Cambridge University Press, 1996.

Rosenzweig, Roy, Steve Brier, and John Brown. *Who Built America? From the Centennial Celebration of 1876 to the War of 1914.* New York: Voyager, 1993. CD-ROM.

Sanford, Christy Sheffield. *Safara in the Beginning.* http://gnv.fdt.net/~christys/safara.html.

Seid, Tim. *Interpreting Manuscripts.* Environment: HyperCard. 1990. (Providence, R.I. Unpublished.)

Tamblyn, Christine, Marjorie Franklin, and Paul Tompkins. *She Loves It, She Loves It Not: Women and Technology.* San Francisco: 1993. CD-ROM.

Thomas, Brian. *If Monks Had Macs.* Environment: HyperCard. Portland, Oreg.: RiverTEXT.

Vizability (Alpha version). Boston: PWS Publishing, 1995.

Winter, Robert. *CD Companion to Beethoven Symphony No. 9.* Environment: HyperCard. Santa Monica, Calif.: Voyager, 1989.

The Wrong Side of Town. Source and date unknown. Interactive video.

Index

Library of Congress Cataloging-in-Publication Data

Landow, George P.

Hypertext 2.0 / George P. Landow. — Rev., amplified ed.

   p.   cm. — (Parallax)

   Rev. of: Hypertext. c 1992.

   Includes bibliographical references and index.

    ISBN 0-8018-5585-3 (alk. paper). — ISBN 0-8018-5586-1 (pbk.: alk. paper)

    1. Criticism.   2. Literature and technology.   3. Hypertext systems.   I. Landow, George P.

Hypertext.   II. Title.   III. Series: Parallax (Baltimore, Md.)

PN81.L28   1997

801'.95—dc21   97-1642 CIP